Beyond Babel

In the seventeenth-century, black linguistic interpreters and spiritual intermediaries played key roles in the production of writings about black men and women. Focusing on Peru and the southern continental Caribbean, *Beyond Babel* uncovers long-ignored or lost archival materials describing the experiences of Africans and their descendants in the transatlantic slave trade and the colonial societies where they arrived. Brewer-García's analysis of these materials shows that black intermediaries bridged divisions among the populations implicated in the slave trade, exerting influence over colonial Spanish American writings and emerging racial hierarchies in the Atlantic world. The translated portrayals of blackness composed in collaboration with these intermediaries stood in stark contrast to the pejorative stereotypes common in literary and legal texts of the period. This book reconstructs the context of those translations and traces the contours of the notions of blackness they created, which were characterized by physical beauty and spiritual virtue.

Larissa Brewer-García is Assistant Professor of Latin American Literature at the University of Chicago.

Afro-Latin America

Series editors

George Reid Andrews, *University of Pittsburgh*
Alejandro de la Fuente, *Harvard University*

This series reflects the coming of age of the new, multidisciplinary field of Afro-Latin American Studies, which centers on the histories, cultures, and experiences of people of African descent in Latin America. The series aims to showcase scholarship produced by different disciplines, including history, political science, sociology, ethnomusicology, anthropology, religious studies, art, law, and cultural studies. It covers the full temporal span of the African Diaspora in Latin America, from the early colonial period to the present and includes continental Latin America, the Caribbean, and other key areas in the region where Africans and their descendants have made a significant impact.

A full list of titles published in the series can be found at: www.cambridge.org/afro-latin-america

Beyond Babel

*Translations of Blackness in Colonial Peru and
New Granada*

LARISSA BREWER-GARCÍA

University of Chicago

CAMBRIDGE
UNIVERSITY PRESS

University Printing House, Cambridge CB2 8BS, United Kingdom

One Liberty Plaza, 20th Floor, New York, NY 10006, USA

477 Williamstown Road, Port Melbourne, VIC 3207, Australia

314–321, 3rd Floor, Plot 3, Splendor Forum, Jasola District Centre,
New Delhi – 110025, India

79 Anson Road, #06–04/06, Singapore 079906

Cambridge University Press is part of the University of Cambridge.

It furthers the University's mission by disseminating knowledge in the pursuit of
education, learning, and research at the highest international levels of excellence.

www.cambridge.org
Information on this title: www.cambridge.org/9781108493000
DOI: 10.1017/9781108632416

First published 2020

A catalogue record for this publication is available from the British Library.

ISBN 978-1-108-49300-0 Hardback

Para La Boquilla, Cartagena de Indias

y

Sam

Contents

Figures

Acknowledgments

Financial support for research and writing came from the University of Pennsylvania, a Mellon/ACLS dissertation completion grant, the Cotsen Postdoctoral Fellowship at Princeton University, a Princeton Program in Latin American Studies Faculty Research Grant, a Princeton University Committee on Research in the Humanities and Social Sciences Faculty Grant, and the Humanities Division of the University of Chicago. Sections of Chapter 4 appeared in an essay published in *Envisioning Others: Race, Color, and the Visual in Iberia and Latin America* and are reproduced here with permission of Brill.

I am extremely grateful for the support I received from mentors, colleagues, friends, and family while writing this book. Yolanda Martínez-San Miguel and Barbara Fuchs supported this project since its inception and continue to be sources of advice for which I will happily always be in debt. For reading and critiquing the complete book manuscript, I sincerely thank my dear friends and colleagues Agnes Lugo-Ortiz and Miguel Martínez. My gratitude extends to Rachel Sarah O'Toole and the other readers for Cambridge University Press who made such careful recommendations for improvements.

It is with grateful admiration that I remember Padre Tulio Aristizábal, whose scholarship and generosity contributed to the development of the chapters about Cartagena. I owe similar thanks to Padre Francisco de Borja Medina at the Archivum Romanum Societatis Iesu. I am also very grateful to the friends and colleagues whose questions and feedback on pieces of research from this book affected its final shape, including Paulina Alberto, Liliana Angulo, Gavin Arnall, Wendy Belcher, Herman Bennett, Susanna Berger, Wallace Best, Dain Borges, Claudia Brittenham,

Sherwin Bryant, Kathryn Burns, Sidney Chalhoub, Anne A. Cheng, Tom Cummins, Rachel DeLue, Alejandro de la Fuente, José Carlos de la Puente, Jessica Delgado, Caroline Egan, Ann Farnsworth-Alvear, Brodie Fischer, Cécile Fromont, Claire Gilbert, Matthew Goldmark, Pablo Gómez, Michael Gordin, Karen Graubart, Andrew Hamilton, Mary Harper, Dirk Hartog, Tamar Herzog, Ruth Hill, David Kazanjian, Bob Kendrick, Emilio Kourí, Laura Llerena León, Valeria López Fadul, María Elena Martínez, Mónica Martínez, Michelle McKinley, Erika Milam, Kenneth Mills, Michelle Molina, Anna More, Daniel Nemser, Gabriela Nouzeilles, Ricardo Padron, Naomi Paik, Pamela Patton, Matthew Restall, Ana Sabau, Mario Santana, Victoria Saramago, David Sartorius, Daniel Sheffield, Ana Silva, Amara Solari, Michael Solomon, Justin Steinberg, Susan Stewart, Fidel Tavárez, Mauricio Tenorio, Sonia Velázquez, Tamara Walker, Adam Warren, Judith Weisenfeld, Sophie White, Danielle Terrazas Williams, and Yanna Yannakakis. In addition, Allison Bigelow, Fred de Armas, Katharine Gerbner, Daniela Gutiérrez Flores, John Lipski, Joanne Rappaport, Gabriel Rocha, and Rubén Sánchez-Godoy kindly answered research queries along the way. I am thankful for the members of the Working Group on Slavery and Visual Culture at the University of Chicago, including Allyson Field, Isabela Fraga, Agnes Lugo-Ortiz, Andrei Pop, Danielle Roper, and Chris Taylor, who led me to sharpen my thinking about this project in many ways.

Maxim Rigaux and Veronica Vegna helped me review and correct my transcriptions and translations from Latin and Italian, respectively. Kathryn Joy McKnight generously shared her transcriptions of documents from the Archivo General de Indias which I have cross-referenced with the manuscripts. I am also exceedingly grateful to Nancy van Deusen for her meticulous work transcribing, editing, and providing context for Úrsula de Jesús's spiritual diary and *Vida anónima*, for sharing her transcriptions with me, and offering feedback on an almost final version of Chapter 5.

In June 2019, I had the privilege of watching a performance in the Santuario San Pedro Claver in Cartagena prepared by artist Liliana Angulo and the contemporary Afro-Colombian dance group Permanencias, directed by Nemecio Berrio Guerrero. As part of a colloquium organized by the Working Group on Slavery and Visual Culture, Permanencias performed a response to some of the documents about Claver and his interpreters that I analyze in Chapters 3 and 4 of this book. Seeing the dancers enact and react to stories from those documents in the same corridors and courtyard walked by the Jesuits' black interpreters in the seventeenth century was beyond moving. For the experience, I am grateful to Padre Jorge Camacho, the Santuario San Pedro Claver, Danielle Roper, Liliana, Nemecio, and dancers Héctor Jesús Contreras Marimon, Sebastián Díaz Gómez, Fairladis Díaz Zúñiga, Kaytrin Miranda Vargas, Jorge Palomeque Dueñas, María José Salcedo Gómez, and Yiseth Alejandra Urzola Ospino. The cover photograph of this book was taken by Maruja Parra during a rehearsal for that performance.

Finally, for their constant encouragement, I thank the friends and family not yet mentioned: María Angélica Bautista, Laurel Beversdorf, Nathan Blom, Graham Brewer, Andrea Cote Botero, Leticia Cruz, Alli Cuentos, Eric Brewer Cuentos, Abby Evans, Will Evans, Ben Goldberg, Fred Goldberg, Jake Goldberg, Melissa Goldberg, Rachel Goldberg, Wendy Goldberg, Adam Goodman, Yara Hudgson Oliveira, Gerriet Jenssen, Rony Monsalve, Aurea Oliveira Santos, Waidis Ortega Miranda, Iliana Pagán-Teitelbaum, Carlos Riobó, Elsa Romero, Gerald Slevin, Bindu Suresh, and Jennie Taylor. Raquel García Brewer and Robert Brewer sustained me throughout this effort as model translators, careful proofreaders, and adoring grandparents. Last but not least, I thank Sam, Nico, and Diego for giving me the very best reasons "to wake up from work."

Note on Transcriptions and Translations

The primary texts analyzed in this book were written in Spanish, Portuguese, Italian, Catalan, Latin, and French. My citations keep the spelling and punctuation from the original printed and manuscript texts, with the exception of modernizing u/v and i/j reversal, and unifying split words erroneously separated by the typesetter. Any other modifications, such as making explicit content elided in abbreviations, are marked with brackets. In the English translations, I have standardized capitalization. All translations into English are my own unless otherwise specified.

Introduction

Linguistic and Spiritual Mediations in the Earlier Black Atlantic

On a May morning in 1659 in the Caribbean port of Cartagena de Indias, a man from Angola named Andrés Sacabuche testified before a notary and a judge in the city's Jesuit church. Sacabuche was serving as a witness in a formal inquiry into the potentially saintly life of Jesuit priest Pedro Claver, his recently deceased supervisor. In his lengthy testimony, Sacabuche provided details about his own life as a survivor of the Middle Passage and an enslaved evangelical interpreter in Cartagena: after arriving in Cartagena as a young man on a slave ship, he was purchased by the city's Jesuit school to help its priests evangelize the new black arrivals from central Africa disembarking in the port by the hundreds almost every year during this period.[1] As a speaker of the languages of Kimbundu and Anchico, Sacabuche became an important member of a group of enslaved black interpreters owned by the Jesuits in Cartagena. Sacabuche's testimony and related Jesuit writings about missionary efforts in colonial Lima and Cartagena offer windows onto how black men and women in the diaspora used linguistic and spiritual mediation to communicate with each other and adapt to their New World surroundings.

---

[1] *Proceso de beatificación de Pedro Claver* [hereafter *Proceso* 1676], Biblioteca Nacional de Colombia, manuscrito 281 [1658–1669], trans. Claudio Louvet [1676], Andrés Sacabuche, 99v–109v. For a transcription and translation of a selection from Sacabuche's testimony, see Appendix B. For details regarding numbers and places of provenance for slave ships to Cartagena, see David Wheat, "The Afro-Portuguese Maritime World and the Foundations of Spanish Caribbean Society, 1570–1640" (PhD diss., Vanderbilt University, 2009), 252–56.

While Sacabuche narrated his testimony in 1659, some 1,050 miles away in the Pacific coastal city of Lima, Úrsula de Jesús, a Peruvian-born black religious servant in the Convent of Santa Clara, was fashioning another kind of testimony. Úrsula's narration took the form of a spiritual diary about her visions and conversations with holy voices and souls in purgatory that she related out loud to nuns in her convent at the request of her confessor.[2] Úrsula was a different kind of intermediary than Sacabuche: rather than translate between distinct languages, she served as a respected visionary and relayer of messages between God, souls in purgatory, and the living. Two posthumous biographies written about her shortly after her death in 1666 use her spiritual diary to fashion their own accounts about her. The biographies selectively repeat her diary's portrayals of how black men and women should be perceived in and beyond her religious community.

Andrés Sacabuche and Úrsula de Jesús are two of the black intermediaries from colonial Spanish America who are the focus of this book. By examining texts by and about them, *Beyond Babel* highlights the influence black men and women had on the production of written texts in their respective communities through the work of linguistic and spiritual mediation. In the case of the evangelical interpreters in Cartagena such as Sacabuche, linguistic mediation describes the transposition of messages across the many different languages spoken by the black men and women disembarking from slave ships to facilitate their arrival in the port as well as their catechisms and baptisms. In the case of Úrsula de Jesús in Lima, spiritual mediation describes the labor of relaying messages communicated to her by God and other otherworldly interlocutors to her spiritual community and to serve as an advocate for the salvation of the souls of the living and the dead. This book will demonstrate that these black intermediaries used linguistic and spiritual mediation to shape notions of blackness in written texts that have been overlooked by previous scholarship on colonial Latin America and the African diaspora. Specifically, these intermediaries helped document and circulate notions of black

---

[2] *Diario espiritual de la venerable Úrsula de Jesús, escrita por ella misma*, Archivo de Santa Clara de Lima, 8r–60r. This document has been edited and published by Nancy van Deusen in Spanish and English. Nancy van Deusen, *Las almas del purgatorio: El diario espiritual y vida anónima de Úrsula de Jesús, una mística negra del siglo XVII* (Lima: Pontificia Universidad Católica del Peru, 2012); *Souls of Purgatory: The Spiritual Diary of a Seventeenth-Century Afro-Peruvian Mystic, Úrsula de Jesús* (Albuquerque: University of New Mexico Press, 2004). Úrsula's diary dates from 1650 and concludes in 1661.

virtue and black beauty even as racial hierarchies stigmatizing blackness were increasingly cohering in seventeenth-century Spanish America.

Men and women of African descent first arrived in the territories that would become Peru and New Granada along with the first Spanish expeditions to these areas in the sixteenth century. In some cases, they were conquistadors themselves, and in others they were servants to conquistadors.[3] The importation of large numbers of enslaved Africans to the Caribbean for commercial purposes began in 1518 after the Spanish Crown authorized the first large shipment to Hispaniola.[4] Then, when the Spanish Crown assumed control of Portugal in 1580, the volume of the transatlantic slave trade to Spanish America increased significantly until 1640. The enslaved black men, women, and children who survived the sea voyage during this period were taken to work in farms, fields, and mines or to serve as servants in domestic spaces and convents. Some already knew skilled trades on arrival in Spanish America; others learned

---

[3] Frederick Bowser, *The African Slave in Colonial Peru, 1524–1650* (Stanford, CA: Stanford University Press, 1976), 4–6. A trickling arrival of enslaved Africans as personal servants in the early years of the Peruvian viceroyalty resulted from the permits for the importation of African slaves from Iberia that the Crown awarded Pizarro and his men for the conquests in Peru. For example, when Pizarro returned to Spain and signed the Capitulations of Toledo in 1529, the Crown authorized him to import duty-free fifty African slaves into the land. Other men who went with him were granted similar permits for a modest fee. Then, between 1529 and 1537, the Crown granted more people to import at least 363 slaves. Black servants were coveted in the early viceregal period, as they would be throughout the following centuries, because they were considered a symbol of prestige for their owners (8). On the prestige of owning black slaves in the Andes, see also Tamara J. Walker, *Exquisite Slaves: Race, Clothing, and Status in Colonial Lima* (New York: Cambridge University Press, 2017), 26–42. For a recent synthesis of historiography on Iberian and Mediterranean antecedents to the transatlantic slave trade, see William D. Phillips, Jr., *Slavery in Medieval and Early Modern Iberia* (Philadelphia: University of Pennsylvania Press, 2014), 10–78. On black soldiers in the early European settlement of the Spanish Caribbean, see Jane Landers, *Black Society in Spanish Florida* (Chicago: University of Illinois Press, 1999), 21–23; Matthew Restall, *The Black Middle: Africans, Mayans, and Spaniards in Colonial Yucatan* (Stanford, CA: Stanford University Press, 2009), 6–13.

[4] In 1518, the Spanish Crown agreed to the shipment of 4,000 captive African laborers from western Africa to the Caribbean over an eight-year period. On the early history of the trade to Spanish America, see David Wheat, *Atlantic Africa and the Spanish Caribbean, 1570–1640* (Chapel Hill: University of North Carolina Press, 2016); Alex Borucki, David Eltis, and David Wheat, "Atlantic History and the Slave Trade to Spanish America," *American Historical Review* 120, no. 2 (2015): 433–461; José Luis Cortés López, *Esclavo y colono: Introducción y sociología de los negroafricanos en la América Española del siglo XVI* (Salamanca: Ediciones Universidad, 2004), 1–44; Robin Blackburn, *The Making of New World Slavery from the Baroque to the Modern, 1492–1800* (New York: Verso, 1997), 134–37; Bowser, *The African Slave in Colonial Peru*, 26–30.

them afterward.[5] Some became free through their owners' selective manu-mission, their own supplemental work as day laborers, or physical escape.[6] Many more stayed enslaved. By the early seventeenth century, free and enslaved black men and women came to form a significant percentage of the population in these regions.[7]

The texts examined in this book were produced in the sixteenth and seventeenth centuries in the urban centers of Lima and Cartagena, two coastal cities connected by empire, commercial routes, and evangelical projects.[8] Together, as ports, Lima and Cartagena were tied to other cities across the globe such as Seville, Luanda, Lisbon, Veracruz, Portobello, Buenos Aires, and São Tomé. Colonial Peru and New Granada, the broader areas surrounding Lima and Cartagena, are usually studied separately, but by focusing on both in conversation in this book I can

[5] On black men and women in the skilled trades, see Bowser, *The African Slave in Colonial Peru*, 125–146.

[6] For recent scholarship on the varying forms of access to freedom throughout colonial Spanish America, see Bianca Premo, *The Enlightenment on Trial: Ordinary Litigants and Colonialism in the Spanish Empire* (New York: Oxford University Press, 2017), 191–223; Michelle McKinley, *Fractional Freedoms: Slavery, Intimacy, and Legal Mobilization in Colonial Lima, 1600–1700* (New York: Cambridge University Press, 2016); Sherwin Bryant, *Rivers of Gold, Lives of Bondage: Governing through Slavery in Colonial Quito* (Chapel Hill: University of North Carolina Press, 2014), 115–42; Jane Landers, "The African Landscape of Seventeenth-Century Cartagena and Its Hinterlands," in *The Black Urban Atlantic in the Age of the Slave Trade*, ed. Jorge Cañizares-Esguerra, Matt D. Childs, and James Sidbury (Philadelphia: University of Pennsylvania Press, 2013), 147–62; Alejandro de la Fuente, *Havana and the Atlantic in the Sixteenth Century* (Chapel Hill: University of North Carolina Press, 2008), 170–79.

[7] For scholarship on Lima as a majority black city for most of the seventeenth century, see Bowser, *African Slave*, 340–41; José Ramón Jouve Martín, *Esclavos de la ciudad letrada: Esclavitud, escritura y colonialismo en Lima, 1650–1700* (Lima, Peru: IEP, 2005), 21–52. On the changing demographics of blackness in Lima toward the end of the seventeenth century, see Nancy van Deusen, "The 'Alienated' Body: Slaves and Castas in the Hospital de San Bartolomé in Lima, 1680–1700," *The Americas* 56, no. 1 (1999): 1–30. According to David Wheat, for all of the seventeenth century Cartagena's free and enslaved black population outnumbered its native and Spanish/white populations (*Atlantic Africa*, appendix 1, 277–81).

[8] Travel between these two cities during this period was typically realized by sailing from Cartagena to Portobello, crossing the Panamanian isthmus by land, and sailing south from Panama to Lima. For Iberians seeking to reach Peru as well as west African captives forced to travel the same route, stopping in Cartagena was often the first stop after crossing the Atlantic. See Nicolás del Castillo Mathieu, *La llave de las Indias* (Bogota: El Tiempo, 1981); Wheat, *Atlantic Africa*; and Linda Newson and Susie Minchin, *From Capture to Sale: The Portuguese Slave Trade to Spanish South America in the Early Seventeenth Century* (Boston: Brill, 2007). For a narrative of a voyage from Iberia to Peru via Cartagena, see Gerónymo Pallas, *Missión a las Indias* [1619], ed. José Hernández Palomo (Sevilla: Consejo Superior de Investigaciones Científicas, 2006).

attend to some of the ways the movement of people, material goods, and evangelical projects between them were frequent and mutually influential.[9] For example, most of the routes of the legal and illegal slave trades to Peru during this period passed through Cartagena such that the black men and women who arrived in Peru from Iberia or western Africa had to stop in Cartagena before resuming their voyage. As I will show in Chapter 2, people, materials, and evangelical projects also went in the other direction: missionary strategies that were first developed for indigenous populations in Peru in the late sixteenth century then served as models for Jesuit missionary efforts among black men and women in Cartagena when the order expanded northward into New Granada from Peru in the early seventeenth century. Focusing on both areas in this book allows me to examine a shared discourse about blackness produced in collaboration with distinct kinds of black intermediaries across different areas of colonial Spanish America. The juxtaposition demonstrates that the notions of black virtue and black beauty that circulated in each city were not merely local phenomena. They were shared across regions as well as among recent arrivals from Africa *and* black men and women born in the Americas. The bifocal frame of my study also offers an alternative to "Atlantic-only" readings of the African diaspora by foregrounding ways in which policies and practices developed to incorporate black men and women into colonial societies in the Atlantic were directly connected to precedents established in the Andean highlands and the Pacific littoral.[10]

The time period covered by this book begins in the late sixteenth century and closes toward the end of seventeenth century, a stretch of time that coincides not only with the demographic boom of Africans in

[9] In the sixteenth and seventeenth centuries, Peru corresponded to the contemporary territories of Peru, northern Chile, and Bolivia, whereas New Granada corresponded to today's Colombia, Ecuador, Panama, and Venezuela. The Spanish began their conquests in the Andes in 1532 and incorporated Peru as an official viceroyalty in 1542. The region of New Granada took on its name starting in 1539, although sometimes it was also referred to as Tierra Firme. Santa Fe (Bogota) became the seat of the Audience of New Granada in 1550, but the Spanish Crown did not officially incorporate the "New Kingdom of Granada" as a separate viceroyalty (from that of Peru) until 1718.

[10] While Paul Gilroy's "Black Atlantic" and Joseph Roach's "circum-Atlantic world" trace important geographies of New World blackness, they emphasize English and French Atlantic iterations of the diaspora from the eighteenth century forward and therefore omit earlier and concurrent Iberian-controlled geographies of the slave trade that connect the early Atlantic world with the Pacific Ocean. See Paul Gilroy, *The Black Atlantic: Modernity and Double Consciousness* (Cambridge, MA: Harvard University Press, 1993); Joseph Roach, *Cities of the Dead: Circum-Atlantic Performance* (New York: Columbia University Press, 1996).

colonial Spanish America, but also with the onset of the influence of Iberian Renaissance humanism and Counter Reformation theology in these areas.[11] As I will show in Chapter 1, the confluence of Renaissance humanist ideology and Counter Reformation theology had a profound effect on the way written texts began to codify blackness in early and mid-colonial Spanish America. In particular, I identify and analyze the work of a pervasive set of interlocking associations between black men and women and the uncivilized body, a limited capacity to speak, and a redeemable soul. Important alternatives to this set of stereotypes appear in the textual portrayals of black intermediaries who are described or describe themselves as masters of language, models of Christian virtue, and privileged relayers of religious signs. Their texts offer a set of aesthetic and moral valences that blackness held in this period that have gone unrecognized by scholarship on racial hierarchies of the more secular eighteenth and nineteenth centuries.

For this analysis, it is crucial to note that one of the key ways blackness took shape in Spanish America in the sixteenth and seventeenth centuries was through comparisons with indigeneity. Especially in the first two chapters, this book engages how attitudes and policies developed by Spanish missionaries to evangelize black and indigenous populations helped structure colonial ideas of race. In taking this approach, I join a growing number of scholars integrating the study of Africans and their descendants with that of indigenous peoples in Latin America, examining these groups' social and political histories side by side or examining interactions between them.[12] While mine is not a full comparative study,

---

[11] The period of the unification of the Spanish and Portuguese Crowns (1580–1640) gave Spanish America immediate access to the Portuguese slave trade. For more on the demographic changes of black populations in Spanish America during this period, see Wheat, *Atlantic Africa*, 267–81. The Bourbon takeover of the Hapsburg reign at the beginning of the eighteenth century and the British assumption of political and economic primacy in the Atlantic changed the demographics of the slave trade and the distribution of military and economic power on all sides of the Atlantic.

[12] For studies adopting comparative social and political histories of indigenous and black populations, see Rachel Sarah O'Toole, *Bound Lives: Africans, Indians, and the Making of Race in Colonial Peru* (Pittsburgh: University of Pittsburgh Press, 2012); Marcela Echeverri, "Popular Royalists, Empire, and Politics in Southwestern New Granada, 1809–1819," *Hispanic American Historical Review* 91, no. 2 (2011): 237–69; Aline Helg, *Liberty and Equality in Caribbean Colombia* (Chapel Hill: University of North Carolina Press, 2004); and James Sanders, "'Citizens of a Free People': Popular Liberalism and Race in Nineteenth-Century Southwestern Colombia," *Hispanic American Historical Review* 84, no. 2 (2004): 233–312. For studies that focus on the interactions between the two groups, see Patrick J. Carroll, "Black-Native Relations

it demonstrates that the Jesuit missionary strategies among black men and women in the Americas grew out of and then in distinction from evangelical projects among indigenous populations in the same regions. More specifically, I show that the roles assigned to and adapted by black linguistic and spiritual intermediaries in colonial evangelical projects were initially based on and then expressly different from those assigned to indigenous intermediaries.

The unique roles assumed by the black intermediaries examined in this book relate to the different treatment of black populations compared with indigenous populations in early colonial Spanish America. Key to this difference were the distinct juridical categories given to black and indigenous populations based on their perceived relationships to territorial possession by the Spanish Crown.[13] While the Crown made efforts to legally protect indigenous populations of the Americas and to establish a separate governing system of *la república de los indios* to function parallel to *la república de los españoles*, there was no comparable legal space created for black political collectivities in Spanish American colonial governments.[14] As has been noted by several scholars, black men and women

and the Historical Record in Colonial Mexico," in *Beyond Black and Red: African-Native Relations in Colonial Latin America*, ed. Matthew Restall (Albuquerque: University of New Mexico Pres, 2005), 245–68; Andrew B. Fisher, "Creating and Contesting Community: Indians and Afromestizos in the Late-Colonial Tierra Caliente of Guerrero, Mexico," *Journal of Colonialism and Colonial History* 7, no. 1 (2006); Matthew Restall, *The Black Middle*; O'Toole, *Bound Lives*; Pablo Miguel Sierra Silva, "From Chains to Chiles: An Elite Afro-Indigenous Couple in Colonial Mexico, 1641–1688," *Ethnohistory* 62, no. 2 (2015): 361–84.

[13] O'Toole, *Bound Lives*, 64–87; Herman Bennett, *Colonial Blackness: A History of Afro-Mexico* (Bloomington: Indiana University Press, 2009), 212; Laura Lewis, *Hall of Mirrors: Power, Witchcraft, and Caste in Colonial Mexico* (Durham: Duke University Press, 2003), 49–54; Peter Wade, *Race and Ethnicity in Latin America*, 2nd ed. (London: Pluto, 2010), 27; María Elena Martínez, *Genealogical Fictions: Limpieza de Sangre, Religion, and Gender in Colonial Mexico* (Stanford, CA: Stanford University Press, 2008), 100 and 143.

[14] While in the case of the indigenous populations, there was a bureaucratic mechanism (*protector de indios*) established to protect native subjects, there never existed a *protector de negros* in the American viceroyalties (Jouve Martín, *Esclavos de la ciudad letrada*, 100). Laws from the Spanish American viceroyalties frequently discouraged association between indigenous and black populations due perhaps to a perceived threat posed by the development of a collective consciousness among the two groups as well as the fact that black populations were often cast as aggressors to indigenous communities. See Bowser, *The African Slave in Colonial Peru*, 150; Lewis, *Hall of Mirrors*, 99; and Wade, *Race and Ethnicity in Latin America*, 27–28. O'Toole's *Bound Lives* provides an excellent study of the limits of those perceived divisions between black and indigenous populations.

were thus legally included as part of Spanish American viceregal societies without giving them means of collective representation and protection within them.[15] Indeed, the Spanish Crown debated and defended indigenous rights by the mid-sixteenth century, making native slavery mostly illegal in principle (if not in practice) precisely at a time when black slavery began to grow. Contrary to the critiques of indigenous enslavement and violent evangelical methods that characterized the mid-sixteenth-century debates about Spanish treatment of New World natives, before the late seventeenth century few comparable critiques were made of the ownership of and trade in black men and women in the Iberian empire.[16]

As religious subjects in Spanish America, black men and women also differed from indigenous men and women. The Church in Spanish America administratively considered black men and women to be Old World peoples who had at least technically already converted to Christianity before crossing the Atlantic, whereas indigenous peoples were considered neophytes. Historians have attributed this phenomenon to the many Iberian contacts with Ethiopians, North Africans, and sub-Saharan Africans before and after Iberian colonization of the Americas began.[17] (Ethiopia had long been an independent Christian kingdom and the

---

[15] Martínez, "The Black Blood of New Spain: Limpieza de Sangre, Racial Violence, and Gendered Power in Early Colonial Mexico," *William and Mary Quarterly*, 61, no. 3 (July 2004): 479–520; Jouve Martín, *Esclavos de la ciudad letrada*, 53–74; O'Toole, *Bound Lives*, 122–25; Bryant, *Rivers of Gold, Lives of Bondage*, 8; Graubart, *Republics of Difference*. On indigenous slavery in the Iberian world after the mid-sixteenth century, see Nancy van Deusen, *Global Indios: The Indigenous Struggle for Justice in Sixteenth-Century Spain* (Durham, NC: Duke University Press, 2015).

[16] See Bowser, *The African Slave in Colonial Peru*, 110–24; David Brion Davis, *The Problem of Slavery in Western Culture* [1966] (Oxford University Press, 1988), 165–96. On the late seventeenth-century critique of black slavery by two Capuchin priests in Cuba, see José Tomás López García, *Dos defensores de los esclavos negros en el siglo XVII: Francisco José de Jaca y Epifanio de Moirans* (Caracas: Universidad Católica Andrés Bello, 1982); Miguel Anxo Pena González, *Francisco José de Jaca. La primera propuesta abolicionista de la esclavitud en el pensamiento hispano* (Salamanca: Universidad Pontificia, 2003), among other secondary studies.

[17] Solange Alberro, *Inquisición y sociedad en México, 1571–1700* (México: Fondo de Cultura Económica, 1946), 8–9, 455; Martínez, *Genealogical Fictions*, 220–21; Herman Bennett, *African Kings and Black Slaves: Sovereignty and Dispossession in the Early Modern Atlantic* (Philadelphia: University of Pennsylvania Press, 2018); Herman Bennett, *Africans in Colonial Mexico: Absolutism, Christianity, and Afro-Creole Consciousness, 1570–1640* (Bloomington: Indiana University Press, 2003), 4, 54; Joan Cameron Bristol, "The Church and the Creation of Christian Subjects in Spanish America," in *Christians, Blasphemers, and Witches: Afro-Mexican Ritual Practice in the Seventeenth Century* (Albuquerque: University of New Mexico Press, 2007), 64.

Kongo had become Christian by the early sixteenth century.)[18] Before and during the sixteenth century, it was not uncommon for peoples from what we now consider the African continent to arrive in Iberia as royal visitors, diplomats, servants, or slaves.[19] Many of these were already Christian; others, especially if they were servants or enslaved, became Christian soon after arrival due to evangelization efforts inside the homes in which they worked.[20] These precedents contributed to the fact that black men and women in the early modern Iberian world were often rarely *categorically* identified as New Christians.

Indigenous populations of the Americas, in contrast, were cast as neophytes. The missionaries, theologians, and Crown officials committed to evangelizing New World populations generally agreed on the need to use different policies and practices than those developed for the Old World populations of Jews and Muslims, many of whom were forcibly converted to Christianity in Iberia in the fifteenth and early sixteenth

[18] On the early history of Christian Ethiopia beginning in the fourth century, see Sergew Hable Sellassie, *Ancient and Medieval Ethiopian History to 1270* (Addis Ababa: United Printers, 1972). On advent of Christianity in the Kongo, see John Thornton, "The Development of an African Catholic Church in the Kingdom of the Kongo, 1491–1750," *The Journal of African History* 25, no. 2 (1984): 147–67; Thornton, *Africa and Africans in the Making of the Atlantic World, 1400–1800*, 2nd ed. (New York: Cambridge University Press, 1998), especially 254–62; Linda Heywood and John Thornton, *Central Africans, Atlantic Creoles, and the Foundation of the Americas* (New York: Cambridge University Press, 2007), 60–67; and Cécile Fromont, *Art of Conversion: Christian Visual Culture in the Kingdom of the Kongo* (University of North Carolina Press, 2014).

[19] On the travelers and diplomats to Europe from Africa, see Kate Lowe, "'Representing' Africa: Ambassadors and Princes from Christian Africa to Renaissance Italy and Portugal, 1402–1608," *Transactions of the Royal Historical Society* 17 (2007): 101–28; Matteo Salvadore, *The African Prester John and the Birth of Ethiopian-European Relations, 1402–1555* (New York: Routledge, 2017); Paul H. D. Kaplan, "Italy, 1490–1700," in *The Image of the Black in Western Art from the "Age of Discovery" to the Age of Revolution: Artists of the Renaissance and Baroque*, ed. David Bindman and Henry Louis Gates, Jr. (Cambridge, MA: Harvard University Press, 2010), 93–190; Fromont, *The Art of Conversion*, 109–71; Bennett, *African Kings and Black Slaves*. On free black men and women who requested permission to travel to and from Iberia and the Spanish American territories in late sixteenth and early seventeenth centuries, see Chloe Ireton, "'They Are Blacks of the Caste of Black Christians': Old Christian Black Blood in the Sixteenth- and Early Seventeenth-Century Iberian Atlantic," *Hispanic American Historical Review* 97, no. 4 (2017): 579–612.

[20] See Bianca Premo, "Familiar: Thinking beyond Lineage and across Race in Spanish Atlantic Family History," *William and Mary Quarterly* 70, no. 2 (2013): 295–316, on the slave as a part of the Iberian family.

centuries.[21] One important perceived difference between the Old World conversions of Jews and Muslims and those of the New World natives was that, unlike Old World Jews and Muslims, New World natives had not known of Christianity before the arrival of the Spanish and therefore could not be considered guilty of rejecting it or descending from those who had rejected it.[22]

The black men and women in Spanish America who arrived with the boom in the trade to the region in late sixteenth and early seventeenth centuries were caught in between these distinct models. Some missionaries sought to evangelize black men and women using the coercive practices employed for Jews and Muslims in fifteenth- and early sixteenth-century Iberia, but others looked to accommodate policies and techniques developed for indigenous evangelization.[23] To complicate matters further, the Inquisition in Spanish America had jurisdiction over black men and women but not over indigenous populations.[24] This policy, historians

[21] For a study of the policies and practices developed to convert Jews and Muslims at the end of the fifteenth century and through the sixteenth century, see Seth Kimmel, *Parables of Coercion: Conversion and Knowledge at the End of Islamic Spain* (Chicago: University of Chicago Press, 2015). Kimmel explains that a key moment occurred in 1525–26 when the Council of Madrid agreed that while no more forced conversions should happen in the future, those of the past should be considered legitimate. This ruling, according to Kimmel, was largely about defining jurisdiction for the governing of New Christian populations. It brought the forcibly converted under the purview of the Inquisition, who would then be in charge of monitoring New Christian beliefs and behaviors.

[22] On the emergence of such prejudice against descendants of New Christians in Iberia, see Benzion Netanyahu, *The Origins of the Inquisition* (New York: Random House, 1995); David Nirenberg, "Race and the Middle Ages," in *Rereading the Black Legend: The Discourses of Religious and Racial Difference in the Renaissance Empires*, ed. Margaret R. Greer, Walter D. Mignolo, and Maureen Quilligan (Chicago: University of Chicago Press, 2007), 71–87; Nirenberg, "Was There Race before Modernity? The Example of 'Jewish' Blood in Late Medieval Spain," in *The Origins of Racism in the West*, ed. Miriam Eliav-Feldon, Benjamin Isaac, and Joseph Ziegler (New York: Cambridge University Press, 2009), 232–64.

[23] For a critique of the Old World model of mass baptisms, see José de Acosta, *De procuranda indorum salute*, vol. 2, 367–69; and Alonso Sandoval, *Naturaleza, policia sagrada*, book 3, chap. 4, 242v–249r.

[24] See Bristol, *Christians, Blasphemers, and Witches*, 63–91; J. Jorge Klor de Alva, "Colonizing Souls: The Failure of the Indian Inquisition and the Rise of Penitential Discipline," in *Cultural Encounters: The Impact of the Inquisition in Spain and the New World*, ed. Mary Elizabeth Perry and Anne J. Cruz (Berkeley: University of California Press, 1991), 3–23; Nicholas Griffiths, "Inquisition of the Indians?: The Inquisitorial Model and the Repression of Andean Religion in Seventeenth-Century Peru," *Colonial Latin American Historical Review* 3, no. 1 (1994): 19–38. Bristol notes that in 1518 King Charles I required all enslaved Africans imported to the New World to have already become Christians before arrival (68).

have speculated, originated from the fact that before 1580 most black men and women taken to Spanish America arrived by way of Iberia (and would have therefore been already considered Christian on arrival in the New World).[25]

The failure to update Inquisition policy on black men and women in Spanish America after 1580 when most black men and women began to arrive directly from Africa likely reflects the marginal priority black populations represented for New World missionaries and the Crown compared with indigenous populations. This was the case, in large part, because the basis for Spanish sovereignty in the Americas originally depended on indigenous evangelization, while African evangelization held no such connection to sovereignty.[26] A secondary, but also crucial, reason is that unlike missionary efforts among indigenous populations that had clear funding sources (from *repartimiento* labor and substantial tributes to the Crown), black men's and women's evangelization was not a lucrative enterprise in itself. Slaveholders were supposedly responsible for recompensing priests who tended to their slaves' spiritual care, but in practice slave owners were often reluctant to do so.[27] And even though free black men and women were supposed to pay tributes to the Crown in recognition of the costs related to "civilizing them," recent research has shown that they were not a significant source of revenue as many freed black individuals avoided tribute through exemptions related to military service or demonstrated poverty.[28]

[25] Martínez, *Genealogical Fictions*, 220–21; Bristol, *Christians, Blasphemers, and Witches*, 65–68.

[26] Alexander VI's papal bull of 1493 gave Spain and Portugal custodianship of the areas that were divided between the two in the Treaty of Tordesillas in 1494. See Anthony Pagden, *Spanish Imperialism and the Political Imagination: Studies in European and Spanish-American Social and Political Theory 1513–1830* (New Haven, CT: Yale University Press, 1990), 13–15. According to Pagden, by the mid-sixteenth century, Thomist Spanish theologians articulated a new justification of Spanish sovereignty in the Americas based on natives' voluntary submission to the Spanish Crown and the Catholic Church.

[27] A 1545 royal ordinance required slave owners to teach their black slaves to speak Spanish and to Christianize them within the first six months of arrival in the Americas. The ordinance reminds owners of the importance of tending to their enslaved black servants' spiritual care. See Richard Konetzke, *Colección de documentos para la historia de la formación social de Hispanoamérica, 1493–1810* (Madrid: Consejo Superior de Investigaciones Científicas, 1953–58), 1: 237. On complaints of slaveholder negligence regarding the spiritual care of the enslaved, see Alonso de Sandoval, *Naturaleza, policia sagrada i profana, costumbres i ritos, disciplina i catechismo evangelico de todos etiopes* (Seville: Francisco de Lyra, 1627), book 2, chap. 3, 137r–140r.

[28] See Cynthia Milton and Ben Vinson III, "Counting Heads: Race and Non-native Tribute Policy in Colonial Spanish America," *Journal of Colonialism and Colonial History* 3, no. 3 (2002); Karen Graubart, "African-Descent Self-Governance and the Paradigms for

For related reasons, black men and women in Spanish America also occupied a significantly more marginalized position in relation to the production of written texts than indigenous peoples. For example, whereas there are many examples of missionary efforts to compose narratives of the pre- or post-conquest memories, histories, and beliefs of indigenous populations as part of New World evangelical projects – many of which involved the participation of indigenous assistants and intermediaries – very few comparable works were produced to study Africans and their descendants in the Americas.[29] There exists for this period a comparatively small corpus of narrative texts composed in Spanish America to describe black men's and women's beliefs and backgrounds before or after their arrival in Spanish America in *any* amount of detail.[30] The

Racial Order," in *Republics of Difference: Racial and Religious Self-Governance in the Iberian Atlantic, 1400–1650* (forthcoming). For the eighteenth century, see Norah L. A. Gharala, *Taxing Blackness: Free Afromexican Tribute in Bourbon New Spain* (Tuscaloosa: University of Alabama Press, 2019).

[29] Some of the best-known narrative accounts of indigenous cultures from this period that are thought or known to have been composed by missionaries and native informants are Bernardino de Sahagún, *Historia general de las cosas de la Nueva España*; the *Popol Vuh*; the Chilam Balam; and the Huarochiri Manuscript. On the written corpus produced by Sahagún and his indigenous assistants, see Louise M. Burkhart, *The Slippery Earth: Nahua-Christian Moral Dialogue in Sixteenth-Century Mexico* (Tucson: University of Arizona Press, 1989) and Diana Magaloni Kerpel, *The Colors of the New World: Artists, Materials, and the Creation of the Florentine Codex* (Los Angeles, CA: Getty Museum, 2014). The best-known narratives about pre-conquest indigenous beliefs composed by Andean authors identifying as *indio* or mestizo are Inca Garcilaso de la Vega, *Los comentarios reales de los incas*; Guaman Poma de Ayala, *Primer nueva corónica y buen gobierno*. For a typographical study of such narratives, see Rolena Adorno, "The Indigenous Ethnographer: The 'Indio Ladino' as Historian and Cultural Mediation," in *Implicit Understandings: Observing, Reporting, and Reflecting on the Encounters between Europeans and Other Peoples in the Early Modern Era*, ed. Stuart B. Schwartz (New York: Cambridge University Press, 1994), 378–402.

[30] See Jesuit *cartas annuas* from New Granada, Paraguay, and Peru; Gerónymo Pallas's *Missión a las Indias* (1619); Alonso de Sandoval's *Naturaleza, policia sagrada i profana, costumbres i ritos, disciplina i catechismo evangelico de todos etiopes* (1627); Sandoval's *Historia de la Aethiopia* (1647), Estefanía de San José's hagiography (1646), Pedro Claver's beatification inquest (1658–60), Úrsula de Jesús's spiritual diary and hagiographies (1650–61, 1666, 1686), Martín de Porras's hagiographies (1673, 1675, 1680–81, 1696), Miguel de Santo Domingo's hagiography (1680–81), and Juan de la Cruz's and Juana Esperanza de San Alberto's hagiographies composed toward the turn of the eighteenth century. Another set of texts that could form part of this corpus but are not strictly narratives are the surviving records of the Inquisition in the New World on the practices and beliefs of black individuals in the Americas. For scholarship on New Granada Inquisition documents about black men and women, see Jaime Humberto Borja Gómez, *Rostros y rastros del demonio en la Nueva Granada: Indios, negros, judíos, mujeres y otras huestes de Satanás* (Bogota: Ariel, 1998); Luz Adriana Maya Restrepo, *Brujería y la reconstrucción*

comparable dearth of sources derives from the fact that on the whole missionaries perceived the black men and women arriving in the New World as displaced and dispossessed individuals, not members of coherent communities that persisted in meaningful ways in the New World.

A related feature of blackness that separated it from indigeneity in colonial Spanish America is the multilingual nature of the African diaspora. Especially in ports such as Cartagena, Lima, and Veracruz that received ships from an especially diverse set of African ports, there was no consistent common language shared by the black populations passing through them. In the absence of a common language, newly arrived black men and women spoke to each other and to other inhabitants of colonial societies through interpreters and improvised creole languages (often called *lenguas medias* in Spanish documents).[31] Eventually, Spanish or Portuguese became the common language if not the only one used by most black men and women in these areas.[32] While indigenous men and women were also enslaved and displaced in Spanish America, as Nancy van Deusen and others have shown, they were enslaved in much lower numbers.[33] The common missionary strategy of relocating indigenous populations en masse (as seen in processes of *reducción* and *congregación*) allowed for many of these communities to preserve their languages

de identidades entre los africanos y sus descendientes en la Nueva Granada, Siglo XVII (Bogota: Ministerio de Cultura, 2005); Sara Vicuña Guengerich, "The Witchcraft Trials of Paula de Eguiluz, a Black Woman in Cartagena de Indias, 1620–1636," in *Afro-Latino Voices: Narratives from the Early Modern Ibero-Atlantic World, 1550–1812,* ed. Kathryn Joy McKnight and Leo Garofalo (Indianapolis, IN: Hackett, 2009), 175-194; Nicole von Germeten, *Violent Delights, Violent Ends: Sex, Race, and Honor in Colonial Cartagena de Indias* (Albuquerque: University of New Mexico Press, 2013); Pablo F. Gómez, *The Experiential Caribbean: Creating Knowledge and Healing in the Early Modern Atlantic* (Chapel Hill: University of North Carolina Press, 2017); and forthcoming work by Ana María Silva Ocampo. On black men and women in the Inquisition in Lima, see the brief references throughout Paulino Castañeda and Pilar Hernández, *La Inquisición de Lima (1570–1635)* (Madrid: Deimos, 1989), 253-283, 456, 506.

[31] Jean-Pierre Tardieu, "Los jesuitas y la 'lengua de Angola' en Perú (Siglo XVII)," *Revista de Indias* 53, no. 198 (1993): 627–37, 627.

[32] In the Peruvian context, Jouve Martín argues that another motivation for learning Spanish was that it facilitated the access to written documents and the power they upheld as well as eliminated the linguistic barriers between black men and women and colonial officials (*Esclavos de la ciudad letrada,* 79). See also John M. Lipski, *A History of Afro-Hispanic Language: Five Centuries, Five Continents* (New York: Cambridge University Press, 2005), 1–3; and Tardieu, "Los Jesuitas y la 'lengua de Angola,'" 627, for similar arguments. Some examples of black communities that developed and preserved creoles in the Americas are Palenquero, Papiamento, San Andrés Island Creole, and Garifuna.

[33] Nancy van Deusen, "Diaspora, Bondage, and Intimacy in Lima, 1535–1555," *Colonial Latin American Review* 19, no. 2 (2010): 247–77; Van Deusen, *Global Indios.*

as opposed to the more fragmented displacement and diaspora of African languages in the Americas that resulted from the transatlantic slave trade in black men and women.[34]

In the context of the fragmentation and dispersal of linguistic groups among black populations reaching the New World, the importance of the work done by black intermediaries to facilitate communication among new arrivals is hard to exaggerate. We can imagine that long before the black men and women who disembarked from ships in Spanish America learned to speak Spanish they were in constant communication with each other and with other inhabitants of those colonial locations. These communications would have occurred through linguistic and spiritual intermediaries. Curiously, however, no extended study has examined the work of translation among black populations in colonial Spanish America.[35] Instead, scholarship on translation in colonial Latin America has focused entirely on the roles of native, *mestizo*, and Spanish intermediaries.[36]

---

[34] On the strategy of the *reducción*, see William Hanks, *Converting Words: Maya in the Age of the Cross* (Berkeley: University of California Press, 2010), and Daniel Nemser, *Infrastructures of Race: Concentration and Bio-politics in Colonial Mexico* (Austin: University of Texas Press, 2017).

[35] For the studies that do exist, see Wheat, *Atlantic Africa*, 229–238; Paola Vargas Arana, "Pedro Claver y la evangelización en Cartagena: Pilar del encuentro entre africanos y el Nuevo Mundo, siglo XVII," *Fronteras de la historia* 11 (2006): 293–328; and Joan Fayer, "African Interpreters in the Atlantic Slave Trade," *Anthropological Linguistics* 45, no. 3 (2003): 281–95. For studies of the use of translation in European encounters with west Africa, see P. E. H. Hair, "The Use of African Languages in Afro-European Contacts in Guinea: 1440–1560," *Sierra Leone Language Review* 5 (1966): 5–26; Wiley MacGaffey, "Dialogues of the Deaf: Europeans on the Atlantic Coast of Africa," in *Implicit Understandings: Observing, Reporting, and Reflecting on the Encounters between Europeans and Other Peoples in the Early Modern Era*, ed. Stuart B. Schwartz (New York: Cambridge University Press, 1994), 249–67; and George E. Brooks, *Eurafricans in Western Africa: Commerce, Social Status, Gender, and Religious Observance from the Sixteenth to the Eighteenth Century* (Athens: Ohio University Press, 2003), 31–53.

[36] There are too many works pertaining to this subfield in colonial Latin America to cite all of them here. For the classic assessment of the "indio ladino" as cultural and linguistic intermediary in colonial Spanish America, see Adorno, "The Indigenous Ethnographer." For a typology of kinds of translation in colonial Spanish America, see Larissa Brewer-García, "The Agency of Translation: New Assessments of the Roles of Non-European Linguistic Intermediaries," in *Routledge Companion on Colonial Latin America and the Caribbean*, ed. Santa Arias and Yolanda Martínez-San Miguel (2020). Some of the seminal monographs of the field are Rolena Adorno, *Guaman Poma: Writing and Resistance in Colonial Peru* (Austin: University of Texas Press, 1986); Louise Burkhart, *The Slippery Earth: Nahua-Christian Moral Dialogue in Sixteenth-Century Mexico* (Tucson: University of Arizona Press, 1989); Stephen Greenblatt, *Marvelous Possessions: The Wonder of the New World* (Chicago: University of Chicago Press, 1991); and Alida

Beyond Babel addresses this lacuna and opens the field of colonial translation studies to consider the lives, labor, and influence of black linguistic and spiritual intermediaries in the African diaspora in the Americas. Similar to Louise Burkhart's argument that translation in Nahuatl produced negotiated notions of Christianity in sixteenth-century New Spain, I will show in Chapters 3–5 that black men's and women's participation as linguistic and spiritual intermediaries created opportunities for them to shape understandings of Christianity and language related to blackness in seventeenth-century colonial texts.

Like other recent studies of colonial translation, this book examines colonial encounters that do not easily map onto a linear narrative of a unidirectional success in which Europeans harnessed language to establish colonial domination in the Americas.[37] For example, Alessandra Russo's concept of the untranslatable image, Anna Brickhouse's notion of the motivated mistranslation, and Allison Bigelow's examination of composite vernacular languages of science in colonial mining treatises underscore the highly mediated and multiply negotiated nature of translation in many distinct settings in early Spanish America. Focusing on New World material culture, Russo borrows Barbara Cassin's concept of the untranslatable philosophical term to demonstrate about how technes and aesthetics employed by artists on both sides of the Atlantic influenced each other. Brickhouse takes another approach, harnessing the power of conjecture to read European texts about native intermediaries to highlight

Metcalf, *Go-betweens and the Colonization of Brazil* (Austin: University of Austin Press, 2005). Some of the more recent works in this subfield are Nancy Farriss, *Tongues of Fire: Language and Evangelization in Colonial Mexico* (New York: Oxford University Press, 2018); Kerpel, *The Colors of the New World*; Anna Brickhouse, *The Unsettlement of America: Translation, Interpretation, and the Story of Don Luis de Velasco, 1569–1945* (New York: Oxford University Press, 2015); Alessandra Russo, *The Untranslatable Image: A Mestizo History of the Arts in New Spain, 1500–1600* (Austin: University of Texas Press, 2014); José Carlos de la Puente, "The Many Tongues of the King: Indigenous Language Interpreters and the Making of the Spanish Empire," *Colonial Latin American Review* 23, no. 2 (2014): 143–70; John Charles, *Allies at Odds: The Andean Church and Its Indigenous Agents, 1583–1671* (Albuquerque: University of New Mexico Press, 2010); Yanna Yannakakis, *The Art of Being in-between: Native Intermediaries, Indian Identities, and Local Rule in Colonial Oaxaca* (Durham, NC: Duke University Press, 2008); Camilla Townsend, *Malintzin's Choices: An Indian Woman and the Conquest of Mexico* (Albuquerque: University of New Mexico Press, 2006); Allison Bigelow, *Mining Language: Racial Thinking, Indigenous Knowledge, and Colonial Metallurgy in the Early Modern Iberian World* (Chapel Hill: University of North Carolina Press, 2020).

[37] See Brickhouse's survey of the typical narrative in "Mistranslation, Unsettlement, La Navidad," *PMLA* 128, no. 4 (2012): 938–46.

numerous instances in which native intermediaries undermined Spanish efforts at settlement. Allison Bigelow, for her part, examines colonial mining treatises to demonstrate how indigenous languages and mining techniques were constitutive of the development of colonial mining science.[38] In different ways, all of these scholars use colonial translation as a means of indexing a remainder of difference that is not fully subsumed by a narrative of univocal and unidirectional Spanish conquest and domination in the Americas.

The cases of black men and women who served as intermediaries in the documents analyzed in this book provide distinct challenges and rewards for colonial translation studies than the precedents mentioned above. On one hand, few identifiable material art objects designed by black men and women in Spanish America have survived, so Russo's approach, which depends primarily on the analysis of such objects, is hard to apply.[39] Furthermore, contrary to the native intermediaries about whom Brickhouse writes, the black men and women in the documents I analyze do not on the whole appear as actors with overtly anticolonial intentions. Instead, the black linguistic and spiritual intermediaries examined in this book appear to have worked *within* sanctioned spaces of colonial Christianity to articulate notions of blackness that are nonetheless different from those voiced by Church officials and slave-owning elites. And whereas Bigelow explores the discursive world of colonial mining for the influence of black and indigenous participation in the extraction and refining of the metals of the Americas, I consider the discursive world of Christianity in a multilingual black Atlantic that began earlier than has previously been considered. As I will show in Chapters 3 and 4, the black evangelical intermediaries' unique linguistic abilities in Cartagena allowed them to hide the real points of negotiation of spiritual conversion from those limited to European languages such that the exact terms of acceptance or rejection of Christianity are hard to detect in surviving documentation. What we can see from written evidence of their oral mediations in these documents is the emergence of new notions of blackness that reverberated in and beyond spaces of evangelical translation.

---

[38] Bigelow, *Mining Language.*

[39] Black men's labor was instrumental to the building of the convents, walls, streets, and buildings in many areas of colonial Latin America. These constructions, despite their longevity, are usually analyzed as products of European, *mestizo*, or indigenous architects' designs. See Frank Tannenbaum, *Slave and Citizen: The Negro in the Americas* (New York: Vintage, 1946), and Gilberto Freyre, *Brazil: An Interpretation* (New York: Knopf, 1945), 155–62.

In addition to bringing the study of black intermediaries to colonial translation studies, *Beyond Babel* contributes to two more debates that cut across colonial Latin American studies and African diaspora studies. One has to do with the question of cultural continuity and authority among black communities in the Americas. Contesting Orlando Patterson's argument about the social death experienced by enslaved black men and women forcibly taken to the Americas, a steady stream of studies over the last three and a half decades has sought to demonstrate that enslaved Africans brought with them certain traditions and recreated others in their areas of arrival in the Americas.[40] A different track has been taken by some historians of colonial Latin America who examine Inquisition records for the appearance of black men and women rejecting Christianization, arguing that the vitality of black colonial social life be read from archival glimpses of unorthodox religious behavior.[41] Critiques of this latter approach note that reading Inquisition sources for resistant black subjects can reify the colonial gaze of the Inquisition archive even as it tries to offer insight into black life.[42] *Beyond Babel* treads a new path in the debates about the social lives of black men and women in the diaspora by considering how black men and women served as intermediaries in the

---

[40] See Orlando Patterson, *Slavery and Social Death* (Cambridge, MA: Harvard University Press, 1982). Another line of research followed an alternative route charted by Sidney Mintz and Richard Price in *The Birth of African American Culture: An Anthropological Perspective* (Boston: Beacon, 1976), which prioritizes tracing how the culturally fragmented enslaved populations in the Americas created new creole cultures. Subsequent scholars have noted that Mintz and Price overemphasized the amount of fragmentation among diaspora cultures. For critiques of Mintz and Price, see Stephan Palmié, "Ethnogenetic Processes and Cultural Transfer in Caribbean Slave Populations," *Slavery in the Americas*, ed. Wolfgang Binder (Würzburg: Königshauser und Neumann, 1993), 337–64, 186; David Scott, "That Event, This Memory: Notes on an Anthropology of African Diasporas in the New World," *Diaspora* 1 (1991): 261–84.

[41] See Colin Palmer, *Slaves of the White God: Blacks in Mexico, 1570–1650* (New York: Cambridge University Press, 1976); Maya Restrepo, *Brujería y la reconstrucción*. More nuanced approaches can be seen in Javier Villa-Flores, *Dangerous Speech: A Social History of Blasphemy in Colonial Mexico* (Tucson: University of Arizona Press, 2006), especially 127–47, 129); James Sweet, *Domingos Alvares, African Healing, and the Intellectual History of the Atlantic World* (Chapel Hill: University of North Carolina Press, 2011); Gómez, *The Experiential Caribbean*.

[42] Bennett, *Africans in Colonial Mexico*, 51–78; Bristol, *Witches*, 188–189. Also see Marisa Fuentes, *Dispossessed Lives: Enslaved Women, Violence, and the Archive* (Philadelphia: University of Pennsylvania Press, 2016), 1–12, for a critique of how historians tend to reify power dynamics of the colonial archive in the Anglophone Caribbean context.

articulation of Christian identities in texts beyond those produced by the Inquisition.

This approach is informed by the work of Herman Bennett, Joan Bristol, Karen Graubart, José Ramón Jouve Martín, Michelle McKinley, Nancy van Deusen, and Javier Villa-Flores, whose respective studies of people of African descent in New Spain or Peru focus on ways Christian categories were activated in colonial legal settings to shape black subject-hood.[43] *Beyond Babel* builds on their efforts by examining the notions of blackness that appear in a collection of narrative texts produced about or in collaboration with black linguistic and spiritual intermediaries. In doing so, it demonstrates that the projects, spaces, and language support-ing the Christian salvation of black men and women in Spanish America served as venues for black men and women to craft new social lives and articulate notions of blackness beyond the negative stereotypes increas-ingly circulating in Iberian texts in the late sixteenth and seventeenth centuries.

In analyzing these sources and addressing the construction of blackness within them, *Beyond Babel* also contributes to the ongoing debate about the emergence of race in the early modern world. This debate has many strands, and while there are too many to describe all at length here, I will signal a few of particular importance to this book's argument. One important strand elaborated by David Nirenberg, among others, locates the emergence of modern discourse on race in mid-fifteenth-century Iberia at a moment when anticonverso polemicists began borrowing language from animal husbandry regarding inherited differences and disease in livestock to justify treating converted Jews and their offspring with suspi-cion even after becoming Christian.[44] Building on this argument, María

---

[43] In their respective studies, Bennett and McKinley take Frank Tannenbaum's observation in *Slave and Citizen* that the Church in Spanish America bestowed a "moral personality" on the slave as a point of departure. Bennett deviates from Tannenbaum's emphasis on the Church's potential to ameliorate slavery's excesses in Spanish America (in comparison to Anglo-America) by focusing on its role in regulating the lives of slaves (*Africans in Colonial Mexico*, 35). McKinley also echoes earlier critiques of Tannenbaum's naiveté regarding the living conditions of enslaved black men and women in colonial Spanish America while adding a gendered dimension to Tannenbaum's examination of the moral personality given to slaves in ecclesiastical law (*Fractional Freedom*, 8–13). For earlier important critiques of the Tannenbaum thesis as it relates to Spanish America, see Alejandro de la Fuente, "Slave Law and Claims-Making in Cuba: The Tannenbaum Debate Revisited," *Law and History Review* 22, no. 2 (2004): 304–69.

[44] See Yosef ayim Yerushalmi, *Assimilation and Racial Anti-Semitism: The Iberian and the German Models* (New York: Leo Back Institute, 1982); Netanyahu, *The Origins of the*

Elena Martínez and Max S. Hering Torres place late medieval Iberian anticonverso discourse into conversation with descriptions of human difference in colonial Spanish America, tracing how language and institutional forms developed in fifteenth- and sixteenth-century Iberia transformed in sixteenth- and seventeenth-century Spanish America to differentiate between people based on skin color rather than creed.[45] These scholars joined an older but still ongoing debate about the origins and meanings of race specific to the Americas. Aníbal Quijano, for example, proposed that the modern epistemology of race was born in Spanish America from the first encounters between the New and Old Worlds in the late fifteenth century, such that a coherent system of oppression (conceived of as "coloniality of power") can be traced from 1492 to the present.[46] In contrast, Irene Silverblatt and Daniel Nemser have argued in their different respective studies that racialization emerged in Spanish colonial enterprises of the mid-sixteenth and seventeenth centuries through particular practices of colonial administration.[47] Another strand of the debate relates specifically to identifying modern forms of racial categorization and discrimination as emergent in the eighteenth century along with the epistemological changes of the European Enlightenment.[48] Finally, Ruth Hill and Eduardo Restrepo, among others,

Inquisition; David Nirenberg, "Race and the Middle Ages"; Nirenberg, "Was There Race before Modernity?"

[45] Martínez, *Genealogical Fictions;* Max Hering Torres, "Cuerpo, misoginia y raza. España y las Américas en los siglos XVI–XVII," in *Desvelando el cuerpo: Perspectivas desde las ciencias sociales y humanas,* ed. Josep Martí and Yolanda Aixela (Madrid: CISC, 2010), 145–56; Nikolaus Böttcher, Bernd Hausberger, and Max S. Hering Torres, "Introducción. Sangre mestizaje y nobleza," in *El peso de la sangre. Limpios, mestizos y nobles en el mundo hispánico,* ed. Böttcher, Hausberger, and Hering Torres (Mexico City: El Colegio de México, 2011), 9–28; Hering Torres, "Purity of Blood: Problems of Interpretation," in *Race and Blood in the Iberian World,* ed. Max S. Hering Torres, María Elena Martínez, David Nirenberg (Zurich: Lit Verlag, 2012), 11–38.

[46] Aníbal Quijano, "Colonialidad del poder, cultura y conocimiento en América Latina," *Capitalismo y geopolítica del conocimiento: El eurocentrismo y la filosofía de la liberación en el debate intellectual contemporáneo,* ed. Walter Mignolo (Buenos Aires: Signo, 2001).

[47] Irene Silverblatt, *Modern Inquisitions: Peru and the Origins of the Civilized World* (Durham, NC: Duke University Press, 2004); Nemser, *Infrastructures of Race.* James Sweet, for his part, identified what he called "racialization without race" in the Hispanic world in the sixteenth century that resulted from prejudices against black peoples originating in Iberian Islamic culture. James Sweet, "The Iberian Roots of American Racist Thought," *William and Mary Quarterly* 54, no. 1 (1997): 143–66.

[48] See María Elena Martínez, along with María Eugenia Chaves, and Robert Schwaller. Another aspect of this trend has to do with the changing perceptions regarding the malleability of the body in relation to color, climate, the stars, and behaviors in the

identify the nineteenth century as the beginning of modern racial classification in Spanish America.[49]

   This book's intervention in these debates does not look to change our understanding of when race as we know it today began. I support others' arguments for reading early modern portrayals of human hierarchies as approximate cognates for contemporary racial categories while attending to the specificities of the languages, time, and place in which they appear in colonial sources. As Kathryn Burns so clearly explains, race "has long organized notions of fixity but has never itself been stable."[50] Instead of focusing on *when* exactly race "happened," *Beyond Babel* demonstrates

---

New World. For different angles related to the malleability of New World bodies, see Jorge Cañizares-Esguerra, "Demons, Stars, and the Imagination: The Early Modern Body in the Tropics," in *The Origins of Racism in the West*, 313–25; Ilona Katzew, "White or Black? Albinism and Spotted Blacks in the Eighteenth-Century Atlantic World," in *Envisioning Others: Race, Color, and the Visual in Iberia and Latin America*, ed. Pamela A. Patton (Leiden, 2016), 142–86; and Rebecca Earle, *The Body of the Conquistador: Food, Race and the Colonial Experience in Spanish America, 1492–1700* (New York: Cambridge University Press, 2012).

[49] Ruth Hill, *Hierarchy, Commerce, and Fraud: A Postal Inspector's Exposé* (Nashville, TN: Vanderbilt University Press, 2005), 198–200; and Eduardo Restrepo, "Eventalizing Blackness in Colombia" (PhD diss., University of North Carolina, Chapel Hill, 2008). For a review of these debates, see Kathryn Burns, "Unfixing Race," in *Rereading the Black Legend: The Discourses of Religious and Racial Difference in the Renaissance Empires*, ed. Margaret R. Greer, Walter D. Mignolo, and Maureen Quilligan (Chicago: University of Chicago Press, 2007), 188–204; and Andrew B. Fisher and Frank O'Hara, "Racial Identities and their Interpreters in Colonial Latin America," in *Imperial Subjects: Race and Identity in Colonial Latin America*, ed. Fisher and O'Hara (Durham, NC: Duke University Press, 2009), 1–38. For the debate related to the emergence of classificatory systems in relation to "class" and "casta," see Douglas Cope, *The Limits of Racial Domination: Plebian Society in Colonial Mexico, 1660–1720* (Madison: University of Wisconsin Press, 1994). For studies on the role gender plays in the construction and manipulation of casta categories, see Leo J. Garofalo and Rachel Sarah O'Toole, "Introduction: Constructing Difference in Colonial Latin America," *Journal of Colonialism and Colonial History* 7, no. 1 (2006); Martínez, *Genealogical Fictions*; and O'Toole, *Bound Lives*. For key works on the debate on the comparative study of race in the Americas and its complications, see Tannenbaum, *Slave and Citizen*; Michael Hanchard, *Orpheus and Power: The Movimiento Negro of Rio de Janeiro and Sao Paolo, 1945–1988* (Princeton: Princeton University Press, 1994); Howard Winant, *Racial Conditions: Politics, Theory, Comparisons* (Minneapolis: University of Minnesota Press, 1994); Peter Wade, "Images of Latin American Mestizaje and the Politics of Comparison," *Bulletin of Latin American Research* 23, no. 1 (2004): 355–66; Micol Seigel, *Uneven Encounters: Making Race and Nation in Brazil* (Durham, NC: Duke University Press, 2009). For a thorough literature review, see Wade, "Race in Latin America."

[50] Burns, "Unfixing Race," 188. See also David Nirenberg's incisive analysis of race in the medieval period compared with the present, "Race and the Middle Ages" and "Was There Race before Modernity?"

how black men and women participated in shaping what blackness meant as it happened. To do so, I underscore how the language black intermediaries helped produce about blackness overlaps with contemporary religious discourses related to territorial and political sovereignty of the Spanish Imperial project in the sixteenth and seventeenth centuries. A key point of this overlap will demonstrate that the growing discrimination associating black men and women with enslaved or minimally paid labor in late sixteenth- and seventeenth-century Spanish America was actually based on gestures of inclusion in the Christian category of the human, not exclusion.[51] This inclusion, while limited and hierarchical, became a condition of possibility of and a point of emphasis in black men's and women's own notions of what it meant to be black in colonial Spanish America: all people, even black people, are equal before God.

The term "blackness" itself (referenced in Spanish as *lo negro* or *la negrura*) rarely appears as an abstract concept in the sources I examine. While the abstraction itself is mine, it is done in close dialogue with the primary sources so as to attend to the differences between the distinct terms that make up the category and the reasons why the terms can be productively collapsed to make an argument about blackness in colonial Spanish America. More precise and contextualized definitions of what I mean by blackness will emerge from the individual chapters, but for the sake of establishing a common vocabulary as a point of departure, the remainder of this introduction offers working definitions of the most common terms associated with blackness in texts written about and from New Granada and Peru in the sixteenth and seventeenth centuries: *negro/a*, *etíope*, *moreno/a*, *pardo/a*, and *mulato/a*.

Individuals identified with any of these terms were perceived in relation to two interlocking criteria: (1) coming from or descending from at least one parent originating from what we now consider the African continent and (2) having some form of dark skin tone. As I will show in the next chapter, there were other linguistic, legal, and physical associations with blackness beyond place of origin and skin color circulating in this period, too, but they were not sine qua non criteria as these two were. While the five terms named above share these two criteria, it is also crucial to note that the different terms are by no means merely equivalent to each

---

[51] On the "differential inclusion" of *indios* and *mestizos* in New Spain, see Nemser, *Infrastructures of Race*, 88, 99–100.

other.[52] Although texts sometimes use more than one term to describe the same person or group, each name tended to carry specific valences and values with different relationships to hierarchy and stigma.[53] I will therefore keep the terms in their original in italics to avoid ignoring important specifications. To attend to these specifications, below I survey their typical uses around the turn of the seventeenth century in Spanish America. In doing so, I will note how they increasingly although not exclusively began to associate people of African descent with displacement, enslavement, and servitude.

Many of the colonial valences and values associated with *negro/a*, *etíope*, *moreno/a*, *pardo/a*, and *mulato/a* began to appear in Spanish discourse and visual art after the sixteenth century witnessed the arrival of unprecedented numbers of enslaved men, women, and children from Africa in the Iberian Peninsula and the Spanish American territories, as mentioned earlier in this introduction.[54] For example, although there existed a late medieval aesthetic tradition in visual and written texts of figures such as Saba (the queen of Sheba), the black magus, and Prester John that associated blackness with faraway wealth, power, and spiritual virtue, references to this tradition are absent from all definitions related to black men and women in Sebastián de Covarrubias's *Tesoro de la lengua castellana*, a dictionary published in Madrid in 1611. Instead of referring to any illustrious black figures of the late medieval and early modern imagination of blackness in Europe, Covarrubias explains in his definition for "negro" [black] that it is not only the term used for "el etiope de color negra" [the black Ethiopian] but also a term for a color considered "infausta y triste, y como tal usamos desta palabra, diziendo: Negra ventura, negra vida, etc." [unlucky and sad, like when we say: Black luck,

---

[52] Sherwin Bryant, Ben Vinson III, and Rachel Sarah O'Toole justify analyzing similar terms together insofar as they demonstrate a "politics of blackening cross-cut with gender at work in the colonial era" ("Introduction," in *Africans to Spanish America: Expanding the Diaspora*, ed. Bryant, O'Toole, and Vinson [Urbana: University of Illinois Press, 2012], 1–26, 13).

[53] In the "Vida de la Venerable Madre Ursula de Jesucristo," Franciscan Archive of Lima, Registro 17, No. 45, n.d., ff. 585r–607v, the narrator describes Úrsula as a "morena criolla" and "negra criolla" in the same paragraph, reflecting the interchangeability of the terms *morena* and *negra* in this text (f. 585v).

[54] For a study of earlier classifications and descriptions of black men and women arriving in Iberia in the late medieval Mediterranean trade, see Debra Blumenthal, *Enemies and Familiars: Slavery and Mastery in Fifteenth-Century Valencia* (Ithaca: Cornell University Press, 2009).

black life, etc.].⁵⁵ Covarrubias directly connects the color's symbolism to what he presumes to be the lowly position of black people themselves in Iberian societies by then citing the proverb "Aunque negros, gente somos" [Although we are black, we are people].⁵⁶ Meanwhile, Covarrubias describes white as representing "castidad, limpieza, alegría" [chastity, cleanliness, and happiness]⁵⁷ and expressly identifies black as its opposite: "Uno de los dos estremos de las colores, opuesto a blanco" [One of the two color extremes, the opposite of white].⁵⁸ Covarrubias's dictionary thus associates black men and women with servility, bad luck, and corruption, demonstrating key ways color symbolism affected the values assigned to individuals called *negros* in early seventeenth-century Spanish discourse. Such uses of the terms *negro* and *negra* traveled to Spanish America, appearing in now well-known texts composed by Spanish and indigenous authors before and after the turn of the seventeenth century.⁵⁹

Negro and *negra* also had a series of ambivalent religious associations on both sides of the Atlantic during this period. On one hand, there existed an association between the color and sin as seen in texts that

⁵⁵ Sebastián de Covarrubias, *Tesoro de la lengua castellana* (Madrid: Luis Sánches, 1611), 1: 562. Jack Forbes, *Africans and Native Americans: The Language of Race and the Evolution of Red-Black Peoples* (Chicago: University of Illinois Press, 1993), 71–72, gives an account of the use of *negro* in Portuguese in the sixteenth century to refer to New World natives. I do not include this alternative usage in my analysis as it does not appear to affect the use of *negro* in Peru and New Granada.

⁵⁶ Covarrubias, *Tesoro de la lengua castellana*, 1: 562. Two additional longer variations of this proverb appear in Gonzalo Correas, *Vocabulario de refranes y frases proverbiales* [1627] (Madrid: Olózaga, 1924): "Aunque somo negro, hombre somo, alma tenemo" and "Aunque somos negros, gente somos, alma tenemos" (73).

⁵⁷ Covarrubias, *Tesoro de la lengua castellana*, 1: 140r.   ⁵⁸ Ibid.

⁵⁹ For an early example, see Bartolomé de Las Casas, *Historia de las Indias* [1527–1559], ed. Agustín Millares Carlo (Mexico: Fondo de Cultura Económica, 1951), book 5, chap. 129. For a later example, see Felipe Guaman Poma de Ayala, *Primer nueva corónica y buen gobierno* [1615], ed. John V. Murra and Rolena Adorno (www.kb.dk/permalink/2006/poma/info/en/frontpage.htm), 940–941. On Las Casas's portrayals of black men and women as a plague in the New World as well as innocent victims of an unjust slave trade, see Rubén Sánchez Godoy, *El peor de los remedios: Bartolomé de las Casas y la crítica temprana a la esclavitud en el Atlántico ibérico* (Pittsburgh, PA: Iberoamericana, 2016), and "Mercancía, gentes pacíficas y plaga: Bartolomé de las Casas y los orígenes del pensamiento abolicionista en el Atlántico" (PhD diss., Pennsylvania State University, 2009), 54-55 in particular. For examinations of Guaman Poma's pejorative portrayals of blackness, see O'Toole, *Bound Lives*, 157–61; Valérie Benoist, "La conexión entre casta y familia en la representación de los negros," *Afro-Hispanic Review* 29, no. 1 (2010): 35–54; Jean-Pierre Tardieu, "L'integration des noirs dans le discours de Felipe Guaman Poma de Ayala," *Revue de CERC* 4 (1987): 40–60.

invoke the stain of sin as a mark that could be either washed out through confession or continuously suffered as a literal and permanent trace of God's curse of Cham for mocking his father.[60] A related connotation sometimes projected onto black men and women in early modern Spanish and Spanish American texts is an association with the devil and threatening sexuality. While this association has some precedents in early Christian and then medieval Europe, it became particularly prevalent in Spanish American texts in the seventeenth century.[61] For example, several

---

[60] For texts that speak of symbolically whitening African's souls, see Sandoval, *Naturaleza, policia sagrada*, and Pedro de Mercado, *Historia de la provincia del Nuevo Reino y Quito de la Compañía de Jesús* [c. 1688] (Bogota: Biblioteca de la Presidencia de Colombia, 1957), 1: 233; 3:13. Chapter 4 will discuss this tradition at greater length. On the emergence of the use of the curse of Cham as a justification for black enslavement, see A. J. R. Russel-Wood, "Before Columbus: Portugal's African Prelude to the Middle Passage and Contribution to Discourse on Race and Slavery," in *Race, Discourse, and the Origins of the Americas: A New World View*, ed. Vera Lawerence and Rex Nettleford (Washington, DC: Smithsonian, 1995); Benjamin Braude, "The Sons of Noah and the Construction of Ethnic and Geographical Identities in the Medieval and Early Modern Periods," *William and Mary Quarterly* 54, no. 1 (1997): 103–42; David M. Goldenberg, *The Curse of Ham: Race and Slavery in Early Judaism, Christianity, and Islam* (Princeton: Princeton University Press, 2003); David M. Whitford, *The Curse of Ham in the Early Modern Era: The Bible and the Justifications for Slavery* (New York: Routledge, 2009); and Larissa Brewer-García, "Imagined Transformations: Color, Beauty, and Black Christian Conversion in Seventeenth-Century Spanish America," in *Envisioning Others: Race, Color, and the Visual in Iberia and Latin America*, ed. Pamela A. Patton (Leiden: Brill, 2016), 111–41, 134.

[61] For early Christian instances of this stereotype, see Robert Hood, *Begrimed and Black: Christian Traditions on Blacks and Blackness* (Minneapolis: Fortress Press, 1994), 73–90; David Brakke, "Ethiopian Demons: Male Sexuality, the Black-Skinned Other, and the Monastic Self," *Journal of the History of Sexuality* 10, nos. 3–4 (2001): 501–35; Gay Byron, *Symbolic Blackness and Ethnic Difference in Early Christian Literature* (New York: Routledge, 2002). For primary sources demonstrating this phenomenon across medieval Europe, see Peter Abelard, "Letter 4 to Héloise," and Bernard of Clairvaux, "On the Song of Songs," in *Race in Early Modern England: A Documentary Companion*, ed. Ania Loomba and Jonathan Burton (New York: Palgrave Macmillan, 2007), 60–62, and *Cantiga* CLXXXVI of Alfonso X's thirteenth-century *Las Cantigas de Santa María*. For secondary studies of the phenomenon in Iberian medieval texts, see Andrew Beresford, "Sanctity and Prejudice in Medieval Castilian Hagiography: The Legend of S. Moses the Ethiopian," in *Medieval Hispanic Studies in Memory of Alan Deyermond*, ed. Andrew M. Beresford, Louise M. Haywood, and Julian Weiss (New York: Boydell and Brewer, 2013), 11–37. For the circulation of this stereotype in the New World in the sixteenth and seventeenth centuries, see Borja Gómez, *Rostros y rastros*, 103. Other examples of this kind of demonization of black men and women are referenced by Walter Hawthorne, *From Africa to Brazil: Culture, Identity, and an Atlantic Slave Trade, 1600–1830* (New York: Cambridge University Press, 2010); Laura Mello e Souza, *The Devil in the Land of the Holy Cross: Witchcraft, Slavery, and Popular Religion in Colonial Brazil*, trans. Diane Grosklaus Whitty (Austin: University of Texas Press,

life writings from the Andes describe protagonists encountering the devil in the form of a black man. The motif appears most often in texts by or about white men and women who report having conversed or copulated with the devil in the form of a black man (in dreams, visions, or possessions).[62] Blackness in these cases is conceived not only as sinful but as a demonic sexual threat.

On the other hand, there existed a competing religious connotation that associated black men and women with an innocent ignorance of God. This association conceives of the knowledge of God as "light" and the ignorance of God as "darkness." Employing this dichotomy, many visual and discursive representations of blackness present black men and women as innocent victims of ignorance who need missionaries to save them from their own darkness. Art historians Tanya J. Tiffany, Victor Stoichita, and Carmen Fracchia, in distinct studies, analyze the effects of this ideology on the representation of black religious subjects in Hispanic art, baptismal manuals, and sermons from the late sixteenth and seventeenth centuries.[63] This notion of blackness differs from the demonization mentioned above because it conceives of blackness as related to the blamelessness of the soon-to-be or recently converted, not the intentional (or inherited) guilt of a willful rejection of God and association with the devil. This particular Christian conception of blackness imagines black men and women as the ideal objects of evangelical efforts: like unconquered territory for the colonizer, they contain the promise of glory for

---

2004); and James Sweet, *Recreating Africa: Culture, Kinship, and Religion in the African-Portuguese World, 1441–1770* (Chapel Hill: University of North Carolina Press, 2003).

[62] See descriptions of the devil in *Vida de la V. M. Francisca Josefa de la Concepción* (Philadelphia: T. H. Palmer, 1817), chap. 39, 162. See also Rachel Sarah O'Toole, "'The Most Resplendent Flower of the Indies': Making Saints and Constructing Whiteness in Colonial Peru," in *Women, Religion, and the Atlantic World, 1600–1800*, ed. Daniella Kostroun and Lisa Vollendorf (Toronto: University of Toronto Press, 2009), 136–55.

[63] Victor Stoichita, "The Image of the Black in Spanish Art: Sixteenth and Seventeenth Centuries," in *The Image of the Black in Western Art, vol. 3: From "Age of Discovery" to the Age of Abolition: Artists of the Renaissance and Baroque* (Cambridge, MA: Harvard University Press, 2010), 191–234; Tanya J. Tiffany, "Light, Darkness, and African Salvation," *Art History* 31, no. 2 (2008): 33–56; Carmen Fracchia, "(Lack of) Visual Representation of Black Slaves in Spanish Golden Age Painting," *Journal of Iberian and Latin American Studies* 10 2004): 23–34. Margaret Olsen, in *Slavery and Salvation in Colonial Cartagena de Indias* (Gainesville: University Press of Florida, 2004), has also studied how Sandoval employs this imagery in *Naturaleza, policia sagrada*, explaining how in some passages Sandoval portrays black men and women as innocently ignorant of God (83–91).

missionaries capable of converting them.[64] Whereas the blackness associated with the devil reflects the fear of seduction by a black man or woman, the blackness associated with an innocent ignorance of Christ reveals the missionary fantasy of seducing black souls in a glorious spiritual conquest.

The notion of the black Christian, in fact, often circulated under another name: the *etíope* [Ethiopian]. The legends of Prester John, Moses's Ethiopian wife Sepphora, and the black magus provide important precedents for this use of the term *etíope*. "Ethiopia," during the sixteenth and seventeenth centuries, could refer to a variety of geographic locations, and therefore those described as *etíopes* were not necessarily tied to a fixed geographic area. Even though the term sometimes referred specifically to people from the kingdom of Ethiopia located in what is today's northeastern Africa, it was also used more broadly to refer to any dark-skinned Christian people.[65] Uses of this term for the latter purpose relate to the fact that several passages in Scripture mention the promise of Ethiopian conversion to Christianity.[66] Sandoval's treatise *Naturaleza, policia sagrada* manipulates the distinction between the different peoples of the African continent by referring to *etíopes* in the title of his text and then clarifying in the first

---

[64] See Sandoval, *Naturaleza, policia sagrada*, book 3, chap. 1, 230r–v, on the paramount glory of evangelizing *negros bozales*. Baltasar Fra Molinero, "Ser mulato en España y América: Discursos legales y otros discursos literarios," in *Negros, mulatos, zambaigos: Derroteros africanos en los mundos ibéricos*, ed. Berta Ares Queija and Alessandro Stella (Seville: Escuela de Estudios Hispano-Americanos, 2000), 123–47, describes this particular archetype of black men and women as "a means of reaching glory" (125). Regarding the manifestation of similar ideology in colonial New Spain, see Nicole von Germeten, "Corporate Salvation in a Colonial Society: Confraternities and Social Mobility for Africans and Their Descendants in New Spain" (PhD diss., University of California Berkeley, 2003), 15–61.

[65] See Luis de Urreta, *Historia eclesiastica, politica, natural, y moral, de los grandes y remotos Reynos de la Etiopia, Monarchia del Emperador, llamado Preste Juan de las Indias* (Valencia, 1610), for an example of the more geographically limited use of "Etiopia" [Ethiopia] and "*etíope*" [Ethiopian] in early seventeenth-century Spanish discourse. On Urreta's notion of Ethiopia, see Brewer-García, "Hierarchy and Holiness in the Earliest Colonial Black Hagiographies: Alonso de Sandoval and His Sources," *William and Mary Quarterly* 76, no. 3 (2019): 477–508.

[66] For example, "Ethiopia shall soon stretch out her hands unto God" (Psalm 67:32 Vulgate; 68:31 KJB). See also Jean Marie Courtès, "The Theme of 'Ethiopia' and 'Ethiopians' in Patristic Literature," in *The Image of the Black in Western Art, vol. 2: From Early Christianity to the "Age of Discovery": From the Demonic Threat to the Incarnation of Sainthood* (Cambridge, MA: Harvard University Press, 2010), 199–214.

book of the treatise that *etíopes* are also commonly called *negros* or *morenos*.[67]

Moreno/a also had a variety of meanings in late sixteenth- and seventeenth-century Spanish-language texts. Those composed in Spanish America generally use the term differently than contemporary texts from the Iberian Peninsula. For example, in Iberia Covarrubias defines *moreno* as a color with an uncertain approximation to black, relating it to the color of Moors.[68] This association coexists with another popular connotation for *morena* that appears in popular lyric from the period as the object of affection or the beloved. Scholar of Iberian popular lyric Margit Frenk argues that this association relates to the symbolism of the dark-skinned woman as colored by her loss of virginity.[69] In contrast to such uses common to the Iberian Peninsula in the sixteenth century, in Spanish America *moreno/a* explicitly referred to dark-skinned people from western Africa or descending from those who originated there. Sometimes *moreno* or *morena* appear to be synonyms for *negro* or *negra* (or *etíope*), as when Alonso de Sandoval describes the baptisms of *morenos* on the shores of western Africa before their shipment to the Americas.[70] Other times, *moreno/a* appears in Spanish American texts in distinction with *negro* and *negra* to name individuals of African descent who were not

---

[67] See the chapter in Sandoval's *Naturaleza, policia sagrada*, titled: "De la naturaleza de los Etiopes, que comunmente llamamos negros" [Of the nature of Ethiopians, whom we commonly call blacks] (book 1, chap. 2, 10r). See also Brewer-García, "Hierarchy and Holiness in the Earliest Colonial Black Hagiographies."

[68] "Color, la que no es del todo negra, como la de los moros, de donde tomó nombre, o de mora" [A color that is not completely black, like that of the Moors, from which it took its name, or that of the blackberry] (Covarrubias, *Tesoro de la lengua*, 1: 555). See Valentín Groebner, *Who Are You?: Identification, Deception, and Surveillance in Early Modern Europe* (New York: Zone, 2007), 131–32, on a distinct notion of "brown" in medieval European texts that associates the color with humoral traits of an individual instead of an ascription to a broad status-related type.

[69] Margit Frenk, "Símbolos naturales en las viejas canciones populares," in *Poesía popular hispánica: 44 estudios* (Mexico, DF: Fondo de Cultura Económica, 2006), 239–352; Frenk, "La canción popular femenina en el Siglo de Oro," in *Poesía popular hispánica*, 336–37; Daniel Devoto, *Cancionero llamado Flor de la rosa* (Buenos Aires: Francisco A. Colombo, 1950), 126–32; Alfonso Alegre Heitzmann, "El color de la Sulamita en las Biblias medievales romanceadas," *Anuario de Filología* 5 (1979): 239–56; José M. A. Alín, *El cancionero español de tipo tradicional* (Madrid: Taurus, 1968), 253–57; Wardropper, "The Color Problem in Spanish Traditional Poetry," *Modern Language Notes* 75, no. 5 (1960): 415–21; Wardropper, "The Impact of Folk Song on Sacred and Profane Love Poetry in Post-Tridentine Spain," *The Sixteenth Century Journal* 17, no. 4 (1986): 483–98.

[70] Sandoval, *Naturaleza, policia sagrada*, book III, chap. 4, 234r.

enslaved or who held a higher social status. For example, Gerónymo Pallas's description of the different kinds of black populations living around Cartagena in the early seventeenth century employs *moreno* in distinction with *negro* to name people of African descent who occupied positions of higher status: "De los negros criollos (esto es los nacidos acá en las Indias) muchos son libertos, los cuales están alistados en compañía[s] de soldados con su capitán y oficiales morenos" [Of the black *criollos* (that is those born here in the Indies) many are freed. These participate as soldiers of militias with *moreno* captains and officials].[71] Even though Pallas uses the term *moreno* to refer to individuals of a higher status than that of other *negros*, he includes all of them in the category of *negros criollos*.[72] In another important example, Graubart's study of black confraternities in seventeenth-century Lima notes that free or freed people of African descent sometimes chose to call themselves *morenos* to set themselves apart from enslaved black men and women.[73]

Mulato/a is yet one more term used to describe people of African descent in texts from this period.[74] Compared with *negro/a* and *moreno/a*, however, *mulato/a* does not expressly refer to a color-related

---

[71] Pallas, *Missión a las indias*, 114. On the multivalent uses of the term *criollo* in late sixteenth century and seventeenth century, see Karen Graubart, "The Creolization of the New World: Local Forms of Identification in Urban Colonial Peru, 1560–1640," *Hispanic American Historical Review* 89, no. 3 (2009): 471–99.

[72] On free black men in the military in colonial Spanish America and the use of the term *moreno*, see Ben Vinson III, "Race and Badge: The Free-Colored Militia in Colonial Mexico," *The Americas* 56, no. 4 (2000): 471–96, 472; Jean-Paul Zúñiga, "'Morena me llaman . . .' Exclusión e integración de los afroamericanos en Hispanoamérica: El ejemplo de algunas regiones del antiguo virreinato del Perú (siglos XVI–XVIII)," in *Negros, mulatos, zambaigos: Derroteros africanos en los mundos ibéricos*, ed. Berta Ares Queija and Alessandro Stella (Sevilla: Publicaciones de la Escuela de Estudios Hispano-Americanos, 2000), 105–22, 109. An important clarification is offered by Joanne Rappaport's study of the use of the term *moreno* in travel documents from seventeenth-century New Granada. Rappaport finds that *moreno* as an adjective is never used to describe the traits of those identified as *negros* in the travel documents, but it was used as an adjective for the complexion and hair and eye color for some indigenous peoples and Spaniards (*The Disappearing Mestizo: Configuring Difference in the Colonial New Kingdom of Granada* [Durham, NC: Duke University Press, 2014], 171–204). This fact reveals the importance of differentiating between the use of these terms as adjectives and as nouns in colonial texts.

[73] Graubart, "So color de una cofradía." On "negro" as a synonym for slave at the turn of the seventeenth century in Iberia, see Fracchia, "(Lack of) Visual Representation."

[74] On *mulatos* in Spanish America in the sixteenth and seventeenth centuries, see Martínez, *Genealogical Fictions*, 164–65; Berta Ares Queija, "Mestizos, mulatos y zambaigos (Virreinato del Perú, siglo XVI)," in *Negros, mulatos, zambaigos*, 75–88; and Fra Molinero, "Ser mulato."

category but instead to a person's mixed parentage when one of the parents is of African descent. As a result, a *mulato* or *mulata* in sixteenth- and seventeenth-century Spanish texts could be described as "light" or "dark."[75] Covarrubias confirms that *mulato/a* refers to mixed parentage rather than a precise color when he defines the term as "El que es hijo de negra y de hombre blanco, o al revés y por ser mezcla extraordinaria la compararon con la naturaleza del mulo" [The child of a black woman and a white man, or the reverse; for being an extraordinary mix they compare it to the nature of the mule].[76] Comparing the *mulato/a* to the degeneracy and hybridity of the mule invokes animal husbandry language to describe new "kinds" of people emerging in the early modern period through global contact.[77] Additionally, in the Americas, *mulato/a*, like *negro/a*, had its more positively inflected euphemism that grew in popularity in the mid- to late seventeenth century: *pardo/a*.[78] As with the abovementioned phenomenon of *morenos,* Jouve Martín's study of the self-representations of *mulatos* in seventeenth-century Peru finds that people identifying as *mulatos* sometimes tried to distance themselves from the label of *negro* because of the latter's association with servitude and enslavement.[79]

The term *mulato* carried with it an additional legacy tied to darkness: the stain of infamy related to the suspicion of having been born of an adulterous union. Associations between *mulato/a* and illegitimacy appear, for example, throughout Solórzano y Pereira's *Política Indiana* from the

---

[75] Forbes, *Africans and Native Americans*, 148–50; Richard Boyer, "Negotiating *Calidad*: The Everyday Struggle for Status in Mexico," *Historical Archaeology* 31, no. 1 (1997): 64–72, 68–69.

[76] Covarrubias, *Tesoro de la lengua castellana*, 1: 117v.

[77] On the use of animal husbandry terms to describe human differences in early modern Spanish, see Hill, *Hierarchy, Commerce, and Fraud*, 205, 259–60; and Javier Irigoyen, "Diana and Wild Boar Hunting: Refiguring Gender and Ethno-Religious Conflict in the Pastoral Imaginary," *Bulletin of Hispanic Studies* 88, no. 3 (2011): 237–87. Rappaport specifies that *mulatos* could be born of a range of specific combinations of mixed parentage: "indigenous–African or European–African in the Americas, but also European–North African in Spain" ("'Asi lo paresçe por su aspecto: Physiognomy and the Construction of Difference in Colonial Bogotá," *Hispanic American Historical Review* 91, no. 4 [2011]: 601–31, 603).

[78] Ann Twinam, "Purchasing Whiteness: Conversations on the Essence of Pardo-ness and Mulatto-ness at the End of the Empire," in *Imperial Subjects*, 141–66, explains that "Pardo usually means 'dark skinned' although the term can be used interchangeably with 'mulato'" (161).

[79] Jouve Martín, *Esclavos de la ciudad letrada*, 47. See also Jouve Martín, "Public Ceremonies and Mulatto Identity in Viceregal Lima: A Colonial Reenactment of the Fall of Troy (1631)," *Colonial Latin American Review* 16, no. 2 (2007): 179–201.

mid-seventeenth century. In following passage, the Iberian jurist writing in Peru states that the infamy attributed to *mulatos* did not necessarily result from the mixture itself of which they were born, but rather from the presumed illegitimacy of the unions that produced them:

si estos hombres huviessen nacido de legitimo matrimonio, y no se hallasse en ellos otro vicio, u defecto, que lo impidiesse, tenerse, y constarse podrán, y deberian por Ciudadanos de dichas Provincias, y ser admitidos a honras, y Oficios de ellas ... [p]ero porque lo mas ordinario es, que nacen de adulterio, o de otros ilicitos, y punibles ayuntamientos: porque pocos Españoles de honra ay que casen con Indias o Negras, el qual defecto de los Natales les hace infames.

[if these men were born of legitimate matrimonies, and if no other vice or defect that might limit him is discovered, they can and should be considered and included as citizens of these provinces and awarded honors and titles thereof ... but it is most common for them to be born of adultery or of other illicit and punishable unions; because there are few honorable Spaniards who marry Indians or black women; this defect of the offspring makes them *infame*.][80]

Although *mulatos* were not always born out of wedlock, Solórzano y Pereira suggests that the suspicion of illegitimacy accompanied all *mulatos/mulatas* and *mestizos/mestizas* regardless of the actual marital status of their parents. For similar reasons, Baltasar Fra Molinero states that in seventeenth-century dramas performed in Iberia, *mulatos/mulatas* often appear as objects of ridicule due to the illegitimacy of which they were assumed to have been born.[81] References to the darkness or blackness of a *mulato/a* in colonial Spanish American texts, then, could refer to an individual's skin tone and/or to the metaphoric obscurity of his or her lineage or conditions of birth. The double interpretation of the *mulato/a*'s darkness is supported by Covarrubias's definition of "claro" [light]: "Lo que se opone a lo escuro, tenebroso y dificultoso. Claro linage, el ilustre y generoso" [The opposite of that which is dark, shadowy, and difficult. Light lineage, illustrious and generous].[82] For such a presumed lack of clarity and the additional infamy of having being born into slavery or descending from a parent who had been enslaved, invocations of *limpieza de sangre* in the New World began to exclude *negros/as*, *mulatos/as*, and other "mixed populations."[83]

---

[80] Juan Solórzano y Pereira, *Política Indiana* (Madrid: Diego Diaz de la Carrera, 1648), 246.

[81] Fra Molinero, "Ser mulato," 127.

[82] Covarrubias, *Tesoro de la lengua castellana*, 1: 215.

[83] Fra Molinero, "Ser mulato," 135–37; Martínez, *Genealogical Fictions*, 220–26; Carmen Bernand, *Negros esclavos y libres en las ciudades hispanoamericanas* (Madrid: Tavera, 2000), 100–106.

In contrast, by the early seventeenth century in Spanish America, documents employ the terms *blanco/a* [white] as synonyms for *español/a* [Spanish]. Like the double meaning of the darkness of a *mulato*, the association between *blanco/a* and *español/a* was related not only to the presumed lighter skin tone of Spaniards but also to the supposed clarity of their lineage in comparison to those born of mixed parentage in the New World.[84] Joanne Rappaport, building on work by Ann Twinam, suggests that whiteness was first used as a color term before appearing as a category in late seventeenth-century Spanish America.[85] Yet there are earlier uses of *blanco* as a color-related category. For example, Pallas's 1619 narrative demonstrates that by the second decade of the seventeenth century people in Spanish America used the terms Spaniard and *blanco/a* as synonyms to refer categorically to any European-born person of a presumed higher class who was free of the reputation of being "contaminated" with mixed or illegitimate parentage:

es de advertir que por español se entiende cualquier hombre blanco nascido en Europa y otras provincias o islas de los que acá passan y viven en estos reynos, porque el nombre español fuera de significar la naçión es título de honra, y vale lo mesmo que hombre no indio, ni mestizo, ni quarterón, ni mulato, ni negro ettz. sino como en Castilla se dize un hidalgo.

[It should be noted that Spaniard is understood as any white man born in Europe or other provinces and islands from which they originate and come here to live in these kingdoms, because the name Spaniard, other than meaning a nation, is an honorable title and is like saying a man who is not Indian, mestizo, *quarterón*, *mulato*, or black, etc., like the term nobleman used in Castile.][86]

Pallas's explanation thus defines *blanco* as a category shaped by color, class, and geographic place of origin in Spanish America. Contrary to its use in the Iberian Peninsula, Pallas demonstrates that language to describe class differences (specifically related to the status of nobility compared with that of a commoner) was redeployed by the early seventeenth century to describe emerging racial hierarchies in the Americas. Pallas's description implies that a person considered *negro/a*, *indio/a*, or *producto de alguna mezcla* would have limited access to whiteness's categorical associations with nobility in the New World, whether it be nobility tied to

---

[84] Martínez, *Genealogical Fictions*, 268. Martínez explains that the emerging association between whiteness and Spanishness in New Spain resulted from the adaptation of Peninsular *limpieza de sangre* discourse to Spanish American circumstances.

[85] Rappaport, *Disappearing Mestizo*, 197; Ann Twinam, "Purchasing Whiteness," 154.

[86] Pallas, *Missión a las Indias*, 163–64.

wealth, titles, or merely the prestige of coming from or descending from white European parents.[87]

Documents from this period demonstrate that the distinctions between *negro/a*, *moreno/a*, *etíope*, and *mulato/a* surveyed here were far from consistent. For example, some enslaved people called themselves *morenos/as* and some non-enslaved people called themselves *negros/as*; other times, both terms are used in the same text to refer to the same individual.[88] Such variations show that these different terms for blackness were not clear static markers of status and value, but that like "woman" and "lady" in today's English they could at times demarcate the same person, while in other instances they could distinguish between people of different social statuses. Nor do the common distinctions between the terms reviewed above revolve around a single coherent ideology of *limpieza de sangre* or color gradation. Rather, they show the confluence of different generic norms and aesthetic and moral values that circulated in the early modern Hispanic world.[89] As a whole, their use evidences the prevalence of what Ruth Hill calls the "norm of inequality" that existed in viceregal societies in the Americas: "a written and unwritten hierarchy that *ostensibly* mirrored nature and its laws but was in fact a social construct."[90]

The chapters of this book will explore how such a "norm of inequality" that by the late sixteenth century tended to place black men and women on the lowest end of colonial social hierarchies coexisted with the Christian ideology that *all* people are equal before God. In its

---

[87] Covarrubias's definition of white adds yet another facet to this association between whiteness and prestige by describing the virtues of whiteness in relation to the shining holy garments of prophets and angels as well as the noble robes of Roman dignitaries (Covarrubias, *Tesoro de la lengua castellana*, 1: 140r).

[88] In addition to the examples provided in notes 53 and 70, enslaved Biafada interpreter Manuel Moreno is described in *Proceso 1676* as the least acculturated black interpreter owned by the Jesuits in Cartagena; yet he is the only one who uses *moreno* as his last name (*Proceso 1676*, Manuel Moreno, 98v–99v).

[89] For studies on the baroque plurality of colonial Spanish American societies that provide context for this confluence, see Karen Graubart, *Republics of Difference* (forthcoming); Tamar Herzog, *Frontiers of Possession: Spain and Portugal in Europe and the Americas* (Cambridge, MA: Harvard University Press, 2015); Lauren Benton, *Law and Colonial Cultures: Legal Regimes in World History, 1400–1900* (New York: Cambridge University Press, 2002); Joanne Rappaport and Tom Cummins, *Beyond the Lettered City: Indigenous Literacies in the Andes* (Durham, NC: Duke University Press, 2012); and Alejandro Cañeque, *The King's Living Image: The Culture and Politics of Viceregal Power in Colonial Mexico* (New York: Oxford University Press, 2004).

[90] Hill, *Hierarchy, Commerce, and Fraud*, 197.

examination of this juxtaposition, *Beyond Babel* will show that the ideology of Christian equality was leveraged by certain black linguistic and spiritual intermediaries in seventeenth-century Spanish America to identify with and articulate notions of black virtue and black beauty in colonial texts. Engaging these notions with care allows us to tell new stories about the making of blackness in colonial Spanish America.

Black Types between Renaissance Humanism and Iberian Counter Reformation Theology

During an ocean voyage from Panama to Lima in December 1618, young Jesuit student Gerónymo Pallas's party reached shore at the port of San Mateo, on the coast of contemporary Ecuador, after surviving a menacing storm. According to his account, upon arrival in San Mateo, Pallas and his weary fellow travelers encountered a community of *indios mulatos* inhabiting the area. By speaking to one who knew Spanish, the Jesuit pilgrims learned the history of the community. According to the informant, more than a generation earlier, African survivors of a shipwrecked slave ship founded the community after swimming ashore and fighting against the men of the indigenous community inhabiting the coast at the time. The new community consisted of the children born to the indigenous women of the area and the African castaways: "Los hijos pues destos negros conquistadores y de aquellas indias son los que hasta oy duran y se llaman indios mulatos" [The children of these black conquistadors and those indigenous women who live there today and are called *indios mulatos*].[1] Throughout the rest of his description of the inhabitants of the area near San Mateo, Pallas variably refers to the members of this community as *negros, mulatos,* and *indios mulatos.*[2]

---

[1] Pallas, *Missión a las Indias,* 164.

[2] For more on texts produced about the black populations on the coast of today's Ecuador such as the one that Pallas describes, see Ruben Sánchez Godoy, "Early African-Amerindian Subjectivities in Miguel Cabello Balboa's *Verdadera descripción de la provincia de Esmeraldas* (1583)," *Comparative Literature* 49, no. 2 (2012): 167–85; Charles Beatty-Medina, "Rebels and Conquerors: African Slaves, Spanish Authority, and the Domination of Esmeraldas, 1563–1621" (PhD diss., Brown University, 2002); Beatty-Medina, "Between the Cross and the Sword: Religious Conquest and Maroon Legitimacy

Despite the variety of terms used for its people, Pallas invokes a universal definition of blackness to signal what he considers one of the community's most salient characteristics – the linguistic plurality of its members:

Algunos ay que saben hablar en lengua española porque van y vienen a la ciudad de Quito, que dista pocas leguas, y destos era uno el que habló con los padres en la plaia. Los otros hablarán un lenguage que no avrá calepino que lo interprete, porque será mesclado y corrompido de una lengua india y de treynta differencias de Guineo, porque cuantas castas vienen de negros tantas son las diversidades de lenguas que ay entre ellos, y por esto se dize todos somos negros y no nos entendemos.

[There are some who know how to speak the Spanish language, because they come and go from the City of Quito, which is only a few days' travel away. And one of those spoke with the fathers on the beach. The others spoke a language that no dictionary could interpret, as it is a mixture and corruption of one indigenous tongue and thirty different kinds of Guinean, because there are as many different languages among blacks as there are *castas* among them. And that is why it is said: we are all blacks, and we do not understand each other.][3]

By invoking the adage "todos somos negros y no nos entendemos" [we are all blacks, and we do not understand each other], Pallas associates blackness with diverse, corrupt, and incomprehensible speech and implies that all black men and women are *bozales*.[4]

First used in the mid-fifteenth century as a term for an undomesticated horse, *bozal* emerged soon afterward as a label for black men or women

in Colonial Esmeraldas," in *Africans to Spanish America*, 95–113; Tom Cummins, "Three Gentlemen from Esmeraldas: A Portrait Fit for a King," in *Slave Portraiture in the Atlantic World*, ed. Agnes Lugo-Ortiz and Angela Rosenthal (New York: Cambridge University Press, 2013), 119–46. For studies of black populations of colonial Quito and surrounding areas, see Kris Lane, "Captivity and Redemption," in *Quito, 1599: A Colony in Transition* (Albuquerque: University of New Mexico Press, 2002); Sherwin Bryant, *Rivers of Gold*; and Jean-Pierre Tardieu, *El negro en la Real Audiencia de Quito, ss. XVI–XVII* (Quito: Abya-Yala, 2006).

[3] Pallas, *Missión a las Indias*, 164.

[4] This adage appears in Gonzalo Correas, *Vocabulario de refranes y frases proverbiales*, 483. An inversion of this adage is used in present-day Dominican Republic, Puerto Rico, and Venezuela: "Ellos son blancos y se entienden" [They are whites so they understand each other]. Speakers employ this expression to describe people who should be left alone to resolve their differences or problems. Both expressions invoke the listener and the speaker as not white – though the adage quoted by Pallas suggests a lack of comprehension among black men and women vis-à-vis each other, and the latter suggests a lack of understanding by nonwhites of whites. The two expressions similarly locate black subjects in a colonial context of nonsignification.

with limited ability to communicate in Iberian languages.[5] The term was used frequently in the latter sense in the seventeenth century as evident in Covarrubias's definition: "Es el negro que no sabe otra lengua que la suya" [He is the black person who does not know another language but his own].[6] Pallas's use of the expression "todos somos negros y no nos entendemos" [we are all blacks and we do not understand each other] demonstrates how the terms *bozal* and *negro* often stood in for each other in this period such that the nonnormative speech of the *bozal* had become a common marker of blackness in general. As this chapter will show, such an association brought with it a set of negative values according to Iberian Renaissance humanist ideology. And yet, Pallas's description of the community near San Mateo also hints at a different possible relationship between blackness, language, and civility. He notes that the African castaways had become conquistadors in their own right ("negros conquistadores" [black conquistadors]) and that some members of the resulting community had learned Spanish through their intermittent contact with Quito, demonstrating an awareness that black men and women were not forever condemned to *bozalidad* but rather were capable of settling territory and learning European languages, hinting at a possible evangelical project Jesuits could undertake in the area in the future.

While Pallas's narrative demonstrates how one text can juxtapose different typological portrayals of blackness, this chapter compares three different black types that circulated in distinct genres of texts in sixteenth- and seventeenth-century Spanish America, focusing on the types that were most prevalent in Peru and New Granada. The three types surveyed in what follows are (1) the *bozal* of literary stereotype, (2) the black person of legal ordinances, and (3) the black Christian or proto-Christian of evangelical treatises. Comparing these three types will show that even though literary, legal, and theological treatments of blackness generally present black men and women as the least civilized type of human, conceived in relation to unruly bodies rather than intellectual capacities, a unique angle for conceiving of black men and women appears in evangelical texts. Due to the demands of a particular strain of Iberian Counter Reformation theology in Spanish America, typological portrayals of black Christians or proto-Christians in missionary texts acknowledge black men's and

---

[5] Blumenthal, *Enemies and Familiars*, cites notarial documents from the late fifteenth century identifying certain individuals as so "uncivilized" (*molt boçal*) that they could not provide testimonies regarding the legitimacy of their captivity (42–43, nn. 95–99).

[6] Covarrubias, *Tesoro de la lengua*, 1: 143.

women's intellectual capacities, whatever their level of civility, as a means of justifying their ability to become Christians. The juxtaposition of the three generic types will demonstrate that even as racial hierarchies in the Iberian world were cohering and increasingly associating blackness with bodies direly in need of civilizing tutelage, theological discourse left open a loophole for conceiving of black intellectual capacities and spiritual virtue.

My conception of the Renaissance humanism that informs these three black types draws on Margarita Zamora's notion of it as both a method of study (a hermeneutic philology that proposed returning to the original languages of classical texts in order to recover the intention of their original authors) and an ideological program that encouraged restructuring the ultimate goals of systematized education to privilege proficiency in eloquent speech and writing.[7] As humanist ideas spread throughout Europe in the early Renaissance, the cultivation of eloquent language became increasingly important to standard educational programs. By the end of the fifteenth century in Iberia, for example, curriculum reform at universities had replaced the medieval *trivium* of grammar, logic, and rhetoric with the *studia humanitatis* model that subsumed logic under the category of rhetoric.[8] This change, according to Lisa Jardine, reflects humanists' subordination of reason to its development and expression in persuasive language.[9] It follows that if reason was conceived and expressed in language, then a person without the ability to use language

---

[7] Margarita Zamora, *Language, Authority, and Indigenous History in the* Comentarios reales de los Incas (New York: Cambridge University Press, 1988), 12. The term "humanism" itself was not actually employed by those who are now considered to have practiced humanism, however. The vernacular term "humanist" (*umanista*) came into use much earlier than any version of "humanism." The first uses of *umanista* appear in the fifteenth century to refer to teachers of classical literature and then also to their students. See Augusto Campana, "The Origin of the Word Humanist," *Journal of the Warburg and Courtauld Institutes* 9 (1946): 60–73; R. Avesani, "La professione dell'umanista nel Cinquecento," *Italia medioevale e umanistica* 13 (1970): 205–32.

[8] The humanist educational program focused on language training was explicitly stated in Lorenzo Valla's *De linguae latinae elegantia*. On university curricular reform and the increased attention to classical texts and attempts to translate them in the Iberian Peninsula, see Ottavio di Camillo, "Humanism in Spain," in *Humanism beyond Italy, Renaissance Humanism: Foundations, Forms, and Legacy*, vol. 2, ed. Albert Rabil, Jr. (Philadelphia: University of Pennsylvania Press, 1988), 55–108. See also Jeremy N. H. Lawrence, "Humanism in the Iberian Peninsula," in *The Impact of Humanism in Western Europe*, ed. Anthony Goodman and Angus MacKay (London: Longman, 1990), 220–58.

[9] Lisa Jardine, "Logic and Language: Humanist Logic," in *Cambridge History of Renaissance Philosophy*, ed. Charles B. Schmitt, Quentin Skinner, Eckhard Kessler, and Jill Kraye (New York: Cambridge University Press, 2008), 173–98.

or with limited linguistic proficiency could be considered of little intellectual capacity.[10] Yet although language was man's most coveted faculty according to humanist ideology, those who did not display proficient use of language were not considered nonhuman, but rather humans most in need of a civilizing education.[11]

Renaissance humanists of the Mediterranean world inherited a hierarchical continuum of humanity along with the Greek and Roman texts they coveted. For example, Cicero's *De inventione*, a rhetorical manual for orators that was popular throughout late antiquity and then among preachers in medieval and early modern Europe, hypothesizes that people first became civilized through the persuasion of the first man to master eloquent language:

[Q]ui dispersos homines in agros et in tectis silvestribus abditos ratione quadam compulit unum in locum et congregavit et eos in unam quamque rem inducens utilem atque honestam primo propter insolentaim reclamantes, *deinde propter rationem atque orationem studiosius audientes ex feris et immanibus mites reddidit et mansuetos.*

[Men were scattered in the fields and hidden in sylvan retreats when he assembled and gathered them in accordance with a plan; he introduced them to every useful and honorable occupation, though they cried out against it at first because of its novelty, and *when through reason and eloquence they had listened with greater attention, he transformed them from wild savages into a kind of gentle folk.*][12]

Cicero thus identifies that first orator as the agent responsible for the development of cities and civilization. Through reasoned and eloquent speech, the first orator inspired his listeners to domesticate their bodies, adopt sedentary lives, and learn useful trades and civil demeanors.

---

[10] Of particular importance to Renaissance philologists was Aristotle's consideration of the close relationship of language and humanity. Anthony Pagden describes this Aristotelian notion: "Logos, language, is more characteristic of man than the use of the body" (*The Fall of Natural Man: The American Indian and the Origins of Comparative Ethnology* [New York: Cambridge University Press, 1982], 211, n. 5).

[11] Rolena Adorno, *Polemics of Possession in Spanish American Narrative* (New Haven, CT: Yale University Press, 2007), 106; Padgen, *Fall of Natural Man*, 165.

[12] Marcus Tullius Cicero, *De inventione*, 1.2.2. The Latin original and English translation are cited from *On Invention: The Best Kind of Orator*, trans. H. M. Hubbell, Loeb Classical Library (Cambridge, MA: Harvard University Press, 1949), 6–7; my emphasis. On the intellectual background of Cicero's argument in *De inventione* and its posthumous wide reception in late Antiquity and medieval Europe, see George A. Kennedy, *A New History of Classical Rhetoric* (Princeton: Princeton University Press, 2009), 56–58. On the reception of Cicero generally in colonial Latin America, see Andrew Laird, "Cicero in Colonial Latin America," in *The Afterlife of Cicero*, ed. Gesine Manuwald (London: Institute of Classical Studies, University of London, 2016), 121–43.

As other scholars have noted, in the case of early portrayals of indigenous peoples of the Americas, such a hierarchical notion of humanity relating eloquent language to the civility and virtue of the city-dweller was extremely influential in the way indigenous peoples were codified in writings produced for European audiences in the sixteenth and seventeenth centuries.[13] Writers garnered authority to judge and describe the level of "civilization" and "virtue" of New World peoples by basing their criteria on such classical ideals.

Juan Ginés de Sepúlveda's famous Aristotelian portrayal of New World natives as iterations of the category of the natural slave is just one of many instances in which such associations were central to describing indigenous populations of the Americas. Bartolomé de Las Casas, as Anthony Pagden has noted, did not reject the humanist continuum employed by Sepúlveda but rather contested Sepúlveda's positioning of New World natives at the continuum's most barbarous extreme.[14] In another example, Las Casas refers directly to Cicero's first orator in his *De unico vocationis modo* to emphasize the importance of using rhetoric, not violence, to persuade potential converts in the New World.[15] Jesuit theologian José de Acosta, whose evangelical treatise *De procuranda indorum salute* will be examined at length in the final section of this chapter, opted for a middle ground between Sepúlveda and Las Casas. Similarly keeping to the Renaissance humanist continuum of civility, Acosta presents some indigenous groups as barely needing civilizing tutelage before being Christianized, while insisting that others would need much more. Inca Garcilaso de la Vega would also invoke Cicero's first orator in his *Comentarios reales* to elevate the estimation of Inca culture according to humanist values, implying that the Inca empire was able to

---

[13] See Pagden, *The Fall of Natural Man*, 73–80, 127–97; Pagden, *Lords of All the World: Ideologies of Empires in Spain, Britain, and France, c. 1500–c. 1800* (New Haven, CT: Yale University Press, 1995), 19–25, 94–102; Adorno, *Polemics of Possession*, 93–98, 103–24; Lewis Hanke, *Aristotle and the American Indians: A Study of Race and Prejudice in the Modern World* (Chicago: Regnery, 1959); Brian Tierney, "Aristotle and the American Indians, Again," *Cristianesimo nella storia* 12 (1991): 259–322, among others.

[14] In his *Apologética historia*, for example, Las Casas defines different categories of barbarians and fashions his historical narrative around proving that indigenous peoples of the New World belong to the most "civilized" category of barbarians (Pagden, *The Fall of Natural Man*, 122–23).

[15] On Las Casas's use of Cicero, see Ruth Hill, "Hearing Las Casas Write: Rhetoric and the Facade of Orality in Brevísima relación," in *MLA Approaches to Teaching Bartolomé de las Casas*, ed. Santa Arias and Eyda Merediz (New York: MLA, 2008), 57–64, 58; Laird, "Cicero in Colonial Latin America," 123–25.

civilize other indigenous groups before the arrival of the Spanish through persuasive speech.[16] Despite their different positions regarding where indigenous peoples fit on the humanist continuum, all of these authors endorse the continuum itself and its connections between eloquent speech, intellectual capacity, moral virtue, and behavioral civility. They also share the Aristotelian premise that the intellect, if adequately educated, can govern the body, which in turn develops virtuous character.[17]

While black men and women were rarely the focus of comparable extended narrative reflections in New World writings, when they were, they were assessed along the same Renaissance humanist continuum. A concrete case in point is Pallas's introduction to his chapter on the *indios mulatos* near the port of San Mateo. Even before his description of the community cited above, the account begins with a reference to Pliny the Elder: "Dize Plinio de natural istoria en el capítulo 43. del libro 8, que no ay animal manso de cuya especie también no se halle animal fiero, *lo cual se verifica hasta en la especie humana,* que tiene gentes y naciones silvestres, como políticas y urbanas" [Pliny says in chapter 43 of book 8 of his natural history that every kind of domestic animal has a corresponding savage type, too. *This is true even in the human species* that encompasses wild peoples and nations as well as political and urban ones].[18] Basing his descriptions on criteria from Pliny, Pallas presents the community of *indios mulatos* as the "nondomesticated" kind of human.[19] Pallas's adaptation of Pliny coincides with his citing and glossing of the adage "todos somos negros y no nos entendemos" [we are all blacks and cannot understand each other], both activating a universal

---

[16] On Inca Garcilaso de la Vega's use of Cicero, see Zamora, *Language, Authority, and Indigenous History,* 110–28; Laird, "Cicero in Colonial Latin America," 127–28. Inca Garcilaso was not the only Spanish American author to recognize the eloquence of certain New World indigenous groups. Several early and mid-colonial missionaries praised, for example, the eloquence of the Nahua oratory tradition of the *huehuetlahtolli* (words of the elder). See book 6 of the Florentine Codex for Bernardino de Sahagún's attempt to capture and translate some *huehuetlahtolli* for future missionaries to emulate. On Cicero and Sahagún, see Laird, "Cicero in Colonial Latin America," 129–30. On the broader tradition of which Sahagún's effort is part, see Valeria López Fadul, "Languages, Knowledge, and Empire in the Early Modern Iberian World (1492–1650)," PhD diss., Princeton University, 2015, especially 87–157.

[17] Aristotle, *Nicomathean Ethics,* ed. Roger Crisp (New York: Cambridge University Press, 2000).

[18] Pallas, *Missión a las Indias,* 163; my emphasis.

[19] For more on theories of hybridization in classical writings, see Pietro Li Causi, *Generare in commune: Teorie e rappresentazioni dell'ibrido nel sapere zoologico dei Greci e dei Romani* (Palermo: Palumbo, 2008).

notion of blackness as uncivil and ineloquent to describe a local group of black inhabitants of the New World.

Pallas's portrayal of the category of blackness as commensurate to that of the *bozal* finds a complement in the literary stereotype of the *bozal* that circulated in the same regions throughout the seventeenth century in ecclesiastical *villancicos de negro*, a kind of vernacular polyphonic song performed throughout Iberia and Spanish America. The *bozal* stereotype of these *villancicos*, like Pallas's narrative descriptions, invokes blackness in relation to incivility, unruly bodies, and poor speech.

LITERARY *BOZALES*

The literary stereotype of the *bozal* began to appear in Iberia as a motif in poetic texts in the mid-fifteenth century, emerging from a trend in medieval *pastorela* that aestheticized the speech of shepherds and other commoners for the amusement of elite audiences.[20] The earliest examples of the *fala do preto* in Portuguese poetry date from 1455, and the earliest known Castilian examples of the *habla de negro* date from the first decade of the sixteenth century.[21] By the mid-sixteenth century, the motif spread from poetry to theatrical productions, evident in dramatic works by Jaime de Huete, Diego Sánchez de Bajadoz, Gil Vicente, and Lope de Rueda.[22]

---

[20] Peter Dronke, *The Medieval Lyric*, 3rd ed. (Rochester, NY: D. S. Brewer, 1996), defines the *pastorela* as a range of songs that typically feature a shepherdess as a protagonist: "Usually they take the form of a lyrical dialogue: a man of some status in the outer world, a knight or clerk, enters the Arcadian landscape, sees a pretty shepherdess there, and tries to win her love" (200). Dronke attributes the genre to a "learned offshoot of Latin bucolic poetry" that first appeared in Provençal and Italian romance dialects. See Justin Steinberg, *Accounting for Dante: Urban Readers and Writers in Late Medieval Italy* (Notre Dame: University of Notre Dame Press, 2007), for an analysis of the aestheticized "common speech" of the *pastorela* among elite writers in fourteenth-century Italy (107).

[21] The earliest Portuguese example appears in a poem by Fernã da Silveira, written around 1455 and published in *Cancioneiro Geral de García de Resende* (Lisbon, 1516). One of the earliest Spanish examples is Rodrigo de Reinosa's "Comiençan unas coplas a los negros y negras" from 1510–11, reproduced in Jeremy Lawrence, "Black Africans in Spanish Literature," in *Black Africans in Renaissance Europe*, ed. Thomas F. Earle and Kate J. P. Lowe (New York: Cambridge University Press, 2005), 80–93. See Nicholas Jones, *Staging* Habla de Negros: *Radical Performances in the African Diaspora in Early Modern Spain* (University Park: Pennsylvania State University Press, 2019), 10–11, for a recent redesignation of a corpus of *habla de negro* in Spanish. Jones, unlike Lawrence cited above, attributes the first example of the genre to Reinosa's "Gelofe, Mandiga" from 1501 (10).

[22] For analyses of the *habla de negro* in dramatic works from the sixteenth century, see Edmund de Chasca, "The Phonology of the Speech of the Negroes in Early Spanish

Lope de Vega and Simón Aguado, among others, would continue the tradition in the second half of the sixteenth and seventeenth centuries, such that by the mid-seventeenth century Francisco de Quevedo could make the declaration that one of the skills the dramatist and poet needs to know is how to make some of his characters speak "guineo" [Guinean].[23]

Beyond the world of theater and profane poetry, the *habla de negro* motif appeared prominently in the *villancico*, which grew in popularity across social classes in Iberia in the mid-sixteenth century. *Villancicos* began as secular songs, but became sacred compositions over the course of the sixteenth century.[24] The subgenre of *villancico* composed in *habla*

Drama," *Hispanic Review* 14 (1946): 323–39; Juan Castellano, "El negro esclavo en el entremés del Siglo de Oro," *Hispania* 44, no. 1 (1961): 55–65; Frida Weber de Kurlat, "El tipo cómico del negro en el teatro prelopesco: Fonética," *Filología* 8 (1962): 139–68, and "Sobre el negro como tipo cómico en el teatro español del siglo XVI," *Romance Philology* 7, no. 2 (1963): 380–91; Germán de Granda, *Estudios linguisticos hispánicos, afro-hispánicos y criollos* (Madrid: Gredos, 1978); Consolación Baranda Leturio, "Las hablas de negros. Orígenes de un personaje literario," *Revista de Filología Española* 69, nos. 3–4 (1989): 311–33; Baltasar Fra Molinero, *La imagen de los negros en el teatro del siglo de oro* (México: Siglo XXI, 1995); Jeremy Lawrence, "Black Africans in Spanish Literature"; Jerome Branche, *Colonialism and Race in Luso-Hispanic Literature* (St. Louis: Missouri University Press, 2006), 32–81; Dong-Hee Chung, "Imagen y función de los negros en la literatura española de la primera mitad del siglo XVI: Enfocado en la *Segunda Celestina* (1534), de Feliciano de Silva," *Revista Asiática de Estudios Iberoamericanos* 27, no. 3 (2016): 67–95; Jones, *Staging* Habla de Negros. For analyses of seventeenth-century examples in poetry and drama, see Fra Molinero, *La imagen de los negros*; John Beusterien, *An Eye on Race: Perspectives from Theater in Imperial Spain* (Lewisburg, PA: Bucknell University Press, 2006); Daisy Ripodaz Adarnaz, "Influencia del teatro menor español de los siglos XVI y XVII sobre la imagen peninsular de lo indiano," in *Lo indiano en el teatro menor de XVI y XVII*, ed. Ripodaz Adarnaz (Madrid: Ediciones Atlas, 1991), IX–CXXI; Jones, *Staging* Habla de Negros, among others. Miguel Cervantes's *novela* "El celoso extremeño" evidences the appearance of the motif in Spanish narrative in the early seventeenth century with the characters of Luis and Guiomar.

[23] Francisco de Quevedo, *Obras en prosa festivas y satíricas* (Barcelona: Sociedad Editorial La Maravilla, 1862–63): "Si escrives comedias, y eres poeta, sabràs guineo, en bolbiendo las rr ll y al contrario, como Francisco, Flancisco, Primo, Plimo" (280). Indeed, key characteristics of the *habla de negro* motif on both sides of the Atlantic in the sixteenth and seventeenth centuries are the interchanging of the "r" and the "l" or the "d" for the "l" or "r" and the substitution of "j" or "x" for "s." Other common morphological trends include omitting or adding letters or syllables, replacing masculine endings with feminine endings, and eliminating the "s" of the plural (Ripodaz Adarnaz, "Influencia del teatro menor español," XXVII–XXIX). For more, see Lipski, *A History of Afro-Hispanic Language*; Edmund de Chasca, "The Phonology of the Speech of the Negroes."

[24] See Margit Frenk, "Villancicos de negro en el siglo XVII novohispano," in *El folclor literario en México*, ed. Herón Pérez Martínez and Raul Eduardo González (Zamora: Universidad Autónoma de Aguascalientes, 2003), 45–54, and Antonio Sánchez Romeralo, *El villancico (Estudios sobre la lírica popular en los siglos XV y XVI)* (Madrid:

de negro became known as a *negrilla*, a *guineo*, or a *villancico de negro*. According to musicologists, ecclesiastical *villancicos* of the sixteenth and seventeenth centuries (including *villancicos de negro*) were made by a small group of lettered individuals for mass consumption by audiences across the social hierarchy, which signals a social importance larger than their literary representation would suggest.[25]

In the sixteenth century, ecclesiastical *villancicos* increasingly became a highlight of liturgical ceremonies of high feast days. They could be sung at Mass, the Divine Office, or in paraliturgical ceremonies. They were most often sung as part of Matins of the Divine Office for Church festivals. In these services, the typical seven to nine chanted readings of the liturgy would each be followed by the performance of a *villancico*. These *villancicos* replaced the traditional responsories of Matins, delivering elaborations of the theme of the reading, sung in the vernacular.[26] Because of

Gredos, 1969). The first published *villancicos* of the sixteenth century appear to be Esteban de Zafra's *Villancicos para cantar en la Natividad de nuestro Señor Jesu Christo* (Toledo: Juan Ruyz, 1545), cited in Isabel Ruiz de Elvira Serra, "Introducción," in *Catálogo de villancicos de la Biblioteca Nacional, Siglo XVII* (Madrid: Ministerio de la Cultura, 1992), XI. The first major publication of *villancicos* is Francisco Guerrero, *Canciones y villanescas* (Venice, 1589). Neither text includes a *villancico de negro*. On the debate that developed by the end of the sixteenth century about whether *villancicos* were salubrious additions to liturgy or problematic distractions, see Jaime V. Moll, "Los villancicos cantados en la Capilla Real a fines del siglo XVI y principios del siglo XVII," *Anuario musical* 25 (1970): 81–96.

[25] The change from secular to ecclesiastical topics in *villancicos* overlapped with a change in their generic norms such that the *coplas* of the songs would provide pieces of the answer to the concept or enigma presented in the *estribillo*. On the generic structure of the *villancico*, see Andrew Cashner, "Faith, Hearing, and the Power of Music in Hispanic Villancicos, 1600–1700" (PhD diss., University of Chicago, 2015), xxxii–xxxiii. On authorship of *villancicos*, see Cashner, "Faith, Hearing, and the Power of Music," 454; Geoff Baker, "The Ethnic Villancico and Racial Politics in 17th-Century Mexico" in *Devotional Music in the Iberian World, 1450–1800: The* Villancico *and Related Genres*, ed. Tess Knighton and Alvaro Torrente (Burlington, VT: Ashgate, 2007), 399–408.

[26] The *villancicos'* vernacular verse contrasted with the Latin of services' readings from breviaries and missals. Similarly, the textured, multivoiced music of the songs contrasted with the Gregorian chant of the other parts of the Divine Office. Matins was usually a nighttime service, but for important Church festivals they were performed before sunset so more people could attend. On the structure of the Divine Office, see John Harper, *The Forms and Orders of Western Liturgy: From the Tenth to the Eighteenth Century* (Oxford: Clarendon Press, 1991), 73–108. Sometimes the performances also involved play-acting and or dancing by the singers (Ruiz de Elvira Serra, "Introducción," XV). On ecclesiastical music in colonial Cartagena, see Luis Antonio Escobar, *La música in Cartagena de Indias* (Bogota: Intergráficas, 1985), 38–40. For Bogota, see José Ignacio Perdomo Escobar, *El archivo musical de la Catedral de Bogotá* (Bogota: Instituto Caro y Cuervo, 1976), 80; Bermúdez, "Organización musical y repertorio en la Catedral de Bogotá durante el siglo XVI," *Ensayos, teoría e historia del arte* 3 (1996): 43–54;

their popularity, the quality of the *villancicos* performed for holy days became a growing concern for cathedrals and churches. To prepare for important festivals, chapel masters would often be allotted special time away from their regular duties to compose the *villancicos*.[27] Famous poets were sometimes contracted to assist chapel masters in crafting the lyrics, and after the celebrations the lyrics to the *villancicos* were increasingly printed in the seventeenth century, leading to a growing standardization of the genre.[28]

Villancicos were especially popular at Christmas on both sides of the Atlantic in the Iberian World, as the principal theme of the genre is the celebration of shepherds reacting to the news of Jesus' birth. In the subgenre of *villancicos de negro*, black characters sing the part of the humble shepherds who were the first to receive the evangelical message of Jesus' birth and the first visitors to admire the newborn child. The same association was given to the characters of the other subgenres of Christmas *villancicos* composed in nonnormative speech during the period: the *villancico de vizcaíno*, the *villancico de gallego*, the *villancico de morisco*, and the *villancico de gitano*. Although the *villancico de negro* is just one of these subgenres, its popularity by far eclipsed the others' as many more *villancicos de negro* appear in Iberian and colonial verse and song collections from the late sixteenth through eighteenth centuries than any other *villancico* subgenre.[29] The unparalleled popularity of *villancicos de negro*, compared with the other subgenres, could be attributed to the fact that the music for *villancicos de negro* was known to be especially jovial and

---

Bermúdez, "El archivo de la catedral de Bogotá: Historia y repertorio," *Revista Musical de Venezuela* 16, no. 34 (1997): 53–64; Bermúdez, *Historia de la música en Santafé y Bogotá, 1538–1938* (Bogota: Fundación de Música, 2000); Bermúdez, "Sounds from Fortresses of Faith and Ideal Cities: Society, Politics, and Music in Missionary Activities in the Americas, 1525–1575," in *Listening to Early Modern Catholicism: Perspectives from Musicology*, ed. Daniele V. Filippi and Michael Noone (Leiden: Brill, 2017), 301–25. On Lima, see Andrés Sás, *La música en la Catedral de Lima durante el virreinato, primera parte* (Lima: Unversidad Nacional Mayor de San Marcos, 1971). On Cuzco, see Geoff Baker, *Imposing Harmony: Music and Society in Colonial Cuzco* (Durham, NC: Duke University Press, 2008).

[27] Ruiz de Elvira Serra, "Introducción," XI–XIII.   [28] Ibid., XIII.

[29] For example, according to Margit Frenk, "Cancionero de Gaspar Fernández (Puebla-Oaxaca)," in *Literatura y cultura populares de la Nueva España*, ed. Mariana Masera (Barcelona: Azul Editorial, 2004), 19–35, in the entire 280-folio volume of Gaspar Fernandes's *villancicos* that was composed in Puebla between 1609 and 1615, there are seventeen *villancicos de negros*, nine in "Vizcaíno," four in Nahuatl, a few in Sayaguez, and one in a "Gitano" dialect (23). See also Margit Frenk, "Villancicos de negro en el siglo XVII novohispano," 46.

thus particularly appropriate for celebrations, but there are several other potential causes.[30] One is that the uncouth black caricatures of the songs began to stand in as a catchall category for lower social classes in general. In casting black *villancico* characters as the prototypical pastoral rustics of the nativity imaginary, elite members of the audience might have enjoyed the reification of class distinctions while members of the nonblack lower social classes could have perceived themselves as exempt from explicit mockery through the invocation of the black characters' distinct corporal appearance and implied enslaved legal status.[31]

Some of the most well-known *villancicos de negro* from before the codification of the genre in the mid-seventeenth century appear in Luis de Góngora's "Letrillas sacras," which the poet composed for the Cathedral of Córdoba in 1609 and 1615.[32] Just six months after Góngora's *letrillas* were performed in Córdoba for Corpus Christi in 1609, the first recorded instance of the subgenre appeared in Spanish America.[33] In fact, the first

[30] Most musicologists agree that the music of *villancicos de negro* is in general no different from that composed for other *villancicos* (Carolina Santamaría, "Negrillas, negros, y guineos y la representación musical de lo africano," *Cuadernos de música, artes visuales y artes escénicas* 2, no. 1 (2006): 4–20; Baker, "The Ethnic Villancico"; and John Swadley, "The *Villancico* in New Spain 1650–1750: Morphology, Significance and Development" (PhD dissertation, Canterbury Christ Church University, 2015), 129–49.) Yet Cashner, "Faith, Hearing, and the Power of Music," 454, presents a slightly different position in his analysis of the music of a *villancico de negro* from seventeenth-century New Spain. He suggests that the awkwardness of the "broken speech" of the lyrics was imitated in an affected awkwardness in the music.

[31] Some parallels could be made with the popularity of black minstrelsy among the working class in nineteenth-century United States, as described by Eric Lott, *Love and Theft: Blackface Minstrelsy and the American Working Class* (New York: Oxford University Press, 1993) and Thomas Holt, "Race Making and the Writing of History," *The American Historical Review* 100, no. 1 (1995): 1–20. A related possibility has recently been suggested by Nicholas Jones, who associates the wide-ranging popularity of aestheticized feigned black speech in early modern Iberia with what he calls "Black coolness" (*Staging Habla de Negros*, 24–26).

[32] Luis de Góngora, "Letrillas sacras," in *Todas las obras de Don Luis de Góngora en varios poemas* (Madrid: Hoces y Córdova, 1633), 72–76. Martha Lilia Tenorio, *Los villancicos de Sor Juana* (México: El colegio de México, 1999), 27, gives the dates for the performances for Góngora's two sets of villancicos and explains that *letrillas sacras* is a synonym for *villancicos* during this period. Another famous collection of religious songs published in the early period that contains some *villancicos* is José de Valdivielso's *Romancero espiritual* from 1612. Valdivielso's collection, however, does not contain any *villancicos de negro*.

[33] On the dynamic exchange of *villancicos* across the Atlantic between Iberia and New Spain, see Cashner, "Faith, Hearing, and the Power of Music," 302–11. On cathedral music in colonial La Plata, see Bernardo Illari, "Polychoral Culture: Cathedral Music in La Plata (Bolivia), 1680–1730" (PhD diss., University of Chicago, 2001).

known *villancico de negro* composed in Spanish America is Gaspar Fernandes's "Guineo a 8." It was performed at Christmas in Puebla in the same year as Góngora's first *villancico de negro*.[34] The earliest surviving *villancicos de negro* composed or performed in New Granada and Peru date from the mid-seventeenth century, although future archival research could turn up more and earlier examples.[35]

For my analysis of the *bozal* literary stereotype in New Granada and Peru, I have culled a corpus of the nine *villancicos de negro* that are known to have been performed in these areas in the seventeenth century (Table 1.1).[36] In the case of New Granada, the only extant colonial music from this period was performed in Bogota. While the music from Bogota and other areas of New Granada, such as Cartagena, was likely a little different, as the musicians and the populations ministered to in each urban area were, the relatively close physical proximity of the areas to each other suggests that the music, instruments, and musicians of *villancicos* arriving from Iberia in different cities of New Granada would not have been *that* distinct from each other. I therefore use my analysis on the Bogota *villancicos* to speculate about similar phenomena in other cities of the region.[37] I analyze *villancicos de negro* in particular because they were

---

[34] Other than his "Guineo a 8," Fernandes would write three more *villancicos de negro*, two *villancicos de vizacaíno*, and one *villancico de "mestiso [sic] e indio"* between the years 1609–10, indexing the variety of *villancicos* in nonnormative speech that appear in the earliest known collection of *villancicos* from the New World. See Tello, *Cancionero musical de Gaspar Fernándes*.

[35] On the musicians, instruments, and music that traveled from Iberia to New Granada and Peru in the late sixteenth and seventeenth centuries, see Robert Stevenson, *The Music of Peru: Aboriginal and Viceroyal Epochs* (New York: Pan American Union, 1959); Stevenson, "La música colonial en Colombia," *Revista musical chilena* 16, nos. 81–82 (1962): 153–71; José Ignacio Pedromo Escobar, "Historia de la música renacentista e indo-barroca de la catedral de Bogotá," in *El archivo musical de la Catedral de Bogotá*, 1–69; Bermúdez, "Organización musical y repertorio; Sás, *La música en la Catedral de Lima*.

[36] This corpus was first inspired by the supplemental database John Lipski included in his *Afro-Hispanic Language*. It should be noted, however, that some of the dates and the lyrics included by Lipski for these verses in his database did not match those given in the sources. In particular, many of the songs labeled by Lipski as dating from the seventeenth century actually date from the eighteenth century. In compiling this corpus, I have used the lyrics and dates given by the musicologists who transcribed them from archival manuscripts. As shown in Table 1.1, some of the anonymous songs are hard to date, but have been attributed by the musicologists who transcribed them to the mid- or latter half of the seventeenth century.

[37] Other areas to look would be Tunja and Popayan. Few studies beyond Escobar's above-mentioned *La Música en Cartagena de Indias* exist on ecclesiastical music from colonial Cartagena, likely due in no small part to the poor climate conditions for keeping

TABLE 1.1 Villancicos de negro *from seventeenth-century Peru and New Granada*

Title	Place performed	Composer, date	Occasion/feast	Transcribed by
"Los negritos a la navidad del Sr"	La Plata/Sucre (certain) and Cuzco and Lima (possible)	Juan de Araujo (1646–1712), second half of 17th century	Christmas	Stevenson 1959, 236–249
"Esa noche yo baila"	Monasterio de Santa Clara en Cochabamba	Anonymous, 17th century	Christmas	Claro 1974, LXXV–LXXVII
"Turu lu neglo"	Seminario de Cuzco	Anonymous, 17th century	Christmas	Stevenson 1975, 1–2
"Toca la flauta"[a]	Catedral de Bogotá	Alonso Torices (*maestro de capilla* in Malaga in 1672), late 17th century	Christmas	Claro 1974, LXXVIII–LXXIX; Perdomo Escobar 1976, 568–71
"Cucua, cucua"	Catedral de Bogotá	José de Cascante, second half of 17th century	Christmas	Perdomo Escobar 1976, 227–78
"Teque-leque"	Catedral de Bogotá	Julián de Contreras, second half of 17th century	Christmas	Perdomo Escobar 1976, 558–63
"Que me manda buen zanze"	Catedral de Bogotá	Anonymous, likely mid-17th century	Christmas	Perdomo Escobar 1976, 508–10
"Vengan, que lo plegona la negla"	Catedral de Bogotá	Anonymous, second half of 17th century	Christmas	Perdomo Escobar 1976, 601–3
"Turulu neglo"[b]	Catedral de Bogotá	Anonymous, second half of 17th century	Christmas	Perdomo Escobar 1976, 576

[a] This *villancico* was composed in southern Spain and traveled without its composer to New Granada. Alonso Torices, *maestro de capilla* in Malaga in the mid-seventeenth century, never appears to have traveled to the New World.
[b] This is a different song than the third item in the table with a similar title.

the principal literary productions with typological presentations of black characters circulating in these areas during this period. While it is of course possible that Góngora's *Letrillas* and other theatrical productions from Iberia featuring *habla de negro* also traveled to these areas of Spanish America, I have encountered little proof of their circulation.[38] I end this section by contrasting the portrayal of blackness in the *villancicos* to the few epic poems that included black characters that were composed in these regions.

These *villancicos* were performed for Christmas Matins or Mass in churches and cathedrals throughout Peru and New Granada. Despite the disparity in the locations of composition, performance, and authorship, the typological presentation of the black characters from Peru and New Granada in these texts is formally consistent, showing a particular set of generic patterns for depicting black characters in poetry on both sides of the Atlantic in the seventeenth century.

Juan de Araujo's "Los negritos a la navidad del Sr," performed at Christmas in the Cathedral of Cuzco in the second half of the seventeenth century, exhibits the literary stereotype's common characteristics. The black characters of the song describe themselves as "colfades de la estleya" [confraternity members of the Christmas star]. Their nonstandard speech as well as the diction and imagery they invoke present the characters as far removed from the Renaissance values of eloquence and civility, which as I described above were so coveted in Iberian territories at the time of its composition. The song begins:

> Los coflades de la estleya vamo turus a Beleya
> y velemo a rio la beya con ciolo en lo potal
> vamo vamo currendo aya, oylemo un viyansico que lo compondlá
> Flacico siendo gayta su focico y luego lo cantalá
> Blasico Pellico Zuanico y Tomá y lo estliviyo dilá
> Gulumbé gulumbá guachemo

> [Brothers of the Christmas star, we're all going to Bethlehem,
> We will see there the beautiful boy with heaven in the doorway,
> Let's go, let's go, let's run along; let's listen to a carol Flacisco will compose

---

documents in the city. The city's role as a port suggests it might have had more frequent and dynamic exchanges of music and instruments with other locations in the Atlantic world than Bogota.

[38] One exception is the mention of Enciso's play about Juan Latino by Alonso de Sandoval in his 1647 *Historia de Aethiopia*, 108.

Using his snout as a flute and then singing it
Blasico, Pellico, Zuanico, and Tomás will say the chorus
Gulumbé gulumbá guachemo][39]

In the nonstandard speech of the verse, the *villancico* presents its black characters as comic antitheses to the "civilized" characters implicit in the scene of the song (the holy family) and the elite members of the church audience. In doing so, the song dramatizes the news of Jesus' birth through the celebrations of uncouth shepherds whom it presents as members of a black confraternity, a lay corporate structure in which black men and women participated in urban areas of the Iberian world – including the Andes. By having the members of a black confraternity stand in for the shepherds of the nativity scene, the song actualizes the celebration of Jesus' birth by imagining black men and women from the New World in the space of Bethlehem, singing lyrics to "black" songs. The personas of the black confraternity members celebrate that they will see not only the Lord in the nativity but also the gifts brought from Angola by the three kings: "Bamo a bel que traen de Angola a Ziolo y a siola / Baltasale con Melchola y mi plimo Gasipar" [Let's go see what they are bringing for the Lord and Lady from Angola / Balthazar with Melchor and my cousin Gaspar].

Araujo's *villancico* demonstrates the stereotype's generic tendency to infantilize black characters by frequently referring to them in the diminutive, as the characters call themselves "little blacks" [negliyos]. The other *villancicos* of the Peru and New Granada corpus outlined in Table 1.1 coincide with this trend as they primarily employ the diminutive terms for a black man, a black woman, and a group of black individuals (e.g., "negliyo," "negliya," "negliyos"). The use of the diminutive also appears in the invocation of the names of the black characters, such as "Flaciquilla" in "Vengan que lo plegona la negla" and "Juaniya" in "Teque leque."[40] Furthermore, the black characters often add the diminutive ending to many of the nouns they use, such as "plimiyo" [little cousin]

[39] Stevenson, *The Music of Peru*, 236–49. This *villancico* is often performed and reproduced by contemporary baroque music choirs under the title "Los coflades de la estleya." See Geoff Baker, "Latin American Baroque: Performance as a Post-colonial Act?" *Early Music* 36, no. 3 (2008): 441–48, and John Swadley, "Villancico de negros," for critiques of contemporary reinterpretations of *villancicos de negro* as part of baroque music repertoires.

[40] "Vengan que lo plegona la negla," in José Ignacio Perdomo Escobar, *El archivo musical de la Catedral de Bogotá* (Bogota: Instituto de Caro y Cuervo, 1976), 601–3; "Teque leque" in ibid., 558–63.

in "Cucua, Cucua."[41] The especially abundant use of the diminutive in *villancicos de negro* sets the subgenre apart from any other type of *villancico* in nonnormative speech, reinforcing the infantilizing depiction of the *villancico*'s black stereotype.

Another aspect of the caricature of the poorly speaking and childlike black characters in these *villancicos* is the focus on performances of song and dance. The premise of the majority of the *villancicos de negro* is that the black characters are not only celebrating Jesus's birth, but also traveling to entertain the newborn Jesus, framing their musical performances as a kind of grateful servitude. The passage cited above describes Francisco composing a *villancico* en route to Bethlehem, suggesting the group's mission is to bring that song to entertain the newborn baby Jesus: "aya vamo turu aya, / que pala al niño aleglar" [Let's all go there / to make the boy merry]. Similarly, in "Teque leque," the black characters declare: "tlaemo la flautiya / sacabuche y chilimia / la bajona, colnetiya / sonajiya y cascabé" [we bring the soprano recorder, / the trombone and the shawm, / the *bajona*, cornettino, / rattle, and bells].[42] In the "Turu lu neglo" composed in Bogota, the narrators also describe their plan to play music and dance for the newborn baby in the manger: "saltemo y bay- lemo / colamo, dansemo / y hagamono varas" [we jump and dance / run and dance / and make tunes].[43] The characters of the "Turulu neglo" from Cuzco similarly exhort each other to "Danza y tañe y tañe la guitariya" [Dance and strum and strum the little guitar]" for the newborn child.[44] In "Esa noche yo baila," the characters explain that they will obediently sing to the Christ child: "el manda me a mi canta / yo canta asta amanese" [he commands me to sing / I sing until the sun rises].[45] Throughout this *villancico* corpus, as in most *villancico de negro* prece- dents from Iberia and New Spain, the black characters become caricatures of limited speech as well as obedient and amusing performers of music and dance.

The tendency to associate the black body with a propensity for dancing, playing music, and an impaired ability to speak is evident in Araujo's *villancico* where the "instrument" invoked is a black character's

---

[41] Ibid., 277–78.

[42] Ibid., 558–63. The *bajona* is a small high member of the dulcian family.   [43] Ibid., 576.

[44] Robert Stevenson, *Latin American Colonial Music Anthology* (Washington, DC: Organ- zization of American States, 1975), 1–2.

[45] Samuel Claro, *Antología de la música colonial en América del sur* (Santiago de Chile: Universidad de Chile, 1974), lxxv–lxxvii. On metamusical *villancicos* that are about composing *villancicos*, see Cashner, "Faith, Hearing," especially chaps. 1 and 5.

mouth: "siendo gayta su focico" [using his snout as a flute]. The portrayal pejoratively refers to Flacico's "mouth" in two significant ways. First, the character turns his mouth into an object, an instrument of musical expression as opposed to one of verbal communication. Second, the verse refers to Flacico's mouth with a term most commonly used for the snout of an animal. In doing so, Araujo relies on an already existing tradition evident in Covarrubias's definition for "snout": "HOCICO. Comunmente se toma por la estremidad del rostro, quando demasiadamente salen afuera los labios, *como en las negras*: o quando el rostro es largo, *como el de los perros, y el de los puercos, y otros animales*" [SNOUT. Commonly, it is taken for the extremity of the face, when the lips stick out too far, like in black women; or when the face is long, like in dogs, and in pigs, and other animals].[46] Providing a black woman's mouth as the first example for a snout before referring to the mouths of dogs and pigs, Covarrubias's definition suggests an intimate association between the facial structure of black women and those of animals traditionally perceived as domesticated and subservient. Published more than a generation before Araujo's *villancico*, Covarrubias's explanation reflects the already existing tendency in seventeenth-century Iberian discourse to portray black bodies in general (and black women's mouths in particular) in relation to domesticable animals. Araujo's *villancico* combines that trend with that of depicting black men and women as subservient musical performers and nonnormative speakers of Spanish.

In another example from the Peru and New Granada corpus, in "Que manda buen zanze" the black persona of the song describes another man as "un neglo de monicongo / con su caraça de hongo" [a black man from Monicongo / with his big ugly face like a mushroom],[47] echoing a reference that appears in Covarrubias's 1611 definition for *geta* [mug]:

GETA. Llamamos los labios hinchados de los negros, por la semejança que tienen con las setas, o hongos que nacen en el campo. La qual calidad es en ellos tan natural como el color, y como la torcedura de los cabellos que llaman pasillas... *Todas estas son señales ordinarios en los negros:* tener los labios gruessos, los cabellos retorcidillos y las frentes cõ muchas rayas: y ultra desto tienen las narizes anchas y chatas.

---

[46] Covarrubias, *Tesoro de la lengua*, 1: 474; my emphasis. See also Covarrubias's definitions of "Negra" [black woman] (562), and "Baño" [bath] (119), both of which invoke popular sayings that mock black women who go to baths because they will never be washed white. All three defintions ("Hocico" [snout], "Negra" [black woman], and "Baño" [bath]) equate a black woman's mouth or speech with an imperfect body and an inferior social status.

[47] Perdomo Escobar, *El archivo musical de la Catedral de Bogotá*, 508–9.

[The swollen lips of blacks, so named due to the similarities they share with mushrooms or fungi grown in the countryside. These characteristics are as natural to them as their color, similar to the twisted hair that they call kinks... *All of these are typical characteristics of blacks*: having thick lips, kinky hair, and foreheads with many creases; and other than this, wide and flat noses.][48]

Covarrubias's definition shows that "Que manda buen zanze" activates a common pejorative portrayal of black lips as fungus-like in seventeenth-century Spanish. Like Covarrubias's reference to typical black character-istics, the *villancico*'s diction alienates the black body from associations with eloquent speech by emphasizing the incivility of the black character's mouth. Such phenomena demonstrate that skin color was far from the only marker of difference for *negros* during the seventeenth century. The black characters that materialize as a pejorative stereotype in this corpus of *villancicos* do so through an interlocking association with uncouth speech, animal- or fungus-like physical features, dark skin, and the desire to celebrate and obediently entertain.

Some of the implications of the stereotype's collapsing of the black person and the *bozal* are suggested by the next entry for the term *bozal* in Covarrubias's dictionary: a muzzle to restrict animals from biting.[49] The influence of the two definitions on each other is reminiscent of Covarrubias's derisive use of black bodies in his definitions for *hocico* [snout] and *geta* [mug]: all associate black mouths with an inability to speak well and with animal- or fungus-like bodies. Collectively Covarrubias's use of black bodies in *El tesoro de la lengua castellana* shows that the mouth of the black man or woman functioned as a synecdoche to refer to the stereotyp-ical black person's linguistic difficulties speaking Spanish and lowly pos-ition in Iberian social hierarchies, manifested figuratively in his or her emphasized physical body. Influenced by the Iberian Renaissance humanist correlation between eloquent speech, intellectual capacity, and civility, the black literary stereotype employed by sixteenth- and seventeenth-century Iberian and Iberian-American writers cast black men and women as espe-cially alienated from the use of the intellect and civil behavior.

Nicholas Jones suggests a distinct interpretation of the vast popularity of *habla de negro* in theater and verse in Spanish-speaking Iberia than the one I am proposing here. He proposes that the phenomenon should be

---

[48] Ibid., 638; my emphasis.
[49] "Tambien es boçal cierto genero de frenillo que ponen a los perros, y a los demas animales para que no puedan morder" [It is also a certain kind of brace placed on dogs and other animals so they cannot bite] (ibid.).

viewed as celebrations of black sounds, black bodies, and black subjectivity and elite poets' and dramatists' experimentation with baroque contrasts. While Jones's corpus is different from the corpus I analyze here, his
study provocatively foregrounds how distinct audiences of performances
of *habla de negro* might have performed and/or interpreted the performances beyond the mockery which is the focus of my argument here.

Whether or not black men and women participated as composers,
musicians, or audience members in these songs, in fact, is a related subject
of debate across disciplines at this moment. On one hand, linguist John
Lipski has used these *villancicos de negro*, among others from across
Spanish American territories in the colonial and early republican periods,
as evidence of the speech patterns composers overheard black men and
women using in these areas. In contrast to Lipski, José J. Labrador
Herraiz and Ralph A. DiFranco argue that black men and women must
have been the authors of some of the ecclesiastic *villancicos de negro* in
early modern Iberia.[50] Compiling a corpus of Iberian iterations of the
genre in which blackness is spoken of positively, Labrador Herraiz and
DiFranco note that some of them have "less sophisticated lyrics" than
those attributed to authors such as Luis de Góngora and could therefore
have been composed by black authors. Margit Frenk, specialist in popular
and ecclesiastical lyric in early modern Spain and New Spain, is sympa-
thetic to Labrador and DiFranco's interpretation because of the popular
origins of *villancicos*, but she ultimately stops short of endorsing it
because she recognizes that it does not make sense that black poets would
have composed verse in the same standard "broken Spanish" used across
the Iberian world to index black speech.[51] Musicologists, in contrast to
Labrador Herraiz, DiFranco, and Frenk, insist that the music for the
songs would not have been composed by black men and women and
therefore present them as works of elite white authorship.[52] I have not

---

[50] José J. Labrador Herraiz and Ralph A. DiFranco, "Villancicos de negros y otros testimonios al caso en manuscritos del siglo de oro," in *De la canción de amor medieval a las
soleares*, ed. Pedro M. Piñero Ramírez (Seville: Fundación Macado and Universidad de
Sevilla, 2004), 163–87.

[51] Frenk, "Villancicos de negro en el siglo XVII novohispano," 53. Miguel Martínez,
however, makes a compelling point that composers of any *nación* could have learned
the affected patterns of the popular *habla de negro* (email correspondence, August 2018).
For an analysis of some of the Iberian *villancicos* that follows Labrador Herraiz and
DiFranco, see Carmen Fracchia, *"Black but Human": Slavery and Visual Arts in Hapsburg Spain, 1480–1700* (New York: Oxford University Press, 2019), 11–33.

[52] See Baker, "The Ethnic Villancico and Racial Politics in 17th-Century Mexico"; Cashner,
"Faith, Hearing, and the Power of Music in Hispanic Villancicos, 1600–1700," 454.

found evidence to support Labrador Herraiz and DiFranco's thesis in relation to the surviving corpus of ecclesiastic *villancicos de negro* from Peru and New Granada (half of which are credited to known elite authors). None of the songs from this corpus contains the "redemptive" declarations that Labrador and DiFranco focus on as common to the *villancicos* they suspect were composed by black poets. And yet considering black participation in the performances of these or other related *villancicos* is not completely out of the question. The corpus I study in Chapters 2–4 of this book, for example, explains that Jesuits trained black men and women in Lima and Cartagena to play for church services.[53] It follows that black musicians could have played in the church performances of these songs in both cities, seeing as the genre's popularity certainly spread to both.

If black musicians played in the performances of such *villancicos de negro*, it could represent a parallel phenomenon to that of the Corpus Christi festivals celebrated in colonial Cuzco examined by Carolyn Dean. According to Dean, in these celebrations, "For Spaniards, it was not only important to include native Andeans in Corpus Christi celebrations, but it was essential that they perform *as natives*, as the people over whom Christians had triumphed. In performing alterity – usually through Andean costume, song, and dance – they provided the necessary festive opponent whose presence affirmed the triumph [of Christ]."[54] As in the colonial Corpus Christi celebrations analyzed by Dean, black musicians would have been invoked as stereotyped caricatures *and* the musicians performing the music. In such performances, the black caricatures of the Christmas *villancicos* would index the successful spread of Christianity by presenting New World black men and women as obedient and joyful pastoral rustics receiving the Christian message and playing entertaining music. The presence of black musicians in the performance of the *villancicos* would instantiate Christ's promise to save *all* the world, including

---

[53] Andrés Sacabuche, for example, describes himself as a player of the sackbut and mentions other black men owned by the Jesuit school who could play horns, base, and cornet as well as participate in polyphonic singing (*Proceso 1676* manuscript, 106v, 107v). On the Jesuit practice of training its black slaves as musicians, see Luis Martín, *The Intellectual Conquest of Peru: The Jesuit College of San Pablo, 1568–1767* (New York: Fordham University Press, 1968), 70, 137. On Jesuit music training across their South American missions, see Leonardo J. Waisman, "Características y límites de la alfabetización musical en las misiones jesuíticas sudamericanas, siglos XVII–XVIII," *Revista de Musicología* 40, no. 2 (2017): 427–48.

[54] Carolyn Dean, *Inka Bodies and the Body of Christ: Corpus Christi in Colonial Cuzco, Peru* (Durham, NC: Duke University Press, 1999), 15.

the black men and women of the Americas. It would also include them as a means of celebrating the successful Iberian expansion of the project of Christian salvation from Africa into the Americas. If more *villancicos de negro* texts or descriptions of performances were to be uncovered in regional archives from Peru and New Granada, scholars might be able to further analyze the possible meanings the songs had for the distinct performers and audiences implicated in them.

As I mentioned above, the literary stereotype of the *bozal* was not the only way black subjects appear in writing in sixteenth- and seventeenth-century Spanish America. The epic poems of Alonso de Ercilla and Juan de Castellanos, for example, depict black characters from Peru and New Granada who do not fit the stereotype from sung verse. Ercilla's *Araucana*, for example, introduces the figure of the black soldier, and Castellanos's *Elegías de varones ilustres* presents a varied cast of black characters,[55] including uncouth black maroons who impede Spanish settlement and honorable black soldiers who help Spanish military leaders "pacify" new territories.[56] The variety of black characters in these epic poems signals that it was not necessarily a given that black men and women would be stereotyped as *bozales* in literary texts produced or performed in Peru and New Granada throughout the seventeenth century.

It also bears noting that not all authors who used the *bozal* stereotype in the sixteenth and seventeenth centuries explicitly did so to mock black characters. For example, Sor Juana Inés de la Cruz's late seventeenth-century deployment of the *habla de negro* motif in some of her *villancicos* demonstrates a reversal of some of the ideological consequences of the stereotype by making certain black characters capable of intellectual prowess despite their limited speech.[57] Other earlier and concurrent

---

[55] Some black characters mentioned throughout the *Elegías* are, for example, expert soldiers and sailors; others are servants, slaves, freedmen, and maroons. On black soldiers in the sixteenth and seventeenth centuries, see Ben Vinson III and Matthew Restall, "Black Soldiers, Native Soldiers: Meanings of Military Service in the Spanish American Colonies," in *Beyond Black and Red*, 15–52; Ben Vinson III, "Race and Badge"; Ben Vinson III, *Bearing Arms for His Majesty: The Free-Colored Militia in Colonial Mexico* (Stanford, CA: Stanford University Press, 2002). On Castellanos's ideological support of the Spanish colonial project, see Emiro Martínez-Osorio, *Authority, Piracy, and Captivity in Colonial Spanish American Writing: Juan de Castellanos's Elegies of Illustrious Men of the Indies* (Lewisburg, PA: Bucknell University Press, 2016).

[56] For example, one could contrast the portrayal of blackness in Juan de Castellanos, *Elegías de varones ilustres de Indias*, 3rd ed. (Madrid: Ribadeneira, 1874), Parte I, Elegía XII, Canto III, 137, with Parte III, Historia de Cartagena, Canto III, 376.

[57] On Sor Juana's use of the genre, see Nicholas Jones, "Sor Juana's Black Atlantic: Colonial Blackness and the Poetic Subversions of *Habla de negros*," *Hispanic Review* 86, no. 3

variations of the black literary stereotype can be seen in the main characters of Lope de Vega's *El santo negro Rosambuco* (1611), Andrés de
Claramonte's *El valiente negro de Flandes* (1612), and Diego Ximenez de
Enciso's historical play *Juan Latino* (1615), about the black man who
became the grammar chair for the University of Granada in the sixteenth
century.[58] Such works, deservedly, are the focus of other scholarly
research at the moment.[59] The examples provided in subsequent chapters
of this book offer further examples of black men and women who appear
in colonial texts as linguistic experts and venerable spiritual intermediaries. Collectively, they demonstrate that the literary *bozal* stereotype did
not eclipse all written portrayals of black men and women in Peru and
New Granada in this period.

BLACK TYPES IN LEGAL TEXTS

The literary tendency to portray black men and women in Peru and New
Granada in relation to impaired speech, emphasized corporality, and
poor intellect shares certain characteristics with the black type in legal
codes from Peru and New Granada. These legal codes categorically
present black men and women as requiring more tutelage and physical
discipline than any other type of inhabitant of viceregal societies.[60] The

(2018): 265–85; Yolanda Martínez-San Miguel, "(Neo) Barrocos de Indias"; Glenn
Swiadon Martínez, "Los villancicos de negro y el teatro breve. Un primer acercamiento,"
in *La literatura popular impresa en España y en la América colonial: Formas y temas,
géneros, funciones, difusión, historia y teoría*, ed. Laura Puerto Moro, Eva Belén Carro
Carvajal, and Laura Mier Pérez (Salamanca: SEMYR, 2006), 161–68; and Frenk, "Villancicos de negro."

[58] While the exceptional black saintly protagonist of Lope de Vega's play does not speak in
habla de negro, another servant in the play does. On Lope de Vega's and Claramonte's
plays, see Fra Molinero, *La imagen del negro*. On Ximenez de Enciso's play, see Fra
Molinero, *La imagen del negro*; Fra Molinero, "Los negros como figura de negación y
diferencia en el teatro barroco," *Hipogrifo* 2, no. 2 (2014): 7–29; John Beusterein, *An Eye
on Race*; and Emily Weissbourd, "'I Have Done the State Some Service': Reading Slavery
in *Othello* through Juan Latino," *Comparative Drama* 47, no. 4 (2013): 529–51. See
Elizabeth Wright, *The Epic of Juan Latino: Dilemmas of Race and Religion in Renaissance Spain* (Toronto: University of Toronto Press, 2016), 178, for a critique of the
historical inaccuracy of the play.

[59] See, for example, Jones, *Staging* Habla de Negros; Manuel Olmedo Gobante, "'El mucho
número que hay dellos': *El valiente negro en Flandes* y los esgrimistas afrohispanos
de *Grandezas de la espada*," *The Bulletin of the Comediantes* 7, no. 2 (2018): 67–91;
and forthcoming work by Noémie Ndiaye.

[60] The legal codes I examine in this section appear in the following compilation: Manuel
Lucena Salmoral, "Leyes para esclavos: el ordenamiento jurídico sobre la condición,

black types in legal codes appear as dangerous excesses within the colonial social body to be confined to particular physical spaces at particular times, limiting their occupations and economic activities, interactions with other New World groups, and ability to bear arms or wear elegant clothing. While the typological person referenced in legal ordinances exists on a distinct plane of signification than the literary stereotype, it is similarly implicated in the ideology of Renaissance humanism's categorical positioning of black people in a hierarchically inferior position than Spaniards, white *criollos*, or indigenous people. Both black types demonstrate a shared project, conceived in language, to cast black men and women as the least civilized category of person in the Americas. In the case of the literary stereotype, the merry, musical, obedient, but barbarous black body appears as a source of delight; in the legal ordinance the barbarous black body appears as a particularly propitious site for applying civilizing physical violence.

From the mid-sixteenth century, ordinances began circulating in Spanish America requiring owners of enslaved black men and women to treat them as "próximos y cristianos" [familiars and Christians].[61] The first known example of a Royal Ordinance insisting owners care for their slaves' spiritual well-being is from Santo Domingo around 1545, which specifies that owners are responsible for Christianizing and teaching their slaves Spanish within the first six months of arriving in the Americas as a means of ensuring they understand the sacrament of baptism.[62] Requiring pastoral care for black men and women in Spanish America is just one element of the ordinance that promotes the social control that comes with turning black slaves into good Christians. Signaling that social control was a principal priority of this early ordinance, the rest of the requirement outlaws the unregulated circulation by enslaved black men and women throughout the countryside as well as performances of elite status such as riding on horseback or carrying a weapon.[63] Finally, in a legislative move

tratamiento, defensa y represión de los esclavos en las colonias de la América española," in *Tres grandes cuestiones de la historia de Iberoamérica*, ed. José Andrés Gallego (Madrid: Fundación Mapre Tavera, 2005).

[61] "Ordenanzas sobre el tratamiento y sujeción de los esclavos," Santo Domingo [?], 1545 [?] (Lucena, 675–78). On the term "familiar" in Spanish America to conceive of black men and women, see Bianca Premo, "Familiar: Thinking beyond Lineage."

[62] "Ordenanzas sobre el tratamiento y sujeción de los esclavos," Santo Domingo [?], 1545 [?] (Lucena, 675–78, 676).

[63] For later examples of this kind of ordinance that incorporate prohibitions on wearing fine clothing, see "Auto virreinal prohibiendo a las negras y mulatas usar sedas, plata, oro y perlas," Lima, 12 de abril de 1631 (Lucena, 852–53). See Walker, *Exquisite Slaves,*

that seeks to discourage solidarity among black men and women in the colonial context, the ordinance from 1545 ends by describing how to physically punish black men and women who assist runaway slaves.

Similar ordinances would later circulate in Peru and New Granada in the late sixteenth and seventeenth centuries. One trend in the ordinances in Peru and New Granada is a tendency to categorically punish black men and women more severely than Spaniards or indigenous peoples for the same crimes. An important example appears in an ordinance that outlines five different kinds of punishment for individuals found guilty of assisting a runaway slave:

Que cualquier persona español, negro o indio, que se averiguare encubrir cualquiera de los dichos negros cimarrones, por la primera vez, siendo español, caiga e incurra en pena de cien pesos, y por la segunda doscientos pesos y destierro perpetuo de los dichos nuestros Reinos del Perú, aplicados conforme a las demás penas, y siendo cacique, por la primera vez le tresquilen y por la segunda pierda el cacicazgo, y siendo otro cualquier indio le sean dados doscientos azotes, y siendo negro cautivo le sean dados por la primera vez cien azotes por las calles públicas de la dicha ciudad, y por la segunda le capen, y por tercera caiga e incurra en pena de muerte natural, y siendo negro libre, por la primera vez caiga en la dicha pena de cien azotes y por la segunda le ahorquen de manera que muera naturalmente.

[When any Spaniard, black, or Indian is found guilty of hiding any of these black runaway slaves, for the first time, if he is Spanish, he incurs a debt of one hundred pesos, and for the second, two hundred pesos and permanent exile from these Kingdoms of Peru, applied according to the other punishments. If he is a *cacique* [Indian leader], upon the first offense, they shave his head, and upon the second, he should lose his right to rule. If it is any other Indian, they should give him two hundred lashes. If he is a captive black, upon the first offense, he receives one hundred public lashes in this city, upon the second, they castrate him, and upon the third offense, he is sentenced to death. If he is a free black, upon the first offense, they will give him one hundred lashes, and upon the second, he will suffer death by hanging.][64]

The punishments vary in severity depending on the identity and legal status of the individual charged with the crime. Punishments for indigenous men and women (nobles or commoners), for example, are more focused on the physical body than those prescribed for Spaniards; and punishments for black men and women are even more physically severe

---

20–42, on how sumptuary laws restricting fine dress were ignored and implemented by different actors in Peruvian colonial society.

[64] Ordenanzas de negros de la audiencia limeña, Los Reyes, 12 de octubre de 1560. Lucena, "Leyes para esclavos," 725. Similar versions of this law also circulated in New Granada. See ibid., 211–14 and 241–51.

than those prescribed for indigenous peoples. Furthermore, the difference in punishment for the free and enslaved black person is telling of certain nuances related to how the black body was perceived as property in Spanish American legal codes. The fact that an enslaved black man would only be castrated upon a second offense instead of being hanged, as would his free counterpart, shows that the financial importance of the slave as property prolonged his life, despite the fact that the black slave occupied a lower rung on the colonial social hierarchy.[65] In general, whether enslaved or free, the ordinance reveals the prescription for more severe physical punishment for black men and women than any other type of individual.

Another common trait of black types in legal codes from Peru and New Granada during this period is the monitoring of the physical spaces black men and women could enter or occupy. Examples of this phenomenon appear in the ordinances segregating black men and women from other populations in prisons. The following legislation from Cuzco in the late sixteenth century details that Spanish, indigenous, and black prisoners should be jailed separately:

Item, porque es justo que el aposento de las mujeres este dividido de los demás, ordeno y mando que si fueren españolas estén en lo alto de la dicha casa y cárcel que está trazado encima de los calabozos para el dicho efecto, y en lo bajo quedan ocho calabozos para el dicho efecto, con sus puertas fuertes, en el uno de los cuales han de estar las mulatas y negras, en el otro los negros y mulatos, y en el otro las indias, y en el otro los indios, dejando siempre las mejores para los españoles, pues quedan suficientes para el recaudo que es menester que se tenga en todas, para que estén divididos de manera que en la dicha cárcel haya toda honestidad y limpieza.

[Because it is just that women's cells be divided from the rest, I order and demand that if they are Spanish women, they should be kept on the higher floor of this house and jail that is built over the dungeon cells for this purpose. In the lower level, there are eight dungeon cells with locked doors for the following purposes: one of them should house *mulatas* and black women; another black men and *mulatos*; another indigenous women; and another indigenous men, leaving the

---

[65] This prescription for castration of enslaved black men opens up the question of the punishment allotted to enslaved black women for similar crimes. While the legal archive is mostly silent on this question, a contemporaneous law drawn in Chile suggests that the counterpart to the punishment of castration would be to cut off an escaped black woman's breasts: "al varón se le corten los miembros genitales, e a la mujer las tetas" [the male will have his genitals removed, and woman her breasts] (Ordenanzas para los negros del reino de Chile, Santiago, 10 de noviembre de 1577, [ibid., 775]). For a brief analysis of the castration of black men in Spanish legal code in the Peninsula and the Americas, see ibid., 165 and 187.

nicer cells for the Spaniards. This should be done in a manner that leaves sufficient space in each cell for necessary precautions to be taken, and so that prisoners are separated from each other to preserve the honesty and cleanliness of this jail.][66]

The ordinance thus endorses a hierarchical spatial segregation that places black and indigenous men and women in the worst spaces of the jail. Such differential treatment was also sought in other spaces, as seen in an ordinance passed in Quito in 1573 (which claims to be copied from one in Lima) that prohibits elite Spanish women from sitting with *negras, mulatas,* or *indias* in Church.[67] Other examples can be seen in the prohibitions on burying black men and women near Spaniards and those barring entry of black men into certain kinds of lay sodalities and guilds.[68] These ordinances prioritize the reification of what is assumed to be a pre-existing hierarchy among different types of peoples in viceregal societies. The implicit logic of this kind of ordinance is that preserving the propriety of Spanish and indigenous societies requires regulating contact between them and black men and women. A related priority in the codes is limiting upward mobility among black men and women, as seen in the laws restricting their access to certain professions and guilds.[69]

As mentioned in the Introduction to this book, another important distinction of the black type and the indigenous type in legal codes is that unlike the debates, decrees, and ordinances that increasingly circulated in Peru and New Granada to protect native populations from abuses by Spaniards during the sixteenth and the early seventeenth centuries, laws were not made or even debated in these regions to protect black men and women from excessive punishment or abuse.[70] In her examination of the origins and applications of the unequal treatment of black men and

---

[66] Capítulos de las ordenanzas del cabildo de Cuzco relativos a esclavos, Checacupe, 18 de octubre de 1572 [Lucena, 747]. This ordinance was copied two years later for application in La Plata (Sucre) (ibid., 756–57).

[67] Real Cédula ordenando que mujeres de los oidores se sentaran al pie de la capilla mayor donde no hubiera negras, mulatas ni indias, El Pardo (Quito), 13 de diciembre de 1573 (ibid., 751).

[68] In 1614 in Peru measures were taken to prohibit black and *mulato* men and women from being buried in coffins (Provisión del Virrey ratificando el auto del cabildo que prohibió enterrar en ataúd los negros y mulatos, Lima, 26 febrero 1614 [Lucena 832–33]). On prohibitions from joining guilds, see Juan de Solórzano y Pereira, *Política Indiana* (Madrid: Diego Diaz de la Carrera, 1648), book II, chap. 29, 243.

[69] E.g., Capítulos de las ordenanzas sobre negros de Panamá, Panamá, 4 de agosto de 1574 (Lucena, 766).

[70] On the sixteenth-century debates regarding the legitimacy of indigenous enslavement, see Lewis Hanke, *All Mankind Is One: A Study of the Disputation between Bartolomé de Las Casas and Juan Ginés de Sepúlveda in 1550 on the Intellectual and Religious*

women in colonial law, Rachel O'Toole notes, for example, that slave-holders in northern rural Peru were often the same officials in charge of administering legal processes and enforcing laws, which resulted in the application of the legal system to further their own interests.[71] Sherwin Bryant, for his part, argues that due to the design of the colonial legal system to support property owners' interests, even when the enslaved sought to improve their own conditions through advocating for themselves in colonial courts, such appeals functioned to preserve the ideological apparatus supporting slavery itself.[72]

On the whole, the black type in legal codes from colonial Spanish America materializes in the sixteenth and seventeenth century in relation to a disproportionate prescription for physical discipline, restriction of spatial and social mobility, and limited access to rights and status. The black type in Spanish American legal codes thus overlaps with the black *bozal* literary stereotype in these regions insofar as both invoke black men and women as the most physically unruly and least civilized of all populations in Spanish America. While legal codes prescribe disciplining and confining black bodies as ways of ensuring the propriety of colonial societies, the *bozal* stereotype from *villancicos* in the same areas presents black men and women as unsophisticated, entertaining, and servile. Their juxtaposition suggests that the two types might have served to reinforce each other.

THE BLACK TYPE IN NEW WORLD MISSIONARY TEXTS

Similar to the two generic types reviewed above, contemporary missionary texts from Spanish America also construct a typological black subject defined in relation to a presumed unruly black body. Contrary to the first two types, however, evangelical treatments of typological blackness

Capacity of the American Indians (DeKalb: Northern Illinois University Press, 1974); Pagden, *The Fall of Natural Man*; Anthony Anghie, "Francisco Vitoria and the Colonial Origins of International Law," in *Imperialism, Sovereignty, and the Making of International Law* (New York: Cambridge University Press, 2005), 13–31; Adorno, *The Polemics of Possession*; Ruben Sánchez-Godoy, *El peor de los remedios*; Seth Kimmel, *Parables of Coercion*, 55–65. On the specific character this debate took with relation to the extended war against the Mapuche in Chile, see Álvaro Jara, *Guerra y sociedad en Chile* (Santiago de Chile: Editorial Universitaria, 1971), 151–230.

[71] According to O'Toole's examination of rural slavery in northern Peru, black men therefore sought extra-legal means of acquiring justice such as running away or searching for new owners to purchase them. See O'Toole, *Bound Lives*, 122–56.

[72] Bryant, *Rivers of Gold*, 115–42.

produced in relation to developments in Counter Reformation theology leave room to conceive of black men or women as potentially autonomous decision-makers regardless of their level of civility. The distinction between the first two and the third black types derives from the demands of the category of the Christian, which according to most theologians of the late sixteenth century was a universal subject position available to all men and women. In particular, a Jesuit-inflected brand of theology in Iberia and Spanish America argued by the second half of the sixteenth century that to truly become Christian, an individual had to freely and knowingly accept the transformation of conversion.[73] Even the most "barbaric" individual would, according to these criteria, have to knowingly embrace the Christian message to be considered Christian.[74]

Although exercising choice was a central value in discourse on Christian conversion long before the Renaissance, the debates about what criteria to use to interpret that choice took on new life in the fifteenth and sixteenth centuries.[75] The Iberian Renaissance humanist valorization of the freedom of moral choice became especially politically charged around the issue of genuine Christian conversion in Iberian territories in the late fifteenth and early sixteenth centuries, where numerous mass conversions under the threat of violence, exile, or imprisonment occurred and amid the need to evangelize the growing number of enslaved populations arriving in Iberian territories.[76] José de Acosta's *De procuranda indorum salute*, composed in Peru in the late 1570s and published in Salamanca in 1589, evidences the fear some theologians had by the end of

---

[73] As will be discussed below, Acosta argues in *De procurada indorum salute*, book 5, chapter 3, that no one could be saved without explicit faith in Christ, which also requires explicit knowledge.

[74] See Martín, *Intellectual Conquest of Peru*, 66–71.

[75] See Sabine MacCormack, "'The Heart Has Its Reasons': The Predicaments of Missionary Christianity in Early Peru," *Hispanic American Historical Review* 65, no. 3 (1985): 443–66, for some of the connections between the early Christian treatments of conversion and the late sixteenth centuries. For a more nuanced portrayal of the question in relation to sixteenth-century Iberia, see Kimmel, *Parables of Coercion*, 67–94. The classic examination of Renaissance humanism and Counter Reformation theological debates about the criteria for Christian conversion in Miguel de Cervantes's texts is Alban K. Forcione, *Cervantes and the Humanist Vision: A Study of Four Exemplary Novels* (Princeton: Princeton University Press, 1982), 31–92.

[76] I refer to the mass baptisms of Jews resulting from the Spanish Crown's expulsion decrees from 1492, the forced conversions of Muslims throughout the sixteenth century in Iberia, and the expulsion of the *moriscos* between 1609 and 1614. See Kimmel, *Parables of Coercion*, 17–42, for an account of why the mass conversions of Jews and Muslims were defended by Church authorities until the mid-sixteenth century.

the sixteenth century that certain people in the expanding reaches of the Spanish empire might not be able to exercise free choice in their "natural state" to become Christian on their own and so they would first have to be primed through physical discipline to later convert to Christianity "freely." Even in this context, however, Acosta still upholds the principle that the only way for an individual to truly convert to Christianity is by freely and knowingly choosing to do so.[77]

While theologians of the first Salamanca School had argued earlier in the sixteenth century that people of the Indies could be saved without explicit knowledge of Christ, Acosta was a prominent critic of this position.[78] After reviewing the traditional positions on the validity of involuntary baptisms, Acosta concludes that the minimum requirements for a legitimate baptism (of any type of human) in the American missionary setting should be: (1) the individual's knowledge of the baptism's meaning as a Christian ritual, (2) the individual's belief in the Christian message, and (3) the visible or audible consent of the individual being baptized.[79] In the absence of any of these requirements (especially the first and third, which are most easily corroborated), Acosta prescribes that the baptism be deemed illegitimate:

Quodsi nullo modo quid esset baptismus agnovit neque illud a profana et quacumque alia aspersione distinxit, penitus Christi et Ecclesiae fidem ignorans, non magis voluisse intelligendus est, quam si dormiens aut amens baptizaretur, cum nulla antea eius significatio extitisset.

[But if the baptizand was completely ignorant of the meaning of the baptism and could not distinguish it from some other profane sprinkling of water, with total ignorance of the faith of Christ and the Church, it should be considered that he did not desire it more than one baptized in his sleep or when out of his mind, seeing as he never before manifested any desire for it.][80]

The demand for the existence of free and knowing choice for a legitimate baptism does not coincide with an argument for a entirely peaceful

---

77 For this argument, see Acosta, *De procuranda indorum salute,* vol. 2, 362–80. For a study of the logic and language of Acosta's treatise as scaffolding for colonial exploitation of the Americas, see Ivonne del Valle, "José de Acosta, Violence, and Rhetoric: The Emergence of Colonial Baroque," *Calíope: Journal for the Society of Renaissance and Baroque Poetry* 18, no. 2 (2013): 46–72.

78 On the first Salamanca school's position, see Claudio M. Burgaleta, *José de Acosta, S.J. (1540–1600): His Life and Thought* (Chicago: Loyola Press, 1999), 91–92. On Acosta's opposition, see Bugaleta and León Lopetegui, "Influjos de Fr. Domingo de Soto, O.P, en el pensamiento misional del P. José de Acosta," *Estudios Eclesiásticos* 36 (1961): 57–72.

79 Acosta, *De procuranda indorum salute,* vol. 2, 368–70.   80 Ibid., 370.

persuasive evangelical project, however. Expanding on the suggestion made by Ginés de Sepúlveda in *Democrates Alter*, Acosta's treatise prescribes physical discipline for certain neophytes in order to prepare them to eventually freely and knowingly consent to their baptism.

It bears noting that Acosta's insistence on the role of choice by the neophyte convert in the Americas is not the same as the Second Salamanca School's position on human freedom associated with Francisco Suárez and Luis de Molina that erupted after the publication of Molina's *Concordia liberi arbitrii cum gratiae donis* in 1589. Published at the dawn of the fray (known as the *De auxiliis* controversy) regarding whether or not humans could reject God's grace, José de Acosta's missionary treatise focuses much more broadly on the requirements of conversion and legitimate baptism in the Indies.[81] Acosta's foregrounding of free choice in the missionary setting composed before the controversy really took shape is therefore only tangentially implicated in that later unresolved theological conflict.

Central to Acosta's plan for systematizing New World evangelization is the prerogative to be flexible. To outline his standard but flexible strategy, Acosta's treatise begins with a typology of the world's three different types of "barbaros" [barbarians] so as to prescribe a different evangelical approach for each one. The typology categorizes the world's barbarians along a continuum based on criteria associated with the same Renaissance humanist notions of civility, reviewed above.[82] The purpose of Acosta's

---

[81] The *De auxiliis* controversy was never resolved; it was only indefinitely postponed when Pope Clement VIII prohibited either side of accusing the other of heresy in 1607. For a lengthy summary of the *De auxiliis* debate from a Jesuit perspective, see Antonio Astrain, *Historia de la Compañía de Jesús en la asistencia de España* (Madrid: Sucesores Ribadeneira, 1902–9), 4: 115–385. For a much briefer account and a description of Acosta's position, see Burgaleta, *José de Acosta*, 67–69, 123–26. Martín, *Intellectual Conquest of Peru*, 66–67, suggests that there existed a continuity between the *De auxiliis* debate and subsequent critiques of the practice of slavery from Jesuits in Lima in the seventeenth century in the works of Pedro de Oñete and Diego de Avedaño, but does not detail what those continuities might have been.

[82] For extended analyses of Acosta's typology, see Ivonne del Valle, "José de Acosta: Entre el realismo politico y disparates e imposibles, o por qué importan los estudios coloniales," in *Estudios transatlánticos poscoloniales*, ed. Ileana Rodríguez and Josebe Martínez (Barcelona: Anthropos, 2010), vol. 1, 291–324; Pagden, *The Fall of Natural Man*, 158–98; Chaves, "La creación del 'Otro' colonial"; Sabine MacCormack, *Religion in the Andes: Vision and Imagination in Early Colonial Peru* (Princeton: Princeton University Press, 1991), 266–80; and León Lopetegui, *El Padre José de Acosta y las misiones* (Madrid: Consejo Superior de Investigaciones Científicas, 1942), 368–76. For more on humanist criteria for conceiving humanity, see James Hankins, "Humanism, Scholasticism, and Renaissance Philosophy," in *Cambridge Companion to Renaissance*

hierarchy is to prescribe the most effective evangelizing methods for the different peoples in the Indies, by which he means the territories of Spanish America. Although Acosta does not explicitly name black men and women in his initial presentation of the typology in the *proemio*, he provides examples throughout the treatise that reveal the type to which he believes black peoples arriving in the New World generally correspond: the least civilized. The ideology and categories established by Acosta in *De procuranda* would inform later authors' depictions of black souls and bodies, including those of Jesuit Alonso de Sandoval (whose work will be examined in detail in the next three chapters).

Acosta's first category of barbarian is that of the peoples he considers most similar to Europeans. These are the Japanese, Chinese, and other peoples of the "eastern Indies":

Prima classis eorum est, qui a recta ratione et consuetudine generis humani non ita multum recedunt. Hi sunt potissimum quibus et respublica constans et leges publicae et civitates munitae et magistratus insignis et certa atque opulenta commercial sunt, et quod omnium caput est, litterarum celebris usus.

[The first class is of those who are not very estranged from the use of reason and the way of life of the human species. These are above all those who have a stable formal government, public laws, fortified cities, prestigious magistrates, prosperous and well-organized commerce, and what is most important, the well-recognized use of letters.][83]

The statement demonstrates the importance Acosta gives to refined speech formalized in letters as a criterion for possessing higher degrees of humanity, something he assumes is correlated with living in sedentary societies.[84] According to Acosta, missionaries can evangelize peoples of this type through merely spreading the Gospel verbally, as was done in the past when Greek and Roman populations converted to Christianity.[85]

In contrast, Acosta's second and third categories of barbarian require some kind of application of physical discipline *before* being able to choose Christianity freely. The second category pertains to sedentary indigenous groups in the Americas such as the Mexica and the Inca who, according to

---

Philosophical Thought (New York: Cambridge University Press, 2007), 30–48; Oskar Kristeller, "Humanism and Scholasticism in the Renaissance," *Byzantion* 17 (1944–45): 346–74; Pagden, *Lords of All the World*, 17–28; and Mignolo, *Darker Side*, 29–68, 125–217.

[83] Acosta, *De procuranda*, vol. 1: 60–62.

[84] Ibid. Significantly, Acosta attributes the first type of barbarians' high level of civility to an ancient contact he believes they must have had with Europe.

[85] Ibid.

Acosta, had achieved some admirable cultural advancement in the form of eloquent speech, cities, and laws, but still need physical discipline to break them of lingering barbaric customs.[86] Meanwhile, Acosta's third category encompasses those he considers farthest away from European models of civility: the other varieties of "homines sylvestres" [wild humans] of the New World who live in the wilderness and "vix quicquam humani sensus habentes" [who barely possess human sense].[87] For this third type, Acosta prescribes a more severe method of physical discipline than the one proposed for the second type: "Hos omnes homines aut vix homines humana docere oportet, ut homines esse discant, tum puerorum more instituere" [To all of these humans or barely humans, it is necessary to teach them human things so that they learn to be humans, and it is necessary to do so as children are instructed].[88] In this passage, Acosta casts the third type as almost not human. To evangelize them, he identifies the goal of their instruction to be to make them more human, tutoring them as if they were children. This third type, according to Acosta, is human but puerile, the farthest away on the human continuum between the most civilized Christian and the most uncivilized barbarian.

In order to educate the childlike third type of "barbarians" to approximate higher degrees of humanity as a part of their Christianization, Acosta explains that they would need to be disciplined with physical force:

Et si quidem blanditiis sponte ad meliora ducantur, bene; sin minus, deserendi non sunt: sed si adversus salutem suam proterviant et in magistros medicosque suos insaniant, per potentiam et honestam vim quandam, ne Evangelium impediant, coercendi sunt, et in officio continendi, quos de sylvis transferri ad urbes et humanam vitam, et quodam modo invitos ad regnum introire compellere expediet.

[It would certainly be good if they could be spontaneously enticed to better deeds, through soft words, but if not, they should not be forsaken: but if they stubbornly resist their health and go against their magistrates and doctors, unnerving them, it is necessary to oblige the Indians by use of power and a particular honest force so that they do not put up obstacles to the Gospel, and to make them comply with their duty. It is convenient to have them taken from the wilderness to cities and to human life, and to compel those invited in a certain way to enter the kingdom of heaven.][89]

Here Acosta modifies the humanist notion cited earlier from Cicero that men "in agros et in tectis silvestribus" [in fields and sylvan retreats]

---

[86] Ibid., 62–64.   [87] Ibid., 66.   [88] Ibid., 68.   [89] Ibid.

could be coaxed to live in cities through the eloquent speech of an orator. Instead, for Acosta, the third type of barbarians would first need to be impelled by physical force to change their surroundings and behavior before being able to listen to the "blanditiis" [soft speech] of the Gospel. To be clear, Acosta does not propose violent evangelization; he states that violence is a necessary precursor to peaceful catechism that would eventually teach Indians to freely and knowingly convert.[90] In the passage above, Acosta presents missionaries as the spiritual doctors of the Indians, authorizing their physical discipline as if magistrates. Then, a third party (not the missionaries themselves) would exert the civilizing "honestam vim" [honest force] so the missionaries could then successfully preach.

According to Acosta's typology, Cicero's vision of discursive persuasion works initially only for the first type of barbarians. For the second and third types, Acosta prescribes different levels of disciplinary physical force as precedents to the successful verbal administration of the Gospel. The difference between the second and third types is the severity of their barbarity and the corresponding amount of force with which their corporal bad habits would need to be broken. The second type has the advantage of already living in cities and having developed some eloquent forms of speech and civic institutions and so they need less physical discipline. Acosta presents the third type as destitute or almost destitute of such civilizing criteria.

Acosta interpolates black men and women into this typology by associating them with the least civilized type of barbarian.[91] A glimpse at this association appears in an anecdote in which he describes black men's and women's addiction to tobacco in the Caribbean:

Nam in quadam insula cum navigationis commoditatem expectarem, didici ex tabaco contuso (genus id herbae est ad permovendum cerebrum mire efficax) servos aetyopicos naribus exorbere vim solitos gravemque sibi ac diuturnam inde temulentiam excitantes, pro magnis deliciis ducere, ut vix minis plagisque ab ea consuetudine avalli possent.

---

[90] For much more on the colonial missionary technology of resettlement, see Hanks, *Converting Words*, especially 25–58; and Daniel Nemser, *The Infrastructures of Race*, especially 25–64.

[91] The omission of "black" peoples (whom Acosta calls Ethiopians) from the Jesuit's initial presentation of the typology could be due to the fact that they were not considered a "new discovery" in the way the Amerindian populations were at the time, and Acosta primarily composes his treatise to give a new methodology for evangelizing these "new" populations.

[On an island, while waiting for propitious sailing conditions, I learned that Ethiopian slaves usually inhale through their nose crushed tobacco (a kind of plant that excites the mind with surprising efficacy) in order to experience the greatest pleasure from it. With this they excite themselves in a powerful drunken state all day, a habit from which they can barely be removed with threats and whipping.][92]

Placed within the section on the capacity all humans have for free choice, Acosta's anecdote presents black bodies as sites for the propitious application of physical discipline to tame their appetites and prepare them to exercise their intellect. Without physical discipline, Acosta implicitly warns, black men and women would continue to be controlled by their unruly bodies, and their intellect would never be "free" to choose a Christian way of life. According to Acosta, correctly administered disciplinary force would civilize them and allow them to access their freedom of choice.

Acosta's argument for applying physical force to certain types of bodies as a precursor to and reinforcement of conversion was not an original proposition when he composed his treatise. As noted above, although their opinions differ regarding what groups belong to what category, Juan Ginés de Sepúlveda, Bartolomé de Las Casas, and José de Acosta similarly use the Renaissance humanist continuum to compare New World natives to Europeans. Acosta's innovation of the humanist continuum was to develop explicit pedagogical strategies for evangelizing and governing each type. In doing so, Acosta implied that black populations of the New World belong within the most barbaric category.

Yet elsewhere in his treatise Acosta underscores that like all the other types of barbarians found in the Indies, black men and women *can* be taught civility and become good Christians. For example, Acosta invokes the case of black men and women to argue that *even they* can aspire to a higher position on the human continuum: "Ipsos aethiopum liberos, quibus nihil apparet absurdius, in palatio enutritos, adeo promptos ingenio et ad quidvis paratos videas, ut si colorem detrahas, nostros putes" [Even Ethiopian children, who have nothing wrong with them, when raised in a palace, you would see, are so intelligent and capable of any task that if you were to take away their color, you would think of them as our own].[93] While Acosta generally associates blackness with incivility, this declaration demonstrates that for Acosta black men and women are not permanently confined to that association. All barbarians, according to

---

[92] Acosta, *De procuranda*, vol. 1: 550.   [93] Ibid., 150.

Acosta, if removed from the living conditions shaping their barbarity, can be adequately civilized and Christianized. The corporal difference of skin color then remains as an obsolete marker of their original geography-related foreignness. Acosta, therefore, does not suggest that black men and women are irreparably distant from the Renaissance humanist ideal of humanity, but rather introduces them as a limit case to prove his point that all people indeed are capable of salvation.

Acosta hints at his vision of *how* black men and women could ascend on the humanist hierarchy later in his treatise when he criticizes the insufficient care currently taken by slave traders and clergy in western Africa to evangelize the black men and women sent to the New World. In the treatise's previously cited section on the requirements for a genuine baptism, Acosta invokes black men's and women's capacity for correct choice when he complains about their insufficient evangelization before baptism:

Hos enim si convenias an christiani iam sint, audies non raro sese, cum essent impuberes, simul cum aliis plurimis in navi aut litore deprehensos baptizatos esse, cum certe quid secum ageretur ignorarent, nisi quod multis simul a clerico aut milite quopiam aqua aspergebantur; et exinde christianos se fieri audiebant, cum neque hoc etiam ipsum quid esset edocerentur, neque rem ipsam penitus intelligerent et homines barbari iumentis similes minime quid illud esset scire curarent.

[If you summon them to find out if they are already Christian, you will hear not a few times that when they were young they were captured with many others on a ship or a beach and baptized, without really knowing what was being done to them; only that they had in a large group at the same time water sprinkled on them by a cleric or some soldier. From this point on, they heard that they were now Christians without having been taught in the slightest what that meant, without understanding a word of what had happened and without the smallest concern as to why, as if they were savage men, like pack animals.][94]

Such cases, Acosta continues, require returning to debates by theologians as to whether unwilling baptisms can be considered legitimate, and in response he outlines the criteria mentioned earlier that insists that a true conversion requires an expression of free and knowing consent.[95] Implicit in Acosta's critique of the nonconsensual mass baptisms of black men and women in western Africa is the fact these individuals *would be capable* of sincerely converting to Christianity if sufficient pastoral care were taken to procure the legitimating criteria.

[94] Acosta, *De procuranda*, vol. 2, 366–68.   [95] Ibid., 368.

Because Acosta's treatise is primarily concerned with evangelization strategies for the indigenous populations of Spanish America, he does not offer a solution for how missionaries should fix the specific problems related to black evangelization in the Americas even if he mentions them several times in the treatise. If he had taken on this topic, he would have had to address the complicated question of how missionaries might access and interpret the enslaved black person's free will in the midst of the vast language diversity of the Africans taken to the New World and the physical restrictions related to their captivity.[96] In the following decades, Acosta's successors would pick up where Acosta left off by taking steps to systematize the examination of black men's and women's Christian status on arrival in Spanish ports.

In this vein, the baptismal manual *Instruccion para remediar y asse-gurar, quanto con la divina gracia fuere posible, que ninguno de los Negros, que vienen de Guinea, Angola, y otras Provincias de aquella costa de Africa, carezca del sagrado baptismo* (1614) offers criteria to examine the black populations arriving in Iberian ports.[97] The manual explains that priests would not only sin if they were to rebaptize those who had already received legitimate baptisms, but that they would also sin if they were to neglect to baptize those who had not already been legitimately baptized.

The solution proposed by the *Instruccion* provides familiar criteria to learn if black men and women were legitimately baptized before arriving in Iberian ports. The manual states that missionaries must establish (1) whether the black individual was baptized before leaving "su tierra" [his land], (2) if so, whether the priest who baptized the black individual had explained the objective, function, or meaning of the baptism through an

---

[96] He merely concludes this section by stating that peoples deemed to have been insuffi-ciently baptized could and should be re-baptized *subconditione* (ibid.).

[97] *Instruccion para remediar y assegurar, quanto con la divina gracia fuere posible, que ninguno de los Negros, que vienen de Guinea, Angola, y otras Provincias de aquella costa de Africa, carezca del sagrado baptismo* (Seville, 1614; version consulted in ARSI, Fondo General 720, II. 4b). The *Instruccion* is credited to Pedro de Castro y Quiñones, Arch-bishop of Seville from 1610 to 1623, in its original publication as well as the subsequent versions in Sandoval's treatise and a reprinting of the 1614 version in Lima in 1628, cited below. Archival documentation found by Francisco Borja Medina reveals that it was composed in collaboration with Jesuit priest Diego Ruiz de Montoya ("Vita V.P. Iacobi Ruiz de Montoia," appendix to the Carta Annua of 1632, ARSI Baet. 19/II, ff. 118v–119v). See Francisco de Borja Medina, "La experiencia sevillana de la Compañía de Jesús en la evangelización de los esclavos negros y su repercusión en América," in *La esclavitud negroafricana en la historia de España: Siglos XVI y XVII*, ed. Aurelia Martín Casares and Margarita García Barranco (Granada: Comares, 2010), 75–94, especially 84.

interpreter who spoke both his language and Spanish, and (3) whether the black individual had understood anything of what was said. Then, the last point builds off the first three, asking (4) whether the black individual then knowingly and willfully consented to the conversion formalized in the baptism. For this point, the manual specifically demands that priests inquire:

si dieron entonces verdaderamente su libre consentimiento con la voluntad para recibir lo que sus amos, y el cura pretendia darles con aquel lavatorio corporal; o solamente sufrieron a mas no poder lo que sus amos hazian. De suerte, que aunque no contradixeron exteriormente; o aunque fingieron, que tenian voluntad de recebir el baptismo; pero en su coraçon, o no tenian tal voluntad determinada; o dezian entre si, que no consentian.

[*if they truly gave their free consent with their will* to receive that which their masters and the priest attempted to give them with that corporal ablution; or if they only suffered through what their masters did to them without being able to do anything about it. [Priests should inquire if] they had wanted to receive the baptism, or if they just did not visibly object to it or if they only pretended that they wanted it or if in their hearts they did not have such a determined good will or if they said to themselves that they did not consent.][98]

This final point is particularly relevant because it identifies the existence of black men's and women's intellectual capacity to choose to convert sincerely and freely even as enslaved new arrivals with *no* knowledge of Spanish. This point also demonstrates missionaries' anxiety about how to interpret the will motivating that choice.[99] It is significant to note that in the *Instruccion*, like Acosta's *De procuranda*, neither the physical constraints of enslavement nor the difficulties of communicating in Iberian languages impede the recognition of the capacity of black men and women to choose to become Christian freely.

The *Instruccion*'s portrayal of black new arrival's capacity to exercise free will to become legitimate Christians would circulate widely in evangelical texts in the Iberian world in subsequent decades. The *Instruccion* itself would be reproduced verbatim in Sandoval's treatise *Naturaleza, policia sagrada*, which he wrote in Lima and Cartagena between

---

[98] *Instruccion*, f. 929v–930r; my emphasis.

[99] This type of anxiety concerning the difference between "true" belief and its outward expression is comparable to contemporaneous concerns in the Peninsula regarding the return of European Christian captives who had lived as prisoners in Muslim Northern Africa. On returning to European shores, the former captives would have to defend their Christian status, explaining that even though they outwardly appeared to have accepted Islam during their captivity, they never accepted it "in their hearts." See Bartolomé Bennassar and Lucile Bennassar, *Los cristianos de Alá: La fascinante aventura de los renegados*, trad. José Luis Gil Aristu (Madrid: Nerea, 1989).

1618 and 1624 and published in Seville in 1627 to elaborate a theoretical and practical system for black evangelization in the Americas.[100] The *Instruccion* was then again republished as an independent pamphlet in Lima in 1628.[101] According to Jesuit historian Borja Medina, Alonso de Sandoval also sent the *Instruccion* to Father Rodrigo de Cabrero, Provincial Father of Mexico, who then distributed copies to the Archbishop of Mexico City and Puebla.[102] Furthermore, throughout the Americas and the Iberian Peninsula during this period, the Inquisition would intermittently monitor black interiority, seeking to punish and correct heterodox or idolatrous beliefs and behaviors of black men and women, something which required working from the premise that the accused had met the criteria to become legitimate Christians in the first place.

The evangelical texts developed in the New World in the late sixteenth and seventeenth centuries to monitor black men's and women's beliefs signal the circulation of a related but distinct black type than those foregrounded in contemporaneous literary texts and legal codes: that of the black (proto-) Christian who regardless of his or her linguistic abilities and legal status has the interiority and the intellectual capacity to exercise the requisite free will to become Christian. While Acosta's treatise from the late sixteenth century echoes the emphasized physicality and inferior intellectual capacity of the black types of the two other genres by suggesting that heavy amounts of physical discipline would be necessary to prepare black men and women for Christian conversion, his treatise and the *Instruccion* also suggest that black men and women could be fully

---

[100] As will be noted in the following chapter, Sandoval's treatise would be read and cited throughout Spanish America. Jesuit Priest Alonso de Ovalle, for example, cites Sandoval's book and methods in his own text produced twenty years later in Peru: *Historica relacion del reyno de Chile* (Rome: Francisco Caballo, 1646). Luis Martín explains that the Jesuit College of San Pablo in Lima became a distributing center for Sandoval's book that was printed in Seville in 1627, sending many copies to the "four corners of the viceroyalty" between 1628 and 1631 (*Intellectual Conquest*, 52).

[101] A copy of the 1628 *Instruccion* published in Lima is available in microfilm at the Brown University Library. The text cited above comes from the version of the *Instruccion* published in Seville in 1614. There are no significant differences between the Seville and Lima versions.

[102] Borja Medina, "La experiencia sevillana de la Compañía de Jesús," 87. According to Borja Medina, a fragment of the *Instruccion* was also produced and sent to Tucuman between 1616 and 1625 under the title *Instrucción del modo que se debe guardar en el examen, catecismo y Bautismo de los Negros, dada por el Illmo. Sr. D. Julián de Cortázar Obispo e Tucumán conforme a otra que el Illmo. Sr. Arzobispo de Sevilla hizo con parecer de todos los hombres doctos de aquella ciudad para los Negros de la que usan los Padres de la Compañía de Jesús en todas las Indias, con licencia y aprobación de los prelados de ellas.*

capable of exercising their intellect to choose to become Christian. Iberian and Spanish American missionary writings about black evangelization composed in the wake of *De procuranda* similarly acknowledge black men's and women's capacity for free will even as they echo the gesture of positioning them as the least civilized population in Spanish America.

CONCLUSION

The generic typology presented in this chapter demonstrates that black men and women were not categorically excluded from humanity as some have insisted. Instead, they were included as humans while being placed on the lower end of a continuum defined by Renaissance humanist standards for civility. This placement closely identified black types with unruly bodies rather than intellectual capacities or moral virtue. In contrast to the literary *bozal* stereotype and the black type of colonial ordinances, evangelical texts acknowledge black men's and women's potential to possess the characteristics of peoples on the higher end of the human continuum and support black men's and women's ability to legitimately become Christian.

All three generic portrayals of black men and women reviewed in this chapter correspond to a closed circuit of projection and interpretation of black characters and characteristics by nonblack authors and audiences. As I will show in detail in the cases of black linguistic and spiritual intermediaries in the following chapters, such circuits were sometimes interrupted. In the moments of interruption that resulted from black men and women gaining access to the written word and appropriating Christian discourse, other interpretations of blackness emerge in seventeenth-century Spanish American texts. The following chapters consider ways in which black men and women in New Granada and Peru used translation and spiritual mediation to adapt, reject, or ignore the constraints of the black types outlined in this chapter.

2

The Transatlantic Slave Trade and Spanish American Missionary Translation Policy

Most black men and women taken as slaves to the Americas in the first half of the seventeenth century passed through Cartagena de Indias as the first point of entry to the Americas after crossing the Atlantic Ocean. According to the collection of seventeenth-century Jesuit texts analyzed in the following three chapters, when a ship carrying slaves entered Cartagena's harbor, a Jesuit priest and a group of enslaved black interpreters would paddle a small boat to the ship to greet the new arrivals. Once onboard, the interpreters would provide water, food, and medical attention to the enslaved men, women, and children, and then they would explain to them in whatever languages necessary or possible that the ship had arrived in "the land of the whites" and that all the captives would soon become Christian. In a testimony given several decades after his own arrival in Cartagena, black interpreter Andrés Sacabuche narrates his memory of his initial encounter with a group of black interpreters in the city's harbor as a young boy aboard a ship from Angola:

per mezzo delli Interpreti, posto in mezzo del detto naviglio li diceva alli detti mori che esso era venuto ivi per essere Padrino e difesa di tutti, et acciò li trattassero bene li Bianchi, che avvertissero che non li portavano per mangiarli, et ammazzarli, come facevano alle loro terre li negri che li facevano priggioni ma per insegnarli la legge d'Iddio, e che quella mediante si salvassero le loro anime ch'erano immortali, et andassero al cielo e non all'Inferno ove havevano d'andare necessariamente se non fossero Christiani, et acciò servissero li Spagnuoli e che esso faria che l'amassero molto, animandoli et disingannandoli dell'errore nel quale venghono imbeverati [sic] li detti negri, tenendo per certo che li Bianchi li conducono alle loro terre per acciderli e mangiarli, e di far d'essi oglio e polvere, e questo Testimonio e di natione Angola, conforme ha detto, et intese il medesimo quando lo condussero dalla sua terra à questa di Cartagena.

[through the interpreters, in the middle of that ship, the father told those blacks that he had come there to be the father and protector of all, so that the whites would treat them well and so that they [the blacks] would realize that the whites did not take them there to eat and kill them, as the blacks who had imprisoned them in their lands would do, but to teach them the law of God, through which they would save their souls that were immortal so they would go to heaven and not to hell where they would necessarily have to go if they were not Christian. And so they should serve the Spaniards, which would make the Spaniards love them very much. With this, [the father through the interpreters] would encourage them and disabuse them of the lie with which blacks come imbued, firmly believing that the whites take them to their lands to kill and eat them and turn them into oil and powder. This witness is Angolan, as he has already said, and understood this himself when they brought him from his land to Cartagena.][1]

As noted in the Introduction, Andrés Sacabuche's orally delivered account was written down by a Spanish notary for the purpose of documenting Catalonian Jesuit priest Pedro Claver's labor among black men and women in Cartagena for Claver's beatification inquest. The encounter described by Sacabuche would be the first of many exchanges between the Jesuits' black interpreters and the black new arrivals who were beginning their lives as enslaved laborers in Spanish America. As apparent in the passage, the speech delivered in translation through the interpreters on the ship instantiated new meanings for a series of key terms for the men, women, and children arriving in Cartagena: being black, being servants of Spaniards, and being Christian. In particular, Sacabuche's testimony divides being black into two different types: being black in their lands of origin and being black in Spanish lands. Texts that describe the exchanges between black interpreters and black new arrivals from this period, such as this one, indicate the circulation of notions of blackness produced in Spanish America that demand critical attention, as they offer insight into the adoption and transformation of racial categories by racialized individuals themselves. The present chapter argues that the policy developed for evangelizing black populations in Spanish America, compared with that of indigenous populations in the same regions, required uniquely validating black interpreters' roles as evangelical intermediaries. This validation in turn opened a space for important forms of subjectification and authority for black interpreters.

Stories about the Jesuits' black interpreters appear in a set of texts produced in Lima, Cartagena, and Seville about the order's mission

---

[1] *Proceso* 1676, Sacabuche, 101v.

among black populations in the Americas that I will analyze in this chapter and the two that follow.[2] The first printed text from Spanish America to advocate for employing black interpreters for evangelical purposes is Alonso de Sandoval's *Naturaleza, policia sagrada i profana, costumbres i ritos, disciplina i catechismo evangelico de todos los etiopes*, more frequently referred to by its subtitle *De instauranda Aethiopum salute*.[3] This treatise, which Sandoval composed in Lima and Cartagena between 1618 and 1624 and had printed in Seville in 1627, refers to the order's black linguistic assistants with three general names: *intérpretes*, *lenguas*, and *chalonas*. Sandoval uses the first two terms interchangeably to name the facilitators of oral communications between two or more languages, and he uses *chalona* to refer to an interpreter who specifically knows Portuguese as well as one or more African languages.[4] As I will show, the Jesuits' interpreters were not always *negros ladinos* (black men and women who could speak a European language) because, according to Sandoval, interpreters could also be *bozales* (black men and women who

---

[2] Sandoval, *Naturaleza, policia sagrada*; *Proceso 1676*; José Fernández, *Apostolica y penitente vida del P. Pedro Claver de la Compañia de Jesus* (Zaragoza: D. Dormer, 1666); *Proceso Sac Rituum Congregatione sive Eminentissimo et Reverendissimo Domino Card De Abdua Cartagenen, Beatificationis, et Canonizationis Ven Servi Dei Petri Claver Sacerdotis Societ Iesu* (Rome: Sagrada congregación de ritos, 1696).

[3] Sandoval significantly modified the 1627 treatise and republished it in 1647 as *Historia de Aethiopia* (Madrid: Alonso Paredes, 1647). The 1647 edition is an augmented revision of the first two of four books from the 1627 edition. In the twentieth century, two modern editions of the 1627 version were published: *De instauranda Aethiopum salute: El mundo de la esclavitud negra en América* (Bogota: Empresa Nacional de Publicaciones, 1956) and *Un tratado sobre la esclavitud: De instauranda Aethiopum salute*, ed. Enriqueta Vila Vilar (Madrid: 1987). In 2008, historian Nicole von Germeten published a translation into English of highly modified selections from Vila Vilar's edition as *Treatise on Slavery: Selections from* De instauranda Aethiopum salute (Indianapolis: Hackett, 2008). Neither twentieth-century edition fully renders the content of the 1627 text by Sandoval because the first one occasionally paraphrases and inserts orthographical and punctuation marks that are not in the original and the second omits the notes originally published in the margins of the 1627 text and contains many typographical errors. Now that digitized versions of the 1627 text are available (e.g., the copy digitized by the Bibliothèque Nationale de France/Gallica, http://gallica.bnf.fr/ark:/12148/bpt6k73763z), I will be citing from the 1627 text.

[4] See Wheat, *Atlantic Africa*, 229–32, for an etymology of the terms *chalona* (noun) and *chalonear* (verb) that places their emergence in the late sixteenth-century Portuguese contacts with Africa. Wheat explains that *chalonas* were interpreters who facilitated trade, and *chalonear* was used as the Portuguese verb for bartering. Wheat rightly states that *chalona* functions as a synonym for interpreter in Sandoval's treatise (231). I surmise that when Sandoval describes an interpreter as a *chalona*, he was indexing an interpreter who specifically spoke Portuguese.

could not speak a European language), as even *bozales* could serve as crucial links in chains of interpretation between speakers of different west African languages. As interpreters for the Jesuits, *bozal* and *ladino/a* black men and women would play important roles in examining, catechizing, and administering the sacraments that were meant to transform the men, women, and children arriving from western Africa in Cartagena into black Christians.[5]

As an entry into examining the black interpreters' subject positions in seventeenth-century Cartagena, it is first necessary to outline the sixteenth-century colonial missionary translation policies that set precedents for the systematization of black evangelical translation that occurred in Cartagena in the early seventeenth century. By the time the Jesuit order established itself in Cartagena in 1605, it had developed a standard method for evangelical translation among indigenous languages in the Andes. The order codified its methods more than twenty years before as part of the reforms of the Third Lima Council, which enacted a policy that demanded that European priests learn indigenous languages so that New World parishioners could interact with the Church and its sacraments in terms the parishioners could understand. Another goal related to this policy of training European priests to speak indigenous languages was that it would avoid placing such a large part of the responsibility of indigenous evangelization on indigenous catechists or interpreters. The reforms to evangelical language policy and translation in Peru enacted by the Third Lima Council should be understood within the broader context of the debate in the Iberian world about what languages should be used for missionary work and who should be in charge of missionary efforts in areas of colonial expansion. Before the Jesuits arrived in Spanish America in the late 1560s, for example, other religious orders had made progress on the study and transcription of indigenous languages for evangelical purposes.[6] On their own arrival in Lima, the

---

[5] Christianity was not a new religion for all of the black men and women arriving in Spanish America. Many individuals from areas now considered central Africa were already legitimately Christian on arrival (Sandoval, *Naturaleza, policia sagrada*, book 3, chap. 5, 255v). To examine the validity of their baptisms on arrival, Sandoval recommends employing black interpreters.

[6] The first printed grammar and vocabulary in an indigenous Andean language is Fray Domingo de Santo Tomás's grammar of Quechua from 1560. In New Spain, the first printed grammar is Fray Alonso Molina's in Nahuatl from 1571, although much earlier manuscript grammars are known to exist. The Jesuits arrived earlier, in Brazil in 1549. Soon after arrival, they began learning and catechizing in indigenous languages. The bibliography on missionary translation in the colonial Americas is vast. For a broad

Jesuits sought to build on these initial efforts by leading a project to compose standard printed translations of the Christian doctrine in Andean languages to help European priests learn the languages themselves in the early 1580s. The first text of the new standardized catechetic corpus for the Andes was printed by the Third Lima Council in 1584 under the title *Doctrina christiana y catecismo para instruccion de los indios.*[7] As shown in Figure 2.1, the trilingual volume offers same-page renditions of the catechism and prayers in Spanish, Quechua, and Aymara.[8]

The declarations made in the prefatory materials to the *Doctrina christiana y catecismo para instruccion de los indios* reveal that the new

overview of the history of indigenous language texts in Latin America, see Alan Durston, "Indigenous Languages and the Historiography on Latin America," *Storia della storiografia* 67, no. 1 (2015): 51–65; Otto Zwartjes, "The Missionaries' Contribution to Translation Studies in the Spanish Colonial Period," in *Missionary Linguistics V: Translation Theories and Practices* (Amsterdam: John Benjamins, 2014), 1–50. For more specific regional and thematic studies, see Nancy Farriss, *Tongues of Fire: Language and Evangelization in Colonial Mexico* (New York: Oxford University Press, 2018); Lucia Binotti, "'La lengua compañera del imperio'. Observaciones sobre el desarrollo de un discurso de colonialismo linguistico en el renacimiento español," in *Las gramáticas misioneras de tradición hispánica (siglos XVI–XVII)*, ed. Otto Zwartjes (Portada Hispanica, 2001), 259–88; Federico Beals Nagel Bielicke, "El aprendizaje del idioma náhuatl entre los franciscanos y los jesuitas en la Nueva España," *Estudios de cultural náhuatl* 24 (1994): 419–41; Thomas C. Smith Stark, "Rincón y Carochi: La tradición jesuítica de descripción del náhuatl," in *Las gramáticas misioneras de tradición hispánica*, 28–71; Denny Moore, "Historical Development of Nheengatu (Língua Geral Amazonica)," in *Iberian Imperialism and Language Evolution in Latin America*, ed. Salikoko Mufwene (Chicago: University of Chicago Press, 2014), 108–42. For a study comparing Jesuit efforts to standardize and print catechetical materials in indigenous languages across the Iberian Americas, see Andrea Daher, "De los intérpretes a los especialistas: El uso de las lenguas generales de América en los siglos XVI y XVII," en *Saberes de la conversión: Jesuitas, indígenas e imperios coloniales en las fronteras de la cristiandad*, ed. Guillermo Wilde (Buenos Aires: Bibliografika, 2011), 61–80.

7 The two other texts published by the Council are *Tercero cathecismo y exposicion de la doctrina christiana por sermones para que los curas y otros ministros prediquen y enseñen a los indios y a las demas personas* [1585] and *Confessionario para los curas de indios* [1585]. For the production history of the Third Lima Council corpus, see Enrique Bartra, "Los autores del catecismo del Tercer Concilio Limense," *Mercurio Peruano* 52, no. 470 (1967): 359–72; Alan Durston, *Pastoral Quechua: The History of Christian Translation in Colonial Peru, 1550–1650* (Notre Dame, IN: University of Notre Dame Press, 2007), 86–104; Pedro Guibovich, "The Printing Press in Colonial Peru: Production Process and Literary Categories in Lima, 1584–1699," *Colonial Latin American Review* 10, no. 2 (2001), 168–69; and Bruce Mannheim, *The Language of the Inka since the European Invasion* (Austin: University of Texas Press, 1991), 66–67, 141–42.

8 *Doctrina christiana y catecismo para instruccion de los indios* (Lima: Antonio Ricardo, 1584).

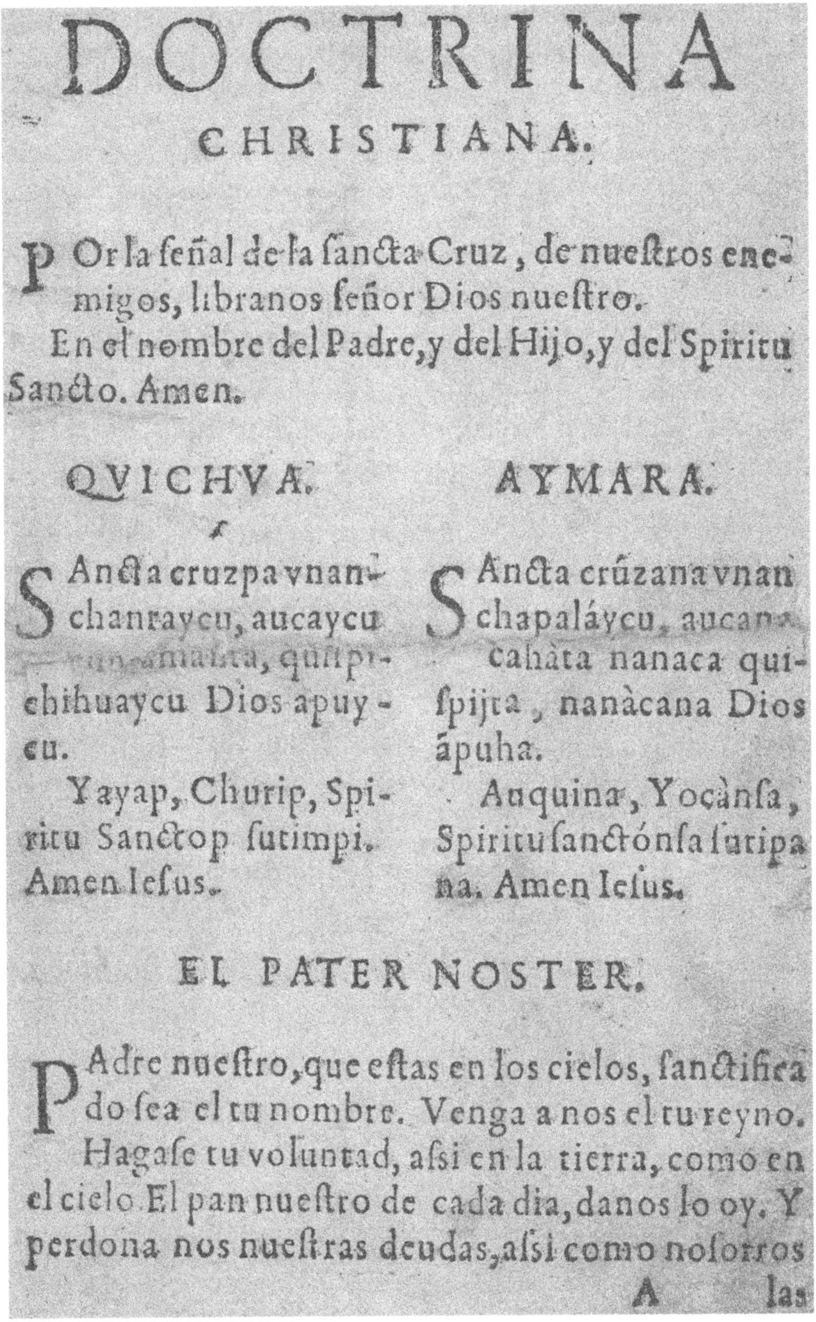

DOCTRINA
CHRISTIANA.

P Or la feñal de la fancta Cruz, de nueſtros ene-
migos, libranos feñor Dios nueſtro.
En el nombre del Padre, y del Hijo, y del Spiritu
Sancto. Amen.

QVICHVA.

S Ancta cruzpa vnan-
chanraycu, aucaycu
~~·~~ ~~amauta, quiſpi~~-
chihuaycu Dios apuy -
cu.
Yayap, Churip, Spi-
ritu Sanctop futimpi.
Amen Iefus.

AYMARA.

S Ancta crúzana vnan
chapaláycu, aucan-
cahàta nanaca qui-
ſpijta , nanàcana Dios
ápuha.
Auquina, Yocànfa,
Spiritu fanctónfa furipa
na. Amen Iefus.

EL PATER NOSTER.

P Adre nueſtro, que eſtas en los cielos, fanctifica
do fea el tu nombre. Venga a nos el tu reyno.
Hagafe tu voluntad, afsi en la tierra, como en
el cielo. El pan nueſtro de cada dia, danos lo oy. Y
perdona nos nueſtras deudas, afsi como nofotros
A   las

FIGURE 2.1 First page of *Doctrina christiana y catecismo para instruccion de los indios* (Lima, 1584).
Courtesy of the British Library

method for evangelical translation among Andean indigenous populations sought to make priests depend much less on native interpreters than
ever before by controlling native interpreters' influence over the translated
message with a codified printed text.⁹ The introductory remarks to the
Doctrina christiana y catecismo para instruccion de los indios declare its
translation to be "autentica" [authentic] by way of its association with the
authority of the Council: "hemos tenido por necessario, (como por diversas personas se ha pedido en este Cõcilio provincial) hazerse por nuestra
orden y cõmision *una traduction autentica* del Catecismo y Doctrina
christiana que todos sigã" [It has been deemed necessary (as many different people have requested it in this Provincial Council) to commission and
compose under our control an *authentic translation* of the Catechism and
Christian doctrine that everyone should follow].¹⁰ Through this statement, the Council characterizes any previously translated doctrinal texts
as specifically unauthorized. Importantly, the authenticity of this printed
text is based on the Council's approval as opposed to individual perceptions of the translation's accuracy. To discourage potential questioning of
the new codified translation by experts in indigenous languages, the
introduction warns that no supplements or elisions should ever be made
to the texts:

parecio a este sancto Concilio Provincial, *proveer y mãdar cõ rigor que ninguno
use otra traduction, ni enmiende ni añada en esta, cosa alguna.* Por que aun que
oviese cosas, q[ue] por ventura se pudieran dezir mejor de otra suerte (que forçoso
es que aya si[em]pre en esto de traduction diversas opiniones) pero hase juzgado, y
lo es menos inconveniente que se passe por alguna menos perfection que tenga por
ventura la traduction: que no dar lugar, a que aya variedad y discordias como en
las traductiones de la sancta Scriptura saludablemente lo ha proveydo la Yglesia
catholica.

[this Holy Provincial Council decided *to declare and to order emphatically that no
other translation than this one be used and that this translation not be amended or
expanded in any way.* Because even if perhaps certain things could be better said
(since regarding translation there are always diverse opinions), the Council judged
that accepting the imperfection of the translation is more important than offering

---

⁹ Elsewhere I have argued that the Jesuit-led codification of translation in the Third Lima
  Council coincided with the exclusion of *mestizos* from becoming Jesuit priests as a double-
  pronged attempt to deauthorize *mestizo* men within the order from claiming status based on
  their proficiency in Andean languages. See Brewer-García, "Bodies, Texts, and Translators:
  Indigenous Breast Milk and the Jesuit Exclusion of Mestizos in Late Sixteenth-Century
  Peru," *Colonial Latin American Review* 21, no. 3 (2012): 365–90.
¹⁰ *Doctrina christiana y catecismo*, n.p. [xvi], my emphasis.

room for variety and discord, as the Catholic Church has devoutly ordered in the case of translations of Holy Scripture.]¹¹

The insistence that the translations be followed to the letter explicitly warns against translations that could incite unhealthy "variedad y discordias" [variety and discord] in indigenous interpretations of Christian doctrine.¹² In fact, some of the most strident disagreements about evangelical translation until this point in the Americas had to do with terms for fundamental concepts such as God, the Cross, and the Holy Spirit.¹³ As a response, the Third Lima Council's translations clarified that it would forevermore be necessary to import Spanish terms for such concepts into indigenous languages, even if certain individuals believed an equivalent term in an indigenous language existed. The opening note on translation to the *Doctrina christiana y catecismo para instruccion de los indios* cited above makes it clear that the new authentic standard text was to function as authority over language experts who might consider themselves to possess the linguistic credentials to contest the Council's translations but were unlikely to have sufficient theological training: "Y aùnque ay algunos expertos en la lengua: ay empero pocos que lo séan juntamente en letras sagradas" [Even though there are some language experts, there are very few who are also experts in theology], and the few who qualify as both nevertheless often disagree over which terms to use.¹⁴ The statement reflects that the move to standardize Andean doctrinal languages and texts involved a devaluing of maternal or native fluency in indigenous languages that was not combined with training in theology and knowledge of the new standardized languages created by the Third Lima Council's texts.

In fact, in printing these standard religious texts, the *Doctrina christiana y catecismo para instruccion de los indios* explicitly created new

---

¹¹ Ibid., n.p. [xvii]; my emphasis.
¹² After the publication of the *Doctrina christiana y catecismo*, the circulation of inauthentic translations of doctrinal texts continued to be a concern, evidenced by the legislation passed two years later to ban manuscript copies of the printed *Doctrina y catecismo* so as to avoid "errors that may result from copying" and intentional modifications to the translations by those making the copies (Durston, *Pastoral Quechua*, 101). From 1584 onward, authority was to rest in the printed text in order to avoid potentially fallacious copying hands.
¹³ See Fray Antonio de Remesal, "Diferencias entre dominicos y franciscanos sobre la traducción del término 'Dios' a idiomas aborígenes" [1551], in Francisco Solano, *Documentos sobre política lingüística en Hispanoamérica (1492–1800)* (Madrid: Consejo Superior de Investigaciones Científicas, 1991), 56–57.
¹⁴ *Doctrina christiana y catecismo*, n.p. [xvi].

variants of the principal indigenous Andean languages for its translations. The additional notes on translation later in the volume explain that the translators chose a stripped-down variant of Quechua spoken in Cuzco for their translations:

De dos extremos se ha procurado huyr en la traduccion de esta Doctrina christiana, y Catecismo, en la lengua Quichua. Que son, el modo tosco, y corrupto de hablar que ay en algunas provincias: y la demasiada curiosidad, conque algunos del Cuzco, y la comarca usan de vocablos, y modos de dezir tan exquisitos, y obscuros, que salen de los limites del lenguaje, que propriamente se llama Quichua, introduziendo vocablos que por v[en]tura se usavan antiguamente, y agora nò, o aprouechandose de los que usavan los Ingas, y señores, o tomandolos de otras naciones con quien tratan.

[In translating the Christian Doctrine and Catechism into the Quechua language, two extremes have been avoided. They are the abrupt and corrupt mode of speech of some provinces, and the excessive peculiarity used by some speakers in Cuzco and its surroundings who use such strange and obscure terms and expressions that they exceed the limits of the Quechua language, introducing words that may have been used long ago, but are no longer used. Or they employ terms that the Incas and lords used, or they use those of other nations with whom they trade.][15]

This new hybrid-yet-purified language is what Alan Durston calls "pastoral Quechua," which was supposed to ensure a straightforward interpretation of the Christian doctrine.[16]

But even though this new standard language was supposed to clarify the communication of the Christian doctrine, its imposition across the Andes also brought with it new complications in the delivery of the message of the text to indigenous audiences. As John Charles has

---

[15] Ibid., 74r [83r].

[16] On the creation of the Third Lima Council's "estilo llano" [plain style], see Durston, *Pastoral Quechua*, 93–95. For more on the variants of Quechua and the Andean general language in the sixteenth century, see John Charles, *Allies at Odds*, 44–48; Durston, *Pastoral Quechua*, 56–59; and Rodolfo Cerrón Palomino, "The Concept of General Language in Garcilaso Inca," in *Garcilaso Inca de la Vega: An American Humanist* (Notre Dame, IN: University of Notre Dame Press, 1998), chap. 9; "Diversidad y unificación léxica en el mundo andino," in *El quechua en debate: Ideología, normalización y enseñanza*, ed. Juan Carlos Godenzzi (Cuzco: Centro de Estudios Regionales Andinos Bartolomé de las Casas, 1992), 205–35. Similar approaches to codifying and purifying native languages for evangelization efforts were adopted across the Spanish territories in the late sixteenth century. On the implementation of such a strategy in Guatemala, for example, see Hanks, *Converting Words*. For complementary essays on the state of the field of New Philology, see Matthew Restall, "A History of New Philology and New Philology in History," *Latin American Research Review* 38, no. 1 (2003): 113–34; and Durston, "Indigenous Languages and the Historiography of Latin America."

demonstrated, the codified Quechua of the *Doctrina christiana y cate-cismo para instruccion de los indios* was sufficiently different from some variants of Quechua in Peru to require that the texts undergo additional supplemental oral interpretation in order to ensure comprehension.[17] Further complications arose in enforcing the codified printed text when missionaries from Peru traveled to provincial areas of the viceroyalty where neither Quechua nor Aymara were spoken.

For example, documents produced shortly after the Jesuits' initial settlement in Bogota in 1604 evidence the attempted spread of the Jesuits' linguistic evangelical strategy to a region with a much more diverse linguistic geography than that of Peru. Despite the distinct situation, Jesuits nonetheless sought to establish a standardized version of the Gospel in the area's principal indigenous languages, which would involve codifying and printing translations and training priests in those languages as they had in Peru. The comparison between Jesuit language policy in Lima and Bogota despite the two areas' distinct linguistic geographies will elucidate how unique the Jesuits' approach to language policies for black evangelization in Cartagena were.

By the time the Jesuits arrived in Bogota, the city had already experienced a frustrating battle over standardizing translation for evangelization. As Juan Fernando Cobo Betancourt explains, one of the biggest problems the city's second Archbishop Fray Luis Zapata de Cárdenas encountered in attempting to make reforms in the 1570s and 1580s to encourage the teaching of Christian doctrine in native languages was that the region lacked general languages like Quechua or Aymara in Peru in which standard doctrinal texts could be composed and disseminated.[18] In 1583, Zapata appointed Gonzalo Bermúdez, a secular *criollo* priest, as language chair to teach the variant of Muisca spoken in Bogota. Bermúdez was to compose a grammar for the language, hold classes to teach the area's clergy to speak it, and produce printed doctrinal texts in it for priests to use in their individual parishes. The regular orders already

---

[17] See John Charles, "More *Ladino* than Necessary: Indigenous Litigants and the Language Policy Debate in Mid-Colonial Peru," *Colonial Latin American Review* 16, no. 1 (2007): 23–47, 33, 34. Charles explains that despite efforts to produce a text that would minimize priestly dependence on non-Spanish interpreters, in certain regions of the Andes, clergy would still need to use native interpreters as language assistants if they were to adjust the *Doctrina christiana* for the comprehension of local audiences.

[18] Juan Fernando Cobo Betancourt, "Colonialism in the Periphery: Spanish Linguistic Policy in New Granada, 1574–1625," *Colonial Latin American Review* 23, no. 2 (2014): 126–29.

established in Bogota (the Franciscans and the Dominicans) resisted
Bermúdez's appointment, however, complaining bitterly about being asked
to learn the native language of the city that would not be useful outside
it and when, they argued, many natives were learning Spanish anyway.[19]

Into this battle over linguistic policy and practice arrived the Jesuits in
1604. They immediately advocated for developing a vernacular compe-
tence system among the area's clergy, similar to the one they helped create
for the Third Lima Council in the 1580s. In 1605 the Jesuits renewed the
effort in Bogota begun by Archbishop Zapata and organized a meeting
among all the religious orders functioning in and around the city to create
an authorized catechism in the Muisca language spoken in Bogota.
A decree signed by the president of the Audiencia of the New Kingdom
of Granada in 1606 details the Jesuits' attempt to apply the Third Lima
Council's strategy of producing a standardized written translation that
would replace any other translations circulating in the area.[20] Following
the model of the Third Lima Council and its Spanish text for the doctrine
and catechism, the Jesuits aspired to create an official translated text in
the Muisca of Bogota. To do so, they sought the help of Bermúdez as well
as that of Italian Jesuit Father José Dadei, who had (apparently) adeptly
learned the city's dialect of Muisca after spending just one year in the city.
Complaints about the validity and the orthodoxy of the terms of their
translation were voiced by people across the social strata of the city,
including authorities of the other regular orders.[21]

In response, the Jesuits resolved to compose a new standardized translation. To do so, they convened another meeting among "lenguas doctas y
peritos de lengua" [educated interpreters and language specialists] in
Bogota. Like the Third Lima Council, this summit of interpreters and
theologians created an official Christian doctrine. The Audiencia president Juan de Borja endorsed this new translation, ordering that:

se promulgue publicamente y se reçiva guarde y observe sin que ninguna persona
de qualquier estado preheminençia o dignidad que sea la pueda ympugnar en
dicho hecho ni palabra ni en otra ninguna manera y en espeçial los que estuvieren

---

[19] Ibid.
[20] "Auto del Sr Presidente del Rey sovre la doctrina en la lengua de los yndios [1606]," in
ARSI, Novi Regni et Quitensis, vol. 14, no. 6, ff. 48r–50r, f. 48r. There are two slightly
different copies of the Auto in ARSI, the second corresponding to ff. 50v–53r. For a
different English translation of the first of the two versions of the decree, see J. Michael
Francis, "Language and the 'True Conversion' to the Holy Faith: A Document from the
Archivum Romanum Societatis Iesu, Rome, Italy," *The Americas* 62, no. 3 (2006): 445–53.
[21] "Auto del Sr Presidente," 48r.

a su cargo doctrinar y enseñar los dichos yndios y por ella y no por otra los enseñen y instruyan de oy en adelante en las cosas de nuestra santa fee catholica...

[it be proclaimed publicly and received and observed without challenge from anyone of any standing or status, in deeds or words, or in any other manner, in particular those who are in charge of spreading the doctrine and teaching said Indians, so they will teach them according to that one and no other from now on in matters relating to our Holy Catholic Faith.][22]

Anticipating the debates caused by the two earlier attempts at language standardization in Bogota, this addendum prescribes different kinds of punishments for those who do not follow the summit's codified translations:

y ninguna persona contravenga segun dicho es a lo que en este auto se refiere *so pena de doçientos ducados y un año de destierro del Reyno cada ves que lo hiciere y siendo persona en quien se pueda executar sea la pena de doçientos açotes.* Para que sea notorio y nadie pueda pretender ignorançia, se pregone en esta corte publicamente y a los officiales reales a cuyo cargo esta la paga de los estipendios de las doctrinas de yndios de la real audiençia corona se les notifica que no paguen al doctrinero el tal estipendio sin que primero preçeda certificaçion del corregidor del partido, por ende les conste que se les enseña a los yndios de tal pueblo la doctrina en su lengua por esta traducçion y a los corregidores se les manda que en las pagas que ellos ubieren de hazer a los doctrineros de pueblos de encomenderos.

[and no one shall disobey this decree, *under penalty of two hundred ducados and one year of exile from the kingdom every time it is disobeyed, and if it is a person who can be so punished, two hundred lashes.* So that this is well known and no one may claim ignorance, it shall be proclaimed in this court publicly, and the royal officials of the Crown's Audiencia in charge of distributing stipends for Indian doctrines are notified that they shall not pay the doctrinal priest without first presenting certification from the local magistrate of the area clarifying that the doctrinal priest will teach doctrine to the Indians in their language by means of this translation. Local magistrates will receive similar orders regarding paying doctrinal priests in *encomendero* towns [Spanish settlements where indigenous peasants live].][23]

The variety of punishments for veering from the authorized translation mentioned above evidences the range of kinds of people assumed to be capable of committing such a crime. In fact, we can infer that the indigenous and *mestizo* language assistants of humble origins who priests generally employed to catechize the indigenous populations of the area would have been the ones subjected to physical punishment if they were caught disobeying the new standard translation. This threat demonstrates how,

---

[22] Ibid., f. 49v.   [23] Ibid., f. 49v; my translation; my emphasis.

despite the vastly heterogeneous linguistic geography of the province of New Granada, the Jesuits still continually attempted to exercise control over the interpreters of indigenous languages to promote orthodox dissemination of the Christian doctrine based on the written word.

The plurality of dialects of Muisca spoken in the highlands of Bogota and the many other indigenous languages spoken in the diverse regions of the province of New Granada required that priests amend the strategy they had used in Peru to recognize that parish priests needed to learn not one standard dialect but rather the particular language of their parish.[24] And yet when the First Provincial Synod of New Granada gathered in 1625, it adopted a very similar policy as that of the Third Lima Council, ordering that all bishops:

cuiden de que en sus respectivas diócesis, con la mayor rapidez posible, sea traducido el mismo Catecismo a las otras lenguas que se hablen en su jurisdicción, por medio de cristianos y competentes intérpretes y que aquella versión, de tal manera aprobada por el Obispo sea acogida por todos sin discusión, no obstante cualquier otra costumbre contraria.

[ensure, as soon as possible, that in their respective dioceses the same Catechism be translated into the other languages spoken in their jurisdiction by Christian and competent interpreters. They must also ensure that this version, once approved by the bishop, is adopted by everyone without challenge, regardless of any previous practice to the contrary.][25]

Like the Third Lima Council, the Provincial Synod of New Granada of 1625 forbade the use of unauthorized or improvised doctrinal translations in indigenous languages by insisting the translations be based on written texts and that the translators composing the texts be authoritative based on the criteria of being Christian and competent.[26] The Provincial

---

[24] Cobo Betancourt, "Colonialism in the Periphery," 119. After the 1606 decree, priests would be assigned a parish only if they could show that they spoke the language of their particular parish itself, not the standardized Muisca of Bogota. Once in their parishes, priests were supposed to compose written texts codifying their translations of the Christian doctrine for their particular area (133). A Cathedral edict from 1610 in Bogota ordered priests to return to Bogota from their posts to present themselves for an audit of their local language proficiency, and a subsequent audit in 1619 required parish priests not only to pass another language proficiency exam but also to provide a copy of the indigenous-language doctrinal documents they had produced that they were using in their parishes (134–36).

[25] Humberto Triana y Añorveza, *Las lenguas indígenas en la historia social del Nuevo Reino de Granada* (Bogota: Instituto de Caro y Cuervo, 1987), 318.

[26] Native interpreters still appear in accounts of Jesuit missionary activities from Peru in the first two decades of the seventeenth century, but when they do the Jesuit priests composing the accounts insist on the importance of curbing their authority with their own

Synod warned that excommunication would be the consequence of a violation of this rule, demonstrating the imposition of an even more severe punishment for interpreters or priests using nonstandardized translations other than those prescribed by the Audiencia of Santafé in 1606.[27]

It is crucial to underscore that despite the overwhelming plurality of indigenous languages in New Granada compared with Peru, religious authorities, backed by the Jesuits, *still* demanded that European priests learn indigenous languages and produce texts in those languages. The language policies adopted in Peru and New Granada for indigenous evangelization in the late sixteenth and early seventeenth centuries stand in stark contrast with the strategies adopted for black evangelization in these regions, where Jesuit priests made minimal efforts to learn African languages or produce evangelical texts in those languages. The following section will detail the unique strategies developed for black evangelization by the Jesuits, and in doing so demonstrate that a key consequence of the alternative strategy adopted by the Jesuits for black evangelization was that it granted black interpreters in Cartagena unparalleled influence over the translation of Christian doctrine into African languages. The practice of translation for black evangelization in Cartagena thereby afforded black interpreters an unchecked position of interpretive authority to shape and circulate evangelical discourse in colonial Spanish America.

AFRICAN LANGUAGES IN NEW GRANADA AND PERU

When the Jesuits began their evangelical efforts among the black populations arriving in and passing through Cartagena in 1605, the most striking practical problem they faced was the variety of languages spoken by the black men and women disembarking from the slave ships in the port. The Jesuits' solution to this problem appears in Sandoval's *Naturaleza, policia sagrada*.[28] After more than ten years evangelizing black men

---

knowledge of the language and through the use of written texts that guide the interpreters and provide the correct vocabulary for their catechetical work. See Brewer-García, "Bodies, Texts, and Translators," 379–81.

[27] Triana y Añorveza, *Las lenguas indígenas*, 318.

[28] Jesuit Alonso de Sandoval was born in Andalusia in 1576. Before the age of five, Sandoval moved to Lima with his father, a bureaucrat of the Peruvian viceroyalty. In Lima, he studied at the seminary of San Martín. Upon completing his education, he was ordained a Jesuit priest in Cuzco in 1593. Sandoval left Cuzco to work at the newly founded Jesuit school in Cartagena in 1605. For more biographical details of Sandoval's life, see Pacheco, *Los jesuitas en Colombia, vol. 1 (1567–1654)* (Bogota: San Juan Eudes, 1959), 248–68; Ángel Valtierra, "El padre Alonso de Sandoval, S.J.," in *De instauranda*

and women on the Caribbean coast of New Granada, the Seville-born
and Lima-raised Spanish Jesuit Alonso Sandoval wrote this treatise to give
instructions on how Jesuits should include the diverse black populations
arriving in the New World within the space of the Catholic Church. He
based his proposed method on his own experiences converting black men
and women in Cartagena, information he gathered from correspondence
with slave traders and Jesuits in other realms of the Spanish empire, and
research he conducted in Cartagena's and Lima's libraries regarding the
histories, political organizations, and religious beliefs of the peoples he
interchangeably calls black or Ethiopian in his treatise. In the preface,
Sandoval states the treatise's principal goal to be to offer spiritual triage to
the new arrivals, which would entail the following three steps:

examinemos sus bautismos, intruyamos su rudeza: y bien enseñados, los baptize-
mos: con lo cual repararemos, y restauraremos la salud que en ellos, por la razon
dicha, estava perdida, y como impossibilitada.

[we examine the validity of their baptisms, instruct them out of their ignorance,
and once they are well-taught, baptize them. With this, we repair and restore their
health that for this reason had been lost and almost rendered impossible.][29]

Sandoval begins by denouncing the present state of the spiritual health of
black peoples in the New World (whom he primarily assumes to be pagan
or Muslim) and criticizing the nonexistent or illegitimate catechisms and
baptisms they received before crossing the Atlantic or on arriving in
Cartagena. The previous and concurrent evangelization of indigenous
populations in Spanish America serves as a precedent and a point of
comparison for Sandoval's project. But unlike the standard protocol
established for indigenous evangelization, Sandoval's solution for ensuring the orthodoxy of black evangelization is not to demand that priests
learn black men's and women's languages and create standard printed
translations of the doctrine in them, but rather to depend entirely on black
interpreters.

    In no uncertain terms *Naturaleza, policia sagrada* calls for priests' full
dependence on black interpreters. Sandoval declares this strategy at the
beginning of the third chapter of the treatise's third book as a warning for
priests to prepare themselves for the effort of locating the right

    Aethiopum salute, V–XXXVII; Vila Vilar, "En torno al padre Sandoval, autor de un
    tratado sobre la esclavitud," in *Église et politique en Amérique Hispanique, XVI–XVIIIe*
    (Bordeaux: Presses Universitaires de Bordeaux, 1984), 65–76; Vila Vilar, "Introducción"
    to *Un tratado sobre la esclavitud*, 15–44.
[29] Sandoval, *Naturaleza, policia sagrada*, Argumento de la obra al christiano letor, n.p.

interpreters. Priest should be ready, Sandoval states, to travel by foot for days at a time to seek them out: "*porque si esta dificultad no se allana, todo el edificio deste levantado ejercicio cae por tierra*, pues es cosa averiguada que cuando las lenguas son extrañas un hombre para otro hombre, es como si no lo fuese" [*for if this difficulty is not overcome, the entire edifice of this lofty enterprise will fall to the ground*, as it is known that when languages are foreign between men, they barely consider each other men at all].[30] Sandoval's instructions underscore the pivotal importance of black interpreters to the Jesuits' pastoral activities in the port city.

In doing so, Sandoval does not completely cast aside the idea of codification at the heart of indigenous language translation policy. Instead of codifying the languages themselves in a printed grammar, Sandoval recommends that priests compose an "abecedario de castas, lengua e interpretes" [primer of the *castas*, languages, and interpreters] of the new arrivals to identify the African languages into which translation would be necessary.[31] Sandoval offers a sketch of such a notebook, organized around the principal ports of origin of the slave ships arriving in Cartagena:[32] (1) the rivers of Guinea and the ports of their mainland banks, (2) the islands of Cape Verde, (3) the island of Santo Tomé, and (4) the port of Loanda or Angola.[33] Sandoval indicates which groups brought from those ports share languages in common and might thus serve as effective interpreters to bridge the linguistic diversity of the peoples coming from those ports. The peoples originating from "the Rivers of Guinea" (Senegambia) Sandoval describes as Jolofo (Wolof), Berbesí (Serer), Mandinga (Mandinka), Fulo, Folupo (Floup), Bañún,

---

[30] Ibid., 234v; my emphasis.

[31] Ibid., book 1, chap. 2, 236r. For contemporary historiography describing the ports of origin for slave ships arriving in Cartagena during this period, see Wheat, *Atlantic Africa*; Newson and Minchin, *From Capture to Sale*; Luz Adriana Maya Restrepo, "Demografía histórica de la trata por Cartagena 1533–1810," in *Geografía humana de Colombia: Los afrocolombianos*, vol. 6, ed. Jaime Arocha Rodríguez, Martha Luz Machado Caicedo, and William Villa (Bogota: Instituto Colombiano de Cultura Hispánica, 2000), 9–52; and Nicolás del Castillo Mathieu, *Esclavos negros en Cartagena y sus aportes léxicos* (Bogota: Publicaciones del Instituto Caro y Cuervo, 1982). Sandoval notes that sometimes shipments arrive with captives from Southeastern Africa and Southeast Asia, too, and he includes them in his survey of the world's "black" populations (Sandoval, *Naturaleza, policia sagrada*, book 1, chaps. 4–9).

[32] See Sandoval, *Naturaleza, policia sagrada*, book 1, chaps. 9–16.

[33] For Sandoval's first general breakdown of these four ports see ibid., book 1, chap. 1, 5r–8v. For Sandoval's more specific descriptions of those coming from Guinea and Cabo Verde, see book 1, chaps. 11–13; for those coming from São Tomé and Sierra Leone, see book 1, chaps. 14 and 16; for the Kongo and Angola, see book 1, chaps. 15 and 16.

Cazanga, Bran (Brame) (which he divides into the Papel, Bojola, Bessi, and Bisau), Balanta, Biafara (Biafada), Bioho, Nalu, Zape, Cocolí, and Zozo.[34] He explains that ships from Cape Verde bring the same as those from the rivers of Guinea because the island was mostly an entrepôt for ships leaving the rivers of Guinea.[35] Further south, ships from São Tomé bring groups pertaining to lower Guinea, such as the Mina, Fula, Arda (Allada), Lucumí (Lukumi), Terranova, Temne, Guere, and Carabali (Kalabar).[36] Finally, Sandoval notes that ships originating from the port of Luanda would bring central African peoples he names as Angola, Kongo, Angico (Anchico), Mongiolo (also spelled Monzolo or Manzolo), Iaga, and Malemba.[37] Sandoval warns priests to expect to encounter complications in finding interpreters for these different peoples because even within the individual groups there can exist an immense variety of languages such that individuals of the same *nación* do not always understand each other.[38] Sandoval estimates the number of different African languages in Cartagena where ships from these four different ports were disembarking as surpassing seventy.[39]

To evangelize in the face of the post-Babelian language dispersion of the transatlantic slave trade and the abysmal physical and emotional conditions of the slave trade itself, the Jesuit cleric discards the possibility of learning African languages and using written texts in these languages to support the evangelical effort. In a chapter titled, "De la precisa necessidad que tienen los obreros destos Etíopes del uso de los interpretes, y lenguas ladinas, y fieles" [Of the extreme need missionaries working among these Ethiopians have for interpreters and acculturated language assistants, who are faithful], Sandoval declares adopting a comparable linguistic strategy to that of indigenous evangelization as "moralmente imposible" [morally impossible]:

a nosotros parece moralmente imposible que aprendamos todas estas lenguas por ser tanta su multitud y no haber alguna general, como por no haber quien pueda enseñarlas ni ser la comunicacion que con los negros tenemos la que baste para pegarsenos naturalmente.

---

[34] Ibid., 37v–41r.   [35] Ibid., 5r–6v.   [36] Ibid., 7r–7v.   [37] Ibid., 8r.

[38] For an analysis and summary of some of the languages that Sandoval notes are sometimes shared in common across distinct groups, including the São Tomé creole, see Antonio Santos Morillo, "La expresión lingüística de los esclavos negros según Alonson [*sic*] de Sandoval," *Actas del Congreso Internacional América Latina: La autonomía de una región*, ed. Heriberto Cairo Carou et al. (Madrid: Trama Editorial, 2012), 1086–93.

[39] Sandoval, *Naturaleza, policia sagrada*, book 3, chap. 2, 236r.

[for us it seems morally impossible to learn all these languages due to their multitude, the lack of a common one spoken among them, and the fact that we have no one who could teach them to us nor do we have such communication with blacks that we might acquire them naturally.][40]

With this declaration, Sandoval insists unequivocally that instead of requiring priests to learn African languages, missionaries should depend entirely on the help of enslaved black interpreters. Sandoval never explains the moral argument to which he alludes. It could refer to his opinion that the Jesuit priests' time would be better spent in other endeavors than trying to learn individual languages spoken by only a small percentage of the black populations arriving in Cartagena. It could also suggest that the prolonged contact priests would have to have with speakers of those languages to learn them sufficiently would be itself morally precarious.[41] Instead of explaining himself, Sandoval moves on to firmly advocate for the central role of black interpreters in his project: "sirve de poco, si no ay interprete o lengua de la nacion del enfermo o adulto sano a quien por su medio se ha de catechizar, baptizar o confessar, si ellos no entienden la nuestra, o nosotros no sabemos la suya" [Our missionary effort will bear little fruit if there is no interpreter who speaks the language of the sick or healthy adult through whom he can be catechized, baptized or confessed, as they do not understand our language and we do not understand theirs].[42] Sandoval then outlines a system wherein a priest would interview new arrivals and record the name, master, and residence of any multilingual slave next to the languages she or he speaks in a little book that would serve as the Jesuit's roster of interpreters. Significantly, Sandoval warns his readers that creating the roster itself is not enough because shipments often bring unprecedented groups to Cartagena, for whom no interpreters can be found in the area. Priests must be willing to search far and wide for appropriate interpreters among the city and surrounding areas.

Texts composed soon after Sandoval finished his treatise in 1624 demonstrate that in addition to renting multilingual enslaved laborers from their owners for days at a time as Sandoval suggests, the Jesuit school in Cartagena began to purchase black men to become in-house

---

[40] Ibid., 234r–v.
[41] I will provide evidence in support of the first set of possibilities later in this chapter in my analysis of the letter "En razon" below. Evidence for the second set of possibilities will be discussed in Chapter 3.
[42] Sandoval, *Naturaleza, policia sagrada*, 234r.

interpreters.[43] Keeping a group of enslaved interpreters on hand in the Jesuit school would have alleviated some of the labor of searching for adequate interpreters among the city's black populations to assist in evangelizing new arrivals.

Sandoval's position, articulated in the early 1620s and published in 1627, strikingly contradicts the efforts made by the Third Lima Council in 1583, the Audiencia of Santafé in 1606, and the Synod of New Granada in 1626 regarding evangelical translation in indigenous languages. As described in the previous section, in Peru and then in the highland interior of the province of New Granada, Jesuits stridently advocated *against* using untrained interpreters and unregulated religious translation in indigenous languages. On the Caribbean coast of New Granada, Sandoval argues for exactly the opposite for black evangelization: to use recently Christianized black interpreters to disseminate doctrine orally to the hundreds and sometimes thousands of black men and women arriving yearly in Spanish America through that port. Furthermore, unlike the approach adopted by the Third Lima Council in Peru, Sandoval's systematization of black interpretation provides minimal guidance regarding how to monitor or control the terms used by the interpreters for key religious concepts in the African target languages.

The previous Jesuit policy had been so clear on the standardization of translated religious texts in non-European languages that some misinformed Jesuits, such as student Gerónymo Pallas, who passed through Cartagena in 1619 on his way to Lima, assumed that the Jesuits would follow the route taken with indigenous evangelization and learn African languages. Pallas thus explains the evangelical duties of Jesuits in Cartagena:

una de las ocupaciones del servicio de Dios y en quien la compañía se ocupa con suma caridad en las Indias es la catequizaçión y enseñança de los morenos, particularmente aquí en Cartagena, donde por ser recién venidos de Guinea son más boçales y *es necessario que los padres trabajen en aprender sus lenguas diferentes para enseñarles el Catecismo y bauptiçar a los que no lo están.*

[one of the duties of those in the Indies in the service of God, whom the Jesuit order serves with great charity, is the catechization and teaching of blacks, particularly here in Cartagena, where because as they are newly arrived from Guinea they are more *bozal, requiring that the priests labor to learn their different languages in order to teach them and to baptize those who are not already.*][44]

---

[43] "Vitelleschi a Claver, 12 de febrero 1624." ARSI, N. R. et Q. 1, Epist. Gen. f. 240, cited in Pacheco, *Jesuitas en Colombia*, vol. 1, 277–78.

[44] Pallas, *Missión a las Indias* , 114–15, my emphasis.

Comparing Pallas's observation with those of the Jesuit priests who actually worked among black populations in Peru and New Granada shows that Pallas was not familiar with the strategies actually adopted by the Jesuits in the city for black evangelization.[45]

Yet Sandoval's proposal was not without precedent. The first Jesuits in Peru who arrived in 1568 borrowed a strategy for black evangelization that Jesuits had employed in Seville when the order established itself there in 1554.[46] This strategy entailed leading black men and women in singing processions through city streets that would end at a Jesuit church where they would listen to a brief sermon.[47] Texts describing early Jesuit missionary labor among black populations from sixteenth-century Peru do not specify the language(s) used for these songs and sermons. The omission is likely due to the fact that Jesuits spoke Spanish to black men and women in this period because before the large-scale adoption of Portuguese *asientos* in the 1580s, the majority of the black men and women in Peru arrived there from the Iberian Peninsula or other regions of Spanish America and were thus more likely to already comprehend Spanish than those arriving directly from western Africa in later years.[48]

---

[45] Some historians have stated that Sandoval and his colleague Pedro Claver eventually learned some African languages in Cartagena to help evangelize new arrivals from Angola. I have found contradictory evidence from the period regarding these claims. Ángel Valtierra cites a section from the Congregación Provincial of 1642 that praises Sandoval as "atento a que sabe la lengua de los negros" [attentive to knowing the language of blacks] ("Introducción" to *De instauranda* [1956], XXII). The statement is less than definitive, however, as it could refer to Sandoval's concern for seeking out interpreters in these languages rather than being able to speak them himself. Furthermore, Sandoval's treatise never suggests he could speak any African languages and only one witness mentions in passing in *Proceso 1676* that Claver could speak some Kimbundu (Vicente de Villalobos, 109v). For a summary and analysis of terms in African languages that appear in *Naturaleza, policia sagrada* that suggest Sandoval had some familiarity with some of these languages, see Antonio Santos Morillo, "La expresión lingüística," 1088.

[46] Francisco de Borja Medina, "El esclavo: ¿Bien mueble o persona? Algunas observaciones sobre la evangelización del negro en las haciendas jesuíticas," in *Esclavitud, economía y evangelización: Las haciendas jesuitas en la América virreinal*, ed. Sandra Negro and Manuel M. Marzal (Lima: PUCP, 2015), 83–124, 84.

[47] Antonio de Egaña, ed., *Monumenta Peruana*, vol. 1 (Rome: Instituto Histórico de la Compañía de Jesús, 1954), 167, 345; qtd. in Borja Medina "El esclavo," 84.

[48] Bowser, *The African Slave in Colonial Peru*, 11, 25. The change in the provenance of the black populations of Lima toward the end of the sixteenth century appears in the names of the black confraternities in the city. In the late 1570s the Jesuits sponsored only one *cofradía de negros*, but by 1590 there existed two separate groups: one for black *ladinos* and *ladinas* and another for black men and women from "Guinea" (Tardieu, *Los negros y la Iglesia en el Perú: Siglos XVI–XVII* [Quito: Centro Cultural Afroecuatoriano, 1997],

As the volume of the slave trade from western Africa grew in Peru and southern Spain toward the turn of the seventeenth century, Jesuits noted that linguistic diversity among black men and women arriving in the ports of the Spanish empire would need to be handled differently than before. In fact, a precursor to Sandoval's stance regarding the necessity of using black interpreters to evangelize black populations appears in the manual *Instruccion para remediar y assegurar, quanto con la divina gracia fuere posible, que ninguno de los Negros, que vienen de Guinea, Angola, y otras Provincias de aquella costa de Africa, carezca del sagrado baptismo* mentioned at the end of Chapter 1. Sandoval cites it verbatim in its entirety as part of book 3 of his own 1627 treatise.[49] The *Instruccion* advocates for using black interpreters in the examinations of baptisms of enslaved black men and women on arrival in Spanish ports. To do so, the manual suggests that priests document the name, legal status, marital status, and place of baptism of each individual black man and woman, along with his or her nation of origin and African languages known:

En todas las parochias hagan los Curas un padron o catalogo, en que se escrivan todos los negros varones, y mugeres captivos, y libres. Escrivase el nombre del negro, declarando si es libre, y si es captivo, declarando cuyo es. Y de todos se escriva, si fue baptizado en España, o no, y si es casado. Item se escriva, si es boçal, o si es tan ladino, y bien instruydo, y con tan buena noticia de alguna lengua de su nacion, que pueda servir de interprete para los boçales de su lengua, y de que lengua es.

[In all parishes, priests shall prepare a census or catalogue, registering all black men and women, captive and free. The name of blacks shall be listed, stating if they are free, captive, and declaring whose they are. With regard to all of them, it shall be recorded if they were baptized in Spain or not, and if they are married. It shall also be recorded if they are *bozales, ladinos,* and well instructed, and if they have sufficient knowledge of any language of their nation to serve as interpreters for *bozales* of that language, indicating which language.][50]

Noting each man's or woman's level of familiarity with Iberian languages and level of instruction was meant to help priests identify possible interpreters among the black population in Spain who might be able to help priests communicate with future new arrivals. This is the extent of the systematization of translation among black men and women suggested by

vol. 1, 427). This diversification of *cofradías* reflects the growing distinction between black men and women who had arrived relatively recently from Africa and those who had lived longer in Spanish- or Portuguese-speaking regions in the late sixteenth century.

[49] Sandoval, *Naturaleza, policia sagrada,* book 3, chap. 22, 326v–334v.

[50] *Instruccion,* f. 926r.

the manual. No comments or guidelines are given regarding how to monitor the linguistic exchanges when communicating the doctrine to new arrivals through black interpreters.

The *Instruccion* nonetheless so encourages the use of black interpreters that a key point to its guidelines, as mentioned in Chapter 1, is to test the legitimacy of black men's and women's baptisms by asking whether or not the catechism had been delivered through an interpreter. Priests were to ask each black new arrival "si por medio de algun interprete, que supiesse su lengua, y la nuestra, les dixeron algo de el fin, o utilidad, o significacion de el baptismo" [if the priest told them the objective, use, or meaning of the baptism *through an interpreter* who knew their language and ours].[51] Here the *Instruccion* suggests a baptism *without* the assistance of an interpreter should be considered invalid.

In adopting the *Instruccion*'s method for use in Cartagena, Sandoval surpasses the flexibility of the manual by justifying using chains of black interpreters to catechize newly arrived black men and women. According to Sandoval, even *bozales* could serve as key links in a chain to communicate with people for whom no *ladino/a* interpreter could be found. He explains the scenario as a way of alerting priests to the fact that *bozales* are often multilingual in several African languages even if they cannot speak a European language:

Y porque assi como las lenguas è interpretes ladinos suelen hablar varias lenguas, assi los negros boçales tambien las suelen hablar y entender, para que assi se les baptize, confiesse y remedie con cualquiera de las que entendieren, sin que haya de ser fuerza buscarseles las suyas genuinas y naturales; y muchas veces sucederá que el enfermo, v.g., nalu, no entienda la lengua del interprete, v. gr., Biafara; busquese en este caso algún otro Nalu bozal, que entienda biafara con el cual podrá (atento a que no todas veces se hallan nalues ladinos ni de otras muchas castas que puedan servir de lenguas e interpretes con los boçales de su casta) sin dificultad bautizar o confesar al otro nalu, que no sabia sino sola su lengua Nalu natural, v. gr., la lengua Biafara, hablará en Biafara al Nalu, que tambien entiende biafara, y este Nalu dirá lo que se le dijo en biafara al otro Nalu en Nalu; y assi se podrà ir advirtiendo de manera que se puede catequizar uno o tres o cuatro y mas lenguas a este modo, como a mí me ha acontecido muchas vezes.

[Just as *ladino* interpreters often speak various languages, so do black *bozales*, who can speak and understand various tongues. Because of this, to baptize, confess, and heal *bozales*, it is not necessary to find interpreters who speak their genuine and native tongue but rather to just find interpreters for any language that they understand. Often it will happen that the sick Nalu man, for example, cannot

---

[51] Ibid., f. 929v.

understand the interpreter who is Biafada, for example; in this case you will find another Nalu *bozal* who does understand Biafada through whom you can baptize or confess the other Nalu man without difficulty. (You must be aware that one cannot always find *ladino* Nalus to serve as interpreters for people of their kind [*casta*], which happens with many other kinds, too). As this Nalu man knows how to speak his native Nalu and Biafada, he will speak in Biafada to the Nalu man who also understands Biafada, and this Nalu man will convey what he was told in Biafada to the other Nalu man in Nalu. You can proceed in this way such that you can catechize one person with three or four or more interpreters, as has happened to me many times.][52]

Unlike the recommendations of the *Instruccion*, which suggest that appropriate interpreters should speak an African language and Spanish or Portuguese, Sandoval advocates for people who have no knowledge of Spanish to also serve as supplemental intermediary interpreters. Far from minimizing "variedad y discordias" [variety and discord] as demanded by the Third Lima Council's evangelical language policy from 1583, Sandoval's method multiplies it through introducing the idea of chains of interpretation to communicate with the newly arrived black men and women. Sandoval celebrates the results of using such chains of transla-tion: "Otro a quien baptizè a lo ultimo de su vida, por medio de cinco interpretes, que unos hablavan a otros, como queda advertido, me lo agradecia, aviendo escapado con la vida" [Another man whom I baptized on his deathbed *through five interpreters*, speaking among themselves as I have previously explained, would thank me every time he saw me, for he had survived his illness].[53] Sandoval emphasizes the successful conversion through translation by focusing on the man's grati-tude. Yet the passage begs the question: What messages were actually passed among those five different interpreters who speak "among them-selves" to catechize and baptize the dying man?

Sandoval's belief in transparent linguistic translation across such mul-tiple orally rendered translations depends on his confidence in the exist-ence of a universal signified, a stable common meaningful reference point between languages. According to Sandoval's system, an interpreter (or a chain of interpreters in sequence) can replace a term in one language with an equivalent in another without altering the meaning of the original message. The stability of this universal referent is so firm for Sandoval that he even suggests that the Christian concepts communicated through

---

[52] Sandoval, *Naturaleza, policia sagrada*, book 3, chap. 2, 236v.
[53] Ibid., book 3, chap. 3, 239r.

translation can be simplified and broken apart into smaller pieces without damaging the integrity of the concepts themselves:

Y en este caso de poca comprehension del interprete, el remedio es a mas no poder, hacer de una pregunta, que se diria a un interprete inteligente entera, tres o cuatro, para que assi como el enfermo que và poco a poco comiendo lo que el sano comeria de una vez, assi estos vayan poco a poco entendiendo para si y repitiendo a los demas.

[In the case of little comprehension of the message by the interpreter, the remedy is, if nothing else, to take apart a question that you would say whole to an intelligent interpreter into three or four questions. Thus, like a sick man eats little by little what a healthy man can eat all at once, these interpreters learn little by little themselves and then repeat it to the rest.][54]

Sandoval's simile thus endorses accommodating the doctrine to the capacities of the interpreter and the catechumens, suggesting that a priest can still spoon-feed a catechism to new arrivals through an untrained or "unintelligent" interpreter. For Sandoval, the Christian message, like a metonym, can be simplified and translated and still arrive intact.

Sandoval's position has precedent in Augustine of Hippo's *De catechizandis rudibus*, which provides guidelines for how to Christianize the uneducated or barely educated. Augustine's text, addressed to the deacon of Carthage, explains that the narration of the catechism may vary in length: "ut alinquando brevior, alinquando longior, sempre tamen plena atque sit" [shorter at one time, longer at another, and yet at all times absolutely complete].[55] Augustine explains that brief accounts are appropriate for the least educated and longer accounts appropriate for those with more education. Such a hierarchy with regard to the length and complexity of catechetical content also underlies the Third Lima Council's official *Doctrina christiana y catecismo para instruccion de los indios* from 1584, which offers a separate, shorter catechism for the "rudos y ocupados" [unlearned and busy], a simplified version of the catechism than the longer one for indigenous catechumens considered to be "mas capaces" [more capable].[56] As prescribed in Augustine's *De catechezandis rudibus*, the Third Lima Council's "Catecismo breve para los rudos y ocupados" [Brief catechism for the unlearned and busy] is an abbreviated version of

---

[54] Ibid., book 3, chap. 2, 236v–237r.
[55] Augustine, *De catechizandis rudibus* (London: Methuen, 1912), 1.4, 20. Translation from Augustine, *First Catechetical Instruction (De catechizandis rudibus)*, trans. Joseph P. Christopher (Westminster, MD: Newman Bookshop, 1946), 1.4, 17.
[56] *Doctrina Christiana y catecismo*, 13r–18r.

catechetical material to meet the assumed inferior capacities and time restraints of the audience. This version is not considered incorrect or incomplete in its brevity. Yet Sandoval stretches the Augustinian logic underwriting the Third Lima Council's distinct catechisms further to argue that not only can the catechism be delivered briefly and still correctly to the black new arrivals in translation; it can be transmitted through multiple intermediaries before reaching catechumens.

It is worth pausing over Sandoval's perception of the benefits and drawbacks of this method of translation. Despite his enthusiastic endorsement of his proposed system for black evangelization in the Americas, Sandoval was not completely ignorant of the possibility of change in the content of the message passed through the multiple interpreters. Regardless of the risks involved in using these chains of translation and the practical challenges they entail, he considers his system a vast improvement over the problematic practice he sought to redress: badly administered translation through a single inappropriately trained black interpreter. The following passage specifies the need for such a remedy. Sandoval documents the answer given to him by a "Visitador de Cacheu" who brought a ship full of slaves to Cartagena claiming they were already baptized. When Sandoval asked him about the way they were baptized, the Visitador purportedly responded:

En entrando en el navio mandè llamar un negro el más ladino, que nunca falta, por lo menos grumete, y díxele que chalonasse a aquella g[en]te, preguntandoles si querian ser como blancos. Habloles y respondió, dizen señor Padre, que si (es aqui de notar si le avrian entendido, pues hablarian en dos, o tres lenguas a lo mas largo a mas de sesenta distintas y diversas). Dixoles mas, que si queriã tomar aquella agua en su cabeça, que serian como blancos; y respondióme el negro que dezian que si, y con esto les baptizé.

[On boarding the ship, I ordered a black man to be called, the most *ladino* possible, which is never hard to find, at least in the form of a deck hand. I told him to speak in translation to those people, asking them if they wanted to be like whites. The interpreter spoke to them and responded: "They say yes, Father" (and here it is important to ask if they had even understood him as they would have spoken two or three languages at least and more than sixty diverse and distinct languages at most). The interpreter spoke to them more and asked them if they wanted to receive that water on their heads and be like whites; the black [interpreter] responded to me that they said yes. And with this, I baptized them.][57]

Using only one interpreter, according to Sandoval's parenthetical critique of the Visitador's reported account, is insufficient for such a group

---

[57] Sandoval, *Naturaleza, policia sagrada*, book 3, chap. 4, 246r–v.

because the formality of the act of translation does not prioritize the catechumens' understanding of the message related in it. To avoid such ineffective evangelical translation in Cartagena, Sandoval argues for using chains of interpreters to ensure each individual knowingly agrees to become Christian in a language he or she can understand.

In doing so, Sandoval's systematization provides only one strategy to control the translated message for the potential converts on the other side of the linguistic chain: asking the interpreters to repeat back to the priest the original message communicated by the priest: "hacer que el interprete repita el misterio preguntandoselo, v.g.: Dime, hijo, ay Dios? Responde que si. Quantos Dioses ay? Responde que uno solo. Dezirle entõces, pues esso mesmo dicelo en tu lengua a este boçal. Dime, quien es Dios?" [make the interpreter repeat the mystery to you, asking him, for example: "Tell me, son, Is there God? He says yes. How many gods are there? He says only one. Tell him then, say the same thing in your language to this *bozal*. Tell me, who is God?]"[58] If one imagines how this dynamic would work in a game of telephone, the interpreter in the chain who speaks directly to the priest could easily relay the same message back to the priest to give the impression of the orthodoxy of a message even when there in fact was none. Far from using a translation based on a written text vetted by language specialists and theologians, as was the case with indigenous evangelical language policy, for black evangelization the messages passing between the individuals or groups in the chains employed by Sandoval appear to have been constantly improvised in oral delivery, multiply transposed, and completely incomprehensible to the priest.

Another aspect of the implicit logic that justifies such a distinct approach to translation for black evangelization compared with that of indigenous missionary projects in Spanish America resides in Sandoval's presentation of this project as a kind of spiritual triage to help remedy the completely illegitimate or nonexistent baptisms of black men and women occurring before or on arrival in the New World. Sandoval underscores the need for such an immediate remedy by describing the horrid physical and emotional state of the black men and women arriving from Africa in Cartagena, many dying soon after arrival. Sandoval suggests that his systematization provides a method to at least ensure the minimal comprehension necessary to preserve the integrity of the sacred rite of baptism so that the individuals who might die soon after arrival could avoid eternal

---

[58] Ibid., book 3, chap. 1, 237r.

damnation. Sandoval implies that more thorough instruction would necessarily follow when the new arrivals had acquired sufficient Spanish to be catechized using the standard catechetical materials and methods used for Spanish-speaking populations.[59]

BEYOND NEW GRANADA

Despite his variation from the norms established by the Third Lima Council, Sandoval's adaptation of the policy of using black interpreters to catechize black men and women in the New World was endorsed by the Jesuit order and soon reached Paraguay and Tucuman, Lima, Chile, and New Spain with the publication of his treatise.[60] Reviewing documentation regarding the practice of evangelical translation among black men and women in other regions of Spanish America after its publication, we catch glimpses of the spread of the treatise's strategies for evangelical efforts among black men and women.

In Peru, for example, we hear echoes of Sandoval's plan in an anonymous Jesuit letter, titled "En razon si conviene entablar en esta Provincia de la Compañía de Jesús del Pirú que aprendan la lengua Angola de los Negros," written in Lima between 1635 and 1638 (Appendix A).[61]

[59] Ibid., book 3, chap. 11, 281v–282r. Sandoval's early efforts in black evangelization in Cartagena resulted in some controversy. For the dossier of the formal complaints made against the Jesuits in Cartagena and the school's defense of its practices, see "Preguntase si es licito baptizar los morenos de Carthagena como los padres de la Compañía los baptizan," ARSI, Nuevo Reino y Quito 14, Epistolario general, Historia, I, ff. 94r–108r. Sandoval himself briefly mentions this defense in his treatise (Naturaleza, policia sagrada, book 3, chap. 12, 282r). For a summary of the controversy, see Tulio Aristizábal, Los jesuitas en Cartagena de Indias (Cartagena: Espitia, 2009), 78–79. The controversy, it is worth noting, did not relate to the Jesuits' use of interpreters, but rather to two complaints: that the Jesuits were taking the task away from secular priests in the city and that the Jesuits might be incorrectly rebaptizing new arrivals.

[60] Sandoval's treatise includes many references and explicit explanations regarding how his method should be used beyond Cartagena. For example, Natualeza, policia sagrada, book 3, chap. 12, 282r, and chap. 13, 286v–291r. Proof of the treatise's use in Chile appears in Alonso de Ovalle, Historica Relacion del Reyno de Chile (Rome: Francisco Cavallo, 1646), book 8, chap. 8, 368. For reference to Sandoval's treatise in the Colegio de San Pablo in Lima in December 1628, see "Libro de Viáticos y Almacén del Colegio de San Pablo, 1628–1631," Archivo General de la Nación (Lima), Fondo Compañía de Jesús, Serie Colegios-San Pablo, box 119, document 468, 30r.

[61] ARSI, FG, Titulus XVIII, Colegia, no. 1488, Perú II, doc. II, ff. 2r–5v. See Appendix A for a full transcription and translation of the letter. According to Tardieu, this undated letter is a response to another by the Father General Vitelleschi, dated November 30, 1634 ("Los Jesuitas y la 'lengua de Angola en Perú [Siglo XVII]," Revista de Indias 53, no. 198 [1993], 634). There is a brief description of Sandoval's efforts to examine the validity of

Composed more than a decade after Sandoval finished the first edition of his treatise, the letter affirms that it would make little sense to adopt a linguistic policy comparable to that of indigenous languages to evangelize black populations of the Peruvian viceroyalty. More specifically, it enumerates nine reasons why Jesuits in Peru *should not* invest time learning the languages of the province's black populations. One of the greatest problems the letter identifies is the displacement of black men and women from their communities of origin and their dispersal among those from different language groups in Spanish America. The following passage (extracted from point number six) discourages learning "black languages" because the priests would never be able to immerse themselves fully in an environment where those languages were spoken:

Pongo caso que un Padre a comenzado a aprender la lengua, y quiera perfecionarse en ella no le sera posible, porque la experiencia nos enseña en la lengua quichua, y en la Aymara de los Indios, que si no las aprenden en los pueblos de las dichas lenguas nunca las podemos aprender.

[Let us assume that a father has begun to learn the language and wants to perfect his use of it, it would be impossible. For experience has taught us in learning Quechua and Aymara of the Indians that if we do not learn them in the towns where those languages are spoken, we can never learn them.][62]

Here the author uses the lessons the Jesuits learned from their language policies for indigenous evangelization to justify a different method for black evangelization. Following this logic, the letter explains that only in locations with a high concentration of people from a single African language group would it make sense for priests to learn the language. Indeed, point number seven explains that:

Sera provechoso aprender esta lengua en la Provincia de Tucuman, y Paraguay donde todos los negros que vienen por el puerto de buenos ayres son Angolas, y por esso el P[adr]e Diego de Torres Bollo desde aquella Provincia a instado tanto que los Padres aprendan la lengua, porq[ue] tienen muy grande empleo en la gobernacion de Tucuman y en ella el de los Indios es muy corto, porque se van

---

black baptisms in Lima during his stay there while writing the first edition of his treatise in Jacinto Barraza's unpublished Jesuit history from later in the century, titled "Historia eclesiástica de la Compañía de Jesús del Perú." For a transcription that includes the section on Sandoval in Lima, see Jimmy Martínez Céspedes, "Los jesuitas y la extirpación de las idolatrías: La historia oficial contada desde la Crónica del Padre Jacinto Barrasa, 1674–1680," *Revista Yuyarccuni* 2, no. 2 (2018): 49–103, 100–101.

[62] "En razon," f. 3r–3v.

acabando a priesa, y en la ciudad donde avia diez mill Indios no ay ya docientos; pero los negros como se van multiplicando por venir cada año de Angola muchos navios de cargazon de ellos son muchos, y cada dia seran mas, conq[ue] es muy acertado que los Padres de aquella Provincia la aprendan como que [*sic*] an començado a aprenderla con mucha gloria de N[uestr]o S[eño]r.

[It will be beneficial to learn this language in the Province of Tucuman and Paraguay where all of the blacks that come through the port of Buenos Aires are Angolas. And because of this, Father Diego de Torres Bollo from that province has vehemently urged that the fathers learn the language because the blacks are of great use for governing Tucuman, whereas the Indians are not because they are disappearing quickly, and in the city that previously had ten thousand Indians there are now no more than two hundred. But blacks are multiplying because every year from Angola many ships come with many of them, and every day there will be more. With this it is very appropriate that the fathers of that province learn the language as they have begun to learn it with much glory to Our Lord.][63]

As suggested here, the high concentration of Kimbundu speakers in Tucuman (today's northern Argentina and Paraguay) during this period resulted from the fact that by the third decade of the seventeenth century slave ships from central Africa were arriving directly in the port of La Plata instead of passing through Cartagena.[64] Indeed, Jesuit correspondence from Buenos Aires and Tucuman during this period confirms that in these areas some Jesuits learned African languages. For example, in 1625 Father General Mutio Vitelleschi in Rome authorized the Visitor of the Peruvian Province to allow Martín de Veras to swear the order's fourth vow because of his ability to speak Kimbundu, "la lengua de Angola" [the language of Angola].[65] As Jean-Pierre Tardieu has surmised, this approval granted by Jesuit Father General Mutio Vitelleschi shows a rare instance in which an African language in Spanish America was

---

[63] Ibid., ff. 3v–4r. See Sue Peabody, "'A Nation Born to Slavery': Missionaries and Racial Discourse in Seventeenth-Century French Antilles," *Journal of Social History* 38, no. 1 (2004): 113–26, on Jesuit reactions to the decrease in the native population in the French Caribbean and the increase of enslaved black men and women in the second half of the seventeenth century.

[64] Even a decade earlier, the Jesuit *carta annua* from 1627–1628 regarding the activities of the Jesuit school in La Plata had called attention to the homogenous "Angolan" origins of the black men and women in the area and the religious instruction being given every Sunday in the "language of Angola" as a result ("Carta annua de 1627–1628," ARSI, Peru 14, f. 104r). For a study of Jesuits' evangelization of Angolans in Paraguay and Tucuman using the *cartas annuas*, see Tardieu, "Los inicios del 'ministerio de negros' en la provincia jesuitica de Paraguay," *Anuario de estudios americanos* 6, no. 2 (2005): 141–60.

[65] Tardieu, "Los Jesuitas y la 'lengua de Angola," 629.

considered *as* valuable to the Jesuit order as an indigenous language, as criteria for promotion within the order.[66]

But according to the anonymous Jesuit author of "En razon," in Peru there were many more indigenous peoples to evangelize and insufficient speakers of the "language of Angola" to justify a similar effort:

> Añado q[ue] los Padres que aprendiessen esta lengua en Lima solam[en]te avian de executarla alli, porq[ue] fuera de Lima como todas las ciudades del Peru estan llenas de Indios ay en ellas poquisimos negros, y essos pocos de diversas lenguas como se a dicho, y un Padre solo bastarà para Lima, porque los demas con mas provecho aprenderan las demas lenguas de los Indios de quienes esta lleno todo el reyno.

> [I add that the fathers who learn this language in Lima will only be able to use it there because outside of Lima and in all of the cities of Peru there are many Indians and so there are very few blacks, and those few speak different languages, as has been said. One father would suffice for Lima because all the other fathers will benefit more from learning the other languages of the Indians with whom this kingdom is full.][67]

The anonymous Jesuit's argument references the fact that the black population of Peru was in fact mostly limited to the capital and its surrounding areas. The letter's opinion that "one priest would be sufficient" to catechize all blacks in Lima also reveals the different value the Jesuits assigned to evangelization among black populations and indigenous populations of the New World. When this letter was written, after all, more than 50 percent of the population of Lima was black or *mulato*,[68] which suggests that the Jesuit author believed a distinct priest for black evangelization would be necessary only as long as the black populations did not speak Spanish. Whereas the indigenous population was to be

---

[66] Ibid., 630. A few other secular and Jesuit priests in Spanish America learned Kimbundu during this period, too. A *carta annua* from the School in La Plata in 1632–34 states that "un hermano portugués" [a Portuguese brother] teaches black men and women the doctrine in Kimbundu (Peru 15, f. 279v; qtd. in Tardieu, "Los jesuitas y la 'lengua de angola,'" 630). Furthermore, Diego de Torres Bollo composed a manual for black evangelization in the region after arriving in Chuquisaca (La Plata) in 1630 (Tardieu, *Los negros y la Iglesia en el Perú*, 490). On November 30, 1634, Vitelleschi ordered the Provincial to print the Kimbundu vocabulary written by López de Castilla, *Scripsit: Grammaticam et Vocabularium lingua Angolanae pro faciliori instuctione Aethiopum, qui ex Africa illuctamquam mancipia deducuntur, ut in fide Christi erudiantur.* This work appears in a catalogue of Jesuit works (Anathanaele Sotuellus, Bibliotheca Scriptorum Societatis Jesu, Roma, 1676), but Tardieu believes it was never published (*Los negros y la Iglesia*, 490). It is likely that this vocabulary is the one referenced in the second half of "En razon" (Appendix A).

[67] "En razon," f. 4v.   [68] Bowser, *African Slave*, 337–41.

cared for separately from the Spanish even after they learned Spanish, the black population, once assimilated linguistically, was to be included as part of the Spanish flock.

In the face of the dismal prospects for learning African languages in Peru described by the Jesuit author of "En razon," the letter proposes a familiar solution. It explains in point eight that finding black interpreters for the languages spoken by newly arrived black men and women is the principal "remedio" [remedy] for catechizing unbaptized *bozales* and confessing Christianized *bozales* who are on the brink of death:

El remedio pues de todas las naciones de negros en las dos necesidades sobredichas no es que sepan una sola lengua, porque esse es un remedio de pocos, el remedio pues General de todos es buscar un negro ladino de cada lengua quan ladino fuere possible por medio del qual se haran las preguntas necessarias para que sepa cada negro lo que es el sacram[en]to del baptismo.

[The remedy then for all of the black nations in these two states of necessity is not that priests learn only one language, because that is a remedy for few. The general remedy for all then is to find an acculturated black of each language, as acculturated as possible, through whom the necessary questions will be asked so that each black person may learn the meaning of the sacrament of the baptism.][69]

Like Sandoval, and the *Instruccion* before him, this letter from Lima presents the black interpreter as the solution for the language challenges of black evangelization in Spanish America. By indicating that the interpreter should be employed to prepare and administer the baptism specifically, the author implies as Sandoval did the decade before that all future interactions with religious ministry could be conducted in Spanish once the black men and women had learned it. The letter does not, however, mention Sandoval's strategy of combining interpreters to form a chain of communication when one *ladino* interpreter could not be found.

Thus, we see that black interpreters occupied a central role in the policies developed for evangelizing black populations in Peru and New Granada during the seventeenth century, a role that was not so explicitly afforded to native language assistants in the same period. The language policy for black evangelization, created first in Seville and then expanded in Cartagena and Lima, demonstrates the vast difference between the attention and methods developed for indigenous evangelization in the New World. Unlike indigenous languages, African languages were not standardized for Christian doctrine in Spanish America; they were not

[69] "En razon," 4r.

used to compose orthodox religious translations; and few priests learned them. As a result, Jesuit priests who employed black interpreters in their missions bestowed on them more authority over the messages translated and much less supervision in moments of evangelical exchange than was the case with indigenous interpreters. Furthermore, the messages communicated as part of black interpreters' labor went unchecked by priests who could understand them. These circumstances granted the Jesuits' black interpreters unique control over the messages they transmitted and a means to negotiate some of their conditions of enslavement, as I will demonstrate in the following two chapters.

ORACIONES TRADUCIDAS EN LA LENGUA DEL REYNO DE ANGOLA

There is an exception to the general absence of printed or written translated texts in African languages regarding the evangelization of black populations in Peru and New Granada that can provide a window through which to speculate about the content of the multiply translated messages relayed by the interpreters mentioned in Sandoval's treatise. The Jesuit order funded the printing of a bilingual prayer book in Spanish and Kimbundu in Lima in 1629 titled *Oraciones traducidas en la lengua del reyno de Angola* (Figure 2.2). A copy of this text survives in the rare book collection of the University of Pennsylvania, though some scholars have considered it lost.[70] According to Jesuit records, the printer sent 1,440 copies of the text to the Jesuit College of San Pablo in Lima in early 1630.[71] The postscript to the sixteen-page pamphlet provides a brief history of its production. It also justifies its importance by echoing reasons established by the Council of Trent and reiterated by the Third Lima Council: people only truly learn the precepts of the Christian faith if they are taught "en su propia lengua" [in their own language]:

Por experiencia, y razon clara se sabe, que ninguna nacion puede hazer concepto puntual de las cosas de nuestra Fé, sino es enseñada en su propia lengua. Lo qual

---

[70] The studies that declare it to be lost are Tardieu, *Los negros y la Iglesia*, 502, and Carlos A. Page, "Iglesias para negros en las estancias jesuitas del Paraguay," in *Fronteiras e Identidades: Encontros e Desencontros entre Povos indígenas e Missões Religiosas*, ed. Graciela Chamorro, Thiago Leandro Vieira Cavalcante, and Carlos Barros Gonçalves (São Paolo: Nhanduti Editora, 2011), 205–22.

[71] "Libro de Viáticos y Almacén del Colegio de San Pablo, 1628–1631," Archivo General de la Nación (Lima), Fondo Compañía de Jesús, Serie Colegios-San Pablo, box 119, document 468, 24r.

ORACIONES

TRADVCIDAS

EN LA LENGVA

DEL REYNO DE

ANGOLA.

POR ORDEN DEL P. MA-
teo Cardoſo Teologo de la Compañia de IESVS,
natural de Lisboa. Impreſſas primero para el Reyno
de Portugal: y aora de nueuo con la declara-
cion en lengua Caſtellana.

Con licencia; En lima, Por Geronymo de Con
treras : junto al Conuento de ſanto Domingo; Año de 1629.

FIGURE 2.2 Frontispiece to *Oraciones traducidas en la lengua del reyno de Angola* (Lima, 1629).
Courtesy of the University of Pennsylvania Library

es mas cierto en Indios, y Negros; porque por su corta capacidad nunca aprendan la Española, quanto es necessario para entender en ella las cosas de la Fè, que de suyo son altas, espirituales, y fuera del comun trato. Por esto se à procurado para el bien de los Negros, que tan distituydos estan de socorros en esta parte, salga a luz este resumen de la dotrina Christiana.

[Through experience, and exercising clear reason, it is well known that no nation can adequately understand the matters of our faith, unless taught in their own language. This is even truer with Indians and blacks because due to their limited intelligence they will never learn enough Spanish to understand in this language matters of the faith, which are high, spiritual, and specialized concepts. So, for the benefit of blacks, who are so poorly endowed with assistance in this respect, we bring to light this summary of Christian doctrine.][72]

Here, contrary to all other Jesuit documents from Peru and New Granada from this period (except for Pallas's description from 1619 cited above), the anonymous Jesuit editor considers linguistic strategies for indigenous and black evangelization as equivalent by providing a *written* text to catechize men and women from Angola in their own language. This unique comparison results from the text's provenance in the Jesuit missions in central Africa and correspondence between Jesuits in La Plata and Brazil. According to the postscript, the text is a compilation of translations taken from a Kikongo–Portuguese Christian doctrine published in Lisbon only five years before.

The Jesuits' evangelical work in central Africa in the sixteenth and seventeenth centuries differed significantly in development, policy, and practice from Jesuit missions in the Americas. The order's first presence in the Kongo lasted from 1548 to 1555, where they arrived almost fifty years after the first Kongolese king had chosen to convert to Catholicism.[73] As

---

[72] *Oraciones traducidas en lengua del reyno de Angola. Por orden del P. Mateo Cardoso Teólogo de la Compañía de IESUS natural de Lisboa. Impressos primero para el reyno de Portugal, y aora de nuevo con la declaración en lengua castellana* (Lima: Geronymo de Contreras, 1629), 15.

[73] For works on Christianity in central Africa in the late fifteenth, sixteenth, and seventeenth centuries, see Georges Balandier, *La vie quotidienne au royaume de Kongo du XVIe au XVIIIe siècle* (Paris, 1965); W. G. L. Randles, *L'ancien royaume du Congo des origines à la fin du XIXe siècle* (Paris, 1968); Richard Gray, "'Come un vero Prencipe Catolico': The Capuchins and the Rulers of Soyo in the Late Seventeenth-Century," *Africa: Journal of the International African Institute* 53, no. 3 (1983): 39–54; Anne Hilton, *Kingdom of Kongo* (Oxford: Oxford University Press, 1985); Wyatt MacGaffey, *Religion and Society in Central Africa: The BaKongo of Lower Zaire* (Chicago: University of Chicago Press, 1986); John Thornton, "Perspectives on African Christianity," in *Race, Discourse, and the Origin of the Americas: A New World View*, ed. Vera Lawrence Hyatt and Rex Nettleford (Washington, DC: Smithsonian, 1995); Thornton, *Africa and Africans in the Making of the Atlantic World*, especially 254–62; Thornton, *The Kongolese Saint*

scholars of early Christian central Africa have explained, during the first period of contact between the Jesuits and the Kingdom of Kongo, Portuguese Jesuits taught some members of the Kongolese nobility to read Portuguese and requested their assistance in catechizing other Kongolese.[74] Jesuit missionary efforts in the region were then paused when the order was forced to abandon the Kongo in 1555. When the Jesuits returned in 1619, Father Mateo Cardoso asked a group of native catechists from the Kongolese court to compose a bilingual catechism in Kikongo and Portuguese titled *Doutrina christãa ... De novo traduzida na lingoa do Reyno de Congo*.[75]

Significantly, in Cardoso's preface to the *Doutrina christãa*, the Jesuit admits that he is not the text's real author: "Et parce que je ne me sentais pas assez compétent pour cette entreprise, j'eus recours aux maîtres les plus insignes qu'il y avait à la Cour, afin que l'oeuvre sorte telle que je la désirais" [Because I did not feel sufficiently competent for this enterprise, I made use of the most noble *mestres* available in court, to make the work turn out as I desired].[76] Although he declares himself inadequate to take

---

Anthony: *Dona Beatriz Kimpa Vita and the Antonian Movement, 1684–1706* (New York: Cambridge University Press, 1998); Sweet, *Recreating Africa*; Heywood and Thornton, *Central Africans, Atlantic Creoles, and the Foundation of the Americas*, esp. 60–67; Fromont, *Art of Conversion*; Linda Heywood, *Njinga of Angola: Africa's Warrior Queen* (Cambridge, MA: Harvard University Press, 2017).

[74] Thornton, "Perspectives on African Christianity," 174–75. On the existence of an earlier catechism by Franciscan Gaspar da Conceição printed in Évora in 1555 that has been lost, see François Bontinck and D. Ndembe Nsasi, *Le catechism kikongo de 1624, Réédition critique* (Brussels: Académie Royale des Sciences d'Outre-Mer, 1978), 17–23. The title to the oldest surviving Kikongo catechism from 1624, referenced in the note below, acknowledges the existence of a previous version: "De novo traduzida na lingoa do Reyno de Congo" [again translated into the language of the Kingdom of Kongo].

[75] I originally consulted this printed catechism in François Bontinck and D. Ndembe Nsasi's edition, *Le catéchisme kikongo de 1624*, but then found a version of the original in the British Library as *Doutrina christãa. Composta pelo P. Marcos Jorge da Companhia de IESU Doutor em Theologia. ... De novo traduzida na lingoa do Reyno de Congo, por ordem do P. Mattheus Cardoso Theologo, da Companhia de IESU* (Lisbon: Geraldo da Vinha, 1624). Strangely, Cardoso's dedication to the King of Kongo, Dom Pedro II, included in translation to French in Bontink and Nsasi's edition, is missing from the copy in the British Library. For a study that mentions this text and the evangelical efforts of Jesuits in central Africa in conversation with those of Jesuits in Cartagena, see Andrea Guerrero Mosquera, "Misiones, misioneros y bautizos a través del Atlántico: Evangelización en Cartagena de Indias y los reinos del Kongo y Ngola, siglo XVII," *Memoria y sociedad* 18, no. 37 (2014): 14–32.

[76] Cardoso's dedication to King of Kongo, Dom Pedro II. See note 75 above. This sentence is absent from the scanned image of the printed book at British Library, but included in the French translation in Bontinck and Nsasi, *Le catéchisme kikongo de 1624*, 12. Bontinck and Nsasi's linguistic analysis in the introduction to their modern edition of the *Doutrina*

on the project by himself, Cardoso describes his editorial power over the Kongolese authors in the prologue to the reader by specifying that he restricted some of their translations for Christian concepts, such as those for the Holy Spirit and the Cross, because they were not sufficiently orthodox:

Chamào os naturais de Cõgo, ao Spirito Sãto Monho Auquissi, & a Cruz, Iqueteqêlo; das quais não quis usar, como nem tambê de outras palavras, porque não explicaõ bem a natureza, & propriedade das cousas, porque Monho Auquissi, quer dizer alma santa, & alma santa, se pode chamar qualquer da dos bemaventurados, & assi não he palavra propia que signifique aterceira pessoa da Sãtissima Trinidade, Iquetequêlo, quer dizer forca. E bem se vè que não significa a Cruz, pelo que me pareceu melhor vsar das propias palavras, Spirito Santo, & Cruz, & de outras que por brevidade deixo de apontar.

[The inhabitants of Congo call the Holy Spirit "Monho Auquissi" and the cross "Iquetequêlo." These terms as well as others cannot be used because they do not explain the nature and essence of things well, for "Monho Auquissi" means "holy soul," but it can also mean a "happy soul" and therefore it is not an appropriate term to refer to the third person of the Holy Trinity. "Iquetelquêlo" means "fork" and it is clear that this term does not mean "cross." Thus, I consider it more appropriate to use the actual words "Spirito Santo" and "Cruz" and others that I omit here for the sake of brevity.[77]

With this comment, Cardoso highlights his presence throughout the text as an editor and censor.[78] But despite this monitoring, unlike works composed in Spanish America by the Jesuits after the Third Lima Council, the Kikongo *Doutrina Cristãa* preserves more Kikongo terms for key Christian ideas. For example, the Kikongo catechism uses the Kikongo term *Zambi* instead of the Portuguese term *Dios* for God. (This continuity stands in contrast to the fact that almost all New World grammars and catechisms import the Spanish word for God into indigenous languages to avoid the potential heresy tied to native terms for divinities.)[79]

---

christãa confirms Cardoso's statement that the Kikongo was written before the Portuguese translation.

[77] Cardoso, *Doutrina christãa*, Prologo ao Leitor, n.p., last paragraph.

[78] The affected humility of the missionary/author/editor of translated missionary documents is a trope that appears in documents from colonial Spanish America as well. I have argued elsewhere that the European missionary/author/editor can disavow his authorship by suggesting his native assistants were the real laborers in the project precisely because the missionary keeps the "real authors" anonymous and still explicitly demonstrates that he exercised editorial control over the terms chosen by his assistants. See Brewer-García, "Bodies, Texts, and Translators," 380.

[79] Cardoso's choice could be related to the fact that he completed a study on Kongolese beliefs in the same year as the Kikongo *Doutrina christãa* that proclaimed that the

Furthermore, Cardoso admits that the native catechists first composed the catechism in Kikongo and then used it as the basis for the interlineal Portuguese translation, as shown in Figure 2.3.[80] The larger font for the Kikongo terms indexes the priority given to the content and delivery of the material in Kikongo, rather than Portuguese. Therefore, even though the title of the *Doutrina christãa* suggests that Father Jorge Marcos was the author of the catechism because his brief catechism served as a template for the Kikongo catechists to adapt, the prefatory materials to the *Doutrina christãa* clarify that the Kikongo catechists were in fact the *Doutrina christãa*'s authors in Kikongo first and translators into Portuguese second.

Some of the differences between the Kikongo–Portuguese *Doutrina christãa* and the majority of the multilingual catechisms composed in South America after the Third Lima Council can be explained by the drastically different conditions for evangelization in central Africa than those in Spanish America. As noted by John Thornton, the Jesuit missionaries in Kongo and Angola were guests in lands still governed by native rulers who had willingly converted to Christianity.[81] Furthermore, the Jesuit presence in central Africa during the sixteenth and seventeenth centuries was relatively sparse. There were never more than seven Jesuit fathers in either of the two kingdoms at one given time during these two centuries,[82] and therefore much of the work of evangelization rested on native catechists.[83] Also, the Jesuits had taught the noble class of the Kongo to read such that the printed text Cardoso published was destined

---

Kongolese believed in the one true God but had not yet learned of Jesus Christ (*História do Reino de Congo* [1624] 1969, 20; cited in Thornton, *Africa and Africans*, 260). Another catechism printed by Capuchins in 1658 for use in Allada (Benin) also used native words for God ("Vodu") and Jesus ("Lisa") (Thornton, *Africa and Africans*, 260).

[80] Cardoso, *Doutrina christãa*, 15.

[81] Thornton, "The Development of an African Catholic Church," 153. Thornton provides further background to understand why such a different approach to religious translation was adopted by the Jesuits in the Kongo than in Spanish America: "the Church tended to be quite exclusive in its attitude toward other religions where it exercised clear political power (such as Mexico) and inclusive where it did not (China). This in turn reflected the degree to which the European priest was secure as opposed to precarious. In Africa, Europeans exercised little power over the local society, and hence, the inclusive approach tended to flourish there" (*Africa and Africans*, 257).

[82] Charles O'Neill, *Diccionario histórico de la Compañía de Jesús: Biográfico-temático I (AA-Costa Rica)* (Rome: Instituto Historicum, S.J., 2001), 172.

[83] Thornton, *Central Africans, Atlantic Creoles*, 246. Jesuit priests were still supposed to perform the sacraments (baptism, marriage, last rites, etc.), but the native catequists (called *mestres*) performed most of the evangelical work.

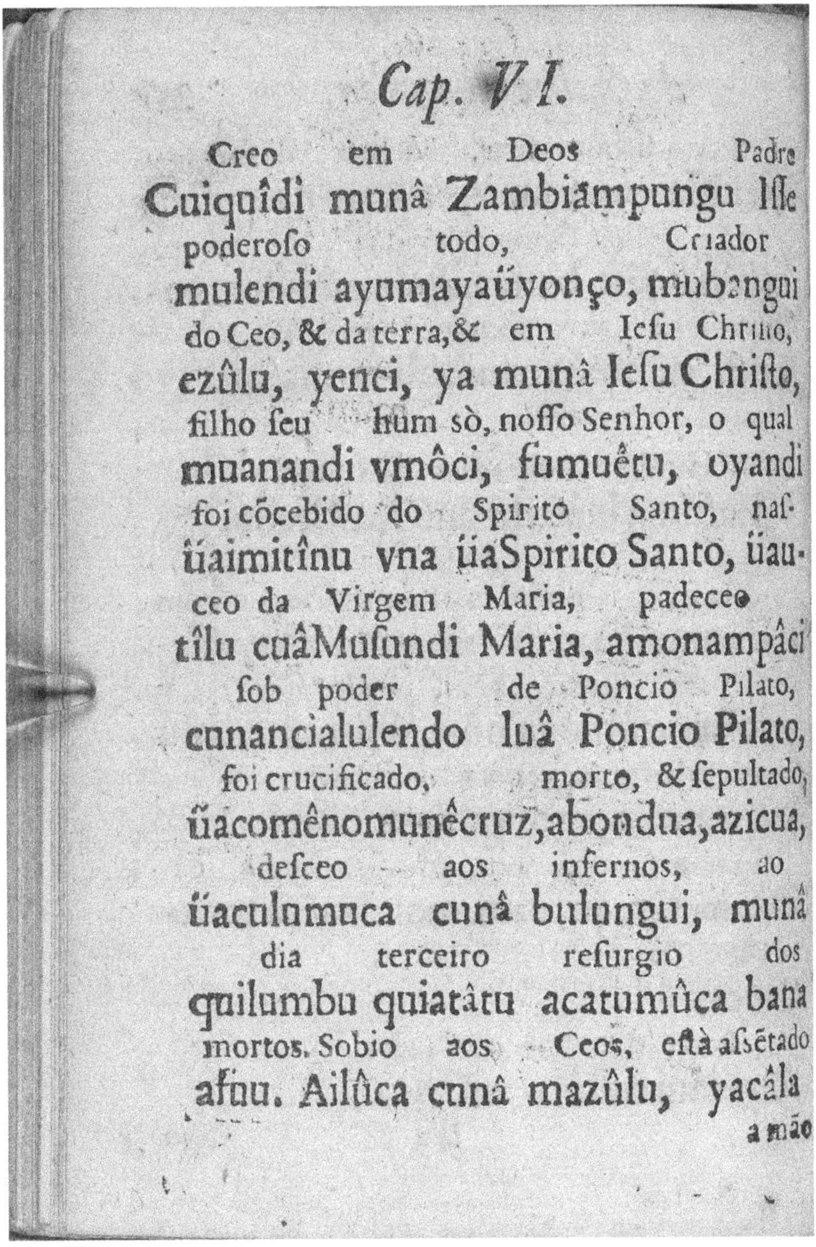

Cap. VI.

Creo   em   Deos   Padre
Cuiquîdi munâ Zambiampungu Iſſe
poderoſo   todo,   Criador
mulendi ayumayaûyonço, mubzngui
do Ceo, & da terra,& em   Ieſu Chriſto,
ezûlu, yenci, ya munâ Ieſu Chriſto,
filho ſeu   hum ſò, noſſo Senhor, o qual
muanandi vmôci, fumuêtu, oyandi
foi côcebido do   Spirito   Santo, naſ-
ûaimitînu vna ûaSpirito Santo, ûau-
ceo da Virgem Maria,   padeceo
tîlu cuâMuſundi Maria, amonampâci
ſob poder   de Poncio Pilato,
cunancialulendo luâ Poncio Pilato,
foi crucificado,   morto, & ſepultado,
ûacomênomunêcruz, abondua, azicua,
deſceo   aos   infernos,   ao
ûaculomuca cunâ bulungui, munâ
dia   terceiro   reſurgio   dos
quilumbu quiatâtu acatumûca bana
mortos. Sobio aos   Ceos, eſtà aſſétado
afuu. Ailûca cunâ mazûlu, yacâla
a mão

FIGURE 2.3 From *Doutrina christãa ... De novo traduzida na lingoa do Reyno de Congo* (Lisbon, 1624).
Courtesy of the British Library

for use not only by Jesuit priests and brothers but also by literate Kongo-lese.[84] These conditions differed from those in Peru where the Jesuit order's presence was much stronger in number and more politically protected by Spanish sovereignty, and where the printed translations of the Christian doctrine in non-European languages were meant for Euro-pean priests to use and deliver orally to native catechumens.

Despite these differences, the Kikongo–Portuguese *Doutrina christãa* made its way to Spanish America for use by Jesuit missionaries evangeliz-ing populations from central Africa. The postscript to the *Oraciones traducidas en la lengua del reyno de Angola* explains the trajectory taken by these translated prayers: "Ellos [los jesuitas] imprimieron estas ora-ciones con la declaracion en Portugues, que embiaron a Buenosayres, para la enseñança de los muchos Negros que por aquel puerto solian entrar" [They [the Jesuits] printed prayers with their explanation in Portuguese that they sent to Buenos Aires to teach the many blacks there that used to enter through that port].[85] Jesuits in Buenos Aires then translated the prayers from Kikongo and Portuguese into Kimbundu and Spanish and sent these translations to Lima to print in 1629. The postscript to the *Oraciones traducidas en la lengua del reyno de Angola* thus describes the text as the product of two coinciding translations: Kikongo into Kimbundu and Portuguese into Spanish. It can be assumed that a Jesuit priest translated the Portuguese prayers into Spanish, but it is possible that a native speaker of either Kikongo or Kimbundu in Buenos Aires rendered the Kikongo into Kimbundu.[86] No record remains of the names of the original Kongolese authors of the Kikongo *Doutrina christãa* or the Kimbundu translator of the *Oraciones traducidas en la lengua del reyno de Angola*, but the latter text's existence itself is a testament to a particular kind of authorship (in translation) that has long been overlooked in the study of African presence in the colonial Americas.

---

[84] This second point is made evident in Cardoso's opening notes that boast that his native language specialists created a work that was "so perfect that its reputation spread, reaching the ears of King Dom Alvaro III, who was in power at that moment, and whom God held in his glory. He asked to see it and after reading it, he lent it out continuously" (Cardoso, *Doutrina christãa*, 14).

[85] *Oraciones traducidas*, 15.

[86] Francesco Pacconio, an Italian Jesuit, composed the first full catechism in Kimbundu in Angola in the mid-seventeenth century (*Gentio de Angola suficientemente instruido no mysterios da nossa sancta Fé* [Lisbon: Domingos Lopes Reza, 1642]). I have found no mention of this text in Spanish American writings from the seventeenth century.

Of particular interest is that the Kimbundu translation for God in the *Oraciones traducidas en la lengua del reyno de Angola* is *Zambi*, as shown in Figure 2.4.[87] The postscript to the text recognizes the contentious nature of preserving the Kimbundu term for such an important concept and merely suggests that the user of the text employ this term at his own discretion:

Quanto al nombre Zambi, Dios, se à dudado, si significa propiamente al verdadero Dios, o algun idolo de esta gente. No sera difilcultoso, si pareciere la duda de consideracion, poner en lugar de Zambi nuestra palabra Dios. Nosotros no quisimos alterar lo que vino impresso de Portugal.

[As far as the name Zambi, God, is concerned, it has been doubted whether it really means the true God, or some other idol of that people. If one's doubt regarding this matter is significant, it will not be difficult to replace our word "God" for "Zambi." We did not want to alter what came in the printed text from Portugal.][88]

The statement would have been a problematic proposition at the time it was printed in Lima because using native words for divinities in religious texts had been outlawed by the Third Lima Council in 1583. Perhaps this discrepancy has something to do with why the text does not appear to have circulated widely. Regardless, the Jesuit editor leaves the Kimbundu term for God as is. By preserving the term *Zambi* in the Kimbundu prayers, the bilingual manual provides a window onto how the use of translation in the evangelization among black men and women in Peru and New Granada functioned very differently than it did among indigenous populations in the Americas and how it resulted in the explanation of Christianity in terms chosen by the black translators, interpreters, and the catechumens themselves with little supervision by priests.

Indeed, this singular example of the use of a printed text in an African language does not diminish the importance of black interpreters in the Jesuit evangelical project. Although the postscript to the *Oraciones traducidas en la lengua del reyno de Angola* suggests that the Jesuits printed it for use among *bozales* from Angola in the Peruvian viceroyalty, there is

---

[87] Kimbundu and Kikongo are distinct Bantu languages that share linguistic structures and many terms. For comparative analyses of the two, see William E. Welmers, *African Language Structures* (Berkeley: University of California Press, 1973); Malcolm Guthrie, *Comparative Bantu*, 4 vols. (Farnborough: Gregg International Publishers, 1967–71), and "Western Bantu Languages," in *Current Trends in Linguistics, vol. 7: Linguistics in Sub-Saharan Africa*, ed. Thomas A. Sebeok (The Hague: Mouton, 1971), 357–66.

[88] *Oraciones traducidas*, 16.

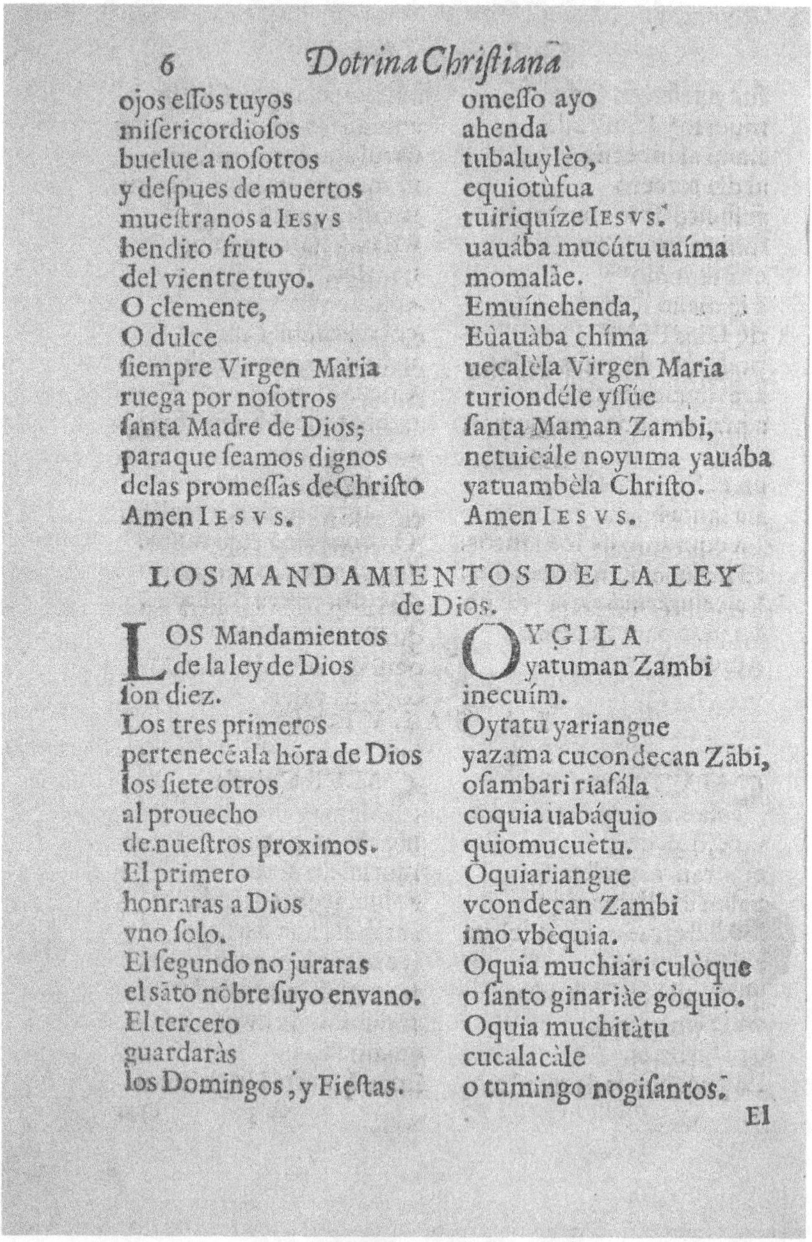

6   *Dotrina Chriſtiana*

ojos eſſos tuyos	omeſſo ayo
miſericordioſos	ahenda
buelue a noſotros	tubaluylèo,
y deſpues de muertos	equiotùfua
mueſtranos a Iesvs	tuiriquíze Iesvs.
bendito fruto	uauába mucútu uaíma
del vientre tuyo.	momalàe.
O clemente,	Emuínehenda,
O dulce	Eùauàba chíma
ſiempre Virgen Maria	uecalèla Virgen Maria
ruega por noſotros	turiondéle yſſùe
ſanta Madre de Dios;	ſanta Maman Zambi,
paraque ſeamos dignos	netuicále noyuma yauába
delas promeſſas de Chriſto	yatuambèla Chriſto.
Amen Iesvs.	Amen Iesvs.

LOS MANDAMIENTOS DE LA LEY
de Dios.

LOS Mandamientos de la ley de Dios ſon diez.	OYGILA yatuman Zambi inecuím.
Los tres primeros pertenecé ala hóra de Dios	Oytatu yariangue yazama cucondecan Zābi,
los ſiete otros	oſambari riaſála
al prouecho	coquia uabáquio
de nueſtros proximos.	quiomucuètu.
El primero	Oquiariangue
honraras a Dios	vcondecan Zambi
vno ſolo.	imo vbèquia.
El ſegundo no juraras	Oquia muchiári culòque
el sãto nôbre ſuyo envano.	o ſanto ginariàe gòquio.
El tercero guardaràs	Oquia muchitàtu cucalacàle
los Domingos, y Fieſtas.	o tumingo nogiſantos.

El

FIGURE 2.4 From *Oraciones traducidas en la lengua del reyno de Angola* (Lima, 1629).
Courtesy of the University of Pennsylvania Library

little evidence that Jesuits employed it to much success.[89] As explained in the second point of "En razon," pronouncing written Kimbundu would have been incredibly difficult for untrained European priests:

aprendiendola pues medianam[en]te como aprendiz no serà de provecho para los negros, porque es gente altiva, colerica, y hablando su lengua con algun yerro se rie luego, y no haze caso de lo que se le dize como tengo experimientado.

[The father having learned the language then half-well as an apprentice will not benefit these blacks because being proud and angry people, if someone speaks their language with some error, they laugh and do not listen to what they are told, as I have experienced.][90]

The statement implies that only with the help of a black interpreter would the priest be able to pronounce the language of the printed text. Preserving the authority of the priest in the eyes of the black catechumens thus required relinquishing linguistic control of the delivery of the message entirely to the black interpreter.

As a whole, the Jesuit policy elaborated in the corpus of texts examined in this chapter envisioned black interpreters as keystones of the Jesuit evangelical project among black men and women; their participation would be necessary as long as linguistically diverse groups of new arrivals continued to reach Spanish American ports. The following two chapters will show that scenes of religious translation mediated by these uniquely authoritative (although mostly enslaved) black interpreters became sites of coexisting cross-purposes through which a new discourse on blackness emerged in the early black Atlantic.

---

[89] An oblique reference to the *Oraciones traducidas* appears in "En razon" (Appendix A), which states that several errors had been found "in the catechism printed in Lima" by those who had tried to use it in Mexico and Lima (4v–5r). Carlos A. Page, "Iglesias para negros," notes that the *Oraciones traducidas* is not listed among the inventory of the Jesuit's school in Córdoba (6).

[90] *Oraciones traducidas*, 2v.

3

The Mediations of Black Interpreters in Colonial Cartagena de Indias

Despite their centrality to the Jesuit missionary project among black men and women in Cartagena, black interpreters are only intermittently visible in Alonso de Sandoval's 1627 treatise. Their presence is implicit whenever Sandoval describes scenes of evangelical communication between the Jesuit priest and newly arrived black men and women, but the interpreters themselves are explicitly mentioned only when Sandoval provides instructions for how missionaries should manage them. One of these key instructions is the reminder that priests need to treat their enslaved black interpreters well to ensure their complicity:

A las mesmas l[en]guas saborearemos con algunas cosas de devocion, teniendolas tambien ganadas por averlas confessado, y buen modo de tratallas, porque se suel [en] cansar con el mucho trabajo y enfado que en este exercicio hallan, para que o el respeto o el premio las detenga o aliente.

[We will sweeten the same interpreters with devotional goods, having also won them over by confessing them and treating them well, because they tend to tire with the hard work and frustration of this ministry. Thus, either respect or reward keeps them with you and encourages them.][1]

By calling them "lenguas" [tongues], Sandoval invokes the interpreters in relation to the organ of speech associated with their labor. Anna Brickhouse has remarked on the use of this term for indigenous interpreters in early Spanish colonial texts, noting that it functions as a synecdoche that disassociates the work of translation from the use of the intellect.[2]

---

[1] Sandoval, *Naturaleza, policia sagrada*, book 3, chap. 2, 237v.
[2] Brickhouse, *The Unsettlement of America*, 18.

Sandoval's use of the term to refer to black interpreters presents them as easily coaxed prosthetic tongues that priests can employ or set aside as needed. Once treated well, Sandoval implies, the black interpreters' complicity in the evangelical project is a given. In making this recommendation, Sandoval indirectly acknowledges that evangelical translation cannot be forced like other forms of enslaved labor.

Despite indirectly raising the question of interpreters' potential noncompliance in the project with this recommendation, Sandoval assures his audience that in practice black interpreters always transparently communicate the priests' messages to new arrivals which in turn always results in legitimate conversions. In fact, Sandoval repeatedly celebrates the conversions achieved through interpreters while portraying the interpreters themselves as exchangeable, replaceable tools. For example, when reflecting on his recommendation for spoon-feeding the catechism piece-by-piece in translation to untrained interpreters (a passage analyzed in Chapter 2), Sandoval describes his method as a foolproof way of making basically *any* interpreter a *good* interpreter: "con lo cual apenas se hallará interprete con quien no se pueda catequizar a necessidad con satisfacion si a la traça dada se junta paciencia y mansedumbre" [with this strategy, one can hardly find an interpreter through whom one cannot catechize as necessary with satisfaction if to the stated strategy one adds patience and humility].[3] If almost *any* interpreter is a good interpreter, Sandoval implies that a particularly ineffective or uncooperative interpreter could easily be exchanged for another.

The broader range of texts describing black interpreters' lives and labor in seventeenth-century Cartagena demonstrates that the men and women employed as interpreters before and after the publication of Sandoval's 1627 treatise were far from the invisible, easily replaceable assistants Sandoval suggests. In fact, the texts analyzed in this chapter and the next provide rich details regarding the biographies and roles assigned to and adapted by the black interpreters in Cartagena. The interpreters' stories, told in part through highly mediated accounts given by some of the black interpreters themselves, present interpreters as linguistic and spiritual intermediaries who are leaders of black communities in the city and influential participants in the Jesuit mission. This chapter argues that the interpreters took advantage of the space of negotiation provided by the mission to acquire privileges unique to enslaved laborers during this period

---

[3] Sandoval, *Naturaleza, policia sagrada*, book 3, chap. 2, 237r.

and became avenues for newly arrived black men and women to make some successful demands through their participation in the Jesuit mission.

THE CORPUS

Extant texts describing the lives and labor of the interpreters can be divided into four sets. The first corresponds to Sandoval's treatise from 1627 and Jesuit correspondence about how to properly administer the missionary project among black men and women in the Americas in the first half of the seventeenth century. These texts make recommendations and are therefore primarily prescriptive. Although they cite practical examples from previous efforts at evangelization to support their arguments and anticipate common problems, their purpose is to propose a model for future evangelical efforts.

The second set of texts is much more descriptive in nature as it consists of Jesuit correspondence and annual reports (*cartas annuas*) from New Granada that describe the evangelical efforts among black men and women recently undergone by Jesuits in Cartagena. These letters offer examples of *how* Sandoval's prescriptions for black evangelization were applied, adapted, or ignored in practice.[4]

The third set of texts focuses on accounts about the life of Jesuit Father Pedro Claver, Sandoval's disciple and contemporary in Cartagena whose dedication to evangelizing black men and women in the city made him a candidate for beatification after his death in 1654.[5] This set comprises works composed from 1657 to 1720. While it is descriptive like the

---

[4] *Cartas annuas* were semi-regularly sent to the Jesuit Father General in Rome and collected in the Archivum Romanum Societatis Iesu. Many of these letters were edited and published in the seventeenth and eighteenth centuries. Three such printed editions of the letters or histories that cite selections from the *cartas annuas* from Cartagena are Sebastián Haza-ñero, *Letras anuas de la Compañía de Iesus de la provincia del nuevo reyno de Granada. Desde el año de mil seiscientos treinta y ocho hasta el año de mil seiscientos cuarenta y tres* [1638–43] (Zaragosa, 1643); Mercado, *Historia de la provincia del Nuevo Reino y Quito de la Compañía de Jesús* [c. 1688]; and José Cassani, *Historia de la provincia de la Compañia de Jesus del Nuevo Reyno de Granada en la America* (Madrid, 1741).

[5] Born in Cataluña, Pedro Claver was educated in Barcelona and the Balearic Islands before setting sail from Seville to New Granada to finish his studies in Bogota and Tunja. He moved to Cartagena in 1614 to work with Sandoval evangelizing black men and women. Claver's beatification inquest began only a few years after his death in 1654. Claver was eventually beatified by Pope Pius IX in 1850 and canonized in 1888 by Pope Leo XIII. Today he is recognized throughout Colombia as the "Slave of the Enslaved." See Tulio Aristizabal's introduction to *Proceso de beatificación y canonización de San Pedro Claver* (Bogota: Javeriana, 2002) for an overview of Claver's canonization process, xiii–xviii.

second set of texts, it is also hagiographic and therefore structured around the demands of documenting the life of an individual celebrated as a potential saint.

Finally, the fourth set of texts is a selection of Inquisition trial summaries and criminal trial transcripts from the 1620s–1640s that demonstrate that some of the Jesuits' black interpreters worked beyond the Jesuit mission as linguistic intermediaries in ecclesiastical and criminal court proceedings in Cartagena.[6]

The network of texts of the third set is particularly complex so I will briefly outline its texts' content, form, and relationship to each other. The items that comprise it are Alonso de Andrade's *Vida del Venerable Padre Pedro Claver* (1657),[7] José Fernández's *Apostolica y penitente vida de V. P. Pedro Claver* (1666),[8] and three surviving versions of a beatification inquest for Claver that was carried out in Cartagena in the second half of the seventeenth century. For the latter, a dossier of testimonies about Claver was gathered by the city's ordinary authorities in collaboration with the city's Jesuit school over two periods, first between 1658 and 1660 and then between 1668 and 1669. The initial inquest produced 154 testimonies given by 152 different witnesses. Once both sets of inquests were completed in 1669, the dossier of testimonies was sent to Jesuits in Aragon, who forwarded it to Papal authorities in Rome.[9]

[6] The Inquisition cases include "Yabel Hernandez [1628]," AHN Inq., book 1020: 293r–295r; "María de Cacheo [1628]," AHN Inq., book 1020: 295r–297r; "Antón Caravali [1628]," AHN Inq., book 1020: 297r–302r; "Phelipa Folupe [1641]," AHN Inq., book 1021: 50r–v. The criminal trial transcripts include "Declaración de Sebastián Anchico," January 23, 1634, and "Declaración de Domingo Anchico," January 23, 1634, Archivo General de Indias, Patronato 234, R. 7, no. 2, 319–329.

[7] Alonso de Andrade, *Vida del Venerable y Apostolico Padre Pedro Claver de la Compañia de Jesus* (Madrid: Maria de Quiñones, 1657). According to the introduction to Andrade's hagiography, the text is based on news of Claver's life in Catalonia before leaving for the Americas and scattered news of Claver that reached Madrid from the Jesuit school in Cartagena. Its stated purpose is to provide a preliminary hagiography until more information about Claver can be gathered to write a longer one (f. 3).

[8] José Fernández, *Apostolica y penitente vida del V.P. Pedro Claver de la Compañia de Jesus. Sacada principalmente de informaciones juridicas hechas ante el Ordinario de Cartagena de Indias* (Zaragoza: Diego Dormer, 1666).

[9] A later phase of the beatification process produced a much shorter collection of testimonies titled "Testimonio de diligencias sobre la causa de beatificación y canonización del venerable padre Pedro Claver de la Compañía de Jesús que floreció" (Cartagena de Indias, 1690), Biblioteca Nacional de Colombia, Bogota, Libros raros y manuscritos, book 401, ff. 1–52. In it twenty witnesses (none of whom is an interpreter) are asked six questions pertaining to the conditions of Claver's death and the existence of a possible unauthorized cult around him in Cartagena.

A translator for the Sacred Congregation of Rites then translated the dossier into Italian in Rome in 1676.[10] A manuscript copy of the Italian translation of the full beatification inquest, now kept in Colombia's National Library in Bogota, is the only extant copy of the full testimonies of the beatification inquest. This manuscript, identified hereafter as *Proceso 1676*, contains the testimonies of almost all of the witnesses who described Pedro Claver after his death for the beatification campaign. In 1696, the Sacred Congregation of Rites printed an edited, abbreviated anthology of these testimonies (hereafter *Proceso 1696*).[11] A second modified version of *Proceso 1696* was published in Rome in 1720 (hereafter *Proceso 1720*).[12]

Of the third set of texts, *Proceso 1676* provides the lengthiest and most substantial accounts of the Jesuits' black interpreters' lives and labor.[13] The other texts of the set are crucial complements to interpreting *Proceso*

---

[10] See *Proceso 1676*, 1r–2v, for an explanation of how the manuscript arrived in Rome via Jesuits in Barcelona. The manuscript names the interpreter who rendered the Spanish manuscript of the dossier into Italian for the Sacred Congregation of Rites as Claudio Francisco Louvet (*Proceso 1676*, 258v).

[11] *Sac. Rituum Congregatione sive Eminentissimo et Reverendissimo Domino Card. De Abdua. Cartagenen. Beatificationis, et Canonizationis Ven Servi Dei Petri Claver Sacerdotis Societ. Iesu* (Rome: Typis Rev. Camerae Apostolicae, 1696). For a contemporary Spanish translation of the Proceso 1696 book, see *Proceso de beatificación y canonización de San Pedro Claver*, trans. Tulio Aristizabal and Ana María Splendiani (Bogota: Javeriana, 2002).

[12] *Sacra Rituum Congregatione Eminentisimo et Reverendissimo D. Card. Zondedario Indiarum seu Carthaginen. Beatificationis et Canonizationis ven servi Dei Petri Claver Sacerdotis Professi Societatis Iesu* (Rome: Typis Rev. Camerae Apostolicae, 1720).

[13] Until now, the little scholarship on the *Proceso* texts that exists has focused on the 1696 version in its 2002 Spanish translation by Aristizábal and Splendiani. There are early twentieth-century currents of hagiography on Claver in English and Spanish that sparingly employ evidence from José Fernández's *Apostolica y penitente vida*, such as Manuel Mejía, *San Pedro Claver de la Compañía de Jesús* (Cartagena, 1918); Arnold Lunn, *A Saint in the Slave Trade: Peter Claver (1581–1654)* (New York: Sheed & Ward, 1935); and Mariano Picón-Salas, *Pedro Claver, el santo de los esclavos* (México: Fondo de Cultura Económica, 1950). Ángel Valtierra's *El santo que libertó una raza: San Pedro Claver* (1954), translated into English in 1960, uses Fernández's hagiography along with a wider selection of printed and archival materials. Juan Manuel Pacheco's sections on Claver in his first volume of *Los jesuitas en Colombia* builds on Valtierra's findings. In more recent scholarship, Aristizábal and Joanne Rappaport and Tom Cummins have worked with Fernández's hagiography. The only published studies on the *Proceso 1676* to date are John K. Thornton, "On the Trail of Voodoo: African Christianity in Africa and the Americas," *The Americas* 44, no. 3 (1988): 261–78; Jaime Humerto Borja Gómez, "Historiografía y hagiografía: Vidas ejemplares y escritura de la historia en el Nuevo Reino de Granada," *Fronteras de la Historia* 12 (2007): 53–78; and Brewer-García, "Imagined Transformations."

1676, however. Andrade's 1657 hagiography, for instance, likely served as a template for many of the questions that witnesses were asked in the inquest in Cartagena because some of the stories told by witnesses in *Proceso 1676* corroborate or elaborate anecdotes in Andrade's brief hagiography. Meanwhile, José Fernández's 1666 hagiography is a narrative synthesis of information from Andrade's hagiography and a now lost preliminary Spanish-language version of the Cartagena beatification testimonies taken between 1658 and 1660. Andrade's and Fernández's hagiographies thus offer clues regarding how distinct Jesuit authors and editors sought to shape the testimonies of the beatification inquest before and after they were compiled in Cartagena.[14] In contrast, the printed books (*Proceso 1696* and *Proceso 1720*) produced from the ordinary inquest in Cartagena demonstrate the editorial labor of the Sacred Congregation of Rites that translated the material extracted from the *Proceso* testimonies into a legally structured brief for Claver's beatification.[15]

The stories about the interpreters related in the four sets of texts demand much more recognition and scholarly inquiry than they have received. Alonso de Sandoval's 1627 *Naturaleza, policia sagrada* is the only one of the corpus that has received extensive scholarly attention. This scholarship can be organized around the two twentieth-century editions of Sandoval's 1627 treatise. The first modern edition was published in Bogota in 1956, under the title *De instauranda Aetihopum salute: El mundo de la esclavitud negra en América*.[16] Scholarship about Sandoval composed in the following fifteen years was mostly authored by Jesuit historians writing from Colombia in both hagiographical and historical modes about Sandoval and Claver until a boom of new studies began to appear in the 1970s and early 1980s by historians and cultural

---

[14] This lost early set of Spanish-language inquest testimonies could be labeled *Proceso 1660* (the date the first round of testimonies was completed). Seeing as we have access to its contents only through Fernández's hagiography from 1666 and the *Proceso 1676* manuscript, I will not be citing it directly.

[15] The *Proceso 1696* is divided into three main parts. The first is the "Informatio," which provides a brief biography of Claver's life and holy works; the second is the "Summario," which anthologizes the testimonies collected from the Cartagena community regarding Claver's holiness, organizing witnesses' anecdotes by theme; the third is an enumeration of possible objections to Claver's beatification, followed by a brief response to each objection. A deliberation of the legitimacy of testimonies given by enslaved witnesses appears in the thirteenth objection in the "Animadversiones" [Objections] section of the *Proceso 1696*. It states that the testimonies of the enslaved are important because they can testify to the many works of faith and charity Claver performed among them (8–9).

[16] Sandoval, *De instauranda Aetihopum salute: El mundo de la esclavitud negra en América* (Bogota: Empresa Nacional de Publicaciones, 1956).

critics in Colombia, Spain, the United States, and France.[17] Then, after Spanish historian Enriqueta Vila Vilar published a new transcription of Sandoval's 1627 treatise in 1987, an even greater number of studies on Sandoval began to emerge.[18] Of all of the aforementioned studies, few

[17] The Colombian Jesuit studies on the treatise include Juan Manuel Pacheco, *Los jesuitas en Colombia*; Ángel Valtierra's three books about Pedro Claver (see the Bibliography); and Jorge Eguren, "Sandoval frente a la raza esclavizada," *Revista de la Academia Colombiana de Historia Eclesiástica* 29–30 (1973): 57–86. The post-1970s secondary works on Sandoval are Vincent P. Franklin, "Bibliographical Essay: Alonso de Sandoval and the Jesuit Conception of the Negro," *Journal of Negro History* 158 (1973): 349–60; David L. Chandler, *Health and Slavery in Colonial Colombia* (New York: Arno, 1981); Marie-Cécile Bénassy-Berling, "Alonso de Sandoval, les jésuites et la descendance de Cham," in *Études sur l'impact culturel du Nouveau Monde*, vol. 1 (Paris: L'Harmattan, 1981), 49–60; Enriqueta Vila Vilar, "En torno al padre Sandoval, autor de un tratado sobre la esclavitud" in *Église et politique en Amérique Hispanique* (Bordeaux: Presses Universitaires de Bordeaux, 1984), 65–76; Vila Vilar, "Introducción," in *Un tratado sobre la esclavitud* (Madrid: Alianza Editorial, 1987), 15–44; and Jean-Pierre Tardieu, "Du bon usage de la monstruosité: La vision de l'Afrique chez Alonso de Sandoval (1627)," *Bulletin Hispanique* 86, nos. 1–2 (1984): 164–78. For more recent secondary studies on Sandoval's treatise, see the following note.

[18] Alonso de Sandoval, *Un tratado sobre la esclavitud (De instauranda Aethiopum salute)*, ed. Enriqueta Vila Vilar (Madrid: Alianza, 1987). More recently, the first edition of Sandoval's treatise has been used to make a range of different arguments across the disciplines related to Cartagena, the institutions and peoples involved in the transatlantic slave trade, and the histories of black men and women in the territories that would become Colombia in the nineteenth century. Historian Jaime Humberto Borja Gómez uses Sandoval to make an argument about the evangelical project among black men and women as a strategy of social control ("Restaurar la salud: La cristianización de los esclavos en el siglo XVII," in *150 años de abolición de la esclavización en Colombia: Desde la marginalidad hasta la construcción de la nación* [Bogota: Aguilar 2003], 292–329). Eduardo Restrepo uses Sandoval to argue for the irrelevance of modern racial terminology to describe black peoples in the seventeenth century. Luz Adriana Maya uses it to trace the reconstruction of black identities in the New World through the reconstruction of African cultural practices in New Granada. María Cristina Navarrete uses Sandoval as one of her primary sources for her histories of slavery in colonial New Granada (see the Bibliography). Manuel M. Marzal and Francisco Borja de Medina, in separate studies, use Sandoval to narrate histories of the systematization of black evangelization in Peru in the early seventeenth century. Brazilian scholar Juana Beatriz Almeida de Souza has compared Sandoval with Las Casas. Meanwhile, María Eugenia Chaves, Christopher Dennis, and Rachel O'Toole, in different studies, use Sandoval to consider the imposition of European categories over black bodies. Other scholars use Sandoval's text as evidence for tracing African origins of black populations in the Americas (Gwendolyn Midlo Hall and David Wheat), the study of witchcraft practiced by black peoples in Cartagena (Andrew Redden; Borja Gómez, *Rostros y rastros del demonio*), and as background information for narrating micro-histories about "ordinary lives" in the port of Cartagena in the seventeenth century (Kristen Block). Literary scholars Mario Cesareo and Margaret Olsen, in their respective monographs, examine Sandoval's use of allegory and the "poly-vocality" of Sandoval's narrative within the

authors have remarked on the presence of the black interpreters at the center of the Jesuit missionary enterprise as presented by Sandoval's treatise.[19] None has compared black interpreters' testimonies from *Proceso 1676* to Sandoval's prescriptions for translation, as I will do here.

THE INTERPRETERS

Far from being the important but anonymous tools of Sandoval's treatise, the broader corpus of texts about the Jesuit evangelization project among black men and women in Cartagena indicates that missionaries and black new arrivals in Cartagena recognized these interpreters' names, unique skills, and capacity to serve as spiritual leaders of the Jesuit missionary project.

context of the Jesuit mission and the Spanish Crown. Historian of religion Ronald Morgan has studied Sandoval's treatise as a spiritual text in his two essays. Linguist Antonio Santos Morillo examines the treatise's reference to the acquisition of Spanish by the newly arrived black men and women. Historian Pablo Gómez uses Sandoval in his study of the medicinal practices and black men's and women's perceptions of the body in the seventeenth-century Caribbean, "The Circulation of Bodily Knowledge in the Seventeenth-Century Black Spanish Caribbean," *Social History of Medicine* 26, no. 3 (2013): 383–402, and *The Experiential Caribbean*. Guerrero Mosquera, "Misiones, misioneros y bautizos a través del Atlántico," places Sandoval's treatise in conversation with writings produced by contemporary Jesuits in Kongo and Angola. Anna More examines the pragmatic support of mercantile exchange underwriting Sandoval's treatments of blackness and the legality of slavery in his 1627 treatise. Art historian Grace Harpster analyzes Sandoval's use of material objects to describe the visual appearance of blackness.

[19] Pacheco, *Los Jesuitas en Colombia*, vol. 1, 276–78, cites some selections from *Proceso 1676*, but the focus of Pacheco's analysis is describing Claver's labor, not the role played by his interpreters in the project. Much more recently, Paola Vargas Arana digests the names of the interpreters from the 2002 Spanish translation of the printed *Proceso 1696* book in "Pedro Claver y la labor de evangelización en Cartagena de Indias (Siglo XVII): Fuentes claves para analizar a los africanos en el Nuevo Mundo," *Revista de Historia* 155, no. 2 (2006): 43–79. Father Tulio Aristizábal's *Los Jesuitas en Cartagena de Indias* (2009) includes a chapter titled "Sacabuche, Yolofo, El Calepino y Compañía" (115–22) describing some of the participation of Claver's black interpreters in the Saint's evangelical mission among black men and women in Cartagena using the printed *Proceso 1696* book and Pedro Mercado's *Historia de la Provincia del Nuevo Reino*. Wheat includes a section on Claver's interpreters as portrayed in the 2002 Spanish translation of the *Proceso 1696* book in the last chapter of *Atlantic Africa*, 229–37. Wheat mentions the interpreters as examples of Africans who served as agents of acculturation for new arrivals. María Cristina Navarrete, *Génesis y desarrollo de la esclavitud en Colombia: Siglos XVI y XVII* (Cali, Colombia: Universidad del Valle, 2005), and Andrew Redden, "The Problem of Witchcraft," also mention the participation of Claver's black interpreters in Cartagena Inquisition testimonies, which I will reference later in this chapter.

The first black interpreter mentioned by name in the Jesuit corpus dates from 1624 when a letter attributed to Father Pedro Claver describes evangelizing with the help of a man named Calepino, who could speak eleven African languages: "junté por la mañana a toda una casta del navío susodicho llamada Erolo, que es una de las once lenguas que un negro llamado Calepino sabe, y fuera de él no la sabe otro en esta tierra, y Dios por su gran misericordia lo ha dado aquí para este santo ministerio" [In the morning I gathered all those of the Erolo *casta* from the aforementioned ship. The language of this *casta* is one of the eleven that the black man named Calepino knows, and beyond him no one else knows in this land. God, for his great mercy, has brought him here for this saintly ministry].[20] Claver's description suggests that this man was named after Ambrosio Calepino, the Augustinian author of a popular multilingual dictionary intended to help its readers acquire Latin, published numerous times throughout sixteenth- and seventeenth-century Europe.[21] That Claver's description calls him a gift from God demonstrates the priest recognizing the unique value of his interpreter in a way Sandoval's treatise never does. Calepino is mentioned again in a printed summary of a 1638 *carta annua*. Describing the black interpreters at the center of missionary efforts among the city's black populations, the summary states:

saben unos a tres y a quatro lenguas, y otros a seis y a ocho, y uno de ellos alcanzò el nombre de Calepino por saber once, en que conocidamente campea la providencia paternal de Dios, y lo mucho que estima y ampara esta ocupacion y santo ministerio; dandosele como por singular divisa, y honor a este Colegio.

[some of them know three to four languages; and others six to eight. One of them was named Calepino for knowing eleven, through which God's paternal providence evidently fights and shows how much he esteems and protects this occupation and saintly ministry, giving him to this school as a singular insignia and honor.][22]

Contrary to Sandoval's approach of describing enslaved black interpreters as anonymous missionary tools who are replaceable if they turn out to be untrustworthy or unavailable, Claver's letter and the summary of the

[20] Mercado, *Historia de la Provinicia del Nuevo Reino*, vol. 1, 242.

[21] The 1590 Basel edition of Ambrosio Calepino's dictionary provides translations from Latin into ten languages: Hebrew, Greek, French, Italian, German, Dutch, Spanish, Polish, Hungarian, and English. See Ambrosii Calepini, *Dictionarium undecim linguarum* (Basileae: Sebastianum Henricpetri, 1590). This version was republished in 1598, 1605, 1616, and 1627.

[22] Hazañero, *Letras anuas de la Compañia de Iesus de la provincia del nuevo reyno de Granada*, 126.

1638 *carta annua* acknowledge Calepino and his colleagues' irreplaceable skills. One possible cause for the emerging visibility of individual interpreters in texts written after Sandoval finished his treatise in 1624 is that the Jesuit school started purchasing its own enslaved interpreters that year, as mentioned in Chapter 2. The school's financial investment in interpreters would have depended on and reinforced the priests' recognition of the unique skills individual interpreters provided the evangelical project.

The next named mention of the Jesuit school's black interpreters appears in a Cartagena Inquisition trial summary documenting cases from 1628, followed by a set of criminal trial transcripts that resulted from the raid of a maroon settlement in the hinterlands of the city in 1634, which will be discussed later in this chapter.[23] Finally, the most substantial accounts regarding the names, lives, and work of black interpreters in Cartagena between the 1620s and 1650s appear in the testimonies collected in Cartagena between 1659 and 1669, recorded in the *Proceso 1676* manuscript and the printed books *Proceso 1696* and *Proceso 1720*. The testimonies in *Proceso 1676* name thirty different black interpreters, and nine of the witnesses who testify are black interpreters themselves. Through the mediation of an interrogator asking specific questions in front of a judge, a Jesuit priest, and a notary who turned the witnesses' responses from oral first-person accounts into written narratives in the third person, these nine black interpreters described their labor as part of the Jesuit mission among black men and women in Cartagena. Their names are Andrés Sacabuche, Manuel Moreno, Ignacio Soso, Ignacio Angola, José Manzolo, Francisco de Jesús, Diego Folupo, Francisco Yolofo, and María de Mendoza.[24] Another level

---

[23] There are three different black interpreters described as slaves of the Jesuit school who appear by name in the Inquisition archive documents from Cartagena. In 1628 there are two: Bartolomé, "de nación Biafara" [of the Biafada *nación*] (Ysabel Hernandez, AHN, Inqu., book 1020, 293r–295r), and Tomé "de nación Caravalí" [of the Caravalí *nación*] (Anton Caravali, AHN, Inquisición, book 1020, 297r–302r). Then in 1641, Domingo Folupe serves as interpreter for Phelipa Folupe (Phelipa Folupe, AHN, Inq., book 1021, f. 50r–v). There are a few other trials that mention the use of interpreters for black men and women, but they do not specify if they were from the Jesuit School. See, for example, the case of Mateo Arará, who made his second appearance before the Inquisition in 1651 with the assistance of interpreters (AHN, Inq., book 1021, 340v–341r.) On Mateo Arará, see Kathryn Joy McKnight, "'En su tierra lo aprendió': An African Curandero's Defense before the Inquisition," *Colonial Latin American Review* 12, no. 1 (2003): 63–84; Gómez, *The Experiential Caribbean*, 177–83.

[24] The ethnonyms occasionally given in parentheses in what follows correspond to the terminology Wheat employs in *Atlantic Africa*. See O'Toole, "From the Rivers of Guinea to the Valleys of Peru: Becoming a *Bran* Diaspora within Spanish Slavery," *Social Text*

of mediation of their testimonies is added by the fact that they are available to us now only in the Italian translation completed in Rome in 1676. The interpreters whose testimonies appear in *Proceso 1676* vary significantly in their backgrounds, languages, and the length of their testimonies, as outlined in Table 3.1.

Andrés Sacabuche is the most prominent of all the interpreters in *Proceso 1676*, as his testimony is the second longest of any witness in the entire inquest. In his testimony, Sacabuche explains that he had worked for Claver for about thirty years by the time of Claver's death. According to Sacabuche's estimated age at the time of his testimony (forty-five or forty-six) and the fact that he states that he arrived in Cartagena as a young boy, Sacabuche was probably born sometime in the second decade of the seventeenth century and was brought to the city from Angola in the mid-1620s.[25] While Sacabuche declares only being an interpreter of "the language of Angola" (Kimbundu), it is likely that he also spoke Anchico.[26] Although the role of evangelical interpreter is the one for which the school appears to have most valued his labor, Sacabuche curiously insists in his testimony that his "offitio" [job] is that of a trombone player, suggesting that his last name refers to his instrument of speciality, the sackbut, which Sacabuche states he knows how to play "molto bene" [very well]. Such a comment reminds us that far from being the anonymous "tongues" of Sandoval's treatise, the interpreters were well-known participants in the Jesuit mission who had many different roles in the Jesuit school. Indeed, other comments in *Proceso 1676* indicate that Sacabuche was also in charge of making some of the devotional objects the Jesuits used in their mission among black catechumens such as rosaries, cords for self-flagellation, and medals on string necklaces given to the newly baptized. Furthermore, Sacabuche explains that he accompanied Pedro Claver on missions to the countryside to minister to the

---

92, vol. 25, no. 3 (2007): 19–36, for a methodological reflection on how to interpret the last names and origins cited in colonial Spanish American texts for the men and women brought from western Africa. More recently, with reference specifically to the name Kisama, see Jessica Krug, *Fugitive Modernities: Kisama and the Politics of Freedom* (Durham, NC: Duke University Press, 2018), 111–45.

[25] *Proceso 1676*, Andrés Sacabuche, 99v–109v. The citations in this paragraph come from 100r and 101r.

[26] I agree with Wheat (*Atlantic Africa*, 232–233) that Sacabuche is the Angolan interpreter named Andrés owned by the Jesuits who interprets for two men who speak Anchico in the 1634 criminal trials mentioned in note 6 and analyzed at the end of this chapter. For the contested meanings of Anchico in and around Cartagena in the early seventeenth-century, see Wheat, *Atlantic Africa*, 132–40.

TABLE 3.1 *Black interpreters who testify in* Proceso *1676*

Witness number	Name and legal status	Date(s) of testimony; approximate age at testimony; and approximate year of arrival in Cartagena	Stated place of origin; languages spoken	Citation in Biblioteca nacional, MS 281
8	Manuel Moreno, slave of Jesuit school	May 31, 1659; 26 or 27 years old; 1650	Biafara (Biafada); speaks Biafara (Biafada), Bioho, and Spanish	98v–99v
9	Andrés Sacabuche slave of Jesuit school	First: May 19, 1659; second: May 20, 1659; third: June 4, 1659; 45 or 46 years old; early 1620s	Angola; speaks Anchico, Kimbundu, and Spanish	99v–109v
14	Ignacio Soso, slave of Jesuit school	June 30, 1659; 60 years old; unspecified date of arrival in Cartagena – states he knew Claver for "many years"	Soso (Susu); speaks Sosa and Spanish	120v–124r
18	Ignacio Angola, slave of Jesuit school	July 19, 1659; 40 years old; mid- to late 1620s	Angola; speaks Kimbundu and Spanish	132v–140r
19	José Manzolo, slave of Jesuit school	August 8, 1659; 44 or 45 years old; unspecified date of arrival in Cartagena – states he knew Claver for "many years"	Manzolo; speaks Manzolo, Kikongo, and Spanish	140r–143r

(continued)

TABLE 3.1 *(continued)*

Witness number	Name and legal status	Date(s) of testimony; approximate age at testimony; and approximate year of arrival in Cartagena	Stated place of origin; languages spoken	Citation in Biblioteca nacional, MS 281
20	Francisco de Jesús Yolofo, slave of Jesuit school	August 8, 1659; 70 years old; early 1620s	Yolofo (Wolof); speaks Wolof and Spanish	143r–144r
35	Diego Folupo, slave of Jesuit school	September 30, 1659; 48 years old; unspecified date of arrival in Cartagena	Folupo; speaks Folupo (Floup) and Spanish	173r–176v
36	Francisco Yolofo, slave of Jesuit school	October 6, 1659; 50 years old; arrived in Cartagena in 1634	Yolofo (Wolof); speaks Portuguese, Mandinka, Yolofo (Wolof), and Verbesi (Serer)	176v–181v
101	María de Mendoza, free black woman	November 6, 1668; 60 years old; unspecified date of arrival in Cartagena	Biafara (Biafada); speaks Biafada and Spanish	238r

black and indigenous populations beyond the city.[27] His talents as a musician, artisan, and interpreter appear to have earned him particular esteem among the priests of the Jesuit school. Not only is Sacabuche the first interpreter called on to testify for the beatification inquest; his testimony is much longer than that of any other interpreter or almost any other witness. In fact, the testimony, which comprises more than ten folios of *Proceso* 1676, was so long that it had to be compiled over three different days.[28] Its length and detailed content indicate that the officials carrying out the inquest considered him to be a particularly valuable source of information for details about Claver's character, life, and work.

Sacabuche's colleague, Ignacio Angola, explains in his testimony that he was also born in Angola. Like Andrés Sacabuche, he was brought while he was young to Cartagena as a slave. But unlike Sacabuche, Ignacio Angola specifies that he was already Christian when he arrived in Cartagena and that he was taken to Cartagena specifically to serve as an enslaved interpreter for the Jesuit school along with another boy named Alonso Angola.[29] Ignacio Angola explains that Alonso Angola, his childhood companion from the Middle Passage, still lives in the nearby island of Tierra Bomba, located less than 10 kilometers from the city. The comment suggests that Alonso Angola lived at the Jesuit hacienda of San Bernabé, which produced much of the stone used to construct the walls of Cartagena and the Jesuit school. Like Sacabuche, Ignacio Angola also possessed an additional job. He is called "muratore" [bricklayer] and "Ignacio Albañil," indicating that he learned to work in masonry after arriving in Cartagena. Because of this additional job, Ignacio Angola could have had reason to come and go from the Jesuit quarry and hacienda in Tierra Bomba, perhaps allowing Ignacio Angola and Alonso Angola to maintain communication with each other despite being separated after arrival in Cartagena. Ignacio Angola gives the second-to-longest testimony of any of the interpreters; it spans seven

---

[27] For Sacabuche's descriptions of the missions, see *Proceso* 1676, 100r–101r.

[28] He is one of only a handful of witnesses in the dossier whose testimony takes more than one day to relate because of its length.

[29] *Proceso* 1676, Ignacio Angola, 133r. According to Monika Thierren, the Jesuit school in Cartagena purchased the property in Tierra Bomba in 1631 as a site to make tiles, ceramics, and bricks for the use of the Jesuit school and sale among the greater Cartagena area. See Thierren, "Más que distinción, en busca de la diferenciación: Arqueología histórica de Cartagena de Indias en el siglo XVII," in *Cartagena de Indias en el siglo XVII*, ed. Adolfo Meisel Roca and Haroldo Calvo Stevenson (Cartagena: Banco de la República, 2007), 17–66, especially 33–48.

and a half folios of *Proceso 1676*, suggesting that he also held a position of esteem among the surviving interpreters who had worked with Claver at the time of the beatification inquest.

Like Ignacio Angola, José Manzolo, the only other interpreter to testify from central Africa, states that he was also already a Christian before crossing the Atlantic. Manzolo specifies that even though he was already baptized when he arrived, he only learned the Christian doctrine and Christian prayers in Spanish, Manzolo, and Kikongo on arrival in the New World, indicating the use of African languages in Spanish America to deliver standardized teachings and prayers orally among newly arrived black populations.[30] José Manzolo explains that Claver asked the director of the Jesuit school to purchase Manzolo because he knew these two African languages "molto bene" [very well].[31]

Francisco Yolofo, in contrast to the three interpreters named above, identifies himself as originating further north on the African continent, from the area now described as Senegambia by historians of the transatlantic slave trade.[32] Francisco Yolofo notes in his testimony that when he arrived in Cartagena he could speak languages he calls Portuguese, Mandinga (Mandinka), Yolofo (Wolof), and Berbesí (Serer).[33] He explains that at first he was purchased by a non-Jesuit resident of Cartagena but that soon afterward Claver borrowed him to assist in interpreting the confession of an escaped slave condemned to death. Yolofo's proficiency in Portuguese as well as the other Senegambian languages named above incited Claver to request that the director of the Jesuit school purchase him to be one of the school's in-house interpreters.[34]

Ignacio Soso, Diego Folupo, and Francisco de Jesús Yolofo also arrived in Cartagena from Senegambia. Ignacio Soso describes himself to be "Sosoc" and a speaker of "Sosa," indicating, according to Sandoval's

---

[30] *Proceso 1676*, José Manzolo, 140v. He either learned these translated prayers from other interpreters or composed the translations himself as part of his role in the Jesuit mission.

[31] Ibid. Wheat states that "Monzolo" [*sic*] must refer to an Ansiku or Teke language (*Atlantic Africa*, 232). John Thornton, in contrast, says "Monzolo" would be the language of Nzolo, a province in eastern Kongo; Thornton says the language would have been a "a dialect of Kikongo" ("On the Trail of Voodoo," 273).

[32] This region appears in seventeenth-century documents as "la tierra de los ríos de Guinea" [the land of the rivers of Guinea].

[33] According to details provided in his testimony, Francisco Yolofo arrived in Cartagena in 1634, a decade or so after Andrés Sacabuche and Ignacio Angola. Wheat explains that the ethnonym "Berbesí" derives from the Wolof political title *Bur ba Sinn*, meaning the "ruler of Siin," Siin being a Serer homeland (*Atlantic Africa*, 31, 34).

[34] *Proceso 1676*, Franciso Yolofo, 177r.

criteria, that he was a kind of Zape.[35] Meanwhile, Diego Folupo does not explain how many languages he speaks, but his name suggests he served as an interpreter for at least one language associated with Floup people of Senegambia. Francisco de Jesús Yolofo's brief testimony spans only one folio but provides some of the most unique details of any of the interpreters' testimonies because he explains his reason for deciding to convert to Christianity from Islam many years after arriving in Cartagena.[36] The name Yolofo suggests that he served as an interpreter of at least one language spoken by the Wolof in Cartagena.

Finally, Manuel Moreno and María de Mendoza are the two interpreters who testify in *Proceso 1676* who identify themselves as being Biafada. Manuel Moreno is the youngest of all of the interpreters to testify and the most recently arrived. In his testimony, Manuel Moreno explains that he was purchased by the Jesuit school at the beginning of the illness that eventually ended Claver's life. The date that appears elsewhere in *Proceso 1676* for the onset of Claver's illness suggests that Moreno arrived in Cartagena around 1650.[37] Moreno is also the youngest of any of the other interpreters to testify, as the notary guesses his age to be twenty-six or twenty-seven. He explains that he speaks Biafada "molto bene" [very well] because he is Biafada, but that he can also speak Bioho "per essere state molto tempo fra li mori Biohos" [because he lived a long time among the black Biohos] (likely as a slave) before being taken to Cartagena.[38] While his principal labor was that of Claver's physical care, Moreno notes that Claver trained him to serve as an interpreter for new arrivals speaking the languages of the Biafada or the Bioho.

María de Mendoza, interpreter of Biafada, is an outlier in *Proceso 1676* for two different reasons: she is the only female interpreter and the only freed interpreter mentioned in the inquest.[39] Her testimony

---

[35] Wheat states, using Alonso de Sandoval's 1627 treatise as evidence, that Soso (Susu) is a subgroup of Zapes, an ethnonym encompassing certain groups of people from south of the Geba River (Wheat, *Atlantic Africa*, 48–49).

[36] *Proceso 1676*, Francisco de Jesús, 143r–144r. The reason given is Claver's kindness to a man sentenced to death. The account appears first in Andrade's hagiography, 37v–38r.

[37] *Proceso 1676*, Manuel Moreno, 98v–99r.

[38] The Bioho (also sometimes written Bijago or Biojó), according to Wheat, "used their strategic geographic location" (on the islands on the mouths of the Geba and Grande Rivers) "to launch raids on the nearby mainland, resulting in the enslavement and sale of Floups, Nalus, Brames, Balantas, and especially Biafadas" (*Atlantic Africa*, 43). Manuel Moreno was likely a Biafada captive of the Bioho who was sold to Portuguese transatlantic slave traders.

[39] *Proceso 1676*, María de Mendoza, 238r. Witness number 63, Ángela Biafara, describes herself as a slave of the Jesuit school who helped Claver in his evangelical efforts but does not say if she ever interpreted for him (*Proceso 1676*, 220r–v).

demonstrates that Claver worked with black female interpreters despite the fact that no other witness mentions women as forming part of the groups of interpreters who regularly helped Claver. The absence of other mentions of female interpreters in the *Proceso 1676* testimonies could be attributed to the hagiographic purpose of the inquest and its related documents. That is, descriptions of the physical proximity and the many hours of work by the side of enslaved black women could have cast doubt on Claver's virtue. That María de Mendoza was freed could have mitigated some of the suspicion associated with her contact with Claver such that her comment regarding her work as an interpreter could be included in the inquest transcript and its subsequent published versions. Because María de Mendoza does not provide more details about her own life, and because references to her in other texts from Cartagena from the period have yet to surface, we can only guess about other aspects of who she was, how she secured her freedom, and whether laboring as an interpreter for Claver had anything to do with it.[40]

Although María de Mendoza's testimony is the briefest of all of the interpreters' in *Proceso 1676*, it indexes the existence of the many female interpreters who participated in the Jesuit mission in Cartagena in the first half of the seventeenth century but were not asked to testify for Claver's beatification inquest. Mendoza's fleeting appearance demonstrates that not all of the black interpreters who worked as part of the Jesuit mission in Cartagena were slaves and that some were also women. The lack of information about these female interpreters who worked for the Jesuits in Cartagena serves as a reminder of the many lingering silences that remain in the archive of texts composed about black men and women in colonial Spanish America.[41]

---

[40] See Sandoval's defense for using enslaved black women as interpreters in *Naturaleza, policia sagrada*, book 3, chap. 2, 236r. Sandoval's comparison between black enslaved women and Igantius's contact with prostitutes in Rome supports the licentiousness associated with employing female interpreters that the compilers and editors of the *Proceso* corpus would have wanted to avoid. In fact, the reason María de Mendoza's testimony appears in *Proceso 1676* at all appears to be related to her claim that she was once miraculously healed by Claver. (Supporting my speculation about the purpose of her testimony, hers is the only one of the interpreters' testimonies collected between 1668 and 1669, the second session of beatification accounts focused on the miracles performed by Claver.) For mentions of Mendoza and Juana, another female interpreter who spoke Biohó, who worked with Claver, see Fernández, *Apostolica y penitente vida*, 209 and 150–51, respectively.

[41] Many more male black interpreters are named in the inquest but do not testify. They appear in the inquest testimonies given by the interpreters as well as those of other witnesses who describe their work or claim that they could serve as potential witnesses to corroborate their testimonies if they were not dead or did not live somewhere outside Cartagena. The names of these additional interpreters are Alonso Angola, Pedro Angola, Antonio Balanta, Lorenzo

VISIBLE ROLES OF THE BLACK INTERPRETERS

Sandoval provides glimpses of the prominent roles interpreters assumed in the service of the mission when explaining to future missionaries how to stage catechisms for black new arrivals with the assistance of an interpreter. According to Sandoval, in the houses or barracoons where catechism sessions would occur, the priest should seat his interpreter in a chair above the group to be catechized, while relegating himself to the periphery:

Juntos todos por el orden dicho por sus divisiones y señales, sentarase el interprete en un lugar que los vea a todos, principalmente si ha de hablar y catequizar juntamente a tres o más castas y naciones diversas, como muy de ordinario sucede, por entender otras tantas lenguas, con lo cual juntamente se sale con otros tantos catequismos y se ahorra y abrevia, se assegura mas gente y se haze mas fruto. A este se le dirá con claridad, con brevedad, con distincion, con viveza y paciencia, lo que ha de decir a los baptizandos: lo que les ha de preguntar e inquirir, ya a unos en una lengua, ya a otros en otra. Y el catequizante andarà sobre todo vigilante, advirtiendo a los unos, ya a los otros, quietandolos, animandolos, avivando y agazajandolos; y preguntandoles por medio del interprete, con toda presteza, sin pasar de una pregunta o cosa a otra hasta que aquella este entendida de todos y quede con moral satisfacion della.

[Gathered together according to their abovementioned divisions and signs, you should sit the interpreter in a place where he can see all of them, especially if he has to speak to and catechize three or more different *castas* and *naciones* together, as often happens, because they understand several languages other than their own. With this, you can accomplish a great deal more catechisms and save time, redeeming more people and producing more fruit. To this one [interpreter] you will say, with clarity, brevity, distinction, vivacity, and patience, what he must ask and inquire of the different individuals, to some in one language, and then to others in another, etc. The catechizing priest will go about the group vigilantly, warning some and then others, calming them, encouraging them, and giving them gifts; he will examine them efficiently through the interpreter, without moving from one question or topic to the next until it has been understood by all and the priest is morally satisfied with it.][42]

Biafara, Manuel Biafara, Simón Biafara, Domingo Bran, Francisco Bran, Manuel Bran, Lorenzo Cocolí, Ventura Cocolí, Antonio de nación Congo, Francisco Folupo, Ignacio Guayacán, Bartolomé Nalu, Joaquín Nalu, Juan Primero (Folupo), Feliciano de los Ríos, Juan Yarca, Juan Yolofo, and Lorenzo Zape. In almost every case, their last names suggest a west African place of origin. Curiously, no one in the *Proceso* documents mentions anyone named Calepino, which is hard to believe considering how prominent he appears in the Jesuit *cartas annuas*. From this absence, I conjecture that Calepino died long before the inquest. It is also possible that one of the aforementioned already deceased interpreters in this list from Senegambia could have used Calepino as a nickname.

[42] Sandoval, *Naturaleza, policia sagrada*, book 3, chap. 9, 271r.

Here Sandoval recommends the seating arrangement as a way to give the interpreter a better view of the group of catechumens to whom he or she will deliver the catechism. The staging, however, also establishes a hierarchy between the interpreter, the audience, and the priest that situates the interpreter as the most important figure presiding over the scenario. Performance theorist Diana Taylor provides helpful tools for interpreting the mutual constitution of setting, script, action, and audience of a performance in a colonial setting such as this one. Taylor explains that through role reversal and parody such scenarios can produce meanings for the audience other than those intended by the colonial authorities sanctioning the performances. Indeed, although Sandoval explicitly describes the catechism as if he could manage the interpreter from the margins as a puppet master, the details he provides reveal possibilities of a very different dynamic at work: it is the interpreter, not the priest, who could see all the catechumens and their reactions to his messages, and ultimately it is the interpreter, not the priest, who fashions the content and affect of the catechism in the target languages of the new arrivals.[43]

Sandoval's comments and the descriptions of the catechism scenarios described in the *cartas annuas* and *Proceso 1676* suggest that the Jesuit priests in Cartagena likely imagined themselves as exercising ultimate authority in these scenes through the implication that they were so important that they did not need to preside physically over the scenes themselves. Orlando Patterson's remarks about the construction of authority in slave systems, inspired by a Weberian notion of the authority produced through recognition, remind us that a slave owner's authority did not require their constant physical presence or violent coercion over his enslaved laborers.[44] Instead, their authority was often constituted through symbolism or the presence of others who represented them in his stead. The descriptions of the scenes of evangelical translation in Cartagena led by black interpreters suggest that the priests envisioned their own authority as temporarily represented in the interpreters. Surviving evidence suggests some of the consequences of such a delegation of authority to the interpreters. One consequence appears implicitly in the passage above: the profound change of the locus of enunciation of the catechism itself. This change in the locus of enunciation of the catechism from priest to interpreter appears to have become further accentuated as

---

[43] See Diana Taylor, *Archive and the Repertoire: Performing Cultural Memory in the Americas* (Durham, NC: Duke University Press, 2003), 28–32.

[44] Patterson, *Slavery and Social Death*, 35–76, especially 36–38.

the interpreters were given increasingly prominent roles in the Jesuit mission toward the end of Claver's life. The texts that describe the delegation of the priest's authority to the interpreters do so as they present Claver as so exceptionally humble that he would elevate his interpreters as more important than himself.

Adapting James Scott's terminology of hidden and public transcripts to analyze subaltern resistance strategies, we can see that the "public transcript" of the catechism scenario centered around the prominent positioning of the black interpreter is that of a Christian catechism led by a priest whose authority and teachings are delegated to his black evangelical interpreter(s). One of many possible "hidden transcripts" for such scenarios might be the establishment of the black interpreter as a linguistic and spiritual leader over all present in the scene – including the priest himself.[45] There were, we can assume, many more possible hidden transcripts produced during these catechisms that are inscrutable from available evidence. In the next chapter, I will analyze the descriptions the interpreters give of the messages about Christianity that they supposedly transferred in translation as part of the Jesuit mission. For now, I underscore that even Sandoval's prescriptive text provides evidence from which to infer that a secondary effect of the catechism scenario involved establishing the black interpreters as linguistic and spiritual leaders among the group of black catechumens. While their authority appears explicitly in the texts as an extension of the priests', readers of these accounts can imagine other possible horizons of interpretation by the black men and women catechized as part of the evangelical mission.

One possible alternative interpretation of the authority wielded by the black interpreters in the mission is suggested in the work of Cécile Fromont on Christian visual culture in the Kingdom of Kongo during this period. Fromont describes the important roles played by Kongolese *mestres*, elite native church leaders and interpreters, in Kongolese Christianity.[46] Reflecting on *mestres'* appearance in missionary documents and visual culture, Fromont explains that they were key facilitators for European priests' missionary and sacramental work as well as important leaders in the spreading and preserving of Kongo Christianity in the absence of European priests. The eighteenth-century watercolor from Berardino d'Asti, "The Father Missionary... Listens to the Sins of the

---

45 James C. Scott, *Domination and the Arts of Resistance: Hidden Transcripts* (New Haven, CT: Yale University Press, 1990).

46 Fromont, *The Art of Conversion*, 65, 109, 147–48, 203. See also note 83 in Chapter 2.

FIGURE 3.1 Bernardino d'Asti, *The Missionary ... Listens to Sins of the Penitent,* ca. 1750. Watercolor on paper.
"Missione in prattica: Padri cappuccini ne Regni di Congo, Angola, et adiacenti," MS 457, f. 8v, Bibiloteca Civica Centrale, Turin. Courtesy of Bibiloteca Civica Centrale, Turin

Penitent" (Figure 3.1) depicts a confession carried out in the Kongo through a *mestre.* As indicated in the composition of the painting, the kneeling man confessing speaks directly to the *mestre* in a conversation supposedly supervised by the European priest seated to the *mestre*'s side. Fromont notes the disjuncture between the title of this watercolor and what it portrays.[47] The composition depicts the missionary as removed from the immediate conversation between the *mestre* and the confessant, suggesting the missionary understood little if anything of the conversation. Catechumens who came from the partially Christianized areas of Kongo and Angola could very well have perceived the enslaved interpreters working with Sandoval and Claver in Cartagena as New World versions of the Kongolese *mestres,* spiritual leaders whose authority was

---

[47] Fromont, "Collecting and Translating Knowledge across Cultures: Capuchin Missionary Images of Early Modern Central Africa, 1650–1750," in *Collecting across Cultures: Material Exchanges in the Early Modern Atlantic World,* ed. Daniela Bleichmar and Peter C. Mancall (Philadelphia: University of Pennsylvania Press, 2011), 134–54, especially 147–50.

not completely dependent on the delegation of that of the European priests but rather contributed to it.

There were of course some important differences in these New World catechetical assistants that should be noted in making this juxtaposition. The Kongolese *mestres* were members of the nobility and wore characteristic regalia including imported and local luxury goods, most notably the bright white cloth with which they are invariably identified in visual images. In contrast, the Jesuits' interpreters in Cartagena were enslaved men whose clothing is barely remarked on in surviving documentation.[48] And yet the *Proceso* documents indicate the interpreters were treated by the priests and the new arrivals with a great deal of respect. This respect suggests that an unstated Jesuit strategy for effective evangelization in Cartagena could have involved making analogous connections between the central African interpreters and the *mestres*. While perhaps obvious, it bears repeating that across the dislocations of enslavement and diaspora, the men and women evangelized through black interpreters in Cartagena brought with them expectations and experiences that shaped their understandings of evangelical translation and conversion.

Numerous testimonies from *Proceso 1676* confirm that the staging of the catechism scenario involved denoting the authority of the black interpreters over the catechism sessions. Unlike Sandoval's scenario, described above, the testimonies from *Proceso 1676* indicate that groups of interpreters were often seated together in high chairs above catechumens and the priest during the scenes of religious instruction. Francisco Yolofo explains:

faceva portar sedie alte e di appoggio per l'Interpreti mori, et il detto Padre si sedeva in qualche fiasca v[u]ota, ò in qualche banca ò pezzo di legna, e molte volte entrando alcune persone di autorità ... vedendo il detto Padre tanto male accomodato, e mal assiso se ne infastidivano assai dicendo, se come li detti mori interpreti stavano assisi nelle seggie, e con tutta autorità et il detto Padre senza alcuna, e esso si alzava e diffendendo diceva questo Testimonio, et tutti li altri Interpreti erano li più necessarii in quel ministerio e che esso faceva poca figura in quello e che cosi dovevano stare con ogni autorità perche li detti mori nuovi li portassero rispetto e li dassero ogni credito in quello che li dicessero.

[Father Claver would have tall chairs with armrests brought for the black interpreters and he would sit on some empty earthenware jug or some bench or a piece of wood. And many times when people of authority would enter... seeing the

---

[48] On the clothing of *mestres*, see Fromont, *Art of Conversion*, 147–48; Fromont, "Common Threads: Cloth, Colour, and the Slave Trade in Early Modern Kongo and Angola," *Art History* 4, no. 5 (2018): 838–67. For the only reference to black interpreters' clothing in Cartagena, see the "cappe" [capes] mentioned by Sacabuche, *Proceso 1676*, 102v.

father so badly accommodated and seated, they would become very upset, saying how the black interpreters could be seated with such authority and the father without any. Claver would then stand up and say, defending this witness and the rest of the interpreters, that they were more necessary in this labor than he was, that he figured little in it, and that, because of this, they should be seated with all authority so that, the new blacks would respect them and give complete credit to what they told them.][49]

Yolofo's testimony confirms that placing interpreters in high chairs was effective not just because it gave the interpreters increased visibility (as Sandoval suggests) but also because it endowed the interpreters with "tutta autorità" [complete authority] that would inspire respect in the groups of newly arrived black men and women being catechized. While Yolofo's testimony is given in the context of highlighting Claver's humility for beatification purposes, the evidence does not only need to be read as an index of Claver's humility. In fact, the interpolated citation from Claver emphasizes the inversion of expected hierarchies between black interpreters and the Jesuit priest through this staging of the catechism. This inversion, voiced through the interpreter as witness, indicates an indirect way for Yolofo to recount his own important role in the missionary project.

The expected reaction of elite audiences to Claver's acts of humility vis-à-vis his interpreters is anticipated in the testimony itself. For example, Yolofo's testimony narrates a specific encounter that occurred when a Spanish captain observed the aforementioned catechism scenario:

si sdegnò molto con questo testimonio e con li altri mori interpreti il detto capitano e castellano, per amar molto il detto P. Pietro Claver, et esser suo compagno, dicendoli come consentè[,] Compare[,] che questi cani mori stiano assisi in seggie alte e di appoggio e vostra paternità tanto scommodo e senza autorità e il detto Padre rispose in diffesa di questo Testimonio e di tutti li altri Interpreti, quello che rispose a tutti li altri con il che il sopra detto, se ne andò molto maravigliato dell'humilità e mortification del detto Padre.

[the Captain and Spaniard] became very indignant with this witness and with all of the other black interpreters because of his great love for Father Pedro Claver and for being his friend, and he would say to Claver: "How can you, father, consent that these black dogs be seated in high seats with armrests and your paternity be seated so uncomfortably and without authority?" And the father responded in defense of this witness and all of the other black interpreters the same thing he would reply to all of the others [who voiced similar complaints].

[49] *Proceso* 1676, Francisco Yolofo, 178r.

And with this, the Spanish captain left, stunned by [Claver's] humility and mortification.][50]

Yolofo's account explicitly ends by framing the story as an example of Claver's saintly humility – and indeed this account is included in the beatification inquest as evidence of it. But the account also demonstrates an instance in which an enslaved interpreter ventriloquizes his supervisor's voice to state that the interpreter was actually completely in charge of the evangelical labor being performed. Six of the nine interpreters who testify in *Proceso 1676* describe similar conflicts that arose between members of Cartagena's elite and Claver on witnessing the role reversals of the catechisms.[51] Like Yolofo's account, their anecdotes testify to Claver's humility; in doing so they also demonstrate that the performance of the catechism through black interpreters involved promoting respect for the enslaved interpreters among black catechumens, priests, and other members of the Cartagena community. Through such anecdotes, the interpreters' testimonies evidence that the interpreters were far from invisible tongues anonymously relaying the messages of Jesuit priests.

The increasingly prominent roles played by the black interpreters are especially evident in the testimonies from *Proceso 1676* that describe the work the interpreters performed for Claver as his health declined toward the end of his life. For example, Francisco Yolofo explains that when Claver became too weak to lead the expeditions to greet the ships of new arrivals before the enslaved men and women had disembarked, Yolofo and many of his enslaved interpreter colleagues would go to greet the ships *on their own*:

li primi doi ò trè anni, che questo testimonio connobbe il detto P. Pietro Claver, andava con quelli [Interpreti] alli detti navigli à dare la buona venuta alli detti mori, et a dirli tutto il riferito di sopra... mà doppò li rettori di questo Colleggio ordinorno [*sic*] al detto Padre che non andasse alli detti navigli perche era già vecchio e stanco, e che potria augumentaseli per la fatica qualche grave Infermità, al che il detto Padre ubbedi e solamente mandava l'Interpreti alli detti navigli comè si è detto...

---

[50] Ibid.
[51] The other interpreter testimonies in *Proceso 1676* that mention the interpreters seated in high chairs with armrests during catechisms are Andrés Sacabuche, 103r; Igancio Soso, 121v; Igancio Angola, 136v–137r; José Manzolo, 142r; Diego Folupo, 176r. An earlier rendition of the account also appears in Andrade's hagiography, 43r, and in Nicolás González's testimony in *Proceso 1676*, 33r, suggesting that the story was one that the officials presiding over the inquest prompted the interpreters to narrate because of its demonstration of Claver's humility.

[The first two or three years that this witness knew Father Pedro Claver, [Claver] would go with the interpreters to those boats to welcome those blacks and to tell them all that was said above... But later the directors of this school ordered Father Claver not to go to those boats because he was now old and tired and the fatigue of the endeavor might aggravate some grave illness, to which the father obeyed and just sent interpreters to the ships, as has already been said.][52]

Even though the interpreters had to serve the Jesuit mission as enslaved laborers, Yolofo's testimony signals the autonomy the interpreters possessed regarding *how* this translation would occur because they conducted their labor without any Jesuit supervisor. Other testimonies explain that the interpreters would then also independently greet the disembarking slave ships at the port and accompany the new arrivals to their temporary barracoons.[53] Then, at the end of the new arrivals' stay in Cartagena, the interpreters – not the priest – would join the groups again as they returned to the docks where most of the new arrivals would be loaded onto ships taking them to the next stop of their journeys. In serving as arrival and farewell committees, the interpreters would give the captive men and women food, water, and words of encouragement to comfort the new arrivals.[54] In their descriptions of these exchanges for the beatification inquest, the interpreters explain that as Claver grew older they increasingly became more like his representatives who acted in his stead. That is, they no longer acted only as mediators but rather as agents speaking *for* the Jesuit priests. We can imagine that these circumstances also permitted the interpreters to communicate messages that exceeded the limits or expectations of the Jesuit mission.

Even before Claver grew ill, the interpreters' prominent roles were especially apparent in the baptismal ceremonies that would follow the catechism sessions, according to many testimonies of *Proceso 1676*. In these ceremonies, Claver would baptize groups of the black men and women through the interpreters, giving the baptizands Christian names and medals on string necklaces that the interpreters had made to

---

[52] *Proceso 1676*, Francisco Yolofo, 177v.

[53] *Proceso 1676*, Andrés Sacabuche, 102r, Francisco Yolofo, 177v.

[54] *Proceso 1676*, Andrés Sacabuche, 105v, Ignacio Soso, 122v, José Manzolo, 142v, Francisco Yolofo, 179r. The majority of the captive black men, women, and children arriving in Cartagena did not stay in the port city, but rather traveled to Peru via Panama. Others were sent to the interior of New Granada or towns surrounding Cartagena. For the latter, their farewell from the interpreters might not have been the last time they would see them, as interpreters such as Andrés Sacabuche regularly accompanied Claver on his missions throughout the countryside. See section 11 of the Summary portion of the *Proceso 1696* for an anthology of accounts of Claver's missionary work.

distinguish the baptized from the unbaptized.[55] The medals first appear in Sandoval's 1627 treatise as a recommended strategy to help priests distinguish correctly baptized blacks from other new arrivals.[56] Sandoval, however, does not mention that the interpreters were also making the medals before distributing them, a detail added in many of the interpreters' testimonies. Through creating, distributing, and describing the significance of these medals in languages unknown to European priests, the interpreters could have endowed the medals with a wide variety of meanings, most of them undocumented and some barely visible in the written documents about the mission. Literary scholar Margaret Olsen has reflected on the polyvalence of Sandoval's stories about the way new arrivals used their medals. Referencing one of Sandoval's accounts in which an enslaved black man carried his medal in a small taffeta purse on a string of ten beads, Olsen states: "These beads could have been a makeshift rosary, as Sandoval suggests, but could also have been a syncretic object that held other religious or cultural meanings for the slave. It may, for example, have been a haphazard string of Muslim prayer beads."[57] While Olsen does not mention it, the small purse could just as well or additionally describe a *bolsa de mandinga*, a *gbo*, a *nkisi*, or a *grisgris*, amulet-like objects or collections of objects worn by people

---

[55] Interpreter Ignacio Angola, for example, describes the task in his testimony: "le quali dette medaglie fondeva in questo detto Colleggio Andrea Sacabuche et altri Interpreti che la maggior parte di quelli già sono morti" [These medals were made in the school by Andrés Sacabuche and other interpreters, the majority of whom have passed away] (*Proceso 1676*, Ignacio Angola, 137r). Francisco Yolofo declares similar information, explaining that enslaved interpreters Andrés Sacabuche and Juan Primero (now deceased) would make the medals and rosaries that Claver would pass out to black men and women throughout the year (*Proceso 1676*, Francisco Yolofo, 179r). The medals had an image of Mary on one side and Jesus on the other.

[56] Sandoval, *Naturaleza, policia sagrada*, book 3, chap. 12, 284v–285r.

[57] Olsen, *Slavery and Salvation in Colonial Cartagena de Indias*, 144. On *bolsas de mandinga* as *gbo* in the Portuguese Atlantic world, see James Sweet, *Domingos Álvares, African Healing, and the Intellectual History of the Atlantic World* (Chapel Hill: University of North Carolina Press, 2011), 62–63. See also Sweet, *Recreating Africa*, 179–86; Daniela Buono Calainho, *Metrópole das mandingas: Religiosidade negra e inquisição portuguesa no Antigo Regime* (Rio de Janeiro: Garamond, 2008); Souza, *The Devil and the Land of the Holy Cross*; Mathew Rarey, "Assemblage, Occlusion, and the Art of Survival in the Black Atlantic," *African Arts* 51, no. 5 (2018): 20–33; Cécile Fromont, "Paper, Ink, Vodun, and the Inquisition: Tracing Power, Slavery, and Witchcraft in the Early Modern Portuguese Atlantic," *Journal of the American Academy of Religion* (2020, in press), among others. On *nkisi*, see Robert Farris Thompson, *Flash of the Spirit: African and Afro-American Art and Philosophy* (New York: Vintage, 1983). On *grisgris*, see Hawthorne, *From Africa to Brazil*, 218–19.

throughout western Africa and the African diaspora for protection. The interpreters would have been key actors in producing or hiding the polyvalence of the medals and other material goods they circulated as part of their missionary work.

The interpreters' prominent positions in the Jesuit evangelical project did not stop at the scenes of catechism and baptism or the arrivals and farewells from the port. For the black men and women destined to stay in Cartagena, Ignacio Soso explains, the interpreters would serve as their constant means of contact with the Church. Every Sunday and Church feast day the interpreters would gather the black men and women remaining in Cartagena to hear mass at the Jesuit church.[58] Ignacio Angola's testimony describes the pageantry centered around the interpreters, who would process through the city to Mass on Church holidays: "tutte le Domeniche di Quaresma usciva in processione per le strade publiche di questa Città con tutti li suoi Interpreti e molti ragazzi portando avanti uno standardo colorato e questo Testimonio portò molte volte il detto standardo et altre volte lo portò Alonso Angola et alcune volte Gioachino Nalu" [Every Sunday of Lent, Claver would parade through the streets of this city with all his interpreters and many young blacks, carrying in front of the parade a colorful banner. This witness often carried the banner, and other times Joaquín Nalu would do it].[59] During Lent, the interpreters also assisted Claver in confessing the city's black men and women and preparing them for their yearly communion. Collectively, the interpreters explain that they were responsible for not only the process of initial evangelization, but also maintaining the city's black population's connection and communication with the Church and its rites. According to Fernández's *Apostolica y penitente vida*, Claver would also send his interpreters to walk through the streets to search for contraband slaves who had been hidden on arrival and had therefore not yet been baptized.[60] No testimony from *Proceso 1676* corresponds to this anecdote, which Fernández could have taken from a different source (such as a now lost *carta annua*) or something excised from the *Proceso* manuscript sent to Rome. Regardless of its origins, the comment invites reflection about the roles played by the interpreters in the political economy of the slave trade in the port and reminds us of the implication of the Jesuits' evangelical project in the buying, selling, and taxing of the sales of black men and women.

[58] *Proceso* 1676, Ignacio Soso, 122r.   [59] *Proceso* 1676, Ignacio Angola, 135r.
[60] Fernández, *Apostolica y penitente vida*, 158.

THE PRIVILEGES OF ENSLAVED INTERPRETERS

Because of their key roles in the Jesuit mission, the order's black interpreters in Cartagena acquired many privileges unique to individuals
considered enslaved property during this period. Some of the privileges
are the physical comfort, medical care, and material goods that Claver
sought to procure for his interpreters. For example, Andrés Sacabuche
testifies that:

era tanta la sua compassione e carità con li prossimi, che molte volte essendo assai
sudato, questo Testimonio nel ministerio delli detti negri servendoli d'Interprete
nella lingua angola li dava il detto suo fazzoletto, acciò si asciugasse con quello, et
ancorche non lo volesse, per il molto rispetto che se li doveva, persisteva in quello,
e questo Testimonio per condescendere [*sic*] al di lui gusto lo accetava...

[Claver's compassion and charity for others was so great that he would often give
this witness his handkerchief to dry himself with it, as he would perspire a lot
while working in the ministry of the said blacks as his interpreter of the Angolan
language. Even if [this witness] did not want to take it because of the great respect
that he owed the father, Claver persisted and this witness would accept it to
concede to his wishes.][61]

It is impossible to know if the declarative frame of the account that
attributes this habit to Claver's virtue was uttered by Sacabuche or added
by the notary or the translator of the text. Regardless of the frame, the
information conveyed in the anecdote underscores the effort Sacabuche
expended in the service of the mission and the care with which Claver
treated him for it. Earlier in his testimony, Sacabuche mentions that on
Claver's death Sacabuche inherited a painting of a crucifix that Claver
had used in his room for his private devotion: "il quale crocifisso sta hoggi
in poter di questo Testimonio, perche cuando mori il detto Padre lo prese
e lo portó alla sua stanza per sua particolar divotione" [this crucifix is
today in this witness's power because when the said father died he
received it and took it to his room for his individual devotion].[62] Such
supplemental comments speak both to the esteem with which Claver
treated his interpreters in general and to the special treatment given to

---

[61] *Proceso 1676*, Sacabuche, 102v–103r. Another privilege specific to Sacabuche is the fact
that he never boarded the slave ships when they arrived in the port but waited for the
captives to disembark (101v). He does not say why he was exempt from this particularly
grueling part of the evangelical labor of the mission, but Sandoval's comments about
interpreters who refuse to interpret for sick catechumens (*Naturaleza, policia sagrada*,
book 3, chap. 9, 271r) suggest it could have been because Sacabuche refused to go.
[62] *Proceso 1676*, Sacabuche, 100r.

Sacabuche in particular. While included in the dossier as support for Claver's humility and generosity, Sacabuche's comments about his special treatment beg the question of what would have happened if such care had not been provided.

Claver indeed advocated for his captive language specialists by writing letters to Jesuit leaders in Rome to protect them from arduous physical labor and resale. Correspondence from the Jesuit Father General Mutio Vitelleschi to Claver in 1624 demonstrates that Claver had formally requested that his interpreters never be required to perform work other than that of linguistic translation for ministry among the black populations of the city.[63] In a response to another request from Claver four years later, the Father General further sanctioned the enslaved interpreters' protection and special treatment, ordering that no enslaved interpreter working with Claver be sold or traded away from the Jesuit school.[64] This advocacy by Claver for his interpreters and the positive responses from the Father General afforded the interpreters the chance to establish permanence in the city, something few other enslaved servants could count on.[65]

Claver also ensured that his interpreters received special honors in death. According to Fernández, Claver held elaborate funerals for his interpreters that were attended by the priest and groups of black men and women living in and around the city: "Si alguno de ellos se le moria; le llorava, y recibia pesames, como pudieran otros por sus hijos, que tiernamente amaron. Haciale muy onroso entierro de cera, y musica, y conbidava a todas las castas de los Negros, para que lo asistiesen" [If any of the interpreters died, Claver would grieve for them and receive

---

[63] Pacheco, *Los jesuitas en Colombia*, vol. 1, 277.

[64] "Muy justo es que ayudemos en cuanto pudiéremos al P. Padre Claver, que con tan grande caridad y santo celo se emplea en el ministerio de los morenos. V.R. ordene que no se vendan ni truequen, ni le quiten los ocho o nueve intérpretes negritos que tiene, pues son tan importantes para hacer el dicho ministerio" [It is very fair that we should help Father Claver as much as we can, who with such love and saintly zeal dedicates himself to the ministry among *morenos*. Your Reverence should order the eight or nine little black interpreters not be taken from him or traded, for they are so important for that ministry] (Vitelleschi a Ayerbe, February 2, 1628; qtd. in Pacheco, *Los jesuitas en Colombia*, vol. 1, 277).

[65] Pacheco attributes the existence of this second letter to the fact that the Jesuits in Cartagena ignored the Father General's first authorization (*Los jesuitas en Colombia*, vol. 1, 277), but I read it differently. The requests addressed in the two letters are not the same; they signal distinct issues that Claver evidently wanted clarified. One is about the labor the interpreters can perform and the other is about their permanence in Cartagena.

condolences, as others might for children whom they loved dearly. He would give them honorable funerals with candles and music and he would gather all of the *castas* of blacks together so that they could attend].[66] The music referenced here would likely have been sung polyphony at a funerary Mass or perhaps the Office of the Dead. Fernández remarks on Claver's expense on the funerals which would involve paying for candles and musicians (or using the school's enslaved musicians such as Sacabuche and Simón Biafara). Furthermore, the account suggests that the interpreters' value to the priest extended beyond their utility to the Jesuit mission because even in death Claver and the city's black population celebrated and remembered them. This honor not only would have promoted more respect for the surviving interpreters, but also could have reflected and encouraged the construction of a sense of community around the interpreters among "todas las castas de los Negros" [all of the blacks' *castas*] in Cartagena.[67]

PIVOTS AND TENSIONS

Despite the descriptions across the corpus of texts of the Jesuits' good treatment of their interpreters, expressions of the interpreters' frustration with their superiors also occasionally appear. These moments offer glimpses into some ways the linguistic intermediaries might have regularly clashed with the intentions of the supervising priests. Sandoval describes some of the interpreters' frustrations in anecdotes he gives to prepare priests for the many difficulties involved in evangelizing newly arrived enslaved black men and women. He warns his readers that:

dado que se hallen, no quieren catechizar sino tales y tales dias a tales y tales tiempos; a sanos y no a enfermos, temiendo con razon sus enfermedades contagiosas; no quieren yr lexos sino cerca, y si es lexos dan muy de ordinario cantonada, como dicen, a la mitad del camino, hallandose el Padre burlado cuando llega a ella, y obligado a buscar otra.

---

[66] Fernández, *Apostolica y penitente vida*, 170.

[67] See Vince Brown, *The Reaper's Garden: Death and Power in the World of Atlantic Slavery* (Cambridge, MA: Harvard University Press, 2008), on New World communities formed on occasion of a death in the diaspora. Black confraternities in Cartagena are referenced in Jesuit *cartas anuas* from this period but only appear indirectly in *Proceso 1676* when Ignacio Angola describes the "essequie" [funeral rites] performed for Claver, which were attended by "tutti li capitani e principali offitiali" [all the captains and principal officials] of all of "le nationi delli mori" [the black *naciones*] (140r). Such confraternities could have helped contribute funds for the interpreters' funerary expenses.

[even if you find them, they do not want to catechize on certain days, but rather on others, and at such and such times, for healthy people and not the sick, fearing with good reason their contagious maladies; they do not want to go far away, but rather prefer to stay close by, and if it is very far, often they will have a change of heart, as they say, in the middle of the road, leaving the father teased when he arrives and obliged to search for another interpreter.][68]

Sandoval prepares priests for these frustrations, reminding them that interpreters often demand working conditions that will not cause them discomfort, sickness, or inconvenience. While he does not suggest these demands are threats to the mission itself, Sandoval's comments index the possibility that black interpreters regularly employed the scenes of evangelical linguistic translation to address their own needs.

This possibility becomes even more salient in what continues of the passage where Sandoval warns that interpreters sometimes even interrupt the catechetical sessions to voice their disapproval or express their exhaustion with the process:

otras vezes se cansan y enfadan a medio catechismo, pareciendoles que basta lo dicho; haziendo instancia al Padre que bueno està, que le heche el agua, y si no condesciende con su parecer, lo cual no es possible, se van; siendo fuerça bolver a buscar otra para acabarle, con nuevo trabajo y riesgo del enfermo.

[other times, the interpreters grow tired and annoyed in the middle of the catechism, believing what has been said is enough, insisting to the father that the catechism is complete, that he should just pour the water on them; and if the father does not consent to their conviction, which would be impossible, they leave, forcing the father to search again for another interpreter to finish the catechism, creating more work [for the priest] and risk for the sick man.][69]

As in the earlier examples, Sandoval does not acknowledge that the interpreters' unwillingness could ever interfere with orthodox evangelization. In fact, Sandoval responds gingerly to the dissonance introduced by the disgruntled interpreters by proposing that priests resolve these issues by merely remembering to give special care to these language specialists and substituting unwilling interpreters with willing ones.

More tangible descriptions of these frustrations appear in Andrés Sacabuche's testimony. In it, Sacabuche details with exasperation Claver's habit of displaying extreme poverty and humility during their missions to the countryside:

---

[68] Sandoval, *Naturaleza, policia sagrada*, book 3, chap. 9, 271r–v.   [69] Ibid., 271v.

quando arrivava à qualche villa si posava nella cameretta o stanza del moro più povero e separato dall'altri, e se vi n'era alchuna abbandonata, e che non habitasse alchuno in quella per essere vecchia, e scommoda, in quella si accomodava, e diceva che stava molto bene, e questo Testimonio li dispiaceva perche solevano stare d'ordinario molto sporche, et era necessario che la scopassero et accomodassero, et acciò non li dispiacesse tanto, molte volte il detto Padre lo agiutava à scopare detta stanza, e la causa principale del dispiacere di questo Testimonio era, come hà detto, perche il detto Padre allogiandosi nella casa o stantiole delli Spagnuoli che la tenevano limpida, scopata, et ornata [*sic*], gli toglierebbe il detto travaglio, ma esso non lo voleva fare per mostrarsi povero in tutto e perfetto seguace della somma povertà.

[when Father Claver would arrive in a village he would accommodate himself in small room or living space of the poorest and most isolated black person; and if there was an abandoned room that no one lived in because it was old and uncomfortable, he would accommodate himself there, and he would say that he felt very good there. This witness was sorry for this because these rooms tended to be very dirty and it was necessary to sweep and organize them. To not bother this witness so much, often the father himself would help him sweep the room. The principal cause for the displeasure of this witness was that, as he has said, if the father stayed in a house or rooms of the Spaniards who kept them clean, swept, and decorated, it would avoid this witness this work. But the father did not want to do it to show himself to be poor in everything and a perfect follower of extreme poverty.][70]

Sacabuche confesses that Claver's wish to appear humble often caused Sacabuche to perform what he considered unnecessary extra labor. The account's realism interrupts the idyllic register of the hagiographic genre, even inviting some measure of skepticism about Claver's piety. The content of Sacabuche's statement does not condone Claver's humility, but rather shows a rarely visible perspective of a servant annoyed by his superior's requests. That Claver would sometimes attempt to assist Sacabuche in cleaning the dismal spaces does not seem to alleviate Sacabuche's annoyance for the description of his frustration continues even after mentioning Claver's willingness to help. This anecdote from Sacabuche's testimony suggests some of the possible dissonances between the intentions of the interpreters and those of the priests in evangelizing black new arrivals. That is, the interpreters did not necessarily share the same ultimate objectives and priorities as their supervising priests.

Fernández's *Apostolica y penitente vida* accentuates this possibility by describing Claver's suffering at the hands of his interpreters. Paraphrasing Nicolás González's testimony from the beatification inquest, Fernández explains that one of Claver's interpreters constantly "tyrannized" Claver

---

[70] *Proceso* 1676, Sacabuche, 100v.

with verbal injuries. Fernández claims that Claver would silently seek out these insults as an act of humility:

Sobre todas las fineças, que hacia con ellos, era la de sufrirlos, porque abusando de la blandura de su amor, le dieron mucho a padecer. Uno especialmente de condicion arrebatada le exercitò como tirano a un Martir. A este hacia mas frecuente recúrso el V. Padre, en busca de oprobios, y mortificaciones, a pretexto de valerse de èl en algunas haciendas. De verle tan sufrido tomava motivo aquel ombre barbaro para ser mas cruel; pareciendole que con el silencio a sus demasias, se las calificava de razon. Sus atrevimientos no entibiaron el amor de el P. Claver, porque le amava sobre las injurias.... Obligavale a esto a mas de su paciencia ambrienta siempre de trabajos, el zelo de las almas; y porque aquel, y otros interpretes eran utiles en la salvacion de muchas; aun ofendido de ellos no podia dexar de amarlos.

[Above all the graces Claver showed his interpreters, his greatest was that of putting up with them, because they would take advantage of the softness of his love and give him much cause to suffer. One interpreter in particular, who had an aggressive temper, abused him as a tyrant to a martyr. The venerable father would turn to him frequently, in search of insults and mortification, with the pretext of using him in some of the haciendas [as an interpreter]. Seeing Claver suffer gave that barbarous man motive to be even crueler, perceiving that Claver's silent response to his insolence confirmed its veracity. Yet the interpreter's impudence did not cool the love Father Claver had for him which persisted despite the insults.... Claver was obliged to do so because of his zeal for saving souls, which was even stronger than his penitent hunger to suffer. Because this interpreter and the others were useful in the salvation of many souls, even if he felt insulted, he could not stop loving them.][71]

Fernández frames this story as an example of Claver's dedication to the mission of black evangelization and his capacity for penance and unconditional love. Yet reading the details of the passage beyond the hagiographical frame reveals the impressive phenomenon that Claver's enslaved black interpreter repeatedly insulted his superior and made demands on him without punishment. Though Fernández does not explain what kind of insults the interpreter would use to injure Claver, or the potential motives he had for doing so, the passage nonetheless evidences conflict between the Jesuit father and his interpreters. It also suggests the priests' continued dependence on these interpreters for the mission even in circumstances in which the interpreters had expressed explicit hostility toward the supervising priest.

The account from which Fernández drew the above anecdote in fact attests that when Claver became sick at the end of his life, his interpreters

---

[71] Fernández, *Apostolica y penitente vida*, 170–71.

did not show Claver much courtesy: "in luogo di assistere à servirlo con amore, e carità, li davano molte occasioni di meritare con [*sic*] le loro trascuratezze, e poca carità, che esercitavano con lui" [Instead of helping him with love and charity, they gave him many occasions to suffer with the negligence and little charity that they would show him].[72] In particular, Nicolás González's testimony relates, Claver was frequently abandoned and mistreated by interpreter Manuel Moreno: "pareva cosa mirabile à questo Testimonio, che il detto Padre volesse che il detto moro solo l'aiutasse à alzare, poiche lo faceva strapazzandolo, e maltrattandolo, come lo vidde molte volte, e li causò gran compassione, e cordoglio" [It seemed a thing of wonder to this witness that this father would want only the aforementioned black man to help him stand up because he would do it by handling him roughly and mistreating him, as he witnessed many times. It caused this witness great compassion and grief].[73] Like Fernández's anecdote, González's testimony frames the account of Claver's abuse by his interpreters to highlight the priest's patience, humility, and dedication to self-sacrifice. Such conflicts with and demands made by the interpreters also index the negotiated social space of the Jesuit mission in which interpreters were not always compliant. These passages call into question the Jesuit insistence on the transparency of religious translation and the seamless spiritual conversions of black men and women in Cartagena that it achieved.

COLLUSION AND CONFLICT AMONG NEW ARRIVALS

While it is possible that the special treatment that Jesuits afforded their black interpreters fostered resentment, mistrust, or jealousy among other black men and women in Cartagena, I have found no evidence for exploring such possibilities. We do have evidence, however, to reflect on black new arrivals' recourse to the interpreters to request help or otherwise improve their living conditions in Cartagena. Sometimes newly arrived black men and women turned to their interpreters to help achieve personal or collective gains that would have otherwise been unattainable.

Other than the food, water, medical attention, and emotional consolation administered by the interpreters to the new arrivals on the slave ships and in the barracoons where they were temporarily housed after disembarking in Cartagena, one of the goods most often solicited by the new

---

[72] *Proceso* 1676, Nicolás González, 62v.   [73] Ibid.

arrivals through their interpreters were the aforementioned medals that interpreters made at the Jesuit school and would tie around the neck of the newly baptized.[74] Sandoval in fact has to warn priests to be careful not to baptize black men and women more than once because they want more medals. To resolve this problem, Sandoval offers an alternative way for already baptized men and women to acquire more:

el Padre se las reparte a todos, con condicion que cada uno le diga primero su nombre, para que le tengan siempre en promptu, y assi sabiendo ellos y a esto, lo primero que hazen es dezir su nombre a bozes con la medalla en la mano cuando quieren se les dé otra; con lo qual quedan tan contentos como si les diessen un tesoro, y sin duda lo deven de reconocer a su modo por tal, como realmente es, pues tanto lo estiman.

[the father should give out new medals to everyone, under the condition that they first say their Christian name so that they have it always in mind. Because they learn this strategy, the first thing they do is yell out their name with the medal in their hand when they want to be given a new one. With this they are left as happy as if they were given a treasure, and undoubtedly they must recognize it as such in their own way, as it truly is, for they esteem it so much.][75]

Sandoval does not explicitly mention the intercession of interpreters here, highlighting instead the black captives' use of signs and their names to make their requests. Yet, we should ask, how else than through interpreters would new arrivals have learned what the medals were and how to acquire more of them?

In addition to seeking out food, water, medical attention, and medals, newly arrived black men and women appear throughout the corpus making appeals to Jesuit priests through the interpreters for protection from abusive owners or intercession to clarify a misunderstanding with their owners. Examples of these successful demands appear in passages promoting Claver's generosity in *Proceso 1676,* demonstrating the non-spiritual functions evangelization served for the black catechumens. For example, Isabel Folupa, a thirty-eight-year-old enslaved black woman who was not an interpreter but who nonetheless testifies in the *Proceso,* describes having known Claver since her own arrival in Cartagena almost thirty years before. She remembers the name of the interpreter who helped baptize her (Juan Primero Folupo) and then describes the advocacy and protection Claver provided her and other captive black men and women when they had conflicts with their owners:

---

[74] Sandoval, *Naturaleza, policia sagrada,* book 3, chap. 12, 284v–285r.   [75] Ibid., 285v.

era la general diffesa e reffuggio di tutti li mori e more al quale ricorrevano in tutti li loro travagli a chiederli consolatione et aiuto, et esso glielo dava non solo di parole consolandoli et animandoli molto, con fervorose essortationi mà anco con l'opere parlando per quelli alli loro Padroni, e chiedendo con preghiere che non li castigassero ne molestassero superfluamente.

[Claver served as the general defense and refuge for all black men and women. They would turn to him in all of their suffering in search of consolation and help. And he not only consoled them through words with such fervent exhortations, comforting and helping them greatly, but he also did so through action, speaking with their owners to whom he pleaded that they not punish or bother them superfluously.][76]

Although the intercession of Juan Primero Folupo is not explicit in Isabel's testimony as the means of accessing Claver's comprehension and intercession, we know from context that the black interpreters would have been the primary mediators of these exchanges until and perhaps even after the new arrivals learned Spanish. "Claver" in this anecdote thus serves as a metonym for the combination of Claver and his interpreters.

An example of one of these conflicts between slave and master that were resolved through a new arrival's recourse to the black interpreter and Jesuit priest appears in Sandoval's treatise. Sandoval describes an enslaved man's attempt to turn to him (through an implicitly present interpreter) to contradict the word of his master regarding the enslaved man's status as a baptized Christian:

Queriendo una vez baptizar a un negro que me dezia no lo estava, llamè a su amo para ver que razon daba de aquello, y si ambos convenian en lo mismo; el cual informado respondio, que el negro se engañava, porque el mismo lo avia llevado y vistole baptizar (quien con esto no creyera, y aun también se engañara), *di esta respuesta al negro, y contradixola con tan evidente razon y solucion que a todos convencio, y a su mismo amo, que tan constante estava contradiziendo a su esclavo.*

[Wanting to baptize a black man who said he was not yet baptized, I called on his owner to see what reason he gave for it and if their stories concurred; the owner, once informed, responded that the black man was incorrect because he himself had taken him and seen him be baptized. (Who would doubt the owner's claim according to this evidence? And even so, the owner was incorrect). *I gave this response to the black man and he contradicted it with such clear reason and remedy that he convinced us all, even his own owner who had been so firm in contradicting his slave.*][77]

---

[76] *Proceso* 1676, Isabel Folupa, 166r.
[77] Sandoval, *Naturaleza, policia sagrada*, book 3, chap. 3, 238v; my emphasis.

In the account the enslaved man gives to Sandoval through the interpreter, the man strategically acknowledges and reinterprets the signs and
evidence his master provided to deny his request for baptism:

Dixo que era verdad que su amo le avia llevado con los demas sus compañeros en
una canoa pequeña (era esta la principal seña del fundamento del amo) al Padre
para que a todos les echara el agua: pero que a el no se la avia hechado; porque
cuando el estava en su tierra le había dicho el Iangomao [sic] que le tenía en
guarda y prisión, que se llamasse Miguel cuando le baptizassen, y que assi
queriendole el Padre baptizar, como lo hizo a los demas sus compañeros, le
pregunto como se llamaba, porque algunos suelen estar ya baptizados, y como
no saben declararse conocelos el Padre por el nombre, o del toma indicacion para
investigarlo, y como respondi (dixo) Miguel, el Padre entonces replicò y me dixo,
pues te llamas Miguel ya eres Christiano, y me apartó con la priessa que estava y
mi amo dava para embarcarnos, sin echarme agua; y concluyó diciendo no estaba
Christiano, si el serlo consistia en echarle agua, dixese o no dixese su amo, que
estaba presente cuanto quisiesse, con esto le bapticé, viendo que el amo desde
entonces empezo a dudar, pareciendole ser muy verisimil lo que su esclavo dezia.

[The man said that it was true that his owner had taken him with his other
companions in a small canoe (this was the principal claim of the owner) to the
priest so that he would pour water on them all: but [the priest] did not pour it on
him because when the enslaved man was still in his own land the Tangomao that
had him under his charge and captivity told him that his name would be Miguel
when baptized, and so when the father wanted to baptize him as he did his other
companions, he asked him his name because some are already baptized, and as
they cannot explain themselves the father distinguishes them by their name or uses
it as indication to investigate it. Because I responded Miguel (he said), the father
then replied and said to me, well, your name is Miguel, you are already a
Christian, and he set me aside in haste without pouring the water on me, and
my owner was ready to leave. Miguel concluded saying that he was not Christian
if being Christian consisted in pouring water on him, no matter what his owner
says, no matter how much he claims he was present. After this story, I baptized
him, seeing that the owner had begun to doubt himself, perceiving that what his
slave had said was very possible.][78]

Miguel's reported testimony offers a version of his biography that differs
from the one insisted on by his master. This alternative version by Miguel,
whom Sandoval calls a *bozal*, could be voiced only through recourse to
the implicitly present interpreter(s). In particular, Sandoval's account
shows Miguel and/or his interpreter(s) recognizing the requirements of
an authentic Christian conversion to forge a strategic alliance with
Sandoval that ultimately helped Miguel contest his master. Miguel,

[77] Sandoval, *Naturaleza, policia sagrada*, book 3, chap. 3, 238v; my emphasis.
[78] Ibid., 238v–239r.

according to the anecdote, employed the black interpreter(s) and the priest as resources to shape his own identity.

In addition to accessing Jesuit assistance to intervene in conflicts with their owners, black men and women appear to have turned to the interpreters for emotional consolation or other forms of protection. One of the ways they did so was through choosing interpreters as godparents. Numerous accounts in *Proceso 1676* describe the dual role the interpreters served as evangelical assistants and godparents for newly baptized black men and women.[79] Stephen Gudeman's and Stuart Schwartz's analysis of the uses of godparentage among enslaved black men and women in eighteenth-century Brazil suggest that black men and women in colonial Brazil typically picked figures of authority or superiors in rank (i.e., non-enslaved blacks or whites) to be godparents. Employing that logic to analyze these earlier anecdotes from Cartagena would suggest that newly arrived black men and women in Cartagena chose their interpreters as godparents because they recognized them as figures of authority who could offer them certain forms of protection or emotional comfort. An example of the protective role an interpreter conceived of himself as playing for a newly arrived captive as a godparent appears in interpreter Francisco Yolofo's testimony in *Proceso 1676* about serving as a godfather for a mortally ill black captive at his baptism: "questo Testimonio fù suo compare ..., e volendosene venire il detto Padre à questo Colleggio, il detto Infermo chiedè che li lasciasse questo Testimonio in compagnia per sua consolatione et il Padre disse che si, che si rimanesse" [this witness became the man's godfather ... upon the father's departure to the Jesuit school, the sick man asked if this witness could stay with him to serve as his consolation; the father agreed, and said he could stay].[80] Yolofo, as both godfather and interpreter, describes comforting the dying convert on his deathbed, evidencing that black captives being evangelized could make successful demands for additional care through their interpreters. Sometimes new arrivals' demands were precisely to receive more care from their interpreters.

Although scenes of translation and conversion among black catechumens in these texts always resolve harmoniously, some of the tensions

---

[79] *Proceso 1676*, Diego Folupo, 174r. See Stephen Gudeman and Stuart Schwartz, "Cleansing Original Sin: Godparenthood and the Baptism of Slaves in Eighteenth-Century Bahia," in *Kinship Ideology and Practice in Latin America*, ed. R. T. Smith (Chapel Hill: University of North Carolina Press, 1984).

[80] *Proceso 1676*, Francisco Yolofo, 177r.

that manifest before their resolutions provide evidence for speculation about the conflicts that might have persisted between the interpreters and the new arrivals or among the new arrivals themselves. The following example from Sandoval's treatise, for instance, describes a Nalu woman in Cartagena demanding to be baptized even though her assigned interpreter does not think she has understood the catechism. Sandoval explains, admiring the Nalu woman's intelligence, how the woman took it upon herself to find another interpreter to represent her case. This story of maneuvering, negotiation, and broken alliances appears as an example to support Sandoval's argument in book 3, chapter 3, that blacks are "rational humans," worthy of being baptized:

No es animal en verdad la negra bozal de Casta Nalu, a quien aviendola apartado por tres vezes del catechismo con que la disponia para el baptismo, por no entenderla el interprete, aunque ella a lo que despues parecio le entendia a el; viendose ya de rodillas cuarta vez en las ultimas preguntas, que son como la piedra del toque para echarles el agua: *con el desseo que tenia de recebirla no huvo orden ni traça de querer que la hablasse alli otro, que una compañera suya tambien bozal, con quien bien se entendia, y tambien la entendia el interprete*, por cuyo medio vendria a entender dando la razon, que no queria me enojasse, viendo que no respondia, y la apartasse del catechismo como las otras vezes sin echarle el agua de Dios.

[The black *bozal* woman of the Nalu *casta* is truly not an animal, for after I had left her out for the third time from the catechism, the prelude to the baptism, because the interpreter did not understand her even though it later appeared that she understood him. Seeing herself again on her knees during the last questions of the catechism, which are like the touchstone used to discern whether the water should be poured over them or not, *with the desire she had to receive the baptism, there was no way anyone else could speak at that moment but a friend of hers who was also a bozal, whom she did understand and who also understood the interpreter.* Through this means, I would come to learn the reason for the altercation: she did not want to anger me, seeing that she did not respond and then setting her apart from the catechism as I had in the other occasions, without pouring the water of God over her.][81]

Sandoval's anecdote highlights a moment in which the Nalu woman rejects both the priest's and her assigned interpreter's intentions. When Sandoval admits that "no huvo orden ni traça de querer que la hablasse alli otro que una compañera suya" [there was no way anyone else could speak at that moment but a friend of hers], he acknowledges a suspension of his own capacity to speak and that of the interpreter by the Nalu woman's insistence. As the passage continues, it shows that the Nalu woman found a friend to serve as a new interpreter to speak on her

---

[81] Sandoval, *Naturaleza, policia sagrada*, book 3, chap. 3, 241r; my emphasis.

behalf. Sandoval concludes the account by summarizing the lesson the exchange had taught him for future catechisms:

con el cual medio me enseño lo que desde el principio yo avia de aver hecho; y me dió regla y metodo para lo que en semejantes casos devia en adelante de hazer, y tambien se pudo baptizar con gran satisfacion; y quedò tan alegre y contenta, que no cabia de gozo, andandose tras los catechismos de sus compañeras, para dezirles a escondidas lo que avian de dezir y responder, porque no se viessen en la confusion y aflicion que se viò ella.

[This taught me what I should have done from the start and thus gave me a rule and a method for what to do in similar cases in the future [to allow *bozales* to serve as intermediary interpreters for other *bozales*]. She was baptized to her great satisfaction, making her happy and content. Bursting with pleasure, she would then go about the catechisms of her friends, to tell them secretly what they were to say and respond, so they would not find themselves in the confusion and affliction she had experienced.][82]

Sandoval ascribes only the most innocent intentions to the fact that after the woman's baptism she continually attended the catechisms of her friends, whispering her own secret translations. In fact, Sandoval considers this story such an example of success that he not only allows the Nalu woman to convert and to accompany other catechisms as a supplementary interpreter, but also decides that it should be a model for future catechisms where he would allow *bozales* to interpret for other *bozales*. Sandoval's faith in this woman's sincerity begs crucial questions regarding what she was actually saying as she imposed herself as an interpreter for other catechisms and what kind of relationships were being formed and broken among the women in those inaudible conversations.

The aforementioned examples demonstrate some of the ways that black Christian conversion through black interpreters could function as an opportunity for black men and women in Cartagena to access care, goods, and opportunities otherwise denied to them. Not only were the black interpreters able to appeal for better treatment; but in turning to black interpreters as avenues of protection and communication, black new arrivals repurposed the Jesuit mission for their own ends.

BEYOND THE JESUIT MISSION

The influence, advocacy, and the participation of the black interpreters in the Jesuit mission should not be overgeneralized or stretched to suggest

[82] Ibid., 241r–v.

that the interpreters were expressly critical of the Jesuit mission or the Spanish colonial project in Cartagena. Whereas some have speculated that Claver's black interpreters helped black individuals accused of witchcraft in Cartagena receive more favorable sentencing than others accused of similar crimes who did not receive their assistance, the available evidence about the black interpreters in Inquisition cases is too sparse to explore this question well.[83] Mentions of the black interpreters' assistance in Inquisition cases appear only briefly in a few trial summaries. In contrast, the appearance of Andrés Sacabuche as an interpreter in a criminal trial proceeding against recaptured maroons from 1634 warns against characterizations of the interpreters as expressly critical of the Jesuit mission or the Spanish colonial project in Cartagena.

The criminal trial transcripts produced after the Cartagena city council funded a series of raids on several maroon settlements (*palenques*) around Cartagena in 1633 indicate that Andrés Sacabuche served as an interpreter for two Anchico men captured in the raids.[84] Unlike the Inquisition sources, the complete testimonies of these two men given through Sacabuche's assistance survive. In their testimonies, Sebastián Anchico and Domingo Anchico claim that they were involuntary maroons. They were first kidnapped and taken to the Palenque de Polín; then when the Palenque de Polín was raided by the Palenque de Limón, they became captives of the Palenque de Limón. Other witnesses in the dossier, however, claim that Sebastián and Domingo men were in fact leaders of the Palenque de Polín and not its kidnapped slaves. Despite their claims to innocence delivered through Andrés Sacabuche, Sebastián and Domingo were found guilty of *lesa majestad* and executed with four other recaptured maroons the day after their testimonies.[85]

---

[83] Anna María Splendiani, José Enrique Sánchez Bohórquez, and Emma Cecilia Luque de Salazar, *Cincuenta años de inquisición en el Tribunal de Cartagena de Indias 1610–1660*, vol. 1 (Bogota: Centro editorial Javeriano, Instituto Colombiano de Cultura Hispánica, 1997), 145.

[84] "Declaración de Domingo Anchico" "Declaración de Sebastián Anchico," January 23, 1634, AGI, Patronato 234, R. 7, no. 2, 319–329. See note 26.

[85] For studies on the *palenque* dossier of 1634, see Kathryn Joy McKnight, "Elder, Slave, and Soldier: Maroon Voices from the Palenque del Limón (1634)," in *Afro-Latino Voices*, ed. Kathryn Joy McKnight and Leo Garofalo (Indianapolis, IN: Hackett, 2009), 64–81; McKnight, "Confronted Rituals: Spanish Colonial and Angolan 'Maroon' Executions in Cartagena de Indias (1634)," *Journal of Colonialism and Colonial History* 5, no. 3 (2004); McKnight, "Gendered Declarations: Three Enslaved Women Testify before Cartagena Officials (1634)," *Colonial Latin American Historical Review* 12, no. 4 (2003): 499–527; Jessica Krug, *Fugitive Modernities*, 111–45; María Cristina Navarrete, "El palenque de Limón (Cartagena de Indias, siglo XVII): El Imaginario del poder y sus

The transcripts from the criminal trials suggest that rather than help the accused, Sacabuche's participation in the trial actually served to legitimize the executions that followed and shape the narrative colonial authorities wanted to tell through the executions. I base this argument on my reading of the proceedings in light of the comments made three months before the raids by Cartagena city council members (*cabildo* members) about the urgent need to attack the *palenques* to enact exemplary punishment on them to avoid more instances of slave insurrection and insubordination allegedly spreading across the city and surrounding areas. A city council member remarks, for example, that funding military attacks on the *palenques* is necessary because of the "notorious" freedom of the maroons among the city's black populations:

es notoria la libertad con que los negros fugitivos cimarrones andan quemando y destruyendo las estançias cogiendo los negros dellas ya de fuerça ya de grado para con mas fuerça rresistirse y hacer los daños que an comensado con que los negros de las estançias y del ceruiçio de los beçinos desta çiudad no estan seguros y ellos casi lebantados de pensamiento y a la mira del efeto desto para huirse o quedarse y es tan presisa y necesaria [la intervención militar] qve no quiere punto de dilaçion porque ya bemos los daños de muertes y rrouos que an enpesado a hacer.

[The freedom is notorious with which these fugitive maroons go about burning and destroying plantations and capturing blacks – some unwillingly some willingly – with whom they can resist with greater force and cause damages like those that have begun. Because of this, the black slaves on plantations and service slaves in this city are not safe; they are almost rebelled in thought; they are waiting to see what happens so as to flee or stay. [Military intervention] is so urgent and necessary that it must not be delayed because we can already see the deaths and thefts that they have begun to carry out.][86]

The *cabildo* member's declaration underscores the symbolic and tangible meaning of the maroons' freedom that he perceives has the area's slaves "casi lebantados de pensamiento" [almost rebelled in thought]. The principal goal he identifies for funding the military attacks is publicly and

---

jerarquias," in *Visicitudes negro africanas en iberoamerica: Experiencias de investigación*, ed. Juan Manuel de la Serna Herrera (Mexico: UNAM, 2011), 101–34; Enriqueta Vila Vilar, "Cimarronaje en Panamá y Cartagena: Es costo de una guerrilla en el siglo XVII," *Caravelle* 49 (1987): 77–92; Hélène Vignaux, "Palenque de Limón: ¿Subversión o sumisión? Un caso de cimarronaje en el Nuevo Reino de Granada," *Memoria* 7 (2000): 30–57; Brewer-García, "The Agency of Translation."

[86] Lorenço Ramires de Alrellano in "Testimonio del libro del cabildo sobre los cimarrones," September 14, 1633, AGI, Patronato 234, R. 7, no. 2, 16r–26v, 21v.

exemplarily punishing the maroons to discourage the spread of such dangerous ideas. A secondary goal is to recapture and resell the inhabitants of the *palenques* to reimburse the owners' lost property and the city council members' investment in paying for the soldiers to raid the communities.

Using an interpreter in the pageantry of the trials, executions, and reselling of the other recaptured maroons from those military attacks would have helped produce a more convincing perception of the guilt of those who were captured. In fact, as early modern notions of criminal justice suggest, in order for the deterrent effect of punishment to work (an effect referenced as *escarmiento*), the audience of the punishment needs to believe that those punished are indeed guilty of the crime for which they are being punished.[87] In the Cartagena *palenque* trials of 1634, using an interpreter to take the declarations of individuals preselected for public execution provided the appearance of due process to legitimize the violence Cartagena authorities were planning to enact on the recaptured maroons' bodies.[88]

Furthermore, making Sacabuche a witness to the trial as its interpreter would have served as a means of publicizing it among the black populations of the city and surrounding areas, especially among the black men and women owned by the Jesuits. As shown throughout *Proceso 1676*, it was well known among the Jesuits and other prominent inhabitants of Cartagena that Sacabuche and his interpreter colleagues communicated messages broadly among the black men and women of the city and provincial areas as well as the new arrivals who would continue to arrive in Cartagena. It is likely that communicating the story of the capture, trial, and punishment to slaves owned by the Jesuit order was seen as particularly urgent by city authorities as nine black slaves had recently abandoned a Jesuit hacienda near Cartagena in what was perceived as a

---

[87] See Covarrubias's definition of "escarmiento" [punishment]: "la advertencia y recato de no errar por no incurrir en la pena, ejecutada en otros" [the warning and caution to not err to avoid a punishment carried out on others] (1611, I: 364r). The underlying premise of this definition is that the person being punished is guilty of the crime.

[88] A comparison can be made to the critique of procedural safeguards in Naomi Murakawa, *First Civil Right: How Liberals Built Prison America* (New York: Oxford University Press, 2014), which argues that instead of mitigating the racist effects of the criminal justice system, liberal procedural safeguards adopted in the United States in the middle of the twentieth century actually gave the biases of the criminal justice system a heightened appearance of legality.

plan to join a *palenque*.[89] By having him participate in the trial as an interpreter, Sacabuche could have been expected to circulate the story of the capture, trial, and punishment among the broader population of black men and women in the city and surrounding areas. Translation, in this context, functioned to avoid future instantiations of the notorious freedom referenced in the Cartagena *cabildo* minutes from September 1633, not as a means of mitigating or contesting colonial hierarchies or the Spanish colonial project in Cartagena.

While Sacabuche does not comment on his participation in the criminal trials in his testimony in *Proceso 1676*, accounts of his and his colleagues' participation in providing spiritual consolation to those condemned to execution in the trials do appear. According to interpreter Diego Folupo, for example, Sacabuche helped catechize and baptize at least one escaped slave who was condemned to death in the maroon trials of 1634.[90] Francisco Yolofo, for his part, remembers helping Claver confess and provide consolation to a group of six men from these raids:

si offeri [*sic*] che il detto P. Pietro Claver havesse da confessare un moro che stava carcerato nella carcere publica di questa Città e condannato a morte per crassatore famoso ..., il quale si chiamava Giovanni Jolofo, e non potendo il detto Padre confessarlo senza l'Interprete, trovò questo Testimonio per sapere la Lingua Porthogese [*sic*] e lo condusse seco alla detta carcere, acciò li servisse d'Interprete e questo Testimonio lo fece et il detto Padre assistè al detto giustitiato et ad altri cinque compagni suoi li quali erano parimente sententiati a morire tutto il tempo che stiedero nella detta carcere e gli [*sic*] accompagnò per le strade publiche quando li cavarono à giustitiare e non li abbandonò consolandoli con le sue ammonitioni e sante essortationi fino che li appiccorno nella piazza di questa Città la quale chiamano dell'herba.

[It was offered that Father Pedro Claver would confess a black man who was encarcerated in the public jail of this city and condemned to death for being a famous criminal ..., whose name was Juan Yolofo. And because the said father could not confess him without an interpreter, he found this witness because he knew Portuguese and he took him with him to the said jail to serve him as the interpreter, and this witness did so. And the father assisted the said condemned man and his five other companions who were also sentenced to death throughout the entire time that they were in the jail and he accompanied them through the

---

[89] "Auto de Francisco de Murga," January 3, 1634, AGI, Patronato 234, R. 7, no. 2, 7r–8v, 7v.

[90] *Proceso 1676*, Diego Folupo, 176r. The maroon whom Andrés Sacabuche helped baptize before his death was different from Domingo and Sebastián Anchico, who claimed to be already baptized in their testimonies.

public streets when they took them out to execute them. Father Claver did not abandon them, but rather consoled them with his admonitions and saintly exhortations until they were hanged in the plaza of this city that they call La Yerba.][91]

The interpreters (indexed almost entirely in reference to Claver in the passages above) appear as facilitators of the condemned's spiritual redemption on their death. It is hard to know, from available evidence, what the interpreters thought of their roles in this economy of spiritual salvation or the violence enacted by the city authorities to prevent future instantiations of marronage. We do learn from *Proceso 1676*, however, that the interpreters were instrumental not only in helping convert and confess those condemned to death but also in playing music for the funerary services the Jesuit school would hold for the souls of those killed in such exemplary punishments.[92] As the Jesuit school's trombone player, Andrés Sacabuche could have played in the services held for Domingo Anchico and Sebastián Anchico after their deaths. Some scholars have commented on the visual display of the severed body parts of the punished, recaptured maroons as demonstrations of power by the city property owners over disobedient black bodies. The funerary services held for the same individuals after their executions invite speculation about other ways the memories of the deceased and their supposed crimes were invoked in the city.

CONCLUSION

By acting as the greeting and farewell committees, the voice of Christian doctrine, means of regular communication with the Church, occasional mediators in Inquisitorial and criminal trials, eleventh-hour confessors and consolers for those condemned to death, and musicians who would play music for funerary services for executed black maroons, the interpreters appear in these documents occupying roles that far surpass those of the invisible anonymous language assistants explicitly claimed by Sandoval and the other Jesuit authors and editors shaping the texts of this corpus. The interpreters' authority and multivalent roles in the Jesuit project in Cartagena might have ultimately fit within the larger story of

[91] *Proceso 1676*, Francisco Yolofo, 177r. This group of men do not form part of the twelve condemned in the trials transcribed in the dossier. It is possible they were part of a third maroon community identified as Zanaguare in the dossier that was supposedly razed in 1633–34 but about which little information appears in the Patronato 234 dossier.

[92] *Proceso 1676*, Diego Folupo, 175v–176r; Sacabuche, 107v; Ignacio Angola, 138v–139r.

the consolidation of racial violence and racialized labor system in Cartagena, but the texts they helped produce nonetheless evidence that the interpreters used the Jesuit mission to access certain privileges despite their enslaved status and that they were important resources for newly arrived black men and women to do the same.

A significant body of scholarship has examined the existence of similar "middle grounds" created through missionary contact in the Americas with native populations.[93] One of the most relevant is Guillermo Wilde's *Religión y poder en las misiones guaraníes*, which analyzes Jesuit missionary negotiations from the sixteenth through the eighteenth centuries. Wilde's book argues that the Jesuit mission among the Guaraní often used accommodative practices that allowed indigenous groups to achieve extra-missionary goals through their interactions with Jesuit priests as a strategy of noncoercive conversion. He explains that another key strategy employed by the Jesuits was to evangelize new groups through first converting their leaders.[94] By assisting leaders (and their constituencies) in their worldly or political demands, Jesuits hoped to encourage them to actively and enthusiastically convert to Christianity. Some of the important distinctions between the Jesuit missions among the Guaraní examined by Wilde and Jesuit evangelical work among the black men and women of Cartagena relate to the fact that the black populations arriving in Cartagena were mostly enslaved, displaced, and separated from the social and political entities of their places of origin, which minimized their chances to collectively make demands or requests in their interactions with evangelizing priests. The black interpreters, as I have argued in this chapter, are an instance of a distinct approach taken by the Jesuits. In lieu of reaching black new arrivals through political leaders, the black interpreters served as surrogate representatives and means of communication through whom new arrivals could appeal for material goods, spiritual care, and some

---

[93] Guillermo Wilde, *Religión y poder en las misiones guaraníes* (Buenos Aires: SB, 2009); Richard White, *The Middle Ground: Indians, Empires, and Republics in the Great Lakes Region, 1650–1815* [1991] (New York: Cambridge University Press, 2011); David Block, *Mission Culture in the Upper Amazon: Native Tradition, Jesuit Enterprise, and Secular Policy in Moxos, 1660–1880* (Lincoln: University of Nebraska Press, 1994); Vilaça and Wright, *Native Christians: Modes and Effects of Christianity among Indigenous Peoples of the Americas* (Farnham: Ashgate, 2009); Paula Montero, "Índios e missionários no Brasil: Para uma teoria da mediação cultural," in *Deus na aldeia: Missionários, índios, e mediação cultural*, ed. Paula Montero (São Paolo: Globo, 2005), 31–66; Ronaldo de Almeida, "Tradução e mediação: Missões transculturais entre grupos indígenas," in *Deus na aldeia*, 277–304.

[94] Wilde notes that this strategy is a recommendation in Loyola's *Constitutiones*, 93–94.

measure of protection or improved conditions despite their enslavement. The interpreters, like the political and spiritual leaders of the Guaraní studied by Wilde, were able to use their intermediary position to make their own requests and advocate for the requests of the constituencies they were assumed to represent. Identifying instances of Jesuit accommodation through translation in a missionary setting such as Cartagena might not be surprising in the context of other Jesuit missionary work among indigenous populations in the Americas, but it is novel for scholarship on the African diaspora. The space of translation of the Jesuit mission in Cartagena allowed for black men and women to create certain kinship ties, appeal for better treatment, and (as I will show in the following chapter) influence the emergence of a common language about black virtue and black beauty tied to Christian conversion. In the post-Babelian conditions of Cartagena, a major port of the transatlantic and intracolonial slave trades, missionary translation contested some of the "natal alienation" and horrific conditions of the black men, women, and children who arrived in and passed through the city.

Anna Brickhouse analyzes the portrayal of captive indigenous interpreters in her study of Columbus's journeys to the Caribbean, indicating numerous instances where the native interpreters kidnapped by Columbus might have purposefully interrupted the admiral's attempts at successful discovery and settlement.[95] Like Brickhouse's approach, this chapter foregrounds the negotiations at work in moments of linguistic exchange that the authors or editors of colonial texts seek to push aside in favor of presenting linguistic translation as always transparent and the religious conversion it affords as always seamless. But whereas Brickhouse identifies explicit subversions of the European colonial project by interpreters in her sources, the sources examined here signal the existence of a much less dichotomous field of positioning between European priests and their African-born interpreters. While, every once in a while, we catch glimpses of the Jesuits' black interpreters' outright refusal to help or open hostility to their superiors' requests, most of the stories presented in this chapter describe black interpreters as complying with the intentions of their Jesuit superiors in their participation in the mission.

Through thus supporting the Jesuit mission, black interpreters of colonial Cartagena de Indias helped shape the mission's means and goals. One of ways the interpreters did so was by making their physical well-being a

---

[95] Brickhouse, "Mistranslation, Unsettlement, La Navidad," *PMLA* 128, no. 4 (2013): 938–46. See also Brickhouse, *The Unsettlement of America*, 17–45.

priority. Another important way was by providing an avenue for black new arrivals from Africa to communicate with priests and other authorities to affect the conditions of their own conversions. The following chapter will focus on how the interpreters used their prominent positions to influence the creation and circulation of notions of blackness as part of the Jesuit mission.

4

Conversion and the Making of Blackness in Colonial Cartagena de Indias

The previous chapter examined the visible and invisible roles given to and adapted by the black interpreters who assisted the Jesuit mission among black men and women in seventeenth-century Cartagena de Indias. The present chapter analyzes the language the interpreters helped produce about the spiritual and aesthetic dimensions of blackness in the distinct missionary scenarios they led. In identifying and parsing this language in the context of its delivery and comparing it with other writings and images about black Christian conversion from the early modern Iberian world, this chapter argues that black interpreters circulated discourse about black virtue and black beauty that is seldom seen in other Spanish or Spanish American texts. This discourse was created through translations of catechetical content, rituals, and supplemental descriptions of visual images for black new arrivals in Cartagena.

As discussed in the previous chapter, black interpreters led the catechetical sessions in African languages to the new arrivals soon after disembarking in the city. Whether or not a priest was present at the catechetical sessions, the messages shared in them were inaccessible to priests because they were conducted in languages the priests could not understand. As a result, the messages were not written down. By examining some of the scripts priests gave interpreters for these sessions as well as accounts of what some interpreters later *said* they communicated to new arrivals in African languages when they were asked by priests and city authorities about their work, this chapter outlines how the black interpreters in collaboration with black new arrivals crafted language to describe what it meant to become black Christians in Spanish America.

SCRIPTS

Several recommended scripts for the delivery of catechetical content through interpreters appear in Sandoval's 1627 treatise and *Proceso 1676*. Sandoval, for instance, explicitly outlines the tenets of the faith to be taught to unbaptized new arrivals in translation. According to Sandoval, the initial catechism for all newly arrived black men and women who were not already legitimate Christians should be structured around nine points: (1) the purpose of receiving baptismal water, (2) the sacred meaning of baptismal water, (3) the singularity and omnipotence of God, (4) the Holy Trinity, (5) the Immaculate Conception, (6) the existence of heaven and hell, (7) the purpose of Jesus's death, (8) the nature of sin as a violation of God's law, and (9) the immortality of the soul.[1]

The recommended language Sandoval gives to explain these ideas suggests that he asked interpreters to invoke their shared experiences of enslavement with the newly arrived catechumens as a point of reference for teaching Christian tenets in catechism sessions in African languages in Cartagena. Sandoval, for example, recommends that interpreters explain the transformation of a Christian baptism through two comparisons. The first compares the transformation of baptismal water to cleansing themselves of filth and the second compares it to the branding of their bodies. Tell them, Sandoval, explains, "con el agua que les han de echar, se an de bolver sus animas blãcas y limpiarse de los pecados, y [las animas] an de quedar señaladas por hijas de Dios: *assi como quedan señalados por esclavos de sus amos, con la señal y marca con que los hierren*" [with that water that will be poured on them, their souls will become white and cleansed of sin, and will be marked as children of God, *just as the sign and mark with which they are branded shows they are slaves of their masters*].[2] For the interpreters and the black catechumens who had experienced the Middle Passage and the branding of their bodies before and after arrival in Cartagena, such material and corporal explanations would have vividly invoked their own experiences of enslavement.[3] The first analogy associates Christian baptism with acquiring a cleanliness antithetical to the physical conditions of the two-month crossing of the

---

[1] Sandoval, *Naturaleza, policia sagrada*, book 3, chap. 10, 272v–276v.
[2] Ibid., 275r; my emphasis.
[3] On branding as a mark separating the legally traded slave from the contraband slave in Spanish America, see Bryant, *Rivers of Gold*, 75–79.

Atlantic Ocean. The second analogy communicates the permanence of the Christian transformation through reference to the branding of their flesh that marked their bodies as property. It is possible the allusion to branding was also useful because it imparted the connotation that the transformation was inevitable. Both analogies explain baptism by animating experiences related to enslavement the interpreters and the catechumens would have had in common.

Other examples of scripts given by Sandoval for the delivery of catechetical content to interpreters similarly recommend that interpreters make use of their shared experiences of the horrors of captivity and the Middle Passage to teach the promise of Christian salvation. For instance, to explain heaven, Sandoval suggests that interpreters describe it as a place "Donde no han de morir mas, sino estar contentos siempre con Dios, sin captiverio y sin enfermedad" [Where they will never die again but rather be forever happy with God, without captivity and without illness].[4] While there is a long rhetorical tradition, dating from the early Church, that associates Christian conversion with freedom from captivity, such analogies would have had particular relevance to the enslaved interpreters and the newly arrived black captives who were surrounded by sickness and held against their will in the houses that served as temporary barracoons where the captives were evangelized.[5] Heaven thus materializes in Sandoval's script as the antithesis of the emotional and physical experiences of captivity, experiences with which the interpreters and the new arrivals were only too familiar.

Sandoval's script suggests that he was adapting missionary instructions for catechizing in indigenous languages in the Andes for black evangelical labor in Cartagena. For example, the *proemio* to the *Tercero cathecismo y exposicion de la doctrina christiana*, a trilingual collection of sermons printed in Lima immediately after the *Doctrina christiana y catecismo para la instruccion de los indios* analyzed in Chapter 2, stresses that translated evangelical messages should be carefully accommodated to their audiences. Such accommodation, the *proemio* explains, involves

---

[4] Sandoval, *Naturaleza, policia sagrada*, book 3, chap. 10, 275v.

[5] I. A. H. Combes, *The Metaphor of Slavery in the Writings of the Early Church* (Sheffield: Sheffield Academic Press, 1998). Another related analogy Sandoval recommends also references the misery of the experience of captivity as a point of contrast for the promise of baptism. It involves giving jugs of water to the enslaved as part of the catechism sessions in the barracoons and comparing how good it feels to drink that water to how their souls will feel to be baptized (Sandoval, *Naturaleza, policia sagrada*, book 3, chap. 8, 267r–268r).

prioritizing simplicity, clarity, and metaphorical language that would be immediately relevant to the catechumens: "Lo que mas les persuade son razones llanas y de su talle, y algunos similes de cosas entre ellos usadas" [What most persuades them are clear reasons, cut to their size, and some similes of things used among them].[6] The proposed analogies in Sandoval's script suggest that he imagined interpreters making use of similar methods to invoke black new arrivals' and interpreters' common experiences to describe the process and promise of Christian salvation.

Futhermore, the *proemio* to the *Tercero catechismo* recommends that the delivery of catechetical content to indigenous audiences be supplemented with impassioned speeches that reference the spiritual fervor of the catechizing priest so as to provide an inspiration and model for catechumens:

Indios (como los demas hombres) comúnmente mas se persuaden, y mueven por afecto, que por razones. Y assi importa en los sermones usar de cosas que provoquen y despierten el afecto, como apostrophes, exclamaciones, y otras figuras que enseña el arte oratoria, y mucho mejor la gracia del Spiritu Sancto cuando arde el sentimiento del predicador evãgelico.

[Indians (like all other men) are commonly more persuaded and moved by affect than by reason. And so it is important in sermons to make use of things that provoke and kindle affection, such as apostrophes, exclamations, and other figures that are taught in the art of oratory, and even better, the grace of the Holy Spirit when it ignites the emotion of the evangelical preacher.][7]

Sandoval's adaptation of these instructions for black evangelization displaces the work of exhortation from the priest onto the interpreters. He suggests that priests ask experienced black interpreters to supplement the catechism by speaking directly to the catechumens in a testimonial fashion, reassuring them with their own stories about their experience of captivity and conversion to Christianity:

quando el interprete fuere ladino y ent[en]dido, hara q[ue] el de suyo les hable en orden a esto lo q[ue] le pareciere, lo qual suele ser de mucha consideraciõ. It[em] haga les digan de quando en quando en el discurso del cate[c]hismo, que lo que les dizen es la verdad, atestiguandola, con q[ue], como les ha de engañar, o dezir cosa q[ue] no les estuviesse bien el que era de su casta, de su nacion y su pariente, &c.

[when the interpreter is experienced and intelligent, you should make him speak from his own perspective about his experience of captivity and conversion, which tends to be taken into much consideration. For example, from time to time in the process of the catechism, have him remind them that he is telling them the truth,

---

[6] *Tercero cathecismo y exposicion de la doctrina christiana*, 4v.   [7] Ibid., 4r–v.

testifying to it by asking how would he lie to them or say something that was not in their best interest if he is of their same *casta* and *nación,* and their relative, etc.][8]

Sandoval thus implies that the most effective and experienced interpreters marshal their similarities with their audience to better convince new arrivals of the veracity and value of Christian conversion.[9] This supplemental moment in Sandoval's text, like the comparisons to the experience of enslavement, displacement, and dispossession cited above, interrupt the mimetic function of conversion that was typically conceived to encourage new converts to emulate European Christians.[10] Instead, in Sandoval's treatise black interpreters become not only the means through which black men and women were supposed convert to Christianity but the models to which they were encouraged to aspire. Sandoval's recommendation for this practice, which he bases on his many years of experience, offers the earliest recorded reference to spiritual autobiography composed by black men and women in the Americas. These spiritual autobiographies were delivered orally to black new arrivals in African languages, and as such they would have been particularly flexible spaces for sharing all kinds of information related to what it meant to become black Christians in Spanish America.

ADAPTATIONS AND IMPROVISATIONS

Documents related to Pedro Claver's ministry in Cartagena after Sandoval completed his treatise reveal key ways Claver and his interpreters adapted Sandoval's recommendations. For example, Sacabuche's testimony in the *Proceso* divides the key points of the catechism for new arrivals into six categories, rather than Sandoval's nine: (1) how to cross oneself; (2) how to recite the *Pater noster,* the *Ave Maria,* and the *Credo* in African languages; (3) belief in one God who manifests as the Holy Trinity; (4) the Immaculate Conception; (5) the basic outline of the life,

---

[8] Sandoval, *Naturaleza, policia sagrada,* book 3, chap. 8, 268r–v.

[9] For studies of the lack of necessary correspondence or collective between enslaved black peoples of the same linguistic group or area of origin in Africa, see Wheat, *Atlantic Africa,* 235–37; O'Toole, "From the Rivers of Guinea to the Valleys of Peru"; and Stephanie Smallwood, "The Anomalous Intimacies of the Slave Cargo," in *Saltwater Slavery: A Middle Passage from Africa to American Diaspora* (Cambridge, MA: Harvard University Press, 2007), 101–21.

[10] The activation of such a mimetic relationship appears in the first line of the first sermon of the *Tercero catechismo:* "Primeramente, hermanos, bien sabes, q soys hõbres como yo" [First, brothers, you know well that you are men like me] (9r).

death, and resurrection of Christ; and (6) the principal mysteries of the faith, such as the immortality of the soul, the nature of heaven and hell, and the ten commandments.[11] Sacabuche's description of the way catechisms were performed differs from Sandoval's script in several ways. First, Sacabuche's description of the catechisms for new arrivals does not belabor the meaning and purpose of baptism as did Sandoval's, which reflect Sandoval's stated priority of correcting false baptisms. Instead, Sacabuche's description includes a new emphasis on teaching embodied citational behavior and employing visual images to teach key concepts. According to Sacabuche, interpreters would teach the first three points of his list through recourse to the catechumens' bodies as pedagogical, ritual, and mnemonic devices. Then they would teach the last three points by showing new arrivals images while explaining their meaning.[12]

The increased dependence on the catechumens' bodies and use of religious images for the delivery of the catechism in African languages does not contradict Sandoval's recommendations, but rather builds on them. For example, Sandoval recommends using visual supplements in the catechism when describing how to explain the unity of the Holy Trinity to black new arrivals (by using a piece of fabric with three folds to show that even though there are three folds, they are actually made out of one cloth).[13] Claver and the interpreters built on this strategy to include the use of the body as a device for explaining, remembering, rehearsing scripts related to the catechism. This adaptation reflects the greater role that black bodies began to play in producing discourse about a specifically black experience of Christianity.

This adaptation that asked catechumens to remember and use Christian teachings in relation to their own bodies has an obvious precedent in Ignatius of Loyola's *Spiritual Exercises*, written in the 1520s and first published in 1548. Loyola's *Spiritual Exercises* promoted the development of an interior experience of Christianity through imagining and

---

[11] *Proceso* 1676, Sacabuche, 103r–v.

[12] According to Rappaport and Cummins, Claver could have developed his enthusiasm for using visual aids in catechisms from Franciscans in the highlands of New Granada where he spent his first three years in the New World before moving to Cartagena (*Beyond the Lettered City*, 97–101). Missions led by Franciscans in Bogota and Tunja had been exploiting this method to evangelize native populations since their establishment in the Andean highlands in 1550 (97).

[13] Sandoval, *Naturaleza, policia sagrada*, book 3, chap. 10, 274r. Sandoval elsewhere underscores how effective such visual props are for black evangelization: "porque se mueven mucho por estas cosas exteriores" [because they are very moved by such exterior things] (book 3, chap. 8, 268r).

empathizing with Christ's corporal suffering while meditating on religious images and performing daily tasks.[14] Loyola recommended the *Spiritual Exercises* to all Christians – priests and lay Christians alike – and we know from Michelle Molina's work that it was regularly used in missionary settings where Jesuit catechists would break the *Exercises* down into smaller pieces to be administered to neophytes.[15] Several testimonies in *Proceso 1676* indicate that Claver and his interpreters incorporated elements of the *Spiritual Exercises* into the pedagogical experience of the mission among black men and women in Cartagena. For example, Sacabuche explains that he and his interpreter colleagues would teach new arrivals to remember the tenets of the catechsim by using their hands as mnemonic devices. In doing so, they would make their fingers "speak":

dicendo per mezzo delli diti della mano sinistra accennandoli con l'indice della destra ... nel detto police della mano sinistra segnalato con l'indice della dritta Jesus, nell'indice Christo, et in quello di mezzo figliolo di Dio, fè nell'annullare tu eri il mio padre, e la mia madre, e nel piccolo io ti amo molto, molto, molto.

[saying with his fingers on his left hand, noting with the index finger of his right hand ... that the thumb of the left hand signals "Jesus," the index finger "Christ," and the middle finger "Son of God," and the ring finger "you were my father and my mother," and the pinky finger, "I love you very, very, very much."][16]

This strategy, as explained by Sacabuche, taught black catechumens to inscribe meanings onto their own hands in order to "read" them later as a way of remembering the catechism. Teaching black captives to speak with and read their bodies coincides with what Molina calls the "structured ritual actions" of Jesuit missionary activity in colonial Spanish America, actions that "elicited embodied responses that were subsequently/simultaneously harnessed to a discursive regime centered upon salvation."[17]

An illustration accompanying the 1676 *Exercitia spiritualia S.P. Ignatij Loyolae* (Figure 4.1) demonstrates that similar methods were employed by Jesuits in other parts of the world.[18] Figure 4.1, for example, not only offers a template for such a mnemonic device, but also a reminder (through its citation of Psalm 118 from the Vulgate) that one's salvation is, in effect, in one's own hands. Such images and practices were, furthermore, not only

---

[14] According to sexton Nicolás González, Claver himself used a quarto-sized book of images of Christ's passion to meditate on during his prayers (*Proceso 1676*, 13v).

[15] Michelle Molina, *To Overcome Oneself: The Jesuit Ethic and the Spirit of Global Expansion, 1520–1767* (Berkeley: University of California Press, 2013), 105.

[16] *Proceso 1676*, Sacabuche, 106r.   [17] Molina, *To Overcome Oneself*, 105.

[18] *Exercitia spiritualia S.P. Ignatij Loyolae* (Antwerp: Jannem Meusium, 1676).

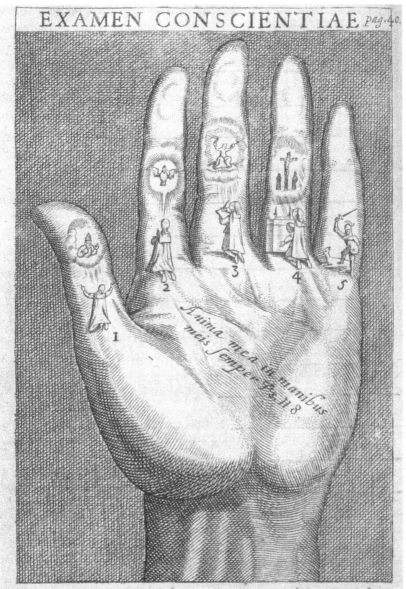

FIGURE 4.1 From *Exercitia spiritualia S.P. Ignatij Loyolae* (Antwerp, 1676).
Courtesy of Loyola University Chicago Library

used by the Jesuits. For example, a bilingual catechism in Huasteco Mayan and Spanish composed by Augustinian friar Juan de la Cruz and published in Mexico City in 1571 offers a similar strategy for using the hand as a mechanism for teaching, translating, and remembering the catechism (Figure 4.2).[19] The adaptation of such a device for black catechisms in Cartagena resulted in the attribution of new uses for enslaved black men's and women's bodies. Even though their bodies were supposed to be the property of slaveholders, the catechisms as described by Sacabuche taught black new arrivals that their souls depended on their bodies and that they should use them to learn and remember catechetical lessons for their own spiritual growth.

The interpreters' testimonies further explain that the bodies of the newly arrived black catechumens were especially important points of reference for the translation of messages about the contrition catechumens should feel for their past sins before being baptized. While Sandoval explains that priests should have interpreters lead catechumens in an Act of Penitence before being baptized, he mentions the difficulties that often arise when trying to determine if catechumens indeed feel any pain or contrition for their past sins. In the face of these challenges, Sandoval merely states that it is enough for interpreters to teach them to act *as if* they feel pain for their sins.[20] In contrast, the interpreters who testify in *Proceso* 1676 describe an adaptation to the Act of Penitence that took the form of a collective corporal performance of a snake molting its skin, signaling the rejection of a bad past life. Ignacio Soso's testimony, for example, underscores this collective performance's function as a means of having black catechumens mark the transformation of becoming Christian in their own bodies:

li faceva fare molti atti di contritione, terminandoli con dire molte volte, Signore, io ti amo molto, molto, molto, dandosi nel dirlo molti e gagliardi colpi nel petto e dicendoli che si havevano da spogliare delli peccati, conforme il serpe si spogliava della pelle vecchia senza ricordarsi mai dell'Idolatrie della loro terra e nel dir questo faceva che con le mani si radessero il corpo dando ad intendere con quell'attione che mutavano la pelle con il che si infervorivano [sic] assai li detti mori nell'Amor di Dio, e nell'abhorrimento del peccato.

---

[19] Juan de la Cruz, *Doctrina christiana en la lengua guasteca c[on] la lengua castellana* (Mexico: Pedro Ocharte, 1571).

[20] For Sandoval on teaching penitence to black men and women, see *Naturaleza, policia sagrada*, book 3, chap. 11, 279r–280r.

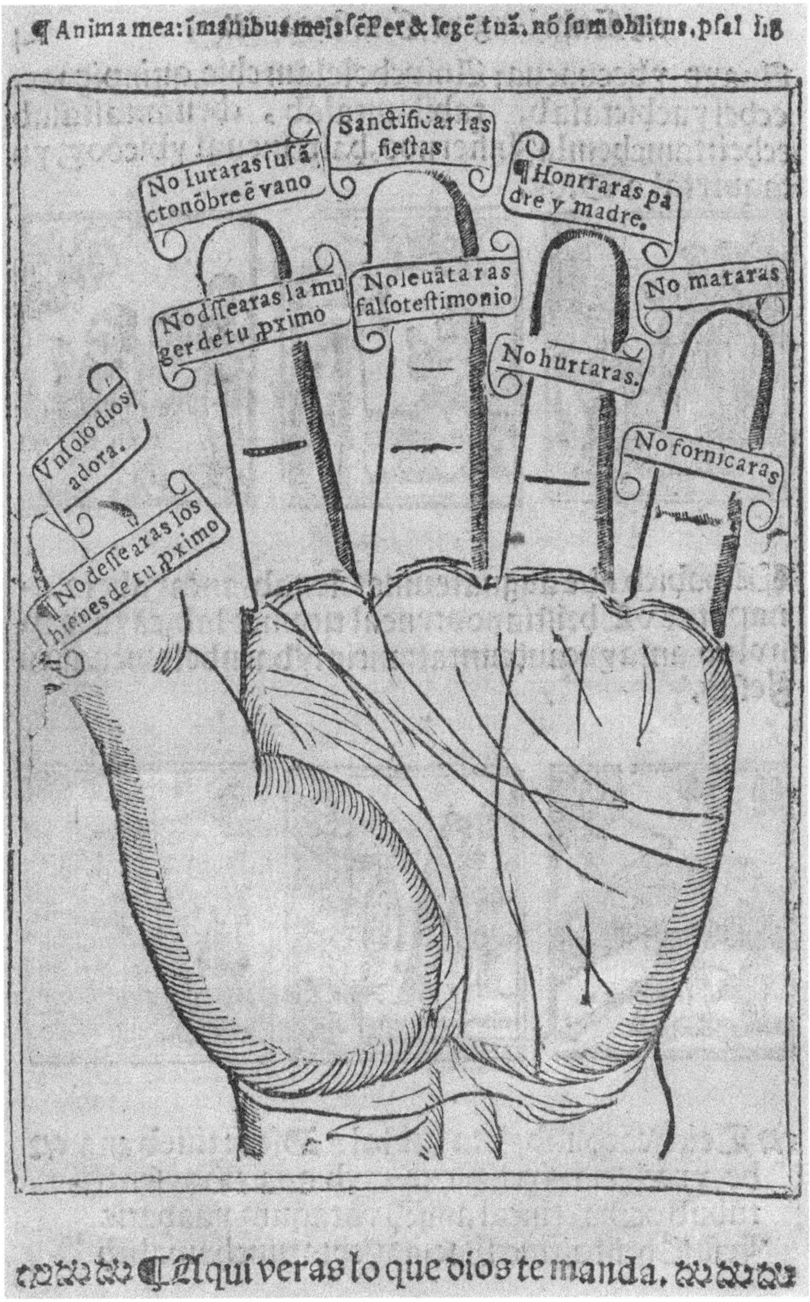

FIGURE 4.2 From *Doctrina christiana en la lengua guasteca* (Mexico, 1571).
Courtesy of the Houghton Library, Harvard University

[He [Claver through his interpreters] would have them perform many acts of contrition, and would finish by having them repeat many times, "Lord, I love you very, very, very much." At the same time, he would give himself many strong blows to his chest and tell them that they should shed their sins as a serpent sheds its old skin, never again remembering the idolatries of their native land. And while he would say this, he would have them scratch at their bodies with their hands, mimicking the action of shedding their skin. In this way, these blacks would stoke their fervor for loving God and loathing sin.][21]

While this performance is a new addition to the missionary script proposed by Sandoval, it follows his proposal for using comparisons with the material world to explain key concepts of the faith. Such comparisons, as mentioned above, were also encouraged by the standard missionary corpus produced in Lima in the 1580s. As a collective preparatory step before baptism in which the priest, interpreters, and catechumens would participate, the ritual in the context of Cartagena displaces the stress of the Act of Penitence from one of performing pain to an act that would symbolically or perhaps actually inflict pain on themselves so as to instantiate a separation from their past selves. This adaptation demonstrates another instance in which the experience of conversion led by black catechumens in Cartagena generated discourse about the catechumens' souls through the direct invocation of the interpreters' and the catechumens' bodies.

According to interpreter Ignacio Soso, the molting performance was supposed to remind the catechumens of their past lives in order to mark a separation from them.[22] As such, Soso's testimony proposes that the performance was framed as an act of remembering to provoke forgetting. Yet we can imagine that in these performances, the catechumens' body movements, as sign carriers, could have had many more meanings than those suggested by the Jesuit priests or even the interpreters. Mary Carruthers's argument that "signs make something present in the mind by acting on memory" invites us to imagine that the black men and women participating in the molting ritual in Cartagena could have understood the performance in relation to a vast variety of personal memories and

---

[21] *Proceso* 1676, Ignacio Soso, 122r.

[22] This double-sided enactment in which participants recall something in order to forget it shares many characteristics with other missionary texts from Spanish America such as the *Manuscrito de Huarochiri* or the *Popol Vuh*, which serve the paradoxical purpose of preserving indigenous traditions, beliefs, and memories for posterity in order to eradicate them.

cultural meanings.[23] Diana Taylor's methodology of scenario analysis referenced in Chapter 3 provides us with some tools to consider how the priests' script of the ritual could have been adapted by the enslaved interpreters and catechumens obliged to participate in it. Indeed, the performance narrated above by Soso could just as well have served as a means of transmitting memories of other rituals of transformation related to snakes, perhaps marking a continuity or a simultaneity of past beliefs and behaviors instead of a means of forgetting them.

Ultimately, however, accessing the wide variety of meanings that the new arrivals generated from performances such as this one is beyond the scope of my analysis. The absence of further evidence about how new arrivals interpreted these performances forces us again to recognize that the interpreters explained and led such performances in dialogues with the new arrivals that remain largely inaccessible. Something we can nonetheless discern from these accounts is that the use of translation in these performances, much like the use of *Zambi* for God in the Jesuit bilingual prayer manual analyzed in Chapter 2, resulted in the use of terms chosen by the black interpreters in negotiation with newly arrived black catechumens. These negotiations were performed beyond the comprehension of the priests supposedly in charge of the mission. Although the Jesuit-sponsored texts try to downplay the heterogeneous construction of the Christian doctrine in non-European languages by insisting that linguistic translations were always entirely transparent and conversions always completely transformative, accounts of translation in practice such as those given by Andrés Sacabuche and Ignacio Soso provide room to reflect on the limits of the priests' ability to control the meaning of Christian conversion as understood by the new arrivals.

BLACK CHRISTIAN BEAUTY, BLACK CHRISTIAN VIRTUE

Until now, this chapter has highlighted examples from the corpus of Jesuit texts that suggest that the adaptations made by the priests, interpreters, and new arrivals to the catechism proposed by Sandoval resulted in an increased use of the new arrivals' bodies as points of reference for the elaboration of language and performances for catechizing black new arrivals. In these examples, the black body appears as a mnemonic device and then a means of enacting a rejection of a past life. While these

---

[23] Mary Carruthers, *The Book of Memory in Medieval Culture* (New York: Cambridge University Press, 1996), 222.

descriptions foreground the use of catechumens' bodies and those of the black interpreters, none of them reflects explicitly on blackness or the black body itself. Such explicit references, however, do appear in the descriptions of how interpreters supplemented doctrinal instruction with reference to images.

The *Proceso* corpus describes Claver and his interpreters using many visual images to supplement catechetical sessions and baptism ceremonies.[24] Some of the most detailed descriptions of these images relate to a painted canvas used in baptism ceremonies for new arrivals. The image is described as that of a black man being baptized in front of a baptismal font filled with Christ's blood. While the painting is no longer extant, the descriptions of it in *Proceso* 1676 offer glimpses into how the interpreters explained the transformation of the baptismal ceremony to black baptizands.[25] Not all testimonies about the painting provide the same level of detail, so I will analyze it here in stages, starting with the aspects of the painting all the testimonies share.

Claver himself briefly describes the painting in a letter from the 1620s as "una imagen de Cristo Señor Nuestro en la cruz, que se levanta de una pila bautismal y de sus sacratísimas llagas caen en ella arroyos de sangre" [an image of Christ our lord on the Cross, erected in a baptismal font and into which rivers of blood fall from his holy wounds].[26] As indicated by Claver, the painting fits the genre of the allegorical image, identifying the water of the baptism with the blood of Christ.[27] The testimonies in

---

[24] Andrade's hagiography says that Claver and his interpreters used a book of prints of the life of Christ by Father Baltasar Ricio for these catechetical lessons (124r). My efforts to find this book have yet to yield results. The *Proceso* 1676 testimonies often reference a particular book Claver and the interpreters used as well as a canvas painting of souls burning in hell. See, for example, Nicolás González, 33v; Manuel Moreno, 99v. Several interpreters mention that Claver delivered sermons for black men and women during holy week before paintings of Christ's passion (Sacabuche, 106r; Soso, 122v; Manzolo, 141r). Some of the content from the following section has already been published as "Imagined Transformations: Color, Beauty, and Black Christian Conversion in Seventeenth-Century Spanish America," in *Envisioning Others: Race, Color, and the Visual in Iberia and Latin America*, ed. Pamela A. Patton (Leiden: Brill, 2016), 111–41.

[25] The witnesses who describe this part of the tableau are temporal coadjutor Manuel Rodríguez, interpreter Andrés Sacabuche, interpreter Igancio Angola, interpreter José Manzolo, and interpreter Francisco Yolofo.

[26] Claver in Mercado, *Historia de la Provincia del Nuevo Reino*, vol. 1, 241.

[27] While not very common, other allegorical images representing the blood of Christ as baptismal water had already been circulating in early modern visual art. An anonymous sixteenth-century Franciscan oil-on-wood painting, described generically as *Genealogía de la Orden Franciscana*, in the Malaga Cathedral Museum depicts a crucifix erected inside an apparently blood-filled baptismal font. A copy of the image appears in *Guía*

Proceso 1676 that were recorded more than thirty years after Claver's letter provide further details about the composition of the image and how it was used in black baptismal ceremonies. Sacristan Nicolás González, for example, relates:

nella parte più decente, metteva una tela da quale era depinta di un Crocifisso il piede della quale era d'entro una pila nella quale cadeva tutto il sangue che correva dalle piaghe e ferite del Crocifisso, formandosi di esso, come una pila di sangue e vicino à quella era dipinto un Religioso della Compagnia con la chierica di sacerdote, che con un boccale, cavava del detto sangue, per battezzare con quello un moro, il quale parimente erà dipinto in ginocchioni, vicino alla detta pila, e dal altro lato ci erano molti Rè, Imperatori, Papi, Cardinali, li quali adoravano in ginocchioni il detto Crocifisso.

[where most appropriate, Claver placed a canvas depicting a Christ on the Cross, its base inside a font into which the blood that streamed down from the wounds and injuries of the crucifix fell, creating a font full of blood. Next to this font appeared a Jesuit with the tonsure of a priest. With a pitcher, he collected this blood to baptize a black man who was also depicted kneeling near the font. To the other side [of the font], there were many kneeling kings, emperors, popes, and cardinals adoring that crucifix.[28]

Displayed as it was above the table, pitcher, and bowl of the baptismal ceremony in Cartagena, the allegorical image of Christ's blood as baptismal water would have associated the water in Claver's pitcher on the altar with the blood of Christ's sacrifice. Furthermore, the Jesuit priest in the painting holding the pitcher would have been associated with Claver and the baptized black man at his feet with the black men and women kneeling before the altar.

The painting thus provided a visual representation of a message often communicated by interpreters to the new arrivals: that Christ's blood promises salvation to *all* mankind, including them. Elsewhere, for example, Sacabuche's testimony says that he described Jesus to new arrivals as "il figliolo di Dio, che per rimediare al genere humano, si era fatto huomo e morto" [the son of God who, in order to save mankind, became a man and died].[29] Communicating the immediate relevance of Jesus's sacrifice to the newly arrived black men and women would have entailed explicitly interpolating black men and women as part of the category mankind. The painting of the black man's baptism before the blood-filled baptismal font offered a visual allegory of the same concept:

that black Christian salvation was made possible through Christ's sacrifice.

Sacabuche's testimony about the canvas includes explanations of the painting that he likely mentioned in his verbal supplementation of the canvas when describing it to black catechumens in Kimbundu and Anchico, including what aspects of the painted Jesuit signify the status of the priest: "vicino al detto vaso stava un Religioso della Compagnia con la chierica [*sic*] scoperta che dimostrava esser sacerdote" [next to this basin stood a Jesuit with his tonsure displayed to show that he was a priest].[30] Sacabuche's description suggests the appositional way he might have interpreted some of the formal signs of the painting as meaningful for new arrivals. That the significance of the image was open to interpretation and verbal supplementation, rather than being incontrovertibly self-evident, can be discerned from the fact that interpreter Diego Folupo's testimony provides an alternate interpretation of the presence of the authority figures than the interpretations that appear in Nicolás González's and Sacabuche's testimonies: "dall'altra parte erano dipinti molti cardinali, vescovi, imperatori, e rè *dando ad intendere che tutti quelli proteggevano e diffendevano* [sic] *il santo battesimo*" [on the other part of the painting, there appeared many cardinals, bishops, emperors, and kings, *demonstrating that they all defended and protected the holy baptism*].[31] Despite such variations in the assigned significance of the authority figures in the painting, most testimonies similarly recall three central themes from the image: the crucified Christ bleeding into the basin below him, the Jesuit priest baptizing a kneeling black man with blood from the basin, and the authority figures present at the scene.

The descriptions given by the four remaining interpreters, another Jesuit assistant, and Fernández's hagiography add a crucial element regarding the appearance of the black man being baptized in the painting: his beauty. Interpreter José Manzolo describes the baptized black man in the painting as exceedingly beautiful: "[Il padre] battezzava un moro che stava in ginnocchiato à suoi piedi, *il quale rimaneva assai bello, con il ricevere il santo battesimo*" [[The father] was baptizing a black man kneeling at his feet, who was *becoming extremely beautiful upon receiving the holy baptism*].[32] Manzolo's detail about the black man's changing

---

[30] Ibid., 103r.   [31] *Proceso 1676*, Diego Folupo, 174r; my emphasis.

[32] *Proceso 1676*, José Manzolo, 142r; my emphasis. Here I read "rimaneva" as a translation of "quedaba" in Spanish.

appearance implies that the baptism produced a transformative effect similar to an alchemical process.

The other remaining testimonies add another crucial detail that the black man's beauty contrasts with the appearance of a group of "molto brutti" [very ugly] black men who had not yet been baptized standing next to him. Interpreter Ignacio Angola's testimony thus explains the aesthetic distinction between them:

vicino à quella stava un Religioso della Compagnia sacerdote con la chierica scoperta, con il superpelliceo e la stola con un boccale nelle mani con il quale cavava il sangue dalla pila per battezzare con quello un moro che à suoi piedi stava in ginnocchiato, *il quale era molto bello con il battesimo e li altri che stavano guardando erano molto brutti perche no si erano battezzati.*

[near the cross stood a Jesuit priest with tonsure, surplice and stole, and a pitcher in his hands with which he took the blood from the font to baptize a black man who was kneeling at his feet. *This black man was very beautiful because of the baptism, and the others who were looking at him were very ugly because they had not been baptized.*][33]

Similar to Ignacio Angola's testimony, interpreter Diego Folupo's testimony describes the difference between the baptized black man and the unbaptized black group in the painting with the same adverbs, describing the baptized black man as "molto bello e gratioso" [very beautiful and full of grace] for receiving the holy baptism and the unbaptized group to his side as "molto brutti" [very ugly].[34] Finally, interpreter Francisco Yolofo's testimony also describes the kneeling black man as "molto bello" in contrast to the "assai brutti" [very ugly] unbaptized blacks.[35] Such contrasts were commonplace not only in Jesuit missionary language, but also in Jesuit architecture, as demonstrated by Evonne Levy's analysis of the composition of the Chiesa del Santissimo Nome di Gesù and Jesuit rhetorical manuals from the period.[36] Like these examples, the composition of this particular painting in Cartagena and the explanations of it provided by interpreters for black new arrivals suggest it served to illustrate a relationship of cause and effect to demonstrate the interior transformation of the converted black Christian.

Francisco Yolofo's testimony about the image of transformation curiously departs from Diego Folupo's and Ignacio Angola's because he

---

[33] *Proceso* 1676, Ignacio Angola, 137v, my emphasis.
[34] *Proceso* 1676, Diego Folupo, 174r.   [35] *Proceso* 1676, Francisco Yolofo, 178v.
[36] Evonne Levy, *Propaganda and the Jesuit Baroque* (Berkeley: University of California Press, 2004) 110–183, especially 155–160.

describes the beautiful black man as *about to be baptized*. Yolofo's reference to the beauty of the man suggests that Yolofo explained this image by stating that the man's desire for the baptism was what produced his external beauty, not the baptism itself: "stava dipinto [...] un religioso della compagnia di Giesù [...], et a suoi piedi in ginocchiato un moro molto bello, il quale voleva battezzare con el sangue che cavava con un boccale dalla detta pila" [a Jesuit priest was painted [...] and at his feet a kneeling beautiful black man whom the priest wanted to baptize with the blood he collected in a pitcher from the font].[37] Although no other testimony about the painting mentions the black man as beautiful before the baptism, all those that recount the man's beauty insist that it was a visible transformation of the soul accepting Christianity.[38]

The practice of placing medals around the necks of baptized black men and women after the ceremony (to mark the difference between the unbaptized and the baptized) evidences that for those involved in the process of catechism and baptism there was no obvious visible difference between a baptized and an unbaptized black person. And yet the beauty of the baptized man is an essential part of the painting according to many of the testimonies of the black interpreters. What did this beauty entail? Was it represented visually on the canvas or was it only a verbal element added to affect its perception? Unfortunately, none of the testimonies in *Proceso* 1676 provides details regarding what formal attributes were employed in the painting to mark the difference between a "beautiful" black convert and an "ugly" unbaptized black person. Without further evidence, we leave the question open and work from the recognition that, however it might have appeared visually in the painting, language to

---

[37] *Proceso* 1676, Francisco Yolofo, 178v.

[38] Luisa Elena Alcalá, "The Image of the Devout Indian: The Codification of a Colonial Idea," in *Contested Visions in the Spanish Colonial World*, ed. Ilona Katzew [New York: Yale University Press, 2011], 227–50; and Jaime Cuadriello, "Winged and Imagined Indians," in *Angels, Demons, and the New World*, ed. Fernando Cervantes and Andrew Redden (New York: Cambridge University Press, 2013), 211–48, have analyzed the visual codification of Christianized natives in colonial Spanish America, but neither scholar mentions the rise of the phenomenon of simultaneously representing the ugliness of the unbaptized and the beauty of the baptized. That paintings like the Jesuit canvas in Cartagena and others that might have been used to evangelize indigenous groups have not been preserved is likely due to the fact that they were paintings produced for missionary settings and not for veneration and consumption as permanent fixtures in churches.

describe extremely beautiful black converts circulated in the Caribbean port as part of black baptismal ceremonies conducted from the 1620s through the early 1650s.

Such language is uncommon in seventeenth-century Spanish and Spanish American texts. Its anomalous nature is reinforced by the fact that when Fernández wrote Claver's hagiography from Aragon in the 1660s using the no longer extant *Proceso 1660* manuscript, he interpreted the same testimonies by changing the description of the painting:

> A un parte de el lienço se veìan Negros hermosamente aseados, representacion de los que avian recibido el Bautismo; otros feroces los que lo reusavan; y entre infernales monstruos, que abrian horribles bocas para hacer presa en ellos.

> [On one part of the canvas there appeared *beautifully composed* blacks, a representation of those who had received the baptism. Other ferocious blacks that rejected it appeared among hellish monsters that opened their horrible mouths to capture them.][39]

The term "aseado" [composed or cleaned] suggests Fernández imagined the transformation being one related to dress or cleanliness or even the skill of the artist. What is most remarkable is Fernández's displacement of "beautiful" from adjective to adverb, which indicates a resistance to reproducing the language of the beautiful black male body from the interpreters' testimonies.

Significantly, it does not appear that the artist of the painting or any of the interpreters who explain it in the *Proceso* corpus conceived of the beautiful baptized black man as *whiter* than the rest of the group. This is remarkable because imagery of black men and women "turning white" through baptism had already been circulating in Europe in literary texts for more than a thousand years and was especially common in Jesuit discourse about evangelical efforts among dark-skinned people.[40] Art

---

[39] Fernández, *Apostólica y penitente vida*, 140–41. Rappaport and Cummins briefly analyze this passage in *Beyond the Lettered City*. In doing so, however, they describe the scene as a compilation of two sets of paintings arranged to face each other: the cross with the baptismal scene of the black man and a distinct portrait of Christian authorities (98–99). Reading the *Proceso* testimonies on which Fernández based his account clarifies that the figures of authority were painted on the same canvas as the baptismal scene. Jesuit historian Antonio Astrain briefly mentions the painting as described in the *Proceso* testimonies in his history of the order in Spanish territories, calling it a "canvas with minimal artistic pretensions" (*Historia de la Compañía*, vol. 5, 487).

[40] See Courtès, "The Theme of 'Ethiopia' and 'Ethiopians' in Patristic Literature," for an overview of the use of whitening imagery to conceive of Ethiopian conversion in early Christian exegesis. See also Jean Michel Massing, "From Greek Proverb to Soap Advert: Washing the Ethiopian," *Journal of the Warburg and Courtauld Institutes* 58 (1995):

historian Jean Michel Massing has traced this trope to the classical proverb about "the impossibility of washing the Ethiopian white," which functioned as a saying to describe unfruitful labor in classical and humanistic texts. Visual images related to this proverb appear in several early modern emblem books. Figure 4.3 is an example of such an emblem that circulated among Spanish readers. Such visual and discursive images eventually influenced visual and written imagery used by Iberian Jesuit missionaries describing the goal of their labor in seventeenth-century texts. For example, a detail from the frontispiece of the second edition of Sandoval's treatise, shown in Figures 4.4 and 4.5, demonstrates a group of "black" men and women being baptized on a beach by a priest above the caption "de albabuntur" [to be turned white].[41] The text of Sandoval's 1647 version of his treatise verbally invokes this imagery when Sandoval explains that Cham's sin resulted in not only leaving his future progeny "obscura y negra" [dark and black], but also "sujeta a cautiverio" [subject to captivity] and condemned to "perpetua servidumbre" [perpetual servitude]:

[El caso de Cam] nos demuestra, que la servidumbre causada de la culpa, y el pecado, es tan continua, y perpetua, que jamas causa libertad a qui[en] la contraxo: porque el que como esclavo siempre sirve, *servuus serviens*, nunca como libre descansa; acabararsele la vida, y no fenecerà su cautiverio, antes se continuarà de generacion en generacion.

[Cham's case shows us that the servitude caused by guilt and sin is so continuous and perpetual, that he who contracts it will never be free: because he who always serves as a slave, *lowest of slaves*, never rests as a free man. His life may end, but his captivity does not; instead it passes on from generation to generation.][42]

180–201; "Washing the Ethiopian or the Semantics of an Impossibility," in *Studies in Imagery*, vol. 2 (London: Pindar, 2007), 315–34; and "Washing the Ethiopian, Once More," in *Studies in Imagery*, vol. 2, 335–58; Fracchia, "*Black but Human*," 28–30, 189.

[41] See Stoichita for an analysis of this frontispiece in relation to other visual representations of black baptisms. According to Stoichita, other contemporaneous representations demonstrate baptized black individuals wearing white clothing after conversion, not changing the color of their skin (201). Also see Fracchia, "La problematización" and "Metamorphoses of the Self: Slave Portraiture and the Case of Juan de Pareja," in *Slave Portraiture in the Atlantic World*, ed. Agnes Lugo Ortiz and Angela Rosenthal (New York: Cambridge University Press, 2013), 147–70, on visual portrayals of whitening in early modern Spanish and Spanish American art.

[42] Alonso de Sandoval, *Historia de la Aethiopia*, 1647, book 1, chap. 3, 21. Sandoval cites God's curse from Genesis 9:25. For citations on the changing associations between black men and women and the sin of Cham, see Introduction, note 60.

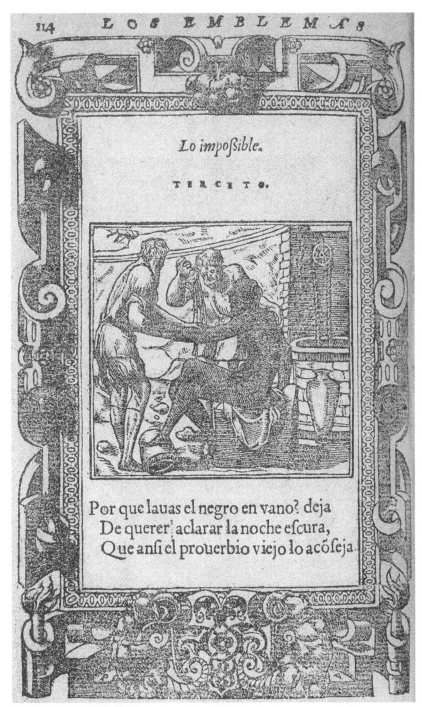

FIGURE 4.3 "The Impossible," in Bernardino Daza's *Los emblemas de Alciato.*
Traducidos en rhimas Españolas (Lyon, 1549).
Courtesy of the British Library

FIGURE 4.4 Juan de Noort, frontispiece to Alonso de Sandoval's *Historia de la Aethiopia* (Madrid, 1647).
Courtesy of the British Library

FIGURE 4.5 "De albabuntur," detail from Figure 4.4, Juan de Noort, frontispiece to Alonso de Sandoval's *Historia de la Aethiopia* (Madrid, 1647).
Courtesy of the British Library

After this condemnation, Sandoval offers a proposed spiritual escape for black men's and women's "dark" worldly enslavement, stating that evangelization and baptism guaranteed their salvation through the whitening of their souls: "lo que es impossible a la naturaleza, le es muy facil a la gracia ... pues tantos quedan con la gracia de los Santos Sacramentos, blancos como el Sol, y de obscuras noches dias claros" [what is impossible for nature is easy for grace ... For the grace of the holy sacraments allows so many of them to become white like the sun, turning dark nights into bright days].[43] By describing evangelical labor as a symbolic whitening process, Sandoval connotes the efficacious nature of Jesuit efforts to evangelize black men and women. This whitening imagery also propagates an association between the ugliness of sin and black bodies.[44] But however apparent in Sandoval's treatise and subsequent histories written about the Jesuit project in Cartagena, whitening imagery is completely absent from all of the descriptions of the transformation depicted in the painting of the black baptism in *Proceso 1676*.

Instead of approximating whiteness, it is likely that one aspect of communicating the beauty of a black Christian convert (perhaps visually and most certainly linguistically) was the notion of radiance. For example, in another part of his testimony, Sacabuche describes the aesthetic transformation of a baptized black soul as becoming more resplendent. According to Sacabuche's testimony, he would explain the transformation of baptism to black men and women with the following language:

arrivando vicino alla detta pila ciascheduno moro da per se di quelli che si havevano da battezzare et al di loro fianche il padrino e con quello parimente la commare, comandava che si ponessero in ginocchioni e postivisi [postovisi] li diceva che quella acqua era l'acqua santa che esso l'aveva detto che dovevano ricevere con la quale ricevendola divotamente e con dolore e dispiacere di haver offeso Dio, saria suo figliolo e Christiano e che daria [*sic*] l'anima sua *assai netta e pura, simile assai al sole materiale nello splendere, e purezza.*

[approaching that baptismal font, he would command every black to be baptized, accompanied by his godfather and godmother, to kneel. And after, he would tell them that that water was the holy water that he had told them they would receive; and by receiving it with devotion, and with pain and displeasure for having offended God, the convert would become a son of God and a Christian, and his soul would become *very clean and pure, much like the material sun in its splendor and purity.*][45]

---

[43] Sandoval, *Historia de la Aethiopia*, book 1, chap. 4, 24.
[44] Mercado, *Historia de la Provinicia del Nuevo Reino*, reuses this imagery, too, 233.
[45] *Proceso 1676*, Sacabuche, 104r; my emphasis.

The verbal explanation of black conversion for Sacabuche does not invoke a distinction in color but rather one of radiance. In fact, Sacabuche's testimony is phrased so as to avoid the association made in Sandoval's treatise between conversion and turning white. Instead, Sacabuche's simile compares the process of conversion to embodying the "splendere e purezza" [splendor and purity] of the sun. The distinction suggests that at least in their oral explanations, black interpreters described black Christian conversion as a process that makes black men and women *radiant* and *beautiful*, not white.

We can surmise some of the possible values associated with radiance in seventeenth-century Cartagena through some definitions in Covarrubias's dictionary, which defines the verb *resplandecer* [to shine] as "echar de si rayos de luz ... Resplandecer en fama, ser ilustre en ella" [to give off rays of light ... To shine in fame, to be illustrious in it].[46] The first of these definitions associates shine not with the reflection of light from an object but with the emitting of light from oneself (like a sun). The second provides the symbolic definition of radiance as being illustrious. Neither of the two invoke color. Sacabuche's account suggests that the black interpreters in Cartagena might have employed such associations alongside others specific to the different African languages in which they delivered their explanations to describe the transformation of becoming black Christians.

As suggested by Sacabuche's reference to becoming radiant and pure through baptism, a perceived literal cleanliness could also have marked the difference between black men and women before and after the ceremony. After all Sandoval as well as the interpreters in their testimonies in the *Proceso*, as mentioned earlier, recount that a key step to preparing for the baptism was having the catechumens wash themselves before the ceremony.[47] Also, the interpreters' descriptions of abject naked and sick bodies of black new arrivals in the other parts of their testimonies suggest that one key way the painting's artist could have visually distinguished baptized and unbaptized blacks from each other was through referencing the physical illnesses, dirtiness, or nakedness of the unbaptized.[48]

---

[46] Covarrubias, *Tesoro de la lengua castellana*, II: 10r.

[47] For Sandoval's description of ablution before the baptism, see *Naturaleza, policia sagrada*, book 3, chap. 12, 282r. For descriptions from *Proceso 1676*, see Sacabuche, 104v.

[48] For descriptions of the bodies of the newly arrived black men and women, see *Proceso 1676*: Andrés Sacabuche, 102v; José Manzolo, 142r; Diego Folupo, 173v; María de Mendoza, 238r. See Walter Johnson, *Soul by Soul: Life Inside the Antebellum Slave*

On a symbolic level, Sacabuche's language about the cleanliness and purity of the baptized soul echoes one that appears in contemporary Spanish texts to describe people of noble lineage who were not marked with any stain of "impure blood" tied to new Christian ancestry. For example, Covarrubias defines "limpieza" [cleanliness] as "mundicia, o sinifica pureza de linage" [immaculateness, or purity of lineage].[49] By association, this could mean that the black interpreters and black catechumens listening to them imagined themselves to be acquiring a nobler lineage because of the baptism.[50] Other kinds of color- or radiance-related symbolism specific to the places of origin and languages of the newly arrived black catechumens could also be considered as points of reference for the explanation of Christian conversion for black new arrivals. Cécile Fromont, for example, describes some of the values attributed to whiteness in the visual culture of the Kongo where even before the arrival of Christian missionaries white was used for royal funerary furnishings and garments worn by indigenous priests.[51] After the Christian conversion of the Kongo, Fromont explains, white figured prominently in the color of churches, *mestres'* uniforms, body paint applied for funerary functions, and the initiation rituals of the Kimpasi to mark those who had died and come back from the dead. If the beautiful black man in the painting from Cartagena had been depicted as dressed in white, it could have served as a useful point of "correlation" for black new arrivals from the Kongo. Such possibilities are suggestive for analyzing the *Proceso* testimonies, especially Sacabuche's, even if the descriptions provided of the painting are limited to mentions of the extreme physical beauty of the painted black baptizand.

PRECEDENTS AND CONTRASTS

Portrayals of beautiful black Christian bodies in earlier texts and images from the Iberian and Iberian American world provide points of contrast to

Market (Cambridge, MA: Harvard University Press), 134–61, for an analysis of the values assigned to black slave bodies by slave traders and slaveholders in the antebellum southern United States.

[49] Covarrubias, *Tesoro*, I: f. 525v.

[50] Another possibility is the notion of *candidez* described by Erin Rowe as a central feature of the linguistic and visual imagery related to some early modern black Christian saints. See "After Death" and *Black Saints in Early Modern Global Catholicism* (New York: Cambridge University Press, 2019), 195–202.

[51] Fromont, "Common Threads," 849–50.

identify what is distinct about the discourse circulated about the painting by the black interpreters in Cartagena. One type of these texts and images relates to the rise of the cults to dark-skinned Virgins in the Iberian Peninsula in the fourteenth century and the transportation of these cults across the Atlantic in the sixteenth and seventeenth centuries. According to Jeanette Peterson, contemporary documents about images of Guadalupe in Iberia evidence "a noteworthy linkage between the authority of the evangelist Luke and the dark color of the images as a marker of antiquity" because they were thought to have been crafted by the evangelist himself from the Virgin's likeness.[52] These images' supposed proximity to the original Virgin was associated with the perception that they had especially efficacious mediating powers.

Over the course of the following centuries as the veneration of these images spread, authors and artists occasionally reflected on the aesthetic dimensions of the Madonna's dark body. Connections were sometimes drawn between the dark images of the Virgin and the dark beauty of the Bride of the Song of Songs. For example, when Gabriel de Talavera's *Historia de Nuestra Señora de Guadalupe* from 1597 notes that "Aunque el color es algo tostado, el rostro es hermoso" [Even though the color is somewhat burnt, her face is beautiful],[53] the marginal note to the text cites "Cant. I," connecting the divine dark beauty of the Virgin Mary to the declaration of the Bride from the Song of Solomon: "nigra sum sed formosa" [I am black but comely].[54]

Songs from popular lyric and José de Valdivielso's *Romancero espiritual*, printed in 1612, make similar allusions to the divine dark beauty of the Virgin Mary. For example, a song from Valdivielso's collection celebrates the Virgin as the dark baker yielding the precious bread of Christ:

> Diréis que morena sois,
> y que la tierra morena
> lleva siempre el pan mejor.
>
> [You will say that you are dark,
> and that dark earth
> always produces the best bread.][55]

---

[52] Jeanette Favrot Peterson, *Visualizing Guadalupe: From Black Madonna to Queen of the Americas* (Austin: University of Texas Press, 2014), 21.

[53] Gabriel de Talavera, *Historia de Nuestra Señora de Guadalupe* (Toledo: Imprenta Tomás de Guzmán, 1597), 159r; qtd. in Peterson, *Visualizing Guadalupe*, 279, n. 66.

[54] Peterson, *Visualizing Guadalupe*, 279, n. 66.

[55] José de Valdivielso, "Romance a Nuestra Señora con el niño Jesús en sus braços," in *Primera parte del romancero espiritual* (Toledo: Loarte, 1612).

Through this conceit, Valdivielso's song cites popular lyric from Iberia that compared the fertility of dark-skinned women to the superior quality of bread produced from wheat grown in dark soil. One rendition of such a popular lyric cited in Valdivielso's song is:

> Aunque soy morena,
> no soy de olvidar,
> que la tierra negra
> pan blanco suele dar.

> [Although I am dark,
> I shouldn't be despised,
> for black earth
> usually produces white bread.][56]

This verse is an elaboration of the popular adage documented in Gonzalo Correas's *Vocabulario de refranes* as "La tierra negra lleva el buen pan" [black earth brings good bread].[57] Another collector of popular language from late sixteenth-century Iberia, Sebasitán de Horozco, glosses the proverb in the late sixteenth century, explaining that:

la tierra blanca es fría y la tierra negra tiene en sí harto calor para llevar frutos. Y de a[hí] viene que la tierra blanca cría serpientes y sabandijas que de su natural son frías y la tierra negra cría panes y otras simientes que son calientes. Y por esta razón se suele aplicar este proverbio a las mugeres morenas y blancas diziendo que la tierra Morena lleva el pan y que la muger baça y Morena es fecunda y por la mayor parte conçibe y pare muchas vezes por la mayor abundançia de calor que tiene.

[white earth is cold and black earth has in itself a lot of heat to grow fruit. From this comes the saying that white earth yields serpents and reptiles who are in their nature cold and black earth yields bread and other seeds that are hot. For this reason, the proverb is typically applied to brown and white women, saying that the brown earth brings bread and that the dark and brown woman is fecund and usually conceives and gives birth much more because of the abundance of heat that she has.][58]

---

[56] *El cancionero español de tipo tradicional*, ed. José María Alín (Madrid: Taurus, 1968), 517, no. 355. The English translation of the lyric is provided by Wardropper, "The Impact of Folk Song on Sacred and Profane Love Poetry," 489. For an alternative interpretation of Valdivielso's contrafacta poems than Wardropper's, see J. M. Aguirre, *José de Valdivielso y la poesía tradicional* (Toledo: Diputación Provincial, 1965).

[57] Gonzalo Correas, *Vocabulario de refranes* [1627] (Madrid: Olózaga, 1924), 78–79, gives ten variations of this proverb. Three are about "tierra morena" [dark earth], one about "tierra prieta" [dark earth], and the other seven – including the most common, which is the one cited in text – are about "tierra negra" [black earth].

[58] Sebastián de Horozco, *El libro de los proverbios glosados* (1570–80), ed. Jack Weiner (Kassel: Edición Reichenberger, 1994), vol. 2, 333.

Borrowing language and logic from agricultural discourse and contemporary humoral theory about female bodies and reproduction, Horozco's gloss connects the fertility of dark soil to that of dark-skinned women. These proverbs from popular speech and lyric specifically tie black or dark-skinned female bodies to an assumed reproductive fertility. These overlapping traditions reviewed here value black women's bodies for their functionality – as conduits either for physical reproduction or for the mediation of the divine.[59]

An additional inversion of values associated with dark to light concludes Horozco's gloss, demonstrating how even in such instances when female blackness was appreciated in early modern Iberia toward the turn of the seventeenth century it was still considered aesthetically inferior to whiteness. Horozco ends his gloss by framing the proverb as a kind of rhetorical compensation for the lack of beauty he associates with dark-skinned women:

Mas este proverbio todavía en la muger no es regla çiertas [*sic*] porque muchas morenas son inútiles y estériles y muchas blancas frutíferas y por el contrario. Mas es una manera de consuelo de las mugeres que no son blancas ni hermosas.

[But this proverb is still not a certain rule for women for many *morenas* [dark-skinned women] are useless and sterile and many white women are fertile and the opposite is true. But the proverb is a kind of consolation for the women who are not white or beautiful.][60]

By casting *morenas* as less beautiful than light-skinned women in principle, Horozco's gloss demonstrates an effort to reify earthly aesthetic appraisals of black skin as less beautiful than light skin even when attempting to appreciate black skin to some degree. The gloss coexists in some tension with the sixteenth-century tendency in popular Iberian lyric (mentioned in the Introduction) to address the female object of affection as a *morena*. Margit Frenk elaborates on this tradition to state that when poets of all social classes laud the dark color of the *morena* or the *negra* in early modern Iberia, they were not always referencing her physical body but rather a symbolic "attractiveness for men of the [sexually] experienced and skillful woman."[61]

---

[59] On the gendered mediating powers of the Virgin Mary in medieval and early modern Christianity, see Marina Warner, *Alone of All Her Sex: The Myth and Cult of the Virgin Mary* [1976] (New York: Random House, 1983), 273–333.

[60] Ibid.

[61] "La canción popular femenina," 371; my translation. Both Frenk in that article and Wardropper in "The Color Problem" argue that the sixteenth-century rise in references to

The traditions surveyed above demonstrate an overlapping set of Iberian traditions for conceiving of dark-skinned women as fertile or particularly effective mediators of the divine, and in some way beautiful in their blackness. Yet unlike any of these examples, the language the interpreters use to describe the painting of the black Christian conversion in Cartagena de Indias specifies that the beautiful black convert is a man. A related innovation is that the interpreters who describe the painting associate the black man's dark skin with spiritual integrity and physical beauty without any connection to his divine mediating powers, sexuality, or fertility. Finally, his beauty is never described as hierarchically inferior to that of a white individual.

Distinct precedents for conceiving of handsome black male bodies can be found in a corpus of visual images that consolidates around two different types: the wealthy black magus who visited Jesus in the manger and the humble black Christian servant. The first type is best represented in the Iberian Atlantic world by the trajectory of the engraved image of the Adoration of the Magi in Jerónimo Nadal's *Evangelicae historiae imagines* from 1593 (Figure 4.6), a popular post-Tridentine text that was sponsored by the Jesuit order and read widely in Spanish America soon after its publication.[62] This image was designed by Flemish artist Martin de Vos, and is typically shown seventh in the collection of 153 plates.[63] De Vos's Adoration depicts the black magus as the third and last king in line to visit the Christ child. His blackness is conveyed less by the color of his skin than by his round facial features and curly hair, as de Vos used hatching in the plate exclusively for shadowing. The black magus's dress in this engraving does not stand out as markedly different from the

the beauty and fertility of dark-skinned women in popular lyric is a completely separate phenomenon from the tradition of glosses of the Bride's beauty in the *Song of Songs*. Other scholars, however, argue that the *Song of Songs* was in fact the inspiration for the proliferation of the theme in popular lyric (Alín, *El cancionero español de tipo tradicional*, 254; Alegre Heitzmann, "El color de la Sulamita"; J. M. Aguirre, "Ensayo para un estudio del tema amoroso en la primitiva lírica castellana," *Cuadernos de Filosofía y letras* 1, no. 54 [1965]: 7–34, 8–14). Regardless of which tradition informed the other, both popular and ecclesiastic traditions should be considered in conversation. After all, as we learn from the marginal citation in Talavara's history cited above, both traditions were employed in the service of celebrating the beauty and efficacious power of dark-skinned Virgins in the Iberian Peninsula.

[62] Nadal, *Evangelicae historiae*, plate 7.

[63] See Maj-Brit Wadell, "The *Evangelicae Historiae Imagines*: The Designs and Their Artists," *Quaerendo* 10, no. 4 (1980), 279–91, for an overview of the author, artists, engraver, and printer who participated in the creation of Nadal's *Evangelicae historiae imagines*.

FIGURE 4.6 Martin de Vos, "Adoratio Magorum," in Jerónimo Nadal's *Evangelicae Historiae Imagines* (Antwerp, 1593).
Courtesy of the Beinecke Library, Yale University

costumes of the other two magi, skipping the trope of portraying the black magus as more "eastern" than the other two kings that sometimes appear in Iberian oil paintings of the black magus.[64] Though the black magus in de Vos's plate is the only one of the three kings still standing and wearing his crown, he is clearly already awestruck by the child before him. His turning torso embodies the action of sudden acknowledgment as his figure assumes a space on the page parallel to Mary's: the positioning of their heads, his crowned and hers haloed, mirror each other as they lean toward the child at the same angle and at almost the same height. The black magus's importance to the image is further underscored by his transitional placement between the narrative scene of the Adoration and the multitudes of people trailing off into the mountainous urban land-scape behind him, all presumably waiting to catch a glimpse of the child.[65] The black magus's admiration of the baby Jesus anticipates the reaction of all those following him in line.

De Vos's image surely circulated as part of Nadal's book in colonial Spanish America, as did copies of the image made by two different artists. One of these copies, composed more than fifty years later, appears on the frontispiece of the second edition of Alonso de Sandoval's treatise. In the detail (Figure 4.7) from Van Noort's 1647 engraved frontispiece (Figure 4.4), the black magus appears first in line to visit the child, reimagining de Vos's composition as if the black magus had skipped ahead of the other two magi before their approach. As in de Vos's design, Van Noort's black magus is not marked by color, but by his stereotypically curved forehead, round nose, prominent mouth, and thick short hair. Van Noort's black magus's regality and authority are also communicated through his elegant dress. The profile perspective of his figure shows that Van Noort assigned this black magus the same placement as that of the oldest white magus in de Vos's image. The similarities between the two engravings suggest not only that de Vos's engraving served as the model for Van Noort's, but that both images had a shared visual language to signal blackness in general and black male regality in particular. As seen in the prints by de Vos and Van Noort, the black magus was not disparaged hierarchically because of his physical differences from the other magi or marginal placement in the composition.

---

[64] Stoichita, "The Image of the Black in Spanish Art," 207.

[65] See Joseph Leo Koerner, "The Epiphany of the Black Magus circa 1500," in *The Image of the Black in Western Art*, vol. 3, part 1 (Cambridge, MA: Belknap Press of Harvard University, 2010), 7–93, specifically 35–47, on the black magus as a threshold device in sixteenth- and seventeenth-century images of the Adoration. On the tradition in early modern Spain, see Fracchia, "*Black but Human*," 60–66.

FIGURE 4.7 "Adoration of the Magi," detail from Figure 4.4, Juan de Noort, frontispiece to Alonso de Sandoval's *Historia de la Aethiopia* (Madrid, 1647). Courtesy of the British Library

The other known copy of de Vos's engraving is an earlier adaptation by Felipe Guaman Poma de Ayala (Figure 4.8) from his *Primer y nueva coronica y buen gobierno*, a missive addressed to the King of Spain, composed in the Andes in the first decade of the seventeenth century. Guaman Poma's drawing "Cristiano negros" demonstrates the borrowing of the iconography from de Vos's black magus to depict a humble black man and woman in the Andes. Guaman Poma's adaptation is, in fact, the earliest surviving example of the second type of portrayal of a black man in visual culture in colonial Spanish America during this period – that of the humble black Christian servant.

Another early instance of such an image that circulated in Spanish America in the late sixteenth century and early seventeenth century is the portrait of the black Franciscan saint, Friar Benedict "the Moor," who was born in Spanish Sicily in the sixteenth century and died a respected leader of the Third Order of Franciscans in Palermo (1526–89). In an account of Benedict's life printed in Valladolid in 1611, Franciscan Antonio Daza reports that an image of Benedict had already developed a reputation for performing miracles in Puebla, New

FIGURE 4.8 "Cristiano negros." Guaman Poma, *Primer nueva corónica y buen gobierno* (1615).
Courtesy of The Royal Library, Denmark

FIGURE 4.9 Relief sculpture of Benedict of Palermo from the Iglesia de San Francisco, Quito, Ecuador.
Photograph by Josh Bunn; used with permission

Spain.[66] While those early images of Benedict that circulated in the Iberian Atlantic have yet to be found, an unknown artist likely used one of them to design the relief sculpture of Benedict of Palermo in Quito's Franciscan Church, installed in the left apse of the nave in the 1640s (Figure 4.9). The image depicts Benedict as a Franciscan friar in a light blue habit: his skin black, his eyes the color of his habit. His light eyes suggest an effort to index the "clarity" of his soul in relation to his eyes, even though the high placement of the panel in the nave of the church makes that detail hard to perceive.

In Seville a couple of decades earlier, Bartolomé de Artiagame, the engraver of the frontispiece of the first edition of Alonso de Sandoval's

---

[66] Antonio Daza, *Quarta parte de la Chronica General de Nuestro Padre San Francisco y su Apostolica Orden* (Valladolid: Juan Godines de Millis y Diego de Cordova, 1611), f. 68. On the rise of the cult of Benedict in Iberia during this period, see Brewer-García, "Hierarchy and Holiness in the Earliest Colonial Black Hagiographies"; Erin Kathleen Rowe, "Visualizing Black Sanctity in Early Modern Spanish Polychrome Sculpture," in *Envisioning Others*, 51–82; Bernard Vincent, "Saint Benoît de Palermo et L'Espagne," in *Schiavitù, religione, e libertà nel Mediterraneo tra mediovo ed età moderna* (Cosenza, 2009), 201–14; Giovanna Fiume, "Saint Benedict, the Moor: From Sicily to the New World," in *Saints and Their Cults in the Atlantic World*, ed. Margaret Cormack (Columbia: University of South Carolina Press, 2006), 16–51, among others.

treatise, included what is likely an image of Benedict of Palermo alongside Francis Loyola, Francis Xavier, and an unknown Jesuit (Figure 4.10). Artiagame's image, which shares compositional similarities to the relief sculpture from Quito (Figure 4.9), portrays Benedict in relation to his shaded face and the cross he holds in his arms (Figure 4.11).[67] His face is surrounded by a halo of light as he stares reverently upward. Unlike the images of the black magus discussed above or the relief sculpture of Benedict of Palermo from Quito, Artiagame's image marks Benedict's blackness only by shading his face, portraying the rest of his facial features as younger but otherwise nearly identical to those of the three Jesuits with whom he shares the frontispiece. By dressing him as an altar boy, however, Artiagame denotes him as a figure of lesser authority than the others on the frontispiece. Diego Velázquez's two paintings of a black scullery maid, *Kitchen Scene* and *Kitchen Servant with Supper at Emmaus,* composed in Seville around 1618–19, trade in similar imagery to portray the humble black Christian servant illuminated by Christian doctrine. Like Aritagame's frontispiece, Velázquez's black scullery maid in *Kitchen Servant with Supper at Emmaus* appears as a humble servant enlightened by Christian conversion.[68] Aritagame's engraving, which reached Cartagena in the late 1620s with the printed copies of Sandoval's book, demonstrates that by the second decade of the seventeenth century an alternative visual language to represent black Christian servants had begun to circulate in Spanish America: the humble black Christian servant.

In summary, there were two different types of portrayals of black men that circulated in visual culture from late sixteenth- and early seventeenth-century Spain and Spanish America: the wealthy black magus and the humble black Christian servant. The discursive collapse of these two visual types into a singular abstraction appears in the widely read and translated *Estado de los bienaventurados en el cielo* by Jesuit theologian Martín de Roa, published in Seville in 1624 by the same editor who printed Sandoval's first treatise three years later.[69] In his book, Roa

---

[67] See also Kaplan, "Italy, 1490–1700" in *The Image of the Black*, vol. 3, part 1, 170.

[68] For studies of Velázquez's paintings in relation to black evangelization, see Tiffany, "Light, Darkness, and African Salvation"; Fracchia, "(Lack of) Visual Representation"; and Stoichita, "Image of the Black in Spanish Art."

[69] Martín de Roa, *Estado de los bienaventurados en el cielo* (Seville: Francisco de Lyra, 1624). Roa's text was widely read, translated, and printed throughout seventeenth-century Europe. In Spanish, seven different editions were published across the Iberian Peninsula between 1624 and 1669. In Italian, six different editions were published between 1626 and 1643. In Latin, at least three different editions were published between 1633 and 1688. And in French, two different editions were published in 1631 and 1645.

FIGURE 4.10 Bartolomé de Artiagame, frontispiece to Alonso de Sandoval's *Naturaleza, policia sagrada i profana, costumbres i ritos ...* (Seville, 1627). Courtesy of the Hispanic Society of America, New York

FIGURE 4.11 "Benedict of Palermo," detail from Figure 4.10, Bartolomé de
Artiagame, frontispiece to Alonso de Sandoval's *Naturaleza, policia sagrada i
profana, costumbres i ritos ...* (Seville, 1627).
Courtesy of the Hispanic Society of America, New York

rejects a theory that states that in heaven black men and women would be
reincarnated as white:

Serà el negro, no deslavado, ni desluzido, sino vivo, resplandeciente, qual fuera
de un azabache quajado con sangre, penetrado todo de luz mas que un Sol,
qual tendran por el dõ de la claridad, que les darà increyble donayre, y gracia.
*Ni desdize lo negro de la hermosura; que no consiste tanto en el color, como en
la suavidad del, que podra ser ygual en lo negro, y en lo blanco, y dar aun
mayor gusto a la vista.* Y como no todos los bienaventurados seran de temple
sanguinos, aunque este sea el mas perfecto de todos; antes cobrarà cada uno el
que tuvo primero; assi tambien sucedera en el color, que no todos tendran
el que mejor fuere en su genero, sino el q[ue] mejor estuviere al sugeto de
cada uno.

[The black man will not be made lighter or less bright, but vibrant and glistening like the color of jet stone, mixed with blood, completely penetrated with a light more brilliant than the sun. Blacks' brilliance, which they will have as a result of the divine gift of light, will give them an amazing air and grace. *Nor will their blackness make them less beautiful, as beauty consists less in color itself than in the soft quality of the coloring that is more pleasing to the sight, which can exist equally in black and white.* Not all of the redeemed will have rosy-complexioned skin, even though it is the most perfect among all. Rather, everyone will take on the complexion they first had. The same occurs with color; not all will have the best possible color, but rather the best possible of their kind.][70]

Roa's description alludes to classical and medieval theories relating the dark hue of certain human groups to an accidental effect of hot climates naturalized over generations instead of identifying darker skin tones with an external sign of moral depravity.[71] For Roa, blackness does not evidence sin and thus whiteness does not evidence salvation. Instead, whether wealthy nobles or humble servants in life, Christian black men and women would be brilliantly and beautifully black in heaven. Roa does not, however, ultimately disrupt the hierarchically inferior positioning of black skin tones compared with lighter tones because he includes the caveat that the saved black man's color is still inferior to that of someone with a "rosy" complexion.

Despite similarly contesting the equivalence of whiteness, beauty, and Christian virtue as the precedents reviewed above, the black interpreters' descriptions in *Proceso 1676* of the painting of the beautiful black Christian convert still differ from them. First the interpreters' descriptions of the baptized black man in the painting tie his color to spiritual devotion and grace without drawing *any* comparisons to whiteness. Furthermore, by describing the beautiful black man as an example of a black person's Christian conversion, the interpreters suggest that his beautiful blackness

---

[70] Roa, *Estado de los bienaventurados en el cielo*, 44–45; my emphasis. Stoichita's citation of this passage in "The Image of the Black in Spanish Art" oddly uses a French translation of Roa's text from 1631 instead of the original Spanish from 1624 (209). The French translation significantly modifies the original Spanish declaration "Ni desdize lo negro de la hermosura" (which I translated above as "Nor will their blackness make them less beautiful" to "Et ce n'est pas une chose messeante à la beauté que le noir," translated by Stoichita as "There is nothing more unbecoming to beauty than black" (209). The French translation offers a superlative negative statement about the color black as the antithesis of beauty, whereas the original Spanish lauds the black beauty of the saved black individual.

[71] For an overview of these classical and medieval theories, see Thomas Hahn, "The Difference the Middle Ages Makes: Color and Race before the Modern World," *Journal of Medieval and Early Modern Studies* 31, no. 1 (2001): 1–37.

is not a unique attribute to the figure on the canvas (as could be conceived in the aforementioned images of Benedict of Palermo) but one achievable by all black Christian converts. Finally, while it is true that the black man in the painting is kneeling to receive the baptism, no description of the painting describes his beauty as contingent on his servility, only on the grace of receiving the blood of Jesus's sacrifice.

FIGURATIVE USES OF BLACKNESS

Additional support for the interpreters' unique descriptions of blackness in relation not only to beauty but to Christian virtue appears in Sacabuche's testimony when he uses blackness figuratively to describe Claver's virtues. In the first example, Sacabuche explains that when Sacabuche became ill, Claver took him to his room and had him sleep in his own bed until he felt well again so that Claver, who would sleep on the floor by his side, could care for him. To characterize the love with which Claver treated him in such circumstances, Sacabuche states: "lo faceva con tanto amore, volonta e schietteza come se fosse stato un altro moro come questo Testimonio" [he did this with so much love, will, and candor it was as if he were another black man like this witness].[72] Significantly, Sacabuche does not state that Claver took care of him as if Sacabuche were white like Claver, but rather that Claver acted as if he were *black* like Sacabuche. With this language, the vignette expresses Sacabuche's perception of Claver's embodiment of the Christian virtues of love, dedication, and sincerity in relation to his proximity to blackness. In addition, the simile invokes a sense of community, constituted by reciprocal good treatment, in relation to Sacabuche's blackness. This positive figurative use of blackness is based on associating blackness with Christian humility, love, devotion, and candor.

Sacabuche's testimony also positively deploys blackness to describe Claver's virtue in a vignette explaining how Claver temporarily became black through a peculiar form of self-mortification with mosquitos. Describing Claver's and Sacabuche's missions to the countryside to minister to the black men and women of the villages surrounding Cartagena, Sacabuche explains that some nights:

erano tante le zampane che se li parevano sopra la detta faccia e mani che di biancho pareva nero, et esso no le amazzava ne faceva movimento ma che le

---

[72] *Proceso* 1676, Sacabuche, 100r.

tolerava e soffriva come se fosse stato insensibile proseguendo de dette sue essortationi con molto fervore e spirito et era tanto il danno e combattimento che li facevano le dette zampane che il giorno seguente rimaneva con la detta faccia e mani piene de molti segni gonfiate e annegrite.

[the mosquitos covering Father Claver's face and hands [while he preached] were so many that though he was white, he looked black. And still he never killed them or scared them away, rather he tolerated them and suffered as if he did not feel them, continuing in his ministry with much fervor and spirit. The harm and damage the mosquitos caused him were so extreme that the next day he was left with his face and hands full of many marks, swollen and blackened.][73]

The turn of phrase stating that although Claver was white, "pareva nero" [he looked black], rings of the verse from the Song of Songs mentioned earlier. In this iteration, however, unlike those that present the Bride's blackness as antithetical to her beauty, Sacabuche's testimony highlights the spiritual value of blackness without framing it as contradictory. He describes Claver's momentary physical blackness as an example of his evangelical zeal and saintly humility. As in Sacabuche's statement regarding Claver's care for him when he was sick, this declaration describes Claver's Christian virtue by associating it with blackness.

Long before the testimonies of the *Proceso* manuscript were recorded in Cartagena, Sandoval's first edition of his treatise cited language similar to the interpreters' notions of radiant and beautiful Christian blackness when describing black men's and women's celebrations after becoming Christian in Cartagena. For example, in one of Sandoval's vignettes celebrating the efficacy of black baptisms in Cartagena, he explains that newly Christianized black men and women often gift each other and their interpreters oil to blacken and shine their skin after the ceremonies. On being baptized:

riendose, alegrandose y regozijandose entresi, y dando de este contento muestras con abraçarse, hac[en] lo mesmo los hombres al Padre, y todos al interprete que les sirvio de lengua, o madrina, preguntandola por su casa, para yrla a ver, y regalar con la miseria que algunos traen de su tierra, y pediran a sus amos, que son unos coroços, coquillos monteses y azeyte de palmas, *conque untados se ponen atesados como azabache.*

[they laugh, make merry, and delight among themselves, expressing this happiness by hugging each other. Then the men do the same to the father, and everyone does the same to the interpreter who served as their translator or godparent, asking her where she lives in order to go see her home and give her a gift of some miserable

[73] Ibid., 101r.

thing they have brought with them from their land or they ask their masters for some *corozos*, little mountain nuts, and palm oil, *with which they paint themselves to become jet black.*][74]

In this passage Sandoval provides proof of black men's and women's acceptance of Christianity by referencing what he interprets for his readers as their celebrations and practices of gratitude, celebrations that entail making black skin blacker and more brilliant. The passage actually recalls an earlier description in Sandoval's treatise, which he borrows from Marco Polo's description of "blacks of Saint Thomas" in the Malabar region of the Indian Peninsula who believe themselves to be more beautiful the blacker they are:

y quanto mas negros, tanto mas lindos, y bellos cre[en] parecer: y assi untã a los muchachos tres vezes cada semana con un cierto azeyte con[que] se ponen muy negros. En resolucion el mas negro es tenido por mas hermoso: y esto es en tanto grado, q[ue] haz[en] las imagines [*sic*] de sus dioses negrissimas, dizi[en]do, que los dioses son negros: y por el cõtrario pintã a los demonios blancos, sinificãdo cõ esta pintura gran fealdad.

[they believe the blacker they are, the more lovely and beautiful. For this reason, three times a week, they rub their children with a certain oil that makes them very black. In general, the blackest is considered the most beautiful, to such an extent that the images they make of their gods are extremely black, saying that their gods are black. On the contrary, they paint their demons white to signify great ugliness.][75]

Passages such as these demonstrate Sandoval attempting to momentarily expand his own readers' symbolic perceptions of the value of skin color to consider the beauty and self-perception of black Christians in Spanish America. He does this to help priests be more effective evangelizers among black men and women, not to change their own aesthetic tastes.

Sandoval underscores the benefits of such an ambivalent approach to valuing blackness when he warns that using language of "whitening black souls" when speaking to black catechumens produces the opposite of the

---

[74] Sandoval, *Naturaleza, policia sagrada*, book 3, chap. 3, 240v; my emphasis.

[75] Ibid., book 1, chap. 29, 106v. This passage first appears in Marco Polo and then is incorporated into versions of Sir John Mandeville's *Travels* to talk about the peoples of Numidia. According to Mandeville, blackness for the Numidians "hold[s] a great beauty, and aye the blacker they are the fairer they think them ... And if they think them not black enough when they are born, they use certain medicines for to make them black withal. That country is wonder hot, and that makes the fold thereof so black" (Mandeville, *Travels, Texts and Translations*, I: 33, qtd. in Alden Vaughn and Virginia Vaughn, "Before Othello: Elizabethan Representations of Sub-Saharan Africans," *William and Mary Quarterly* 54, no. 1 (1997): 19–44, 22–23.

desired effect of convincing black men and women to become Christians. Sandoval notes the rejection missionaries would face in practice if they were to ask black captives if they wanted to receive the water of the baptism to emulate white men and women: "es cierto que no solo no le darían [su consentimiento], pero abominarian en sus corazones el agua, como cosa de blancos, gente que ellos tienen por capitales enemigos" [it is true that not only would they not give their consent to the baptism, but they would hate that water in their hearts as a thing of white people, people who they consider their capital enemies].[76] Instead, Sandoval recommends that priests (and their interpreters) convince black men and women to receive the water of baptism to acquire the esteem of *being Christian*, not of being white:

Tãbien se les dirà luego en este p[un]to q[ue] la causa de ser los blãcos tã estimados de todos, es, por aver recebido esta agua conq[ue] se hizierõ Christianos, q[ue] si no lo fuera[n] no uviera quien hiziera caso dellos. Que la recib[en] ellos tãbien, y serã estimados como ellos, podran yr a los templos y casas de Dios, tratar, y comer con los demas Christianos: y quãdo se mueran los enterraran en la Iglesia si son Christianos, o si no en el muladar, donde sean comidos de perros.

[You will tell them at this point that the reason whites are the most esteemed people of all is because they received this water that made them Christian. If it were not for that water, no one would pay any attention to whites at all. They [the black men and women] should receive the water, too, and they will become *esteemed like them*. They will be able to enter the temples and houses of God and interact and eat with all other Christians. And when they die, if they are Christian they will be buried in the Church; if not, they will be thrown in a pile of trash where they will be eaten by dogs.][77]

In this series of statements, Sandoval acknowledges that the success of the evangelical mission among black men and women involves disassociating Christianity from whiteness to make it enticing to potential black converts. These passages demonstrate the Jesuit's awareness of the limited use of whitening rhetoric in settings where black men's and women's perceptions and value systems had to be taken into consideration to persuade them to accept Christianity willingly. It is possible that his frequent interactions with black interpreters and other newly arrived black men and women helped him understand this necessity, though without more evidence such a conclusion rests in conjecture. Neither can we know what Sacabuche's undeclared intentions were in the

---

[76] Sandoval, *Naturaleza, policia sagrada*, book 3, chap. 5, 254r.
[77] Ibid., book 3, chap. 10, 273v–274r.

narration of his own testimony, or how much was subsequently changed by the notary who put his words into writing or the translator who transformed his testimony into Italian in Rome. What we do know is that testimonies attributed to Sacabuche and his interpreter colleagues describe black men and women in ways that significantly differ from those by other witnesses to the same events and from the broader visual and discursive tradition about black Christians circulating in the Iberian Atlantic world.

The superlative beauty and virtue of blackness are the most salient differences that emerge from the interpreters' descriptions of the transformation of Christian conversion. The similarity between the sections from Sandoval's treatise about black men's and women's attitudes toward conversion and its association with color cited above and the testimonies of Claver's interpreters suggest that the interpreters might have generated their notions of radiant and beautiful black Christian bodies from language and practices that had begun to circulate among black men and women in Cartagena earlier in the century. The next chapter's examination of writings by and about Úrsula de Jesús, a black spiritual intermediary in seventeenth-century Lima, will demonstrate that even though the interpreters' language for beautiful and virtuous blackness was uncommon compared with precedents from the Iberian world reviewed above, it was not entirely unique to Cartagena.

5

Salvation and the Making of Blackness in Colonial Lima

Úrsula de Jesús

As the transatlantic slave trade in the late sixteenth and the first half of the seventeenth century shipped captive black men, women, and children from west African ports to Cartagena and then again to the interior of New Granada and Peru, populations of people of African descent steadily increased in the Andean region. This demographic shift had a significant impact on Lima, where people of African descent outnumbered Spaniards for most of the seventeenth century.[1] Confirming census records from this period, some contemporary narratives describe Lima as a predominantly black city.[2]

Many more texts from the period emphasize the city's reputation for exceptional Christian piety. An example from a mid-seventeenth-century author exalts the city as: "Esta Ciudad de los Reyes ... cuya Liberalidad Caritativa, y Limosnera en sus habitadores excede todo hyperbole ... cuya Fe, Lealtad, y Religion Cristiana puede ser exemplar a muchos Reynos" [This City of Kings ... whose inhabitants' generosity and charity exceeds all hyperbole ... whose faith, loyalty, and Christian religion can serve as a model for many Kingdoms].[3] Lima's fame for fervent religiosity

---

[1] Bowser, *The African Slave in Colonial Peru*, 337–41. See also the demographic discussion in the Introduction.

[2] In 1639, the Jesuit chronicler Bernabé Cobo states that compared with Spaniards, who numbered 5,000–6,000, there were 30,000 black men and women living in and around Lima, half of whom spent most of their time working the fields outside the city. See Bernabé Cobo, *Obras*, vol. 2, ed. Francisco Mateos (Madrid: Biblioteca de Autores Españoles, 1956), 306. A separate indigenous town, named El Cercado, was created to group native populations separately from the Spanish.

[3] "Espejo de religiosas..." (also called *Vida anónima de Úrsula de Jesús*, edited and transcribed by Nancy van Deusen), Archivo Franciscano de Lima, Registro 17, 585r–608r, f. 585v. This hagiography will be identified in the rest of the chapter as the *Vida*

especially grew after the saintly fame of Francisco Solano and Rose of
Lima spread across the Catholic world in the second decade of the
seventeenth century. Rose of Lima's identity as an autochthonous
Limeña, in particular, bolstered the proliferation of the city's reputation
as a "reliquario de santos" [reliquary of saints] by mid-century.[4] Inspired
by the successful global dissemination of the cults of Francisco Solano and
Rose of Lima and the general fervor for accruing spiritual capital in
Spanish American viceroyalties during this period, crafting and collecting
biographies of spiritually venerable individuals became particularly
common among the religious orders active in Lima. These hagiographies
were meant to serve at least two purposes: an edifying one (offering
models of behavior for other Christians to emulate) and a propagandistic
one (celebrating the particular order and the geographic location affiliated
with the individual).[5]

Lima's two reputations – of blackness and exemplary holiness – coincide in a set of narratives produced in the city in the second half of the
seventeenth century about a black woman with a reputation for being a
visionary and an effective spiritual intermediary to save souls in purgatory.
A contemporary of the black interpreters employed by the Jesuits in Cartagena, Úrsula de Jésus was born a slave in 1604 in Lima to her mother Isabel
de los Ríos. When Úrsula was approximately seven years old, her owner
Gerónima de los Ríos died and she was sent to another wealthy household
in Lima where she lived with an elite *beata* and visionary named Luisa
Melgarejo de Sotomayor. *Beatas*, such as Melgarejo, were religious

---

anónima and the second hagiography of Úrsula de Jesús. For more on baroque narrative
praise of Lima's religiosity, see Carlos Gálvez Peña, "La ciudad letrada y santa: La ciudad
de Los Reyes en la historiografía del siglo XVII," in *Urbanismo y vida urbana en
Iberoamérica colonial* (Bogota: Archivo de Bogota, 2008), 71–101.

[4] On the rise of the popularity of the hagiographic mode in seventeenth-century Lima, see
Fernando Iwasaki Cauti, "Vidas de santos y santas vidas: Hagiografías reales e imaginarias en Lima colonial,"*Anuario de estudios americanos* 51, no. 1 (1994): 57–64. On Rose,
her life, texts, and beatification and canonization processes, see Kathleen Ann Myers,
"Redeemer of America: Rosa de Lima (1586–1617), the Dynamics of Identity, and
Canonization," in *Colonial Saints: Discovering the Holy in the Americas, 1500–1800*,
ed. Allan Greer and Jodi Bilinkoff (London: Routledge, 2003), 251–75.

[5] Hagiographies from seventeenth-century Lima were mostly kept as manuscripts in convent
and monastery libraries for local memory and consumption. Some were also published as
stand-alone narratives or as chapters in anthologies sponsored by individual religious
orders. The most well-known hagiographic anthologies from seventeenth-century Lima
are the Franciscan Diego de Córdova y Salinas, *Crónica Franciscana de las Provincias del
Perú* [1650], ed. Lino Canedo (Washington, DC: Academy of American Franciscan
History, 1957) and the Dominican Juan Meléndez, *Tesoros verdaderos de las Indias*
(Rome: Angel Tinasio, 1681).

laywomen who lived outside of convents but nonetheless professed non-binding vows of celibacy and devotion.[6] Melgarejo was born in Tunja to Andalusian parents and then married a prominent doctor residing in Lima. She was considered a visionary because she frequently fell into trances in which she would report having conversations with God.[7] As Nancy van Deusen has explained, due to Úrsula's living in Melgarejo's home between the ages of seven and twelve, Úrsula likely learned from Melgarejo how to "concentrate on and interpret" religious images at an age when other children were learning to read and write.[8] Thus, as many other religious women before and around her, Úrsula became adept at reading God in the world even if she probably never learned to read words.[9]

After about five years of living in Melarejo's home, Úrsula entered Lima's Convent of Santa Clara to serve the niece of Gerónima de los Ríos – Inés de Pulgar – who was joining the religious community as a nun. There, in the convent, Úrsula labored as one of the approximately 100–130 slaves of the religious community for almost thirty years before a different nun in the community purchased her freedom in response to Úrsula's declared intention of leaving the convent to work as a rented

---

[6] We do not know if Úrsula's mother Isabela went with her to Melgarejo's house after de los Ríos's death. On the Iberian-imported tradition of *beatas* in colonial Spanish America, see Jessica Delgado, *Laywomen and the Making of Colonial Catholicism in New Spain, 1630–1790* (New York: Cambridge University Press, 2018), 8–9; Jacqueline Holler, *Escogidas Plantas: Nuns and Beatas in Mexico City, 1531–1601* (New York: Columbia University Press, 2005). Beatas could live in a *beatario* or in their own homes.

[7] For a brief seventeenth-century hagiography of Luisa Melgarejo Sotomayor, see Diego Córdova y Salinas, *Crónica franciscana*, 969–70. For scholarship on Melgarejo Sotomayor, see van Deusen, *Embodying the Sacred*, 47–70; Fernando Iwasaki Cauti, "Luisa Melgarejo de Soto y la alegría de ser tu testigo, señor," *Histórica* 19, no. 2 (1995): 219–51; Iwasaki Cauti, "Mujeres al borde de la perfección: Rosa de Santa María y las alumbradas de Lima," *Hispanic American Historical Review* 73, no. 4 (1993): 581–613. On the currency and means of monitoring otherworldly visions and trances in Europe in the sixteenth and seventeenth centuries, see Moshe Sluhovsky, *Believe Not Every Spirit: Possession, Mysticism, and Discernment in Early Modern Europe* (Chicago: Chicago University Press, 2005).

[8] Van Deusen, *The Souls of Purgatory*, 15.

[9] No record exists that definitively indicates Úrsula learned to read, but she does describe wanting to learn several times in her spiritual diary (11r; 85; 14v; 92). The existence of her spiritual diary itself demonstrates that she participated in a form of "delegated writing," a phrase coined by Armando Petrucci and employed by Kathryn Burns, *Into the Archive: Writing and Power in Colonial Peru* (Durham, NC: Duke University Press, 2010), 126, to describe written interventions made through intermediaries such as notaries or amanuenses. On an African woman who became a religious servant in eighteenth-century Salamanca and wrote her own poetry, see the critical edition translation of Juan Carlos Pan y Agua's hagiography of Sor Teresea Juliana de Santo Domingo (*Black Bride of Christ: Chicaba, an African Nun in Eighteenth-Century Spain*, ed. and trans. Sue Houchins and Baltasar Fra Molinero [Nashville: Vanderbilt University Press, 2018]).

slave.[10] After receiving her freedom, Úrsula eventually chose to stay on in the convent as a *donada*, becoming a novice in December 1645 and swearing her vows in June 1647.[11] *Donadas,* such as Úrsula, were religious servants in early modern convents and monasteries who professed vows but ranked third in importance after nuns of the black veil and nuns of the white veil.[12] Attaining *donada* status required being free, submitting an *auto de ingreso* to be approved by voting members of the community of nuns, and paying a dowry of 500 pesos (a modest sum compared with the 1,500-peso dowry of nuns of the white veil and the dowry of 2,000–3,200 pesos required for nuns of the black veil).[13] It bears noting that despite ranking third after nuns of the black and white veils, *donada* status was the highest position to which women of African or indigenous descent could aspire in Limeñan convents.[14] Questions about the spiritual

---

[10] For the number of slaves in Santa Clara, see van Deusen, *Souls of Purgatory,* 26–27. On slavery inside female convents in colonial Spanish America, see McKinley, *Fractional Freedoms,* 148–52; van Deusen, *Embodying the Sacred,* 95–116; Asunción Lavrin, *Brides of Christ: Conventual Life in Colonial Mexico* (Stanford, CA: Stanford University Press, 2008), 165–68; van Deusen, *Souls of Purgatory,* 26–32; Kathryn Burns, *Colonial Habits: Convents and the Spiritual Economy of Cuzco* (Durham, NC: Duke University Press, 1999), 114–16. For the practice of renting slaves for use by another employer in colonial Lima, see McKinley, *Fractional Freedoms,* 16–17.

[11] All of the biographical information provided in this paragraph comes from the two hagiographies about Úrsula. The second hagiography adds a detail not in the first that she was the legitimate daughter of Juan de Castilla and Isabel de los Ríos, an addition Patrícia Martínez i Àlvarez suggests is related to the second hagiography's effort to present Úrsula in a more favorable light to promote her as a potential saint *La libertad femenina de dar lugar a dios* [Lima: Universidad Nacional Mayor de San Marcos, 2004], 362–63.

[12] In seventeenth-century Lima, as van Deusen has shown, most *donadas* were of African descent. See Nancy van Deusen, "God Lives among the Pots and Pans: Donadas (Religious Servants) in Seventeenth-Century Lima," in *Africans to Spanish America,* 136–60, 140. The chapter also appears in a modified form in *Embodying the Sacred: Women Mystics in Seventeenth-Century Lima* (Durham, NC: Duke University Press, 2018), 95–116. On a different category of *donada,* that of the women and children donated *to* convents as slaves, see van Deusen, "God Lives among the Pots and Pans," 142–43, as well as McKinley, *Fractional Freedoms,* 148–52.

[13] On dowries for nunneries in colonial Lima, see Luis Martín, *Daughters of the Conquistadors: Women of the Viceroyalty of Peru* (Dallas: Southern Methodist University Press, 1989), 180–82; Amaya Fernández Fernández et al., *La Mujer en la conquista y la evangelización en el Perú* (Lima 1550–1650) (Lima: Pontificia Universidad Católica del Perú, 1997), 190; van Deusen, *Embodying the Sacred,* 101. Burns, *Colonial Habits,* 33, and Luis Martín, *Daughters of the Conquistadors,* 181–82, note that sometimes dowries were waived for black veil postulants with valuable social stature (in the case of Cuzco) or talents such as singing (in the case of Lima).

[14] The first and second Councils of Lima stated that only Spanish and *criolla* women could become nuns. Van Deusen, *Embodying the Sacred,* 96, n. 2; Tardieu, *Los negros y la iglesia,* vol. 1, 385. See also Kathryn Burns, *Colonial Habits,* on the emergence of

significance of the worldly hierarchies separating the poorer and darker-skinned slaves, servants, and *donadas* from the wealthier Spanish or *criolla* nuns in convents like hers pervade the corpus of writings produced by and about Úrsula de Jesús in seventeenth-century Lima.

These writings about Úrsula de Jesús depict her as a visionary and spiritual intermediary who conveyed messages between souls in purgatory, God, and the living. Spiritual intermediaries, such as Úrsula, were not uncommon in early modern Catholic societies that believed that almost all souls who were not condemned to hell went to purgatory after death to purify their souls from venial sins committed before death. From purgatory, souls would eventually enter heaven after a determined amount of suffering. It was a common perception that souls in purgatory could be pardoned some suffering in purgatory through an intermediary's prayers on their behalf before God. Úrsula presented herself and was considered by her spiritual community to be such an intermediary. Thus, while she does not translate between languages, like the black interpreters of Cartagena de Indias examined in the previous two chapters, her work as a spiritual intermediary also involved relaying messages to and from distinct interlocutors who would not otherwise understand each other. Also like the black interpreters in Cartagena, her spiritual mediation sometimes involved serving as an advocate for either party in those communications. Finally, and most significantly, like the texts produced in collaboration with the interpreters in Cartagena, Úrsula de Jesús's spiritual diary develops a notion of Christian blackness articulated in relation to both spiritual virtue and corporal beauty. Juxtaposing the texts about Úrsula in Lima to those about the black interpreters of Cartagena suggests the existence of a shared positive language to conceive of blackness among African- and American-born people of African descent in both cities in the seventeenth century.

Mapping the genesis of the three texts composed in seventeenth-century Lima about Úrsula de Jesús is an important element of this juxtaposition. After becoming a *donada*, in 1647 Úrsula's then-confessor Jesuit father Miguel Salazar requested that she keep a spiritual diary to remember and monitor the many otherworldly visions and voices she reported experiencing.[15] Resulting from this request, over the course of

---

racialized hierarchy in the Convent of Santa Clara in Cuzco in the late sixteenth and early seventeenth centuries, 101–31.

[15] *Vida breve de la madre Úrsula de Jesús*, Archivo de Santa Clara de Lima, 3r–6r, 4r; *Vida anónima de la venerable madre Úrsula de Jesús*, Archivo Franciscano de Lima, Registro

at least eleven years between 1650 and 1661, Úrsula related descriptions
of her visions and conversations out loud to nuns of her convent to
transcribe.[16] Fifty-one and a-half of the fifty-seven folios of the diary
survive in the convent's archive. These folios present a series of episodic
entries describing her visions, conversations with holy voices, and reflections about her life as a religious servant. While we admittedly do not
know why some pages of the diary are not included in the version of the
diary that was bound in the eighteenth century in the convent archive, the
surviving pages of the diary do not appear to have been censored or
carefully scrutinized by her confessors who had access to them.[17] Instead,
the diary served as grist for the composition of two anonymous hagiographies about Úrsula de Jesús, composed soon after her death. The first of
the two (cited hereafter as the *Vida breve*) is a short sketch of her life by
an unnamed nun from her convent around 1666 that functionally serves
as a preface to her spiritual diary in the convent archive.[18] The second

17, no. 45, n.d., ff. 585r–607v, f. 587v. The *Vida breve* ends with a list of some of
Úrsula's confessors: Miguel de Salazar (Jesuit), Antonio Ruiz (Jesuit), Francisco Rebelo
(Franciscan), and Antonio de la Calancha (Augustinian), 6r. On hagiographies about
black individuals in the Andes before Salazar asked Úrsula to begin her diary, see Brewer-
García, "Hierarchy and Holiness" and Rowe's analysis of Estefanía de San José's hagi-
ography from 1646 (*Black Saints*, 220–22).

[16] Úrsula de Jesús, *Diario espiritual de la venerable Úrsula de Jesús, escrita por ella misma*,
Archivo de Santa Clara de Lima, 8r–60r. A modernized transcription of the diary in Spanish
has been published by van Deusen as *Almas del purgatorio: El diario spiritual y vida
anónima de Úrsula de Jesús, una mística negra del siglo XVI* (Lima: Fondo Editorial de la
Pontificia Universidad Católica del Perú, 2012). The English translation of the diary is van
Deusen, ed., *The Souls of Purgatory: The Spiritual Diary of a Seventeenth-Century Afro-
Peruvian Mystic, Ursula de Jesús* (Albuquerque: University of New Mexico Press, 2004).

[17] Van Deusen dates the manuscript of her diary from 1650–61 because those dates are
given on different pages in the manuscript. Despite marginal notation of those dates, the
text itself is undated because the episodes do not make references to years, only to the
cyclical Christian calendar, such as "on the eve of the Epiphany" and "on Saint Pedro
Nolasco's feast day." For neither narrator nor the amanuenses it appeared to have
mattered in what year the episodes occurred. As for the identity of the amanuenses, little
is known. The shifts in handwriting, spelling, and narrative voice in the manuscript signal
that its production resulted from the interaction of Úrsula and at least two different nuns
of the convent. Also, as van Deusen has noted, there is a significant shift in narrative voice
from first to third person more than halfway through the text (29v–34r; introduction to
Almas del purgatorio, 150). While most of Úrsula's visions are recounted in the first
person, this portion of the text shifts to the third person. On the likely lack of censorship
of Úrsula's spiritual diary, see van Deusen, introduction to *Souls of Purgatory*, 60;
introduction to *Almas del purgatorio*, 151.

[18] *Vida breve de la madre Úrsula de Jesús*. My transcription of this first hagiography is taken
from the images of Úrsula's spiritual diary included in the CD-ROM supplement to *Las
almas del purgatorio*, ed. van Deusen.

hagiography about Úrsula (cited hereafter as the *Vida anónima*) is a much longer but unfinished narrative composed around 1686.[19] I consider the *Vida anónima* unfinished because its title announces that it will discuss Úrsula's "vida, virtud y muerte" [life, virtues, and death], but the manuscript concludes before reaching the end of her life. The first hagiography, the *Vida breve*, although shorter, includes information about her death and funerary services – standard criteria that hagiographies of this period use to stress the venerable individual's "good death" as proof of their blessed status. The second hagiographer was probably planning on copying, summarizing, or paraphrasing the conclusion to the first hagiography when their efforts were interrupted. This deduction makes sense because entire sections of the second hagiography are taken from the first hagiography, including passages copied verbatim or only slightly modified to elevate the style of its narration or to adjust the interpretation of its thematic content.[20] Both hagiographies base themselves heavily on Úrsula's own spiritual diary.

This chapter compares the three texts about Úrsula to analyze the extent of the influence of her diary's portrayal of blackness on the two posthumous hagiographies composed about her. The comparison will reveal that the spiritual diary's portrayal of blackness was only selectively incorporated into the later narratives about Úrsula, demonstrating competing notions of Christian blackness circulating in late seventeenth-century Lima.

ÚRSULA AND FEMALE AUTOBIOGRAPHICAL CONVENT WRITING IN COLONIAL SPANISH AMERICA

Úrsula's spiritual diary is rather exceptional within the genre of female autobiographical convent writing because texts of this type generally

---

[19] In the Archivo Franciscano de Lima, the document appears under the title "Vida de la Venerable Madre Ursula de Jesucristo," but van Deusen, whose transcription I use, calls it *Vida anónima*. I keep van Deusen's terminology for clarity to distinguish it from the *Vida breve*. Van Deusen approximates the date for the composition of the *Vida anónima* in her introduction to *Souls of Purgatory*, 1.

[20] For a comparison of the style of the two different hagiographies and Úrsula's diary, see Martínez i Àlvarez, *La libertad femenina de dar lugar a dios*; Martínez i Àlvarez, "La oralidad femenina en el texto escrito colonial: Úrsula de Jesús," *Revista Andina* 38 (2004): 201–33; Martínez i Àlvarez and Elisenda Padrós Wolff, "Úrsula de Jesús: La palabra de Dios en el cuerpo propio," in *Catequesis y derecho en la América colonial. Fronteras borrosas*, ed. Roland Schmidt-Riese and Lucía Rodríguez (Madrid: Iberoamericana, 2010), 217–34.

focus on elite women such as the well-known mystics Teresa de Jesús from Ávila, Spain, and Francisca Josefa de Castillo from Tunja, New Granada. The content of Úrsula's diary differs from these examples because, as van Deusen has noted, it does not resort to many of the genre's common tropes that emphasize the autobiographical character's physical weakness and spectacular practices of self-abnegation, which Alison Weber and Kristine Ibsen, among others, have aptly described as ways to validate female experiences and subject positions.[21]

Yet something Úrsula's diary does share with other examples of autobiographical female convent writing from both sides of the Atlantic is the autobiographical narrator's need to negotiate the question of whether her visions are of divine or diabolical origin. Teresa de Jesús famously addresses this suspicion in the *Libro de mi vida* through offering accounts of additional visions to implicitly contradict her confessor, who had diagnosed her visions as diabolical:

Suplicaba mucho a Dios me librase de ser engañada; esto siempre lo hacía y con hartas lágrimas; y a San Pedro, y San Pablo, que me dijo el Señor (como fue la primera vez que me apareció en su día) que ellos me guardarían no fuese engañada; y así muchas veces los vía al lado izquierdo muy claramente, aunque no con visión imaginaria.

[I besought God often to set me free from deception; indeed, I was continually doing so and with many tears. I would also invoke Saint Peter and Saint Paul, for the Lord had told me (it was on their festival that He had first appeared to me) that they would prevent me from being deluded; and I used often to see them very clearly on my left hand, though not in an imaginary vision.][22]

In Teresa's careful response to her confessor's assessment of her visions, she explains that God provided her with even more signs of their divine

---

[21] Van Deusen, introduction to *Souls of Purgatory*, 52. For studies of typical tropes of the genre, see Alison Weber, *Saint Theresa and the Rhetoric of Femininity* (Princeton: Princeton University Press, 1996); Kristine Ibsen, *Women's Spiritual Autobiography in Colonial Spanish America* (Gainesville: University Press of Florida, 1999); Electa Arenal and Stacy Schlau, "Stratagems of the Weak: Autobiographical Prose of the Seventh-Century Hispanic Convent," *Tulsa Studies in Women's Literature* 9, no. 1 (1990): 25–42; Asunsión Lavrin, "Unlike Sor Juana? The Model Nun in the Religious Literature of Colonial Mexico," in *Feminist Perspectives on Sor Juana Inés de la Cruz*, ed. Stephanie Merrim (Detroit: Wayne State University Press, 1991), 61–85; and Kathryn Joy McKnight, *The Mystic from Tunja: The Writings of Madre Castillo, 1671–1742* (Amherst: University of Massachusetts Press, 1997).

[22] Teresa de Jesús, *Libro de la vida*, 349; Teresa de Jesús, *The Life of Teresa of Jesus: The Autobiography of Teresa of Ávila*, trans. E. Allison Peers (New York: Doubleday, 2004), 240. See Ibsen, *Women's Spiritual Autobiography*, 46–47, on adaptations of this strategy in women's convent writing in Spanish America.

origin in the form of new visions of saints. Echoing Teresa de Ávila's accumulative strategy for confirming the validity of her visions, the narrating voice of Úrsula's diary presents Úrsula as an involuntary visionary, wary of being tricked by false visions but nonetheless chosen by God to have them. For example, in a salient episode, Úrsula recounts a recent conversation with God in which she told him she did not want to think about his passion because it provoked visions for her that she feared could be of diabolical origin, noting: "no queria que viniera aquel a engañar" [I did not want that one to trick me].[23] She explains that God answered her by giving her an additional vision:

Y a media ora vi al Señor dentro del sagrario en un sepulcro, orando, y en Él un cuerpo mui grande y estilando sangre por la cabesa y por los pies. Lo demas estaba cubierto con la sabana santa. Despues de media ora se deçianme [sic] que mirase aquellas llagas. Que abia munchos [sic] dias que no estaba io en ellas.

[Within a half hour I saw the Lord within the monstrance, praying in a tomb, His body quite large and discharging blood from His head and feet. The rest of Him was covered with a holy shroud. After half an hour they told me I should look at His wounds, because I had not done so for many days.][24]

Úrsula's diary thus narrates Úrsula's fruitless attempt to avoid having visions and then indirectly endorses them by citing the holy voices who direct her to do precisely what she had been avoiding. While Teresa's manipulation is more carefully plotted to foil the interpretive capacity of the confessor who appears as a character in the narrative, both Teresa and Úrsula similarly present themselves throughout their autobiographical texts as obedient recipients of God's visions, chosen despite their declared distrust in their own abilities to discern their visions' origins.

As evident in the passage above from Úrsula's diary, the typical structure of the narratives of Úrsula's visions begins with a description of the vision immediately followed by the interpretation of that vision by holy voices who give the vision its meaning. The narrator thus presents herself as a carrier of messages of divine authority rather than an authority who dares to interpret the visions herself. To complement this positioning, sometimes Úrsula appears as a character in the episodes, interjecting to ask the holy voices questions about why she deserves to have such visions

---

[23] Úrsula de Jesús, *Diario espiritual*, 35v; 126. The first number provided in parentheses in all citations from Úrsula's diary refers to the folio of the original Spanish manuscript as transcribed by van Deusen in *Las almas del purgatorio*, and the second number refers to the page number from van Deusen's English translation, *The Souls of Purgatory*.

[24] Ibid.

in the first place. For example, in the diary's opening exchange with the soul in purgatory of a Franciscan friar, the narrator states: "Como me pedia [ayuda] con tanto aynco, dije que qué era yo y qué balia para aquello?" [Because he continually insisted, I said to him, Who am I, what worth do I have to do such a thing?].[25] In such instances, Úrsula underscores her humility and anticipates critiques others might have of her descriptions of the visions. In other instances, she speaks back to the holy voices to ask questions about their substance or meaning; but in doing so, she often includes a caveat that her questions are not spoken of her own volition. For example, after describing a dialogue she had with a soul in purgatory belonging to María Bran, a black woman who had lived in her convent and had died more than fourteen years before, Úrsula the narrator interjects to explain to her audience that the questions she asked in the exchange were not her own: "Yo cuando ago estas preguntas, no las ago porque quiero, sino que asi como beo y me ablan sin que quiera, asi me asen ablar sin querer yo" [When I ask these questions I do not do so because I want to but, just as I see them and they speak to me without my wishing it to happen, they make me speak to them without wanting to].[26] Within this mode of self-presentation as an involuntary visionary and obedient carrier of divine messages, Úrsula's diary develops one of its most salient themes: the logic and criteria of divine justice determining who would be condemned to hell, who could go directly to heaven, and who would first have to be purified in purgatory.

DIVINE JUSTICE AND BLACKNESS IN ÚRSULA'S SPIRITUAL DIARY

Úrsula's diary's visions about divine justice reflect a preoccupation with how differences between black, indigenous, and white people in Lima's worldly society relate to the Christian doctrine of the equality of all people before God. Many of Úrsula's visions stress that although God provides *all* people with the necessary tools for saving themselves (memory, understanding, and will),[27] only some souls choose to use them. Those souls who choose redemption can be white, indigenous, or black,

---

[25] Úrsula de Jesús, *Diario espiritual*, 8r; 79–80.   [26] Ibid., 8v; 80, translation modified.

[27] These are criteria elaborated by Augustine in *On the Trinity, Confessions,* and *The City of God,* among other locations. While Úrsula does not cite Augustine, the commentary from her visions demonstrates reflections on the application and implication of Augustine for all Christians.

the diary insists. For example, one of Úrsula's recurring visions involves the appearance of a giant ladder that reaches toward heaven on which "jente de todas nasiones" [people from many different nations] ascend: "bi al pie desta escalera – por todas cuatro partes tan gran multitud de jente de todas nasiones y una gran multitud al rrededor de aquella" [then, I saw, at the foot of the stairway, there, at all four parts, a great multitude of people of all nations and another great multitude surrounding them].[28] The biblical story of Jacob's dream from Genesis 28:10, Psalm 121, and John 1:51 are likely sources for these visions.[29] Holy voices teach Úrsula upon seeing the vision that the variety of people she sees in it means that everyone begins on equal footing when it comes to climbing toward salvation. This teaching resonates with another declaration by a holy voice cited in Úrsula's diary that "aunque [Dios] nos crio de diferentes nasiones" [Although [God] raised us as different nations], these differences do not correlate to differences in spiritual worth: "la boluntad de negros y blancos todo era uno, que en la memoria, entendimiento y boluntad que todos eran unos, que si no las abia criado a todos a su ymajen y semejansa y Redimido con su sangre" [the will of blacks and whites is the same. In memory, understanding, and will, they are all one. Had He not created them all in His image and likeness and redeemed them with His blood?].[30] Through explicitly stating that black people are equally endowed with the ingredients for salvation and equally made in the image of God, the diary implicitly contradicts José de Acosta's argument in *De procuranda indorum salute*, examined in Chapter 1, that black and indigenous peoples in the Americas would have to undergo more physical discipline than others to ensure their salvation because they were generally considered more barbarous. In contrast to Acosta's treatise, neither indigenous nor black men and women in Úrsula's diary are presented as less civilized than the Spanish men and women described in the diary. Civility, in fact, is not a criterion of importance in the diary.

---

[28] Úrsula de Jesús, *Diario espiritual*, 56r; 157.

[29] For example, Psalm 121 (of the Vulgate) invokes Jersusalem as the city toward which God's tribes climb: "Illuc enim ascendrunt tribus, tribus Domini" [For to that place, the tribes ascended, the tribes of the Lord] (121:4). A ladder toward heaven is also invoked in the opening motif of Sor Juana de Inés de la Cruz's *Primero sueño*. In addition to the sources mentioned above, it is possible that both Úrsula's and Sor Juana's uses of this motif were influenced by texts such as Diego Murillo's *Instruccion para enseñar la virtud a los principiantes, escala espiritual de la perfeccion evangelica* (Zaragoza: Robles, 1598).

[30] Úrsula de Jesús, *Diario espiritual*, 52r; 151.

In the diary's development of the theme of the universal capacity for salvation, the narrator and character of Úrsula repeatedly question if the equal footing of all before God affects black women differently than others. For example, on one occasion, Úrsula the character asks a holy voice whether the devotion shown to God by *donadas* was of lesser value to God than that of white nuns: "¿Qué es esto que disen que la profeçion de las donadas no bale?" [What is this? They say that the profession of donadas has no value?].[31] To this question, the voice responds: "diferencias ay de las monjas porque ellas son blancas y de nacion española, mas en cuanto al alma todo es uno, quien mas ysiere baldrá mas" [There [are differences] because the nuns are white and of the Spanish nation, but with respect to the soul, all is one: Whoever does more, is worth more].[32] The voice, which she then identifies as that of Saint Francis, responds to Úrsula by underscoring the ultimate irrelevance of earthly distinctions related to skin color, social status, and place of origin when assessing an individual's spiritual virtue. The next time the diary asks a similar question, a different voice gives Úrsula a similar answer. The episode begins by Úrsula the narrator stating: "Yo e oydo desir que las profesion de las donadas no bale, y pregunteselo" [I have heard it said that what the *donada* professes has no value. I asked Him about this], and the voice responds: "Y dise que como se aga de corason que si bale; que lo demas es engaño" [He said that it has value if it comes from the heart; everything else is deception].[33] In both passages, the diary presents a common opinion about the insignificant worth of *donadas* through citing an anonymous source. Each time the opinion is refuted by Úrsula's holy voices. The refutation in the second citation juxtaposes the sincere heart, a metonym for the compliant will, to the "engaño" [lie] of the hierarchy that considers *donadas* less spiritually valuable than the nuns of the convent. The emphasis on value in both passages in the context of convent hierarchy and the cost of dowries at different levels of it, as described above, suggests that the opinion that *donadas*' vows were worthless could relate to the significantly smaller dowries they paid compared with the elite white members of their religious communities. The holy voices' insistence on the importance of one's acts rather than one's status ("quien mas ysiere baldrá mas" [Whoever does more is worth more]) could be an explicit correction to what the diary presents as a misconstrued equivalence between worldly wealth and spiritual worth. Through the dialogic structure of both accounts, Úrsula's

---

[31] Ibid., 32r; 121.   [32] Ibid. Translation modified.   [33] Ibid., 51r; 149.

diary assures its audience that *donadas* like herself are indeed appreciated by God.

Building on such assurances, a pattern in the diary suggests that black men and women are in fact more likely than white men and women to achieve salvation because of their humility and suffering on earth. In these instances, Úrsula implies that God rewards black women in particular for the special burdens they bear on earth, discounting it from their time in purgatory after death. For example, one day when Úrsula the character declares herself an "esclavita de Santa Clara" [little slave of my mother Saint Claire] in an act of prostration,[34] the holy voices respond with an encouraging maxim: "Quanto mas se abajaren aca, tanto mas subiran alla" [The more you lower your head here, the higher you can ascend there].[35] With this statement, Úrsula suggests to her audience that those of low status in this world, like herself, receive special recognition by God. The maxim could be a gloss of Jesus' teaching cited in Matthew 19:24, Mark 10:25, and Luke 18:25 that states that it is harder for a rich man to enter heaven than a camel to pass through the eye of a needle. The holy voices cited by Úrsula reframe the teaching by suggesting the ease with which the poor achieve salvation. Whereas elites sometimes figuratively occupied the discursive subject position of the spiritually venerable "esclavo" [slave], especially in their participation in confraternities whose members often declared themselves to be slaves of their patrons, Úrsula's diary underscores the humble's intimate identification with that holy subject position. In fact, the declaration suggests her resignification of the term "esclavita" [little slave] to accentuate her humility even further in using the diminutive and to present herself as a bondswoman of her order's patron saint even after becoming a freed *donada*.

The diary's emphasis on the special spiritual recognition given to humble black servants like herself appears most saliently in another example when Úrsula recounts that the holy voices tell her that God's justice vindicates those at the very bottom of the worldly social order: "dísenme de cómo se agradaba dios de los pequeñitos y umildes, y que en esta casa le agrada Florensia Bravo y Antonia de Christo, que son desechadas y nadie ase caso dellas la primera es una mulata chabacana y la

---

[34] Ibid., 40v; 133.

[35] Ibid. For a speculative reading of Úrsula's visions of Christian submission in her diary that consider it in relation Yoruba beliefs, see Rachel Spaulding, "Mounting the Poyto: An Image of Afro-Catholic Submission in the Mystical Visions of Colonial Peru's Úrsula de Jesús," *Early American Studies* 17, no. 4 (2019): 519–44.

otra una negra siega" [the voices told me how much in particular the insignificant and humble ones of this house please God. Florensia Bravo and Antonia de Cristo are outcasts, and no one pays any attention to them. The first is a wretched *mulata* and the other a blind, black woman].[36] Úrsula as narrator thus presents a notion of redeemed female blackness that promises black women increased chances of spiritual salvation in death because of their marginalized status on earth. In identifying the two women and calling them God's favorites, she forces the living to remember them in the present and again references the "engaño" [lie] of the worldly hierarchy that considers them worthless.

Reinforcing this message, the holy voices tell Úrsula that God provides harsher punishment in the afterlife to souls who occupy positions of authority and prestige on earth. Her otherworldly interlocutors explain to her the nature of God's scaled justice in the following way: "a cada uno le pedian cuenta conforme al talento que se le a dado: que al donado como a donado, que al negro como a negro, se le pide quenta de los dies mandamientos. [M]as que al Relijioso le corrian muchas mas obligasiones" [All must account for themselves according to their capacities, the *donado* like a *donado*, the black like a black, and whether they have upheld the Ten Commandments. The religious elites are judged more harshly because they have greater obligations].[37] Úrsula's diary explains through citing these interlocutors that black men and women thus have higher chances of salvation because in purgatory "cada uno tenia su lugar conforme a su estado – que las monjas a una parte, los rreligiosos a otra, los seglares, saserdotes, yndios, negros, todas las jenerasiones y estados de cada uno y las obligaciones que tenian, se les daban las penas" [all had their place and received punishment according to their social position. Nuns were in one part, male religious in another; and lay persons, priests, Indians, blacks, and all other [kinds] were punished according to their conditions and distinct responsibilities].[38] The diary's spatial rendering of hierarchy in purgatory reflects a common perception that certain worldly differences were mirrored in purgatory in the inverse such that those who lived sumptuous lives surrounded by their wealth would eventually have to suffer for those wealth-enabled vanities in death.[39] Úrsula's diary's

---

[36] Ibid., 15v; 93–94.   [37] Ibid., 28v; 116.

[38] Ibid., 24r; 108; my modified translation replaces "generations" with "kinds."

[39] See, for example, Nicolás Díaz, *Tratado del Juyzio Final en el qual se hallaran muchas cosas muy provechosas y curiosas* (Valladolid: Diego Fernandez de Cordova y Oviedo, 1588), 100v–105r.

notion of stratified purgatory comes with a warning: those with more authority on earth would likely suffer more in death because God had higher expectations for them than the humble. Both examples imply that black people would likely suffer fewer punishments in purgatory because they possess less authority and suffer more on earth.

To complement this teaching and its use of spatial language to describe spiritual hierarchies, Úrsula's visions in the diary emphasize that black women have a special place reserved for them in purgatory and heaven. For example, in an account of a vision Úrsula has of the soul of Lucía, a deceased black woman Úrsula had known in life, the narrator explains that she speaks to Lucía as she was processing beside the souls of a group of nuns in purgatory in her vision: "bi benir en aquella prosesión a un lado a la negra Lusia y pregunté si las negras estaban allí tanbién. Respondieronme que así que a un lado estaban apartadas, que allá pasaban las cosas con gran consierto" [in that same procession I also saw a black woman named Lucía off to one side. I asked if black women also went there, and they responded, Yes, they remain separated to one side, and everything there occurs in great concord].[40] The voices' response to Úrsula's question confirms the inclusion of black women in the purifying road to salvation of purgatory. In this instance, the holy voices authorize her interpretation of black women's capacity for salvation.

This is not the first time in the diary that Úrsula communicates that she has learned that black women can reach heaven through purgatory with God's special assistance. For example, in the previously cited conversation Úrsula recounts having with the soul of María Bran, Úrsula asks "si las negras yban asi al cielo?" [if black women go to heaven like that?]. María Bran affirms that God "las salbaba por su gran misericordia" [saved them because of His great mercy].[41] In this episode, the soul of a deceased black woman serves as a witness, testifying through Úrsula that black women *as black women* go to heaven. Úrsula, in relaying the anecdote and the teaching by the holy voices, notifies her audience that God gives special consideration to black women in the eternal life to come. This lesson is reinforced by two visions granted to Úrsula of herself *inside* Jesus' heart.[42]

---

[40] Úrsula de Jesús, *Diario espiritual*, 10v; 84.   [41] Ibid., 8v; 80.

[42] Ibid., 50v–51r; 148–49. These two visions are given on the same day. Úrsula responds by asking God how an "hormiguita" [little ant] like herself can be granted such a gift.

The diary's portrayal of the promise of redemption for black women accompanies its two important descriptions of black female beauty. In Úrsula's exchange with María Bran, for example, Úrsula describes her as a stunning vision of beauty, her face in particular: "Estaba mui linda y un negro lustrosisimo" [was very beautiful, and a most brilliant black].[43] By thus describing María Bran, Úrsula appropriates the typical Christian imagery of holiness associated with light (elaborated in Chapter 4) and relates it to brilliance rather than color. María Bran's resplendent blackness visually signals the potential for black women to be saved, noting that they, too, shine with God's recognition. In another example, Úrsula describes conversing with the soul of Marucha, another deceased black woman from the convent whom Úrsula helped save through her advocacy and prayers. To mark Marucha's redemption after Úrsula's prayers, the narrator recounts that she later saw Marucha with "*el rrostro mui resplandesiente* y me dijo que por la confiansa que abia tenido en la misericordia de dios se abia salvado" [*her face resplendent*. She told me her faith in God's mercy had saved her].[44] Contrary to Alonso de Sandoval's figurative descriptions of black spiritual salvation as turning black men and women "blancos como el sol" [white like the sun] as analyzed in Chapter 4, the portrayals of redeemed black women in Úrsula's diary never suggest blackness could be even figuratively antithetical to embodying Christian virtue or that salvation entails a process of physical or symbolic whitening. Like the black interpreters who testify in Claver's beatification inquest, Úrsula presents the souls of redeemed black Christians as extremely beautiful and resplendent.

The elaboration of this theme of beautiful Christian blackness appears in a later vision described by Úrsula's diary of an extremely beautiful black Franciscan friar:

Estaba un fraylesito negro de nuestro abito – mui lindo hermosisimo = junto al orno – otro abominable el abito paresia desenterrado – ybamelo disiendo para que yo me acordara y dise que aquel que yo bi tan ermoso y Resplandesiente eran los que estaban en grasia/ los obserbantes que guardaban las rreglas y asian lo que les mandaban – la comunidad y que el otro / era de los que estaban por su comodidad – y que no querian ser mandados – ni serbir la comunidad / ni que los apurasen – sino andar a su boluntad.

[I saw a little black friar, very lovely, very beautiful, wearing our habit, near the little dais in front of the lectern. Next to the oven was another abominable one, whose habit looked as if it had been disinterred. He was telling me this so I would

---

[43] Ibid.; translation modified.   [44] Ibid., 24r; 108; my emphasis.

remember. He said the beautiful and resplendent one I saw represented those in grace, the observant ones who obeyed the rules and did what the community mandated. The other one represented those who were in the order for their own selves, but just do what they wished.][45]

The language used in this passage recalls the associations between blackness, beauty, resplendence, and grace crafted earlier in the diary in its descriptions of Úrsula's visions of Maria Bran and Marucha. This particular vision demonstrates that the spiritual diary's notion of Christian blackness includes black men's possibility for redemption, virtue, and beauty. While Úrsula does not mention the black friar's name here, the description could very well refer to Benedict of Palermo, the black Franciscan friar from sixteenth-century Spanish Sicily, mentioned in Chapter 4, whose images and life story became popular in Spanish America by the second decade of the seventeenth century.[46] Unlike Benedict of Palermo, black men in colonial Peru could not become Franciscan friars; the highest position to which they could aspire was that of the *donado*. In this case, the diary's use of the diminutive ("fraylesito") to describe the black friar of Úrsula's vision emphasizes the selflessness about which the holy voice comments in the anecdote. Reminiscent of the diminutive in Úrsula's declaration of herself as an "esclavita de Santa Clara" [a little slave of Santa Clara], the description of the little black friar and the analysis of the image by the holy voices suggest a connection between black beauty and the virtue of letting go of one's will in order to serve one's religious community and God.

A final key way in which Úrsula's diary casts a critical eye on worldly hierarchies related to blackness is its portrayal of Úrsula as a spiritual intermediary for figures across Lima's social strata. In numerous instances, the diary positions Úrsula in relation to the constant pleas she receives from the souls of men and women in purgatory who beg her to intercede on their behalf before God by reminding the living of their memory and asking God for their salvation. When the souls requesting her mediation before God are elite, the diary often includes an indirect critique of their behaviors on earth, noting the sins for which they continue to suffer in purgatory. For example, Úrsula describes witnessing a vision of a soul of a man in purgatory who "abia padesido mucho por Francisca, su negra que la traya arrastrando con mal tratamiento y no cuidando de lo que abia menester" [suffered terribly because of Francisca, his slave whom he had continually mistreated badly, without considering

[45] Ibid., 51r; 149.   [46] On Benedict of Palermo, see Chapter 4, 195–98.

what she needed].[47] Úrsula takes care to describe his torment in purgatory for those sins, as she cites the holy voices who ask her to pray for him:

Bia al licenciado colonia y disenme que por aquella caridad con que nuestro señor jesuchristo bino del sielo a la tierra le encomendara a dios y le pidiese por esa mesma caridad tubiese misericordia del. Encaresio grandemente quan grandes son los trabaxos que se pasan allá. Que ya a él le paresia, que abia mil años que estaba alla.

[I saw Licenciate Colonia. They told me to commend him to God by the love with which Jesus Christ came from heaven to earth. I should ask for that same love, and that He have mercy on him. Colonia spoke very earnestly about the terrible hardship there, and that it seemed like he had been there for a thousand years.][48]

The fact that the holy voices ask her to intercede on his behalf before God evidences an important reversal of status from the worldly hierarchy of the colonial society in which the Licenciado would have been Úrsula's superior. There are, thus, at least two lessons communicated by this vision and its commentary by the holy voices. The first is that the Licenciado should not have overworked his poor slave and taken such poor care of her earthly needs. The second is that Úrsula is considered by the holy voices to be an effective advocate for the soul of someone far superior to her in worldly hierarchies related to gender, education, and status.

Úrsula's capacity to intercede on behalf of the souls of the elite, as presented in the diary, does not stop at individuals whom she personally knew such as the Licenciado Colonia. For example, Úrsula explains in a separate episode that Jesus gave her a vision of the soul of Queen Isabel (Philip IV's wife) in purgatory.[49] In this passage, Christ offers a moralizing commentary that Úrsula relates with surprise to her audience:

A los Reyes que viben conforme a mi ley y tratan a los suditos con caridad y asen justiçia con misericordia, a estos cuando mueren lleboles a mi purgatorio como tengo agora a la reyna de españa. Pasome por el pensamiento, ¿cómo se llamaria? diseme, doña Ysabel ... yo quedé atonita, encomendando a dios a la Reyna y comulgué por ella.

[Those kings who conform to my law and treat their subjects with love, rendering justice mercifully, go to my purgatory when they die, just as I now have the queen of Spain there. I thought to myself, "What do they call her?" They said, *doña* Isabel ... I was dumbfounded but commended the queen to God and received communion on her behalf.][50]

---

[47] Úrsula de Jesús, *Diario espiritual*, 23v; 107.   [48] Ibid., 23v; 106.
[49] Queen Isabel was the Bourbon wife of Philip IV, who died in 1644.
[50] Úrsula de Jesús, *Diario espiritual*, 35r; 125–26.

Similar to how Úrsula presents her role as an intercessor in the encounter with the Licenciado Colonia, Úrsula's vision of Queen Isabel in purgatory ends by presenting herself as an advocate asked to intercede on behalf of a queen. As an intercessor for the imperial elite, Úrsula's diary presents her as a spiritual intermediary for those whose worldly status would have been superior not only to hers but to that of *everyone* in Lima.

And yet, as noted above, Úrsula's diary also shows her to be an advocate for the spiritual salvation of humble black servants like herself. In addition to the previously cited examples, the soul of another black slave from the convent, a different Lucía (one whom she also refers to as "la angola" [the Angolan]), approaches Úrsula to ask for her intercession before God: "que por amor de Dios la encomendase mucho a Dios" [For the love of God, would Úrsula please commend her spirit to God].[51] The reported speech from the exchange specifies that this Lucía had served the convent with good will but that she was still suffering in purgatory for having stolen some of its supplies in her capacity as cook. Such edifying visions reactivate the convent community's memory of a deceased black woman, implicitly reminding current servants of the sins they should avoid as well as convent superiors of the need to provide for servants' material needs so as to ensure the salvation of everyone's souls (theirs included).

A clear way in which the diary demonstrates Úrsula's advocacy for the humble differently than her advocacy for the elite is by including descriptions of Úrsula's efforts to help the souls of the humble even before death. For example, early in the diary Úrsula the narrator describes being concerned about her mother's well-being. She identifies two types of concerns: first that her mother would not be "desnuda" [naked] and second that her soul would be saved. Regarding her first concern, Úrsula thanks God that the last time her mother visited the convent she was dressed, a sign Úrsula reads as God's care for her mother's basic worldly needs so that Úrsula would not have to. Regarding the second concern, Úrsula elaborates: "algunos tienpos que deseo que aga una confesion general, y se lo e aconsejado porque deseo mucho su salvación. Allela mui deseosa de aserla y que lo abia puesto por obra con un padre de la compañía, y que estaba tan de priesa que no yso cosa buena" [sometimes I want her to make a general confession. I realized she had the desire to do so, and she did confess with a Jesuit priest, but he was in such a hurry he did a poor

[51] Ibid., 9r; 82.

job].[52] Unhappy with the unsatisfactory account of her mother's confession before the careless priest, Úrsula intercedes to ensure that her mother would confess again with a more thorough mediator: "Dijele que yo le buscaria un padre que lo aria mui despasio y a su satisfasion, y nonbrele al que le pensaba Rogar que lo ysiese" [I told her I would find a priest who would do it with great care and to her satisfaction, and I named the one I was thinking about to take her confession that night].[53] Later that night in her prayers, Úrsula pleads to God on her mother's behalf. She asks him for guidance regarding her new choice for her mother's confessor. The holy voices respond affirmatively to Úrsula, offering advice for her mother to maximize the benefits of her next confession with the new priest: "Rrespondenme que al que yo le abia dicho le aria que lo quisiese hacer mui de buena Boluntad, y que yo le dijese que pensase sus pecados por las edades y por los tienpos y los años que abia estado en pecado mortal" [The voices responded, The one I already mentioned would do what I what wanted quite willingly. I should tell her to think about her sins at different ages, stages, and years when she had been in mortal sin].[54] In this account, Úrsula not only cites the holy voices' critique of the insufficient efforts of her mother's first confessor, but also offers herself as a supplemental spiritual advocate in this life who arranges for her mother to perform another confession with a more thorough priest. Úrsula's concern for the material and spiritual well-being of her mother and other living black women suggests that while she is an obedient and effective spiritual intermediary for the souls of the elite and the poor in purgatory, she is particularly sensitive to the suffering of the marginalized and lesser privileged like herself.

Significantly, in advocating for and describing the possibility of black spiritual salvation in the spiritual diary, Úrsula never resorts to a devaluation of whiteness. Unlike Covarrubias's oppositional definition of white and black, noted in this book's Introduction, Úrsula's spiritual diary does not present black as white's opposite, implying that white men and women take on characteristics that are the opposite of those attributed to black men and women. Instead, Úrsula's diary elevates the spiritual and aesthetic values of blackness while continuing to appreciate the color white as a symbol of virtue and spiritual integrity. For example, in the scene describing the vision of María Bran in which Úrsula describes her beautiful lustrous black face, María's salvation is also indexed by her

---

[52] Ibid., 15r–15v; 93.   [53] Ibid., 15v; 93.   [54] Ibid.

white clothing: "la bi bestida de una alba albisima, señida con un singulo corto, con unas riquisimas bolas (tanbien el alva estaba mui bien guarnesida) una corona de flores en la cabesa tanbien" [I saw her in a priest's alb, the whitest of whites, beautifully embellished and gathered together with a short cord with elegant tassels. She also wore a crown of flowers on her head].[55] The same superlative suffix to mark the white color of María's richly adorned robe appears in the next line to describe the extreme luster of her beautiful black face, "un negro lustrosisimo" [a most brilliant black], suggesting that both María's white robe and black face index her saved status. In another example from one of Úrsula's more carnal visions of Christ, the diary describes Christ's beauty in relation to his *white* face:

bi dentro del mismo sagrario a nuestro señor jesucristo cruçificado tan grande co-/ mo lo debia de ser. tan al vibo que pareçia de carne con los pechos/ llenos de leche que pareçia que ya queria salir y dijo esto tengo para/ los pecadores umildes y arepentidos. Era de linda figura y blanco.

[I saw the crucified Jesus Christ within the ciborium. He looked alive and as large as life. His breasts looked like they would overflow with milk, and He said, This is for the humble, penitent sinners. His [face] was beautiful and white.][56]

Just as María Bran's face is beautiful and black, Christ's face in this vision is beautiful and white. That his breasts are brimming with milk also associates the salvation of all mankind with a white substance.[57] The persistence of symbolic imagery throughout the diary describing Christ's face, blood, cross, and banners as white does not suggest that salvation is the prerogative of white people. Instead, its use alongside black resplendence demonstrates that the diary's portrayal of Christian blackness is not one of simple inversion in which blackness is more valuable than whiteness. It rather presents an appreciation of blackness such that physical whiteness is neither a requirement for nor an impediment to being considered beautiful and blessed.

---

[55] Ibid., 8r; 80.

[56] Ibid. 34v; 125. Translation modified. I chose "face" rather than "aspect" given in van Deusen's translation based on Covarrubias's definition for "figura" [figure/face] where he states that the term is most commonly used to refer to the face (*Tesoro*, 404r).

[57] Milk was generally considered a form of "cooked" blood in this period (Covarrubias, *Tesoro*, 517r). For the medieval precedents for these kinds of images of Christ with breasts, see Caroline Walker Bynum, *Jesus as Mother*. For a contemporary of Úrsula in Iberia who uses similar images of Christ as nursemaid or mother, see the Augustinian *Vida* of Isabel de Jesús (1586–1648). See Arenal and Schlau, *Untold Sisters*, 187–222, 198–99, for an analysis of Isabel de Jesús's nursing imagery.

In other areas of colonial Latin America in the mid-seventeenth century, comparable discourse regarding the spiritual rewards given to humble dark-skinned slaves in the afterlife circulated. A prominent example appears in a sermon by Antonio Vieira delivered in Salvador, Bahia, in 1633. In this sermon, Vieira addresses both masters and enslaved black men and women in the church audience. In addressing the enslaved, he urges them to recognize the divine favor granted to those who humbly endure their enslavement:

E como o estado, ou religião do vosso captiveiro, sem outras asperezas, ou penitencias, mais que as que elle traz comsigo, tem seguro por promessa do mesmo Deus, não só o premio de bemaventurados, senão tambem a herança de filhos: favor e providencia muito particular é da Virgem Maria que vos conserveis no mesmo estado, e grandes merecimentos delle: para que por meio do captiveiro temporal consigaes, como vos prometti, a liberdade, ou alforria eterna.

[Without any other harshness or penitence beyond that which your status or order, as captives, already has within it, you have the reward of the blessed as well as the inheritance of sons. A very special favor and a providence of the Virgin Mary is that you remain in the same status with its great value, so that, as I promised you, you gain through temporal slavery an eternal freedom and manumission.][58]

Vieira does not criticize the principle of earthly slavery in this passage, but rather suggests, as Úrsula's diary does, that the suffering and humility of the enslaved will grant them easier access to eternal salvation. To make this point, Vieira invokes and repurposes language related to the inheritance of dark color and its ties to slavery that circulated with the story of the sons of Noah and the curse of Cham.[59] By invoking "a herança de filhos" [the inheritance of sons] to refer to the enslaved's dark color, Vieira employs language similar to Sandoval's in his *Naturaleza, policia*

---

[58] Antônio Vieira, "Sermão Vigesimo Setimo" [ca. 1633], in *Obras completas do Padre Antonio Vieira: Sermões*, vol. 12 (Porto: Livraria Chardon, 1907–9), 301–34, 326. The English translation for the sermon here and in what follows is taken from "'Two Slaveries – The Sermons of Padre Antônio Vieira, Salvador, Bahia (ca. 1633) and São Luís do Maranhão (1653)," in Kenneth Mills, William B. Taylor, and Sandra Lauderdale Graham, eds., *Colonial Latin America: A Documentary History*, 2nd ed. (Wilmington, DE: Scholarly Resources, 2002), 218–33, 226–27. Translated excerpts of this sermon also appear in Robert Edgar Conrad's translation in *Children of God's Fire: A Documentary History of Black Slavery in Brazil*, 2nd ed. (University Park: Pennsylvania State University Press, 1994), 163–74.

[59] See Sandoval, *Historia de la Aethiopia*, book 1, chap. 3, 21, as discussed in Chapter 4, 182. See also Introduction, note 60, on early modern Iberian interpretations of the Curse of Cham.

sagrada i profana to suggest that black men and women in the Americas can be saved from eternal bondage in death through Christianization even if they cannot escape the inherited bondage of terrestrial slavery associated with the color of their bodies.

Similar to Úrsula's diary's presentation of the theme of divine redemption, Vieira's sermon's recognition of the possibility of spiritual salvation for the enslaved coexists with reminders of the promise of divine punishment for those who abuse the enslaved. For example, the sermon ends by addressing slave owners, warning them not to ignore the suffering of the enslaved by abusing them: "Mas se os corações, como o de Pharaö, se endurecerem mais, ainda mal, porque sobre ellas não pode faltar o ultimo castigo" [If your hearts, like those of the Pharaoh, are hardened, that is tragic, because you will suffer the ultimate punishment].[60] Nothing less than eternal punishment is the reward Vieira promises to those who abuse their slaves, a sin that Vieira's allusion presents as equivalent to Pharaoh's heavily punished disbelief in God in Exodus.

Yet unlike Úrsula de Jesús's spiritual diary, Vieira's argument about the heavenly favor granted humble slaves is not accompanied by an aesthetic appreciation of blackness as beautiful. Vieira, instead, opts for identifying the enslaved's dark skin with a religious habit that emphasizes their nakedness: "O vosso habito é da vossa mesma côr; porque não vos bestem as pelles das ovelhas e camellos, como a Elias; mas aquellas com que vos cobriu ou descobriu a natureza expostos aos calores do sol, e frios das chuvas" [Your habit is your very color, for you are not clothed in sheepskin nor camel's hair, as was Elijah, but in the very clothes with which nature covered you or uncovered you, exposed to the hot sun and cold rain].[61] Shuffling between metaphor and biblical allusion, Vieira reads the dark skin of the enslaved as a sign of humility and vulnerability, rather than beauty or the mantle of a prophet. In contrast, Úrsula de Jesús's spiritual diary, composed almost two decades after Viera's sermon, incorporates aesthetic beauty to the appreciation of black men's and women's capacity for salvation and portrays herself as an effective divine intermediary. The following section explores the extent to which Úrsula's diary's vision of blackness translates into the two hagiographies written about her soon after her death.

---

[60] Vieira, "Sermão Vigesimo Setimo," 334; "Two Slaveries," 228. For a relevant analysis of the imagery of the hardening of Pharoah's heart in Exodus, see Elaine Scarry, *The Body in Pain: The Making and Unmaking of the World* (New York: Oxford University Press, 1985), 202–4.

[61] Vieira, "Sermão Vigesimo Setimo," 326; "Two Slaveries," 226.

BLACKNESS IN ÚRSULA'S TWO POSTHUMOUS *VIDAS*

The *Vida breve*

The first hagiography composed about Úrsula after her death in 1666 focuses on summarizing her biographical information, including her conditions of birth, conversion, and death, and then providing the names of her confessors and a brief summary of her visions. Its structure follows the typical pattern of spiritual biographies composed across the Catholic world in the seventeenth century. Because it was probably composed by a nun and not a male authority, it does not comment explicitly on Úrsula's virtues. Instead, it ends by noting that her diary will show "las grandes mds que dios le yso a esta sierba suya" [the great favors God granted to this servant of his] and that her confessors attested to the integrity of her spirit: "aprobaron su espiritu" [they approved of her soul]. In providing its overview of Úrsula's life and visions, the first hagiography presents a modified version of her diary's portrayal of blackness. This modified version downplays the theme from Úrsula's diary of the divine justice that promises black men and women increased chances at salvation, focusing instead on the message that God grants even the humble the possibility of salvation.

Instead of including any mention of Úrsula's visions of the great stairway to heaven with black, white, and indigenous souls or the episodes in which Úrsula sees the souls of saved black women, the *Vida breve* only obliquely addresses the theme of black people's chances for salvation by describing one of the visions Úrsula has of herself inside Jesus's heart in the diary:

con la mano derecha [Jesús] le mostraba el corazon y en el se bia ursula- y allandose yndigna de tan gran md le dijo que es esto señor mio, una negra tan gran pecadora. No ay muchas reynas y señoras. Dijo el señor mas de estar en gracia mia que ser Reynas y mostrole el purgatorio donde bido ynumerable jente- y le desian los grandes puestos que abian tenido y las culpas porque estaban en aquellas penas.

[with his right hand, he showed her his heart, and in it Úrsula could see herself. Finding herself so unworthy of such great favor, she said to him, What is this my Lord? A black woman who is such a great sinner? Are there not many queens and ladies? The Lord answered her that it is worth more to be in my grace than to be a queen, and he showed her purgatory where she saw innumerable people, and he explained to her the great roles they had had and their sins that had caused them to be suffering those punishments.][62]

---

[62] *Vida breve*, 4v.

The narration of the episode in the *Vida breve* thus presents Úrsula as an embodiment of Jesus's grace for the humble. By citing Úrsula as questioning her worthiness through declaring herself a sinful *black woman*, the hagiography indexes the vision as one that is not only about Úrsula herself but also about typological female blackness and as such a general reminder that God saves black women, too. The last sentence of the episode only indirectly addresses the comparison pervasive in Úrsula's diary of the increased standards for eternal salvation for the terrestrial elite.

Another distinction from the spiritual diary is that the *Vida breve* describes Úrsula's role as an intercessor only for the souls of the elite, excluding all of the instances of her advocacy for souls of black women in the diary. A potential exception to this exclusion is the incorporation of a detail not included in Úrsula's spiritual diary: her role in founding a lay confraternity for the Virgin of Mount Carmel in the church of her convent.[63] As the first and second hagiographies explain, Úrsula had a special devotion to the Virgin of Mount Carmel because before she became a *donada* she narrowly escaped death after falling into a well with the help of an image of the Virgin of Mount Carmel that she wore around her neck.[64] Although the first hagiography frames the founding of the confraternity as an act Úrsula performed on the request of the Virgin herself, functionally we know from studies about lay confraternities in colonial Lima that the confraternity would have served as a way for Úrsula to work with and on behalf of other black men and women to collectively achieve spiritual salvation by praying for each other's souls after their death and paying for the materials and church fees related to their funerals and requiem masses. This same confraternity was, for example, likely responsible for providing the material support for Úrsula's own good death and funerary services described at the end of the *Vida breve*.[65] That the *Vida breve* describes her role in founding the

---

[63] Ibid.   [64] Ibid., 3r; *Vida anónima*, 586r.

[65] For more on black confraternities in colonial Peru, see Karen Graubart, "'So color de una cofradía': Catholic Confraternities and the Development of Afro-Peruvian Ethnicities in Early Colonial Peru," *Slavery and Abolition* 3, no. 1 (2012): 43–64; Tardieu, *Los negros y la Iglesia*, vol. 1, 509–63; Bowser, *The African Slave in Colonial Peru*, 247–51; Paul Charney, "Sense of Belonging: Colonial Indian Cofradías and Ethnicity in the Valley of Lima, Peru," *The Americas* 54, no. 3 (1998): 379–407. On black confraternities in other regions of colonial Latin America, see Nicole von Germeten, *Black Blood Brothers: Confraternities and Social Mobility for Afro-Mexicans* (Gainesville: University Press of Florida, 2006); Patricia A. Mulvey, "Black Brothers and Sisters: Membership in the Black Lay Brotherhoods of Colonial Brazil," *Luso-Brazilian Review* 17, no. 2 (1980): 253–79;

confraternity as only a service to the Virgin, however, emphasizes the first hagiography's angle of only underscoring Úrsula's advocacy for the elite in the narrative.

Also unlike Úrsula's spiritual diary, the *Vida breve* avoids using any language related to the beauty of redeemed black souls. The only potential mention of black beauty in the text, in fact, comes in a brief description of the appearance of Úrsula's eyes after she had died: "quedo con los ojos abiertos elebados en el sielo – tan claros y tan lindos que en mas de tres oras no la mobieron para amortajarla entendiendo que no abia muerto sino que era algun arrobamiento" [she remained with her eyes open, lifted toward heaven. They were so bright and beautiful that they did not move her to shroud her for more than three hours, thinking that she was not dead but enraptured].[66] The passage suggests that the beauty and vitality of her eyes in death index the celestial destination of her soul. By presenting Úrsula as beautiful only in relation to her eyes and the soul they metonymically represent, the narrative avoids replicating language related to beautiful physical blackness from Úrsula's diary. Therefore, while the first hagiography imparts some aspects of Úrsula's diary's portrayal of Christian blackness by offering a description of a vision of Úrsula as an embodiment of Jesus's grace and mentioning her role as a valuable intercessor for the souls of the elite, it removes the diary's explicit appreciation of beautiful and resplendent blackness and descriptions of her role as an intercessor for the humble.

The *Vida anónima*

Composed twenty years after the *Vida breve*, the second posthumous hagiography about Úrsula, the *Vida anónima*, was written by a male author affiliated with the Franciscan order around 1686. Compared with the *Vida breve*, the *Vida anónima* elaborates more elements of Úrsula's diary's notion of blackness including the theme of divine justice that allots more punishment to the elite and more forgiveness to the humble, Úrsula's capacity to serve as an effective intercessor for the souls of the humble and the elite, and figurative language describing her virtue as a source of light. Even still, unlike the spiritual diary, the *Vida anónima* only obliquely references the possibility of conceiving blackness as beautiful.

Elizabeth W. Kiddy, *Blacks of the Rosary: Memory and History in Minas Gerais, Brazil* (University Park: Pennsylvania State University Press, 2005).
[66] *Vida breve*, 5v.

Marking the second hagiography's emphasis on portraying Úrsula as *blessed and black*, the second hagiography introduces Úrsula as a part of a pantheon of illustrious black men and women recognized by the Church. The list provides a lineage of symbolic descent for Úrsula's own black Christian virtue and divine gift of sight:

Resonaron en los terminos del mundo las Grandezas del Rey Salomon, llegaron las voces al Oriente, y la Reyna Sabâ Ethyopiza, adornada de aromas, y thesoros llegô varonil â los muros de Gerusalên, â postrarse al Rey en su Throno. La sybila Cumanâ, negra, y Gentil anteviô la Encarnacion del Verbo: *Celo demittitur alto,* siendo una negra, sabia Profetiza de tan gran misterio. De los tres Reyes de Oriente, uno fue Negro Oriental, Santo, y sabio. En los Cantares la Esposa se çelebra, que siendo Negra fue hermosa.

[The greatness of King Solomon resounded in the extremes of the world, with voices reaching the Orient, and thus Queen Saba from Ethiopia, donning scents and treasures, arrived in manly fashion at the walls of Jerusalem to kneel before the throne of the king. The sibyl Cumana, black and gentile, foresaw the Incarnation of the Word: *sent down from heaven,* being a black and wise Prophetess of such a great mystery. Of the three Kings of Orient, one was a black from the East, holy and sage. In the Song of Solomon, the Bride is exalted, for in being black she was beautiful.][67]

These three figures (Saba, the queen of Sheba; the sybil of Cumana; and the black magus) are associated with being powerful, prescient, and wise.[68] Significantly, the narrator concludes the list by paraphrasing the declaration of the black Bride from the *Song of Songs* in the third person. This hagiographer's invocation, however, recasts the oppositional conjunction of Jerome's translation. Removing the explicit opposition in "sed" [but] from the declaration in the first person, the *Vida anónima* presents the Bride's blackness as a prefatory subordinate clause to describing her beauty in the third person.[69] As a result, the narrator implies that the Bride was beautiful *in being black*, not in spite of it. Such a statement is the *only* oblique parallel in the second hagiography of the

---

[67] *Vida anónima*, 585r–v. In the margin of the manuscript next to the line describing the sybil and the black magus, the author cites Psalm 67:32 Vulgate; 68:31 KJB (f. 585r).

[68] Descriptions of all three characters appear in an anthology of Ethiopian saints included in a Dominican history written earlier in the century from Valencia. See Luis de Urreta, *Historia de Etiopia* (Valencia, 1610), 624–28. On Urreta, see Brewer-García, "Hierarchy and Holiness in the Earliest Colonial Black Hagiographies."

[69] On the gerund performing the function of a subordinate clause in Spanish from this period, see Hayward Keniston, *The Syntax of Castillian Prose: The Sixteenth Century* (Chicago: University of Chicago Press, 1937), 32–33. For more on interpretations of the Bride in relation to the texts of this book's corpus, see Chapter 4, 189, 192, 203.

way Úrsula's spiritual diary describes María Bran's, Marucha's, and the black Franciscan friar's black beauty, a beauty that indexes and accompanies their souls' spiritual virtue.

While the *Vida anónima* never calls Úrsula beautiful, it does introduce her as black and resplendent. The continuation of the passage cited above highlights Úrsula's capacity, as a venerable black woman, to shine among the other exemplary religious women of her convent: "La Venerable Úrsula de Cristo Negra criolla entre las claras luces de su Convento, *Resplandeciô* esmero de la Gracia, deposito de soberanos dones, sabia Profetiza de altos mysterios, y Esposa muy querida del Altissimo" [The venerable Úrsula of Christ, a black *criolla, shone* with the diligence of grace among the bright lights of her convent; she was a depository of regal blessings, wise prophetess of holy mysteries, and very dear wife of the Almighty].[70] Employing baroque juxtapositions while playing with the metaphoric light-related possibilities of the name of Úrsula's order, the narrator underscores Úrsula's status as a *black criolla* who served as an edifying example in her spiritual community.[71]

To understand the *Vida anónima*'s emphasis on Úrsula as a black *criolla*, it helps to consider the textual portrayals of Martín de Porres in Lima produced in the twenty years between the composition of Úrsula's first and second hagiographies. Martín de Porres was a Dominican *donado* born to a freed black mother and a Spanish father in late sixteenth-century Lima. Although he died in 1639, before Úrsula had changed from enslaved servant to *donada* in the Convent of Santa Clara, Martín de Porres's fame only achieved greater notoriety a little before Úrsula's death in 1666. That is, between 1660 and 1664, the Diocese of the Dominican order in Lima gathered the first round of testimonies about Martín de Porres's life in a preliminary beatification inquest. These recorded testimonies did not circulate widely in Lima until the early 1670s when Dominican author Bernardo de Medina used them and his own interviews of Lima residents to compose a book-length hagiography.[72]

---

[70] *Vida anónima*, f. 585v; my emphasis.

[71] Confirming this claim made by the second hagiography, van Deusen notes that the abbess of the Convent of Santa Clara in 1666 cites Úrsula as a role model for other *donadas* in an *auto de ingreso* for an aspirant to the novitiate Francisca de la Cruz shortly after Úrsula's death (van Deusen, *Embodying the Sacred*, 114).

[72] Bernardo de Medina, *Vida prodigiosa del venerable siervo de Dios Fr. Martin de Porras* (Lima: Juan de Quevedo y Zarate, 1673). On Medina's portrayal of Porres's blackness, see Erin Kathleen Rowe, "After Death, Her Face Turned White: Blackness, Whiteness, and Sanctity in the Early Modern Hispanic World," *American Historical Review* 121,

Medina's hagiography, printed first in Lima in 1673 and soon after reprinted in Madrid in 1675, presents Martín as another potential Lima-based Dominican saint like Rose of Lima.[73] Medina highlights Martín's character as a spiritual and physical doctor to all – elite and humble – and a model for living humbly in the service of others. We know Medina's hagiography was read in Lima because the second set of beatification testimonies collected in Lima between 1679 and 1685 mentions the book and an engraved image from it as having recently performed miracles. While no mention is made of Martín de Porres in Úrsula's *Vida anónima* from 1686, I speculate that the second hagiography's new emphasis on Úrsula as a saintly black *criolla* of the Convent of Santa Clara suggests that the Franciscans in Lima at least momentarily considered presenting Úrsula as their own black Limeñan candidate for beatification.

In crafting the new and longer version of Úrsula's life for a broader audience, the *Vida anónima* curiously does not shy away from reproducing Úrsula's diary's theme of divine justice that stresses not only that all people's souls have access to redemption in death, but that elites have a harder time accessing the Kingdom of Heaven than the humble.[74] The second hagiography develops this theme with two different kinds of references. One pertains to the numerous instances in which the hagiography describes the suffering of religious elites such as convent leaders in purgatory paying for their sins. For example, the hagiography comments on Úrsula's vision of the soul of a dead nun who described having been appointed twice as convent supervisor and was now suffering terribly for the sins she permitted her subordinates to commit.[75] The second kind of

no. 3 (2016): 726–54; Celia L. Cussen, *Black Saint of the Americas: The Life and Afterlife of Martín de Porres* (New York: Cambridge University Press, 2014); and Brewer-García, "Negro, pero blanco de alma: La ambivalencia de la negrura en la *Vida prodigiosa* de Fray Martin de Porras (1663)," *Cuadernos del CILHA* 13, no. 2 (December 2012): 112–45. Note that the year of the first edition is 1673, not 1663.

73   The opening to Medina's hagiography of Porres references Rose explicitly, chap. 1, 2r. This hagiography was subsequently published two more times before the end of the seventeenth century: in Madrid in 1675 and in Juan Meléndez, ed., *Tesoros verdaderos de las Yndias* (Rome: Angel Tinasio, 1681). A modified shorter narrative appears in Alonso Manrique, ed., *Retrato de perfección christiana* (Venice Francisco Gropo, 1696).

74   Evidence that the audience for the second hagiography was perceived to be beyond the very local Franciscan one of the first hagiography can be found in the opening paragraphs of the second hagiography that wax elaborately about the intellectual, spiritual, and material treasures of Lima, which the author lovingly refers to as "ilustre Patria mia" [my illustrious country] (585v).

75   *Vida anónima*, 590v.

reference to divine justice in the *Vida anónima* pertains to Úrsula's recurring visions of the ladder to heaven, specifying, as the holy voices cited by Úrsula's diary did, that the souls who rise and fall on the ladder do not do so because of their color, sex, language, or *nación*, but rather because of their varying commitments and devotions to God. To emphasize that the ability of these different souls to ascend the ladder depends only on their interior devotion to God and not on their terrestrial, corporal status, the hagiographer explains that Úrsula recognized "con mâs individuacion las personas, que iban, por êl de todas Religiones, sexos, y estados, sin ocultarsele el mâs triste negro, y despreciable indio, que subia por la escala" [the individuals on it, of all religions, sexes and conditions of life, without leaving out the poorest black man and the most despicable Indian who climbed the ladder].[76] As "triste" [sad] in seventeenth-century Spanish could mean sad, poor, and broken, its use in this passage conflates the worldly status of the "poorest" black man and the "most despicable" Indian to make the point that God's love is so universal that it includes even the lowliest of worldly society.[77] The imagery of both kinds of references to divine justice in the *Vida anónima* echoes that of Úrsula's diary.

An additional shared strategy for representing Christian blackness in the *Vida anónima* and Úrsula's diary is the appearance of black women as examples of redeemed souls from Úrsula's visions. While all three texts about Úrsula mention the previously cited example of God's gift to her of a vision of herself inside Jesus's heart,[78] a different yet related episode that appears only in the *Vida anónima* recounts that God granted Úrsula the gift of a visit from an angel in the form of a three-year-old black girl:

Un Domingo antes de maytines, divertida con un Crucifixo, que tenia en las manos, se le llegô una negrita de tres años, y diciendole Úrsula, que mirase aquel Señor que avia muerto por ella, y por todo el mundo; fue tal la atencion, devocion, y preguntas, que la haçia aquel inocente, y tierno Angelito, que quedô la Sierva de Dios enbidiosissima de su linda alma, y singulâr inocencia, y cubierta de lagrimas, y sollosos le deçia â Dios.... Y entretenida algun tiempo con estos dulcissimos fervores, y afectuosos suspiros de su corazon, excitados con el coloquio de aquella inocente criatura, se fue â recoger.

---

[76] Ibid.

[77] Miguel Martínez describes the double use of the adjective "triste" in the context of Renaissance Spanish lyric about soldiers in *Front Lines: Soldiers' Writing in the Early Modern Hispanic War* (Philadelphia: University of Pennsylvania Press, 2016), 171.

[78] In the *Vida breve*, this episode appears on 4v. In the *Vida anónima*, it appears on 599r.

[One Sunday before matins, while Úrsula's attention was fixed on a crucifix she held in her hands, a three-year-old little black girl came to her. She asked the little one to look at that Lord who had died for her and for the entire world. The attention, devotion, and questions of that innocent and tender little Angel were such that the Servant of God was left so awed by her beautiful soul and singular innocence that weeping and covered in tears, she bid her goodbye.... Entertained for some time with the sweet fervor and affectionate longing in her heart that had been excited by the conversation with that innocent creature, she withdrew to pray.][79]

The description of this angelic visitor employs a visual program that stands out against the common appearance in colonial visual art of dark bodies to index demonic influences that fight against the light-colored bodies such as those seen in Andean mural paintings of the suffering of souls in hell.[80] Similar juxtapositions that associate dark figures with the devil or the not-yet-Christianized appear in visual doctrinal manuals such as Giovanni Battista Romano's (see Figures 5.1 and 5.2).[81] Assessing the racialized use of similarly chromatically marked images inside church spaces from the colonial Andes, art historian Ananda Cohen Suárez explains:

In particular, Andean religious imagery of the seventeenth and eighteenth centuries frequently resorted to crude formulas in the representation of race that gained intervisual traction through their appearance across a variety of artworks. Indigenous and white bodies were distributed into a binary of sin and virtue whereby brownness became synonymous with transgression and whiteness served as a domain of divinity.[82]

Instead of activating these associations, the hagiography presents the black little girl as an innocent and tender angel, a gift from God for Úrsula. A final example from the *Vida anónima* of this genre of divine gift involves a vision Úrsula has of Christ with an unknown black *donada* by his side. The narrator explains Úrsula's reaction to this vision as one of immense gratitude: "diô Gracias â aquel divino / Señor, porque se dignaba de tener â su Lado â aquella pobrecita" [she gave thanks to that

[79] *Vida anónima*, f. 601r.
[80] See Ramón Mujica Pinilla, "Hell in the Andes: The Last Judgment in the Art of Viceregal Peru," in *Contested Visions in the Spanish Colonial World*, 177–201, especially 179; Mujica Pinilla, *Rosa Limensis. Mística, política e iconografía en torno de la patrona de América* (México, D.F.: Fondo de Cultura Económica, 2005).
[81] Giovanni Battista Romano, *Dottrina christiana, nella quale si contengono i principali Misteri della nostra Fede* (Rome: Giorgio Dagano, 1591), 26 and 76.
[82] Ananda Cohen Suárez, *Heaven, Hell, and Everything in between: Murals of the Colonial Andes* (Austin: University of Texas Press, 2016), 189.

FIGURE 5.1 "The First Commandment." Woodcut print in Giovanni Battista Romano's *Dottrina christiana* (Rome, 1591), 26.
Courtesy of Rare Books and Special Collections, Princeton University

76 DOTTRINA CHRISTIANA.

3.   *L' Inferno.*

SE ben l'inferno è stato preparato da Dio per li demoni, serue però anco per punire i peccatori: Onde considera tra molti altri tormenti che i dannati patiscono, & vederai come Satanasso comanda che vno sia abbruggiato, l'altro arrostito, l'altro circondato da serpi, l'altro battuto con catene, l'altro colatogli la pece in bocca, l'altro cibato di serpi, l'altro stà attaccato per vn piede, ardendo nelle fiamme, &c.

Il Pa-

FIGURE 5.2 "Hell." Woodcut print in Giovanni Battista Romano's *Dottrina christiana* (Rome, 1591), 76.
Courtesy of Rare Books and Special Collections, Princeton University

divine Lord because he deigned to have that poor woman by his side].[83]
Like the visions of María Bran and Marucha in Úrsula's diary, these two
visions from the *Vida anónima* provide examples of black women who
are neither demonized nor stigmatized as ignorant of God but rather
specifically presented as representative of God's favor for black women
generally and for Úrsula in particular. None of these instances, however,
employs language describing the beauty of redeemed blackness as
developed in Úrsula's spiritual diary.

Instead of beauty, the portrayal of Christian blackness in the *Vida
anónima* involves representing Úrsula as an especially effective black
spiritual intercessor. Numerous examples throughout the text emphasize Úrsula's divine power as a black woman to influence the salvation of
the living and the dead. For example, the narrator of the *Vida anónima*
opens a section about her gift for intercession with the following statement: "les constaba â todas [las almas], de quanta efficacia eran las
oraciones, y deprecaciones de esta *Santa Negra* para con la Magestad
Divina; y quanto el fervor de caridad, con que emprendia penitencias,
aplicaba sufragios, ganaba indulgencias, executaba ayunos, repetia
comuniones por su descanso, y alivio" [All souls knew how effective
this *holy black woman*'s prayers and deprecations were before the
Divine Majesty; and how profound her charity, with which she applied
penance, advocated for favors, won indulgences, fasted, and repeated
communion for the sake of their rest and solace].[84] The epithet "Santa
Negra" [holy black woman or black saint] appears here as part of the
description of Úrsula's capacity to advocate for souls before God, connecting Úrsula's especially effective spiritual intercession to her identity
as a black woman, a characteristic the introduction to the hagiography
suggests that she shares with the famous figures of Saba, the queen of
Sheba, and the sibyl of Cumana. The epithet of holy black woman is
particularly impressive because it breaks the rule declared in 1625 and
ratified in 1634 by Pope Urban VIII that states that only figures sanctioned by the Sacred Congregation of Rites should be called "holy"
or "saintly." Had this hagiography been finished and presented for
publication, the epithet would have been censored, most likely replaced
by "venerable" [venerable].

The *Vida anónima* further underscores the efficacy of Úrsula's capacity
for intercession when it describes her advocacy for the soul of Queen

---

[83] *Vida anónima*, 600r.   [84] Ibid., f. 594v; my emphasis.

Isabel by adding the crucial detail that Úrsula's mediation effectively saved the Queen: "Tienese por cierto saliô con brevedad de aquellas penas por las Oraciones de esta Santa Negra" [it is a known fact that her suffering subsided soon because of the prayers of this holy black woman].[85] The repetition of the epithet "Santa Negra" alongside the newly added assurance of her efficacy as a spiritual intermediary demonstrates a key way the *Vida anónima* connects Úrsula's capacity for spiritual mediation to its portrayal of Christian blackness.

Furthermore, unlike the *Vida breve*, the *Vida anónima* explicitly underscores that in being black Úrsula was not only an intercessor for elite figures but also an advocate for the souls of humble black women like herself. For example, in an elaboration of an episode included in the spiritual diary, the *Vida anónima* explains that Úrsula assisted in the salvation of a dying black servant of the convent: "Estando una Negra del Convento para morir por el mes de Marzo de 1659 fue â visitarla la Venerable Úrsula; y excitandola â haçer un acto de Contricion, que hizo muy de veras, con muchas lagrimas, y golpes de pechos, se despidiô la Sierva de Dios muy consolada de averla visto" [When a black woman from the convent was about to die in March of 1659, the venerable Úrsula went to see her. Urged by Úrsula to make an act of contrition, the woman did so with great sincerity, with many tears and beating her chest. This Servant of God bid her goodbye with great consolation for having seen her].[86] Incorporating this anecdote from Úrsula's diary to the second hagiography echoes the theme from Úrsula's diary that Úrsula was a dedicated teacher, healer in the infirmary, and advocate for the souls of black women in her convent. Like the anecdote from Úrsula's diary, proof of Úrsula's successful intercession comes in the form of another vision she has of the woman by Jesus's side:

Y passando de alli â su retiro, â encomendarla con mucho fervor â su Divino Dueño, viô luego un Santo Cristo de muy devota, y admirable estatura, y â sus pies â esta feliz morena amortajada. Con cuya clara vision reconoçiô, era cierta su muerte, y que por la misericordia de Dios se avia de salvar[,] de que le diô muchas gracias, desecha en espirituales dulçuras, y tiernos suspiros.

[On withdrawing to intercede for her before her Divine Owner with great fervor, she saw a Holy Christ of devout and admirable size, and at his feet, this happy black woman in her shroud. With this clear vision she recognized that her death

---

[85] Ibid., f. 589r.
[86] Ibid., f. 594v. See the episode as described in the *Diario espiritual* on 19r; 100.

was certain and that with God's mercy she was going to be saved, for which she thanked Him with great spiritual sweetness and tender longing.][87]

Whereas the episode in Úrsula's spiritual diary attributes the woman's ultimate salvation to God's mercy rather than Úrsula's intercession, the episode from the *Vida anónima* underscores Úrsula's role as the intercessor and the witness who communicated to the rest of the community that the salvation occurred.

An additional intercession by Úrsula in the *Vida anónima* (briefly mentioned in the diary but not in the *Vida breve*) contributes to its particular portrayal of Christian blackness: the passing of reform policies for the convent based on her visions and conversations with God about his displeasure over the lax attitude the religious community had developed toward their confessions and communions. As the episode appears in the *Vida anónima*, Úrsula serves as a conduit for a message from God to the community that all of its members were not preparing for and carrying out their confessions, taking communion, or paying attention at Mass as God demanded. The narrator explains that the convent authorities listened to Úrsula, asking her to dictate a new set of rules to remedy the problem: "Segun lo ordenô el Señor, asi se hizo; tomando â cargo esta diligencia, La Religiosa, â quien comunicaba, y dictaba Úrsula estos escritos, por orden del Señor, y mandato de sus Confessores, como se verâ despues. Y hablando dicha Monja â la Señora Abadeza en secreto, le mandô â Úrsula, hiçiesse las cedulas" [As the Lord ordered, it came to be; this religious woman took charge of the task, and Úrsula communicated and dictated these writings by God's order and by the command of her confessors, as will be seen later. That nun talked to the Abbess in secret, and she ordered Úrsula to prepare the decrees].[88] Úrsula, here, serves not only as a conduit for God's message to her religious community in this account but also as the conveyer of the new rules based on that message. The *Vida anónima* thus suggests that Úrsula's intervention in the written culture of her convent during her lifetime was not limited to her spiritual diary and the constitution of the confraternity to the Virgin of Mount Carmel (mentioned in both hagiographies). It also took the form of transmitting divinely ordained rules for religious observance applicable to her entire convent community. According to the second hagiographer, the reform implemented by the *cédulas* was perceived as effective, offering

---

[87] *Vida anónima*, f. 594v.

[88] Ibid., f. 604r. The reference to the two *cédulas* drafted by Úrsula in the spiritual diary appears at the end of the section narrated mostly in the third person, 34r.

further proof of Úrsula's power to communicate the will of God to her spiritual community: "con que es conoçido el fruto, y cosecha de aquel Labrador Divino en esta su Heredad" [with which the fruit and harvest of the Divine Planter in His Holy Estate is known].[89] Through agricultural language associating spiritual improvements with reaping fruit, the narrator celebrates Úrsula's capacity for spiritual mediation for *all* sectors of her religious community.

The notion of blackness from Úrsula's spiritual diary as described above thus only partly translates into the *Vida anónima*. While avoiding language related to the beauty of the souls of redeemed black men and women that appears in the spiritual diary, it adds a new angle by emphasizing the efficacy of Úrsula's role as a saintly black *criolla*, spiritual intercessor, and divine conduit for rules to reform her spiritual community.

Ultimately, both posthumous hagiographies present notions of blackness that build on and depart from the way it appears in Úrsula's spiritual diary. In interpreting Úrsula's visions and summarizing them for a broader audience, the hagiographies use Úrsula's visions to remind the living that the souls of black men and women are worthy of God's grace, stressing that they can be especially valuable spiritual intercessors. The *Vida anónima*, compared with the *Vida breve*, demonstrates more elements of the spiritual diary's notion of blackness by including numerous anecdotes about Úrsula's power to intercede on behalf of the humble as well as the elite and employing language to describe her as a black beacon for her entire spiritual community.

CONCLUSION

While neither Antonio Vieira nor either of Úrsula's posthumous hagiographers share Úrsula's spiritual diary's notion of virtuous and beautiful blackness, a similar notion appears in the texts produced in collaboration with the Jesuits' black interpreters in Cartagena, examined in Chapter 4. Both sets of texts (the interpreters' testimonies from Claver's beatification inquest from 1659 and Úrsula's spiritual diary from 1650–61) use superlatives to emphasize the extreme beauty of virtuous black Christians. The

---

[89] Ibid., f. 604r. See Kathryn Burns, *Colonial Habits*, 41–69, on the relationship between the rhetoric of *agricultura espiritual* and the acquisition and management of property for agricultural production by the Convent of Santa Clara in Cuzco during the same period of time.

interpreters' testimonies, for example, describe the image of the converted black man as "molto bello" [very beautiful], while Úrsula's spiritual diary describes María Bran's face as "muy linda" [very beautiful] and her face a "negro lustrísimo" [most brilliant black], as if her spiritual beauty were shining through her as if glowing. Neither set of texts suggests that Christian salvation was conceived symbolically or literally as whitening. Together, the two sets of texts offer important instances in which black linguistic and spiritual intermediaries adapted Christian aesthetic traditions to craft visions of what it meant to be virtuous, beautiful, and black in colonial Spanish America. The singularity of this language becomes apparent when comparing it with descriptions of blackness composed by Jesuits, Franciscans, and Dominicans, who, despite advocating for the consideration of black men and women as worthy of God's favor and evangelical attention, never describe black men and women with language related to superlative beauty.

Until now scholarship on meanings and values of blackness in Lima during this period has focused primarily on examples in which black men and women engaged the writing system to try to distance themselves from associations with blackness. For instance, Jouve Martín argues that black men and women used writing in the seventeenth century to file lawsuits and leave last wills and testaments as a way of dissolving their associations with blackness:

Even though it is possible that during a certain period of time and among a small number of people there persisted an oral memory of the traditional communities from which black slaves came, the nonexistence of a colonial black community understood as a cohesive social, ideological, hierarchical and political entity made it such that this entity cannot be found textually or discursively in the documents that have survived to our day.[90]

In this statement, Jouve Martín relegates the expression of a black communal identity to oral ephemera, stressing that interventions by black men and women in colonial written culture index only the dissolution of a black consciousness. Jouve Martín furthermore suggests that the only black communal identity possible would be one tied to African communities from which the enslaved came and not communal identities forged out of experiences in the Americas. Úrsula's diary suggests an important exception to this argument.[91]

---

[90] Jouve Martín, *Esclavos de la ciudad letrada*, 183; my translation.
[91] See McKinley, *Fractional Freedoms*, for examples of litigation on behalf of black men and women in seventeenth-century Lima that index efforts to protect black collective units

Karen Graubart has presented a somewhat parallel vision of a fragmented black consciousness in colonial Lima in two different studies that
signal ways in which freed black men and women sought to separate
themselves from being associated with the category of *negro*. Graubart's
detailed study of the last wills and testaments of women of African
descent composed in Lima between 1565 and 1666 argues that women
of African descent who owned slaves in colonial Lima did not show
empathy for their enslaved laborers based on any kind of shared racial
affiliation.[92] Instead, Graubart explains, women of African descent who
owned slaves present themselves in their wills in terms that emphasize
their hierarchical separation from their servants. In a different study
about the conflicts between confraternities of people of African descent,
Graubart identifies a desire on the part of freed black people to disassoci-
ate themselves with enslaved black men and women by using the terms
moreno or *morena* for themselves and the terms *negro* or *negra* as an
insult for other black men and women. Ultimately, Graubart argues that
in colonial Lima "those who were able to achieve manumission developed
a language that drew upon European colour distinctions to set themselves
off from the less fortunate majority."[93] Graubart's important studies
demonstrate that black men and women sometimes resorted to hierarchical color-inflected language to present themselves as less destitute than
other individuals of African descent in colonial Lima.

The seventeenth-century notions of blackness produced in collaboration with the black linguistic and spiritual intermediaries that I examined
in the previous two chapters speak to the existence of notions of blackness
articulated by black men and women that differ from the negative hierarchical ones that have been identified by Jouve Martín and Graubart.[94]
Attending to these examples can help us map a broader field of signification of blackness in colonial Spanish America that recognizes that even if
some black men and women sought to separate themselves from associations with enslavement increasingly tied to bodies perceived as dark or
black, others sought to identify with and redeem blackness *generally* as

such as marriages or families. For an analysis of comparable legal cases from New Spain,
see Bennett, *Africans in Colonial Mexico* and *Colonial Blackness*.

[92] Karen Graubart, "Los lazos que unen. Dueñas negras de esclavos negros en Lima, siglos
XVI–XVII," *Nueva corónica* 2 (2013): 625–40, 627.

[93] Graubart, "So color de una cofradía," 51.

[94] For the argument about efforts at self-whitening beyond Lima into the eighteenth century,
see Ann Twinam, *Purchasing Whiteness: Pardos, Mulattos, and the Quest for Social
Mobility in the Spanish Indies* (Stanford, CA: Stanford University Press, 2015).

representative of Christian virtue and physical beauty in their interactions with the colonial writing system.

Moreover, the texts examined in this book show that black linguistic and spiritual intermediaries strategically interpreted the Christian tenet of the equality of all people before God to articulate notions of beautiful and virtuous Christian blackness. While there is no doubt that black men and women were increasingly associated with the base worldly condition of slavery in seventeenth-century colonial Spanish America, the textual record produced through the participation of black linguistic and spiritual intermediaries in Spanish America in the seventeenth century shows that there existed competing religious notions of blackness that consider black men and women to be especially beautiful and virtuous.

Coda

Negros literarios

Negro: Persona que trabaja anónimamente para lucimiento y provecho de otro, especialmente en trabajos literarios [Black: A person who works anonymously for the fame and benefit of another, especially in literary works].

—*Diccionario de la Real Academia Española*, 1992, 1015

After *negro* as a term for a captive laborer traveled from Spanish and Portuguese into French in the mid-eighteenth century,[1] it took on a new meaning comparable to that of "ghostwriter" in English with the onset of the literary publishing market in the early nineteenth century.[2] This usage eventually translated back into Spanish (as it did with comparable terms

---

[1] Forbes, *Africans and Native Americans*, 81.

[2] Jacques Savary's *Dictionnaire universel de commerce* from 1723 definitively incorporated the term "nègre" as a synonym of "Pièce d'Inde" and "esclave" (Jacques Savary des Bruslon, *Dictionnaire universel de commerce* [1723], vol. 1 [Paris: Veuve Estienne et fils, 1797], 378, 383, 746–47). For the legacy and politics of translations of the terms "negro" and "nègre" in the twentieth century, see Brent Edwards, *Practice of Diaspora: Literature, Translation, and the Rise of Black Internationalism* (Cambridge, MA: Harvard University Press, 2003), 25–43. See also Simone Delesalle and Lucette Valensi, "Le mot 'nègre' dans les dictionnaires français d'Ancien Régime: Historie et lexicographie," *Langue Française* 15 (1972): 79–104. For a comparison with English, see Lucette Valensi, "Nègre/Negro: Recherches dans les dictionnaires français et anglais du XVIIème au XIXème siècles," in *L'Idée de race dans la pensée politique française contemporaine*, ed. Pierre Guiral and E. Temime (Paris: Editions du Centre National de la Recherche Scientifique, 1977), 157–70. None of these contemporary studies, however, considers the etymology of the usage of the term as ghostwriter.

in Italian, Polish, and Catalan).³ Etymological explanations suggest an association with the set of expressions in Spanish, French, and Italian of "trabajar como un negro," "travailler comme un nègre," "lavorare come un negro" [to work like a slave].⁴ The continued popularity of these expressions in today's spoken language indicates a persistent figuring of blackness around tropes of silence, strenuous unrecognized labor, and dispossession.

A speech made by Pope Francis in Cartagena de Indias in September 2017 demonstrates a related legacy. When invoking the memory of Pedro Claver to his audience, Pope Francis stated that Claver "esperaba las naves que llegaban desde África al principal mercado de esclavos del Nuevo Mundo. Muchas veces los atendía solamente con gestos, gestos evangelizadores, por la imposibilidad de comunicarse, por la diversidad de los idiomas. Pero una caricia trasciende todos los idiomas" [waited for the ships arriving from Africa in the principal slave port of the New World. He often attended to their needs only through gestures, evangelical gestures, because of the impossibility of communicating with them due to the diversity of their languages. But a caring gesture transcends all languages].⁵ Severed from the complex context of Claver's evangelizing project, his "caricia" [caring gesture] stands alone, obliterating the presence and labor of his enslaved black interpreters, who we know not only made possible his mission among black men and women in the port but also served as key witnesses to help beatify him after his death. Such a historical memory erases black men's and women's participation in

---

³ The first time the *Diccionario de la Real Academia* [DRAE] included this definition for "negro" was in 1970: "El que hace trabajos literarios que firma otro; el que trabaja anónimamente para lucimiento o provecho de otro" (1406).

⁴ Ibid.; *DRAE* (1984), 1498; *DRAE* (1989), 1083; *DRAE* (1992), 1015. The fourth edition of *Dictionnaire de l'Academie Française* from 1762 cites a similar expression: "*Traiter quelqu'un comme un nègre*, pour dire, Traiter quelqu'un comme un esclave" [*Treat someone like a black* is to say, Treat someone like a slave] (205). The Italian versions of this expression vary, including "lavorare come uno schiavo" and "lavorare come un condannato." See G. E. Furzi, *Geografia universale fisica e politica: Secondo Arago, Balbi, Ritter, Maltebrun, Vosigien* (Florence: Nuova edicione rivista, 1854), 210; James Middlemore, *Proverbs, Sayings, and Comparisons in Various Languages: Collected and Arranged* (London: Isbister LTD, 1889), 458; Ferdinando Altieri, *Dizionario Italiano ed Inglese* (London: William and John Innys, 1726–27), vol. 2, 528 [SLA-SLI].

⁵ "La recita dell'Angelus presso la Chiesa di San Pietro Claver a Cartagena e la visita alla Casa Santuario di San Pietro Claver," Viaggio Apostolico del Santo Padre Francesco in Colombia (6–11 settembre 2017), http://press.vatican.va/content/salastampa/it/bollettino/pubblico/2017/09/10/0582/01237.html. Translation provided by the Vatican.

Claver's life even as it celebrates an individual who stood out as their ardent advocate.

This book has sought to fill some of the gaps of the historical memory of blackness in Spanish America by turning a critical eye to colonial texts produced with the participation of black interpreters and spiritual intermediaries. Although it is true that elites generally used writing during this period as a mechanism of control to support colonial hierarchies associating blackness with the base status and incivility of the slave, these texts show that the political-ecumenical category of the human also allowed for alternative articulations of black subjectivity in colonial Spanish America to circulate. Indeed, because of the emphasis placed on free choice and informed consent as requirements for legitimate Christian conversion by the end of the sixteenth century, even *bozales* in seventeenth-century Cartagena appear in certain colonial texts as interpreters who help transfer catechetical messages back and forth among new arrivals, shaping notions of beautiful and virtuous blackness in the process. In Lima, Úrsula de Jesús's spiritual diary and related hagiographies present her as an effective spiritual intercessor in her religious community who reminded its members of the "engaño" [lie] of earthly hierarchies that consider black men and women worthless.

At the beginning of the twenty-first century, Gayatri Chakravorty Spivak invited us to attend to "Who slips into the place of the human in humanism at the end of the day?"[6] While Western humanism's structuring categories (and the heavy colonial legacies they carry) cannot be easily repaired, we no doubt need to continue to question them and the ideological work they enable. Studying the human's diverse genealogies before the eighteenth century is an important part of this interrogation. From the documentary record of colonial Spanish America, this means taking black religious discourse and religious subjectivities seriously and foregrounding the influence of black intermediaries in their articulation.

---

[6] Gayatri Chakravorty Spivak, *Death of a Discipline* (New York: Columbia University Press, 2003), 26.

Appendixes

Appendix A
Whether Jesuits Should Learn Kimbundu in Peru
(ca. 1635)

En razon si conviene entablar en esta provincia de la Compa[ñía]
de J[esú]s del Pirú q[ue] aprendan la lengua Angola de los Negros:
Y si conviene imprimir el Vocabulario, Arte y Confessionario
de la dicha Lengua*

Presupongo lo q[ue] es cosa cierta, y q[ue] no se puede dudar, q[ue] si
uviesse algun Padre que supiesse la dicha lengua bien sabida fuera muy
provechosa para enseñar a la nacion Angola las cosas tocantes a su
salvacion porque es cierto que cada nacion las entiende mejor en su
lengua que en la agena, y con este presupuesto dexo de explicar los
muchos bienes que se siguen de confessar y predicar a los negros en su
misma lengua.

Esto supuesto, me resuelvo a dezir q[ue] ni es necessario obligar a los
Padres de la Compañía, ni conveniente aprender la dicha lengua, todo lo
qual probare con distinccion de alg[unos] puntos.

1° Que esta lengua es muy dificultosa de aprender, porque en ella no
ay Maestro que la pueda enseñar que sepa bien la lengua española con
propriedad. [2v] Porque nadie abrà que sepa esta lengua que no sea negro
y la capacidad de los negros es tan corta principalmente los que vienen
adultos: porque la experiencia me a enseñado que como ellos en su tierra
no tratan sino de cosas muy materiales, y toscas; quando se les preguntan
las cosas interiores de el alma de el alma [sic], como tocantes al dolor de
los peccados, o, tocantes a los misterios de la fe, no saben lo que le dizen;

---

* Archivum Romanum Societatis Iesu, FG, Titulus XVIII, Colegia, No. 1488, Perú II,
  documento II.

el aprender pues con negros ladinos de esta capacidad es cosa trabajosis-
sima, porque apenas saben la distinccion de las personas, de los numeros,
de los tiempos, etc., conque es impossible que un Padre por muy cuyda-
doso que sea este seguro que aprende lo cierto.

2° Pero demos caso que este Padre aprenda la lengua con tales Maestros, (que lo pongo en duda como tengo dicho por ser la lengua muy
dificultosa) aprendiendola pues medianam[en]te como aprendiz no serà
de provecho para los negros, porque es gente altiva, colerica, y hablando
su lengua con algun yerro se rie luego, y no haze caso de lo que se le dize
como tengo experimientado.

3° Como ven los negros que son mas estimados los negros ladinos,
tienen increible desseo de saber la lengua española; y assi procuran
hablarla desde luego; y si algún Padre a tomado de memoria alguna cosa
de su lengua para hablarles luego les dizen que no hablen en su lengua,
sino en la lengua española, y es cierto que en seis meses despues de
llegados los boçales a Lima saben lo necessario para confessarse y en
dos dias saben la palabra Hurtar y saben que quiere dezir pecar con
mugeres, que cosa es jurar, y las demas cosas tocantes y la confession
[3r] y lo mesmo digo de las cosas tocantes a la fe q[ue] si ay buen
catequista que quiera ense[ñ]arlos con su media lengua española sabran
lo necessario para salbarse.

4° Si todos los negros hablaran la lengua Angola dixera que era
necessario aprenderla; pero como ay de treinta a quarenta lenguas de
negros, si fuera la una necessaria fueran todas necessarias, lo qual nadie
podra dezir; y los concilios de hombres tan doctos que a avido tres y
quatro vezes en el Peru en los quales tratan muy por extenso de la
salvacion de los negros, ubieran mandado que los curas de ellos aprendiessen sus lenguas, si fuera necess[ario]; y pongo caso que un Predicador
sepa predicar en una lengua de estas como es cierto que todas demas
naciones se le fueran de el auditorio y si se quedassen fuera sin provecho
por no entenderla.

5° En todas las religiones y en el clero ay gente docta, y de mucho zelo
de las almas y nunca xamas les a passado por el pensamiento ser las
lenguas necessarias, ni provechosas ni convenientes, y al cabo de quaresma todos los negros salen catequisados, y confessados, y quanto mas
tiempo estan entre nosotros aprenden mas lengua española haziendose
mas capaçes.

6° Pongo caso que un Padre a comenzado a aprender la lengua, y
quiera perfecionarse en ella no le sera possible, porque la experiencia nos
enseña en la lengua quichua, y en la aymara de los Indios, que si no las

aprenden en los pueblos de las dichas lenguas nunca las podemos aprender; y si dixeren que las aprendemos en [3v] pueblos de españoles, digo q
[ue] en essos pueblos ay mas Indios que españoles y todos hablan una
misma lengua y quando quieren confesar de la mañana hasta la noche en
essa lengua pueden hazerlo, y en esto es donde mas se aprende la lengua, y
las confessiones de los negros entre año son rarissimas; y quando quera-
mos comunicarlos fuera de confession es impossible porque todos los dias
de trabajo estan trabajando, sin perder punto y los dias de siesta quieren
ellos holgarse, y aun p[ar]a obligarlos a un poco de sermon, y dotrina es
fuerça que nosotros Herm[anos] estudiantes, los lleven como yendo a
cosa de ellos, y que los tengan por fuerça juntos solo un breve rato porque
estan rabiando por yr á dançar y cantar con que es impossible tener
communicacion con ellos, y si algun Padre quisiesse yr donde ay cantidad
de negros como a los obrajes, o a las chacras, y heredades tanpoco fuera
de provecho, porque estan trabajando, y demas de esso en cada puesto de
estos ay seis, o ocho lenguas diferentes.

7 ° Sera provechoso aprender esta lengua en la Provincia de Tucuman,
y Paraguay donde todos los negros que vienen por el puerto de buenos
ayres son Angolas, y por esso el P[adr]e Diego de Torres Bollo desde
aquella Provincia a instado tanto que los Padres aprendan la lengua, porq
[ue] tienen muy grande empleo en la gobernacion de Tucuman y en ella el
de los Indios es muy corto, porque se van acabando a priesa, y en la
ciudad donde avia diez mill Indios no ay ya docientos; pero los negros
como se van multiplicando por venir cada año de Angola muchos navios
de cargazon de ellos son muchos, y cada dia seran mas, conq[ue] es muy
acertado que los Padres de aquella Provincia la aprendan como [4r] que
an començado a aprenderla con mucha gloria de N[uestr]o S[eño]r.

8 ° Para los negros pues q[ue] an estado alg[uno]s meses o un año entre
españoles conforme la diligencia que ponen los amos en que aprendan las
cosas necessarias, no es necessaria la lengua Angola como se a dicho pero
fuera necessaria, y provechosa en dos casos solos: el 1° para catequizar a
los negros boçales, rezien llegados de su tierra, para baptizarlos, y para
que entiendan el sacram[en]to que reciben porque no nos emos de fiar de
los baptismos que se dan en Angola, que son de cargazon, sin dezirles
cosa alg[un]a de la fe y el agua que les echan entienden que es p[ar]a
limpiar la cabeça x[por] lo qual es fuerça que se haga aun en Lima porque
aunque an procurado baptizarlos en Cartaxena, muchos passan sin bap-
tizarse, porq[ue] los cargadores, como traen muchos sin despachos legiti-
mos, para que la Justicia no se los lleve por perdidos los esconden y no
permiten que anden publicam[en]te con los que se baptizan; para este

punto fuera cosa del cielo hallarse un Padre que supiesse la lengua Angola, pero este Padre sabra catequizar los Angolas, y no sabra catequizar los Branes, los Biaf[a]ras y las demas naciones que ay; la misma dificultad passa en el otro punto de extrema necesidad, que es in art[icul]o mortis, que fuera de gran gloria de N[uestro] S[eñor] hallar Padre que supiera confessarlos en aquel peligro.

El remedio pues de todas las naciones de negros en las dos necesidades sobredichas no es que sepan una sola lengua, porque esse es un remedio de pocos, el remedio pues General de todos es buscar un negro ladino de cada lengua quan ladino fuere possible por medio del qual se haran las preguntas necessarias para que sepa cada negro lo que es el sacram[en]to del baptismo, con que se baptizara con toda seguridad y en caso que no se hallen estas lenguas el P[adr]e zeloso de las almas se a de aprovechar del poco Romance [4v] que el negro aprendio desde Angola hasta Lima en comp[añí]a de españoles y portugueses, y hablando el P[adr]e la lengua española a lo boçal procurarà hazerlos capazes, como pudiere fiado de la misericorida de Dios, que como no sirve infundirnos las lenguas de los negros, mirara con ojos de clemencia estas pobres almas assi en el baptismo como en la muerte.

9° Añado q[ue] los Padres que aprendiessen esta lengua en Lima solam[en]te avian de executarla alli, porq[ue] fuera de Lima como todas las ciudades del Peru estan llenas de Indios ay en ellas poquisimos negros, y essos pocos de diversas lenguas como se a dicho, y un Padre solo bastarà para Lima, porque los demas con mas provecho aprenderan las demas lenguas de los Indios de quienes esta lleno todo el reyno.

Acerca de la Impression del vocabulario, y arte de la lengua Angola

1° Es cosa dificultosa imprimirle en Lima y fuera trabajo perdido, porque como no ay persona que sepa esta lengua, tanpoco abra quien corrija las probas de la emprenta, conque, aunque se imprima no sera de probecho por los muchos yerros que sacara.

2° El vocabulario y todo lo que esta escrito en esta lengua; digo lo que en Lima tenemos està de tan mala letra que dize el que lo a leydo con cuydado, que muchas letras no se conocen, y es cierto que pondran una por otra; y tanpoco pueden aprobechar en esto los negros ladinos porque el uno pronuncia una palabra de una manera, y el otro de otra con diferentes letras y sonsonete.

3° Item dize quien lo a mirado despasio q[ue] el voca-[5r]bulario es muy diminuto y que le faltan infinitas cosas y estos yerros pueden ser en cosas de mucha importancia, como desde Mexico me avisaron de los yerros que se notaban en el catecismo que se imprimio en Lima, y aqui se an notado otros en el mismo catecismo.

4 ° Por ser esta lengua tan estraña para los impressores piden mucho mas dinero, que si fuera en romançe, o, latin, lo menos que piden son mill y quinientos pesos, y de papel seran menester otros quinientos y este dinero no es tan poco el dia de oy, que se halle tan facilmente, que yo no se de donde avia de salir.

5 ° Dado caso que se imprima no abrà salida deste libro, ni clerigo, ni Frayle que tal compre, porque ellos nunca xamas aprenden lengua ninguna, ni de Indios tanpoco, sino es que quieran alcançar algun beneficio o curato que no le podran alcançar, sin saber lengua de Indios, pero no ay ningun beneficio de negros meram[en]te gente de servicio, a estos tales no los examinan de la lengua de los negros, ni los obligan a que la aprendan, y solam[en]te los obligan a aprender la de los Indios para lo qual tienen todo aparejo, y maestro en la universidad que la lee cada dia, de modo que no abrà hombre que compre tal libro, luego abremos gastado los dos mill pesos en valde y los libros se comeran de polilla.

Sino es que esta Provincia quiera hazer esse gasto de limosna embiando essos libros impressos a la Provincia del Paraguay, porque alli an comencado á aprender esta lengua Angola como arriba dixe. Pero no se si esta Provincia y sus collegios pueden emprender esse gasto, todo lo qual fuera tambien impossible por falta de maestro que assista a la emprenta como [5v] queda advertido.

De todo lo qu[al] infiero q[ue] el P[adre] Ant[oni]o Vazquez Provincial de esta Pronvincia no debe obligar a nadie a que aprenda esta lengua porq [ue] no la podran aprender en muchos años, assi por falta de maestros, como por falta de buenos papeles impresos y por falta de la communicacion necessaria con los negros y porque la consciencia no nos obliga a ello como no nos obliga a aprender las demas lenguas de los negros supuesto que todos ellos aprenden con la lengua media española lo necessario para salbarse y supuesto que en la extrema necessdad que se a referido podemos satisfazer con los interpretes.

Con todo esso si acaso mirando el P[adr]e Provincial este negocio delante de N[uestr]o Señor conforme al zelo que N[uestr]o S[eño]r le á dado hallase que debia cometer esta empreza a algunas personas de nuestra Comp[añí]a; que en tal caso yo me ofresco p[ar]a ello y me dedicare a todo punto a la lengua Angola dando de mano a otro qualquier estudio, y exercicio como si Dios immediatamente me lo mandasse que para ello ni me falta memoria ni voluntad, ni salud.

Whether Learning the Language of Angola of Blacks Should Be Established in This Province of the Company of Jesus of Peru and Whether the Vocabulary, Grammar, and Confession Manual of That Language Should Be Printed

I grant that it is certain and that there is no doubt that if there were a priest who knew the said language very well it would be very beneficial for teaching the nation of Angola matters regarding their salvation because it is certain that each nation understands these things better in their own language than in any other. This said, I leave aside explaining the many benefits that come from confessing and preaching to blacks in their own language. I dare say nonetheless that it is not necessary nor appropriate to require Jesuit fathers to learn this language. All of this I will prove by stressing the following points.

1. This language is very difficult to learn because there is no teacher of it who can speak proper Spanish. [2v] For there is no one who knows this language who is not a black person and the capacity of blacks is so limited, principally those who come as adults, for experience has taught me that because they in their land do not talk about anything more than very material and crude things, when they are asked about the inner things of the soul, such as those regarding the pain of sin, or the mysteries of the faith, they do not understand what they are being told. It follows that learning [the language] from acculturated blacks of this capacity is something extremely arduous because they barely know the difference between persons, numbers, tenses, etc., with which it is impossible for even the most careful father to be sure he is learning what is correct.

2. But let us suppose a case in which this father learned the language with such teachers (which I doubt as I have said above because it is such a difficult language). The father having learned the language then half-well as an apprentice will not benefit these blacks because being proud and angry people, if someone speaks their language with some error, they laugh and do not listen to what they are told, as I have experienced.

3. As blacks see that acculturated blacks are the most esteemed, they have an incredible desire to learn Spanish and so try to speak it quickly. And if a father has memorized something of their language to address them then the blacks say not to speak to them in their language but in Spanish. And it is true that in six months after arriving in Lima, *bozales* know enough to confess, and in two days they know the word *to steal* and they know what it means to sin with women, what it is to swear, and the other things related to matters of confession. [3r] And I say the same

about things related to faith, for if there is a good catechist who wants to teach them with their half Spanish, *bozales* will understand enough to save themselves.

4. If all blacks were to speak the language of Angola I would say that it is necessary to learn it, but because there are thirty to forty languages spoken by blacks, if one were necessary all would be necessary, which no one would endorse. Additionally, if it were necessary, the councils of such learned men that have been held in Peru three or four times in which they extensively discussed the salvation of blacks would have ordered priests to learn their languages. And supposing a preacher were to preach in one of these languages, all of the other black nations would stop listening and would be left out, without any benefit, for not understanding the language.

5. In every religious order and among the clergy there are learned people with tremendous zeal for saving souls and it has never ever occurred to them that these languages are necessary or beneficial or useful. And still at the end of Lent all black men and women are catechized and confessed, and the more time they spend among us the more they learn Spanish, becoming more capable.

6. Let us assume that a father has begun to learn the language and wants to perfect his use of it, it would be impossible. For experience has taught us in learning Quechua and Aymara of the Indians that if we do not learn them in the towns where those languages are spoken, we can never learn them. And if they say that we learn them in [3v] Spanish towns, I say it is because in those towns there are more Indians than Spaniards and everyone speaks the same [indigenous] language. And when the priests want to confess from morning to night in that language they can, for it is in this activity that the language is best learned. In contrast, blacks during the year [outside of Lent] are extremely rare. And when we want to speak with them outside the confession it is impossible because every work day they are working without exception and on their days of rest they want to enjoy themselves. And even if they are required to listen to a little sermon and doctrine, we brothers, students must take them as if going to one of their meetings and yet we still have to keep them there by force just a brief time because they are raging to go dance and sing. With this, it is impossible to maintain communication with them. And if a father wanted to go where there is a significant group of black men and women such as in *obrajes*, farms, or fields, it would be of little benefit because they are working and besides at each post they speak six or eight different languages.

7. It will be beneficial to learn this language in the Province of Tucuman and Paraguay where all of the black men and women that come through the port of Buenos Aires are Angolans. And because of this, Father Diego de Torres Bollo from that province has urged so much that the fathers learn the language because blacks are of great use for governing Tucuman, whereas the Indians are not because they are disappearing quickly, and in the city that previously had ten thousand Indians there are now no more than two hundred. But blacks are multiplying because every year from Angola many slave ships come carrying many of them, and every day there will be more. With this it is very appropriate that the fathers of that province learn the language as [4r] they have begun to learn it with much glory to Our Lord.

8. Thus, for blacks who have been some months or one year among Spaniards, depending on the diligence of their owners in making them learn the necessary things [for their salvation], the language of Angola is not necessary as I have said. It would, however, be necessary and beneficial in only two cases: the first is to catechize black *bozales*, recently arrived from their lands, to baptize them so that they understand the sacrament they receive because we cannot trust the baptisms that are given in Angola, for they are for the whole ship at a time without teaching them anything about the faith such that they think that the water that they are being given is meant to clean their heads. So it is necessary to baptize them even in Lima because although they have tried to baptize them in Cartagena, many get through without being baptized because the ships, many of which carry illegal licenses, hide some slaves and do not let them walk about publicly with those who are baptized so that the law does not take them away. For this point it would be a heavenly gift to find a father who knows the language of Angola. And yet, this father will [only] know how to catechize Angolans and not Branes, Biafadas, and the other nations that there are. The same difficulty occurs with the other point – that of extreme necessity as in the case of *in articulo mortis*.[1] It would be of great glory to Our Lord to find a father who knew how to confess them in such a state of danger.

The remedy then for all of the black nations in these two states of necessity is not that priests learn only one language, because that is a remedy for few. The general remedy for all then is to find an acculturated black person of each language, as acculturated as possible, through whom the necessary questions will be asked so that each black person may learn

---

[1] A Latin phrase used in Spanish texts to refer to an individual at the brink of death, authorized to receive the sacrament of extreme unction.

the meaning of the sacrament of the baptism, and with this they can be baptized safely. If none of these interpreters can be found, the zealous evangelical father can use whatever little Romance [4v] the black person has learned from Angola to Lima in the company of Spaniards and Portuguese. So when the father speaks Spanish in the manner of the *bozal*, he will try to educate them, as best as he can, supported by the mercy of God, for seeing as it is not useful for us to adopt the languages of black men and women, He will look with merciful eyes on these poor souls – both in baptism and in death.

9. I add that the fathers who learn this language in Lima will only be able to use it there because outside of Lima and in all of the cities of Peru there are many Indians and so there are very few blacks, and those few speak different languages, as has been said. One father would suffice for Lima because all the other fathers will benefit more from learning the other languages of the Indians with whom this kingdom is full.

Regarding the Printing of the Vocabulary and Grammar of the Angolan Language

1. It is a difficult thing to print in Lima and it would be a wasted effort because as there is no one here who knows this language, there is no one who can correct the proofs of the printer. With this, even if it is printed it will not be beneficial for the many errors that it would contain.

2. The vocabulary and everything that is written in this language, I speak of what we have in Lima, is written in such bad penmanship that according to the person who has read it carefully, many of the letters are unreadable and it is certain that some letters will be interchanged. Nor will acculturated blacks be able to help with this matter because one pronounces a word in one way and the other in another, with different letters and intonation.

3. The same person who looks at it carefully says that the vocabulary [5r] is very small and an infinite number of things are missing from it. These omissions could be of great importance, as in the case of the errors about which I was notified from Mexico that were found in the catechism printed in Lima and other errors have been found here in the same catechism.

4. Because this language is so foreign to the printers, they ask for a lot of money. If it were in Romance, or, Latin, the least they charge would be one thousand five hundred pesos plus the cost of paper. In this case, we would need five hundred more and this sum is not negligible nor easy to acquire nowadays. I do not know where it would come from.

5. Even if this book were printed, it would not sell; as it would not be purchased by neither clergy nor friars because they never learn a language not even one of the Indians unless they aspire to obtain some benefit or curate that they will not be able to hold if they do not know the language of the Indians. But there is no benefit from preaching to blacks, who are merely service workers. These clergy or friars will not be examined in the language of black populations nor will they be required to learn it. They are only required to learn that of the Indians, for which they have all manner of resources and a teacher at the university who reads out loud in it daily. Thus no one will buy this book and we will have invested two thousand pesos in vain and the books will be eaten by moths.

The exception would be that this province wants to incur this expense as an act of charity, sending these printed books to the Province of Paraguay because there they have begun learning the language of Angola, as I said above. But I do not know if this Province and its schools can take on this expense, all of which in any case would be impossible for the lack of an expert who could assist in its printing as [5v] warned above.

From all of this, I infer that Father Antonio Vázquez, Provincial leader of this Province, should not require anyone to learn this language because they would not learn it in many years, as much for the lack of teachers as for the lack of good printed materials and the lack of necessary communication with these black populations. Also because our conscience does not require us to do it just as it does not require us to learn the other languages of the blacks given that all of them halfway learn the Spanish language enough to save themselves. And if they find themselves in extreme necessity, as has been stated, we can satisfy the need with interpreters.

Having said all of this, if the Provincial father considering this issue according to Our Lord and the zeal Our Lord has given him, finds that this effort should be assigned to some people of our society, in that case I would volunteer to do it, and I would dedicate myself entirely to the language of Angola, with the aid of any other study or exercise, as if God had directly ordered me to do it, for which I am not lacking in memory, will, or health.

Appendix B
Selections from Andrés Sacacuche's Testimony in Pedro Claver's Beatification Inquest (Proceso 1676)

Testimonio Andrea Sacabuche – 19 maggio 1659*

[100r] sempre lo tenne per Religioso di molta virtù et essemplar vita, molto aggiustato alle regole della detta sua Religione. Il che tutto sà questo Testimonio per haverlo visto essere e passar cosi dentro le porte di questo Colleggio ove ha habitato come schiavo di quello e lo possono dire similmente li Padri che lo conobbero che hoggi vivono, e sono fratello Nicolo Gonsalez Sagrestano di questa detta Chiesa et Emanuel Rodriguez Elemosiniero e Pietro Lamparte Procuratore, e si ricorda che in certa occasione, stando infermo, per il molto amore che à questo Testimonio portava il detto Padre, per essere uno delli suoi Interpreti, lo condusse alla sua stanza acciò che in quella si curasse, et esso potesse haver luogho di accorrerli con il necessario, conforme lo faceva con tanto amore, volontà, e schiettezza come se fosse stato un altro moro, come questo Testimonio, et in questo tempo osservò ch' il Padre Pietro Claver prendeva tutti li giorni alle quattro della mattina cuando sonavano ad alzarsi in questo detto Colleggio una molto rigorosa disciplina, nella quale si stava come un quarto d'hora doppo la quale si poneva in ginocchioni, avanti un crocifisso che teneva dipinto in una tela nella detta sua stanza, il quale crocifisso stà hoggi in poter di questo Testimonio, perche cuando morì il detto Padre lo prese e lo portò alla sua stanza per sua particolar divotione...

[1]Parimente si ricorda che l'anno passato del cinquanta, doppo Pasqua di Resurrettione, andò accompagnando il detto Padre a una missione che

---

* Proceso de Beatificación de Pedro Claver, Bilbioteca Nacional de Colombia, Bogotá, Libros raros y manuscritos, manuscrito 281 [1658–1669], trans. Claudio Louvet [1676].
[1] Paragraph break added.

fece à publicar un Giubileo Centesimo per tutte le ville che sono di questa detta città, fino al Rio, che chiamano del Senu che sarà distante più di trenta leghe, et in tutte le ville che vi sono, confessò tutti li mori e more che in quelle erano, e similmente li Spagnuoli et Indiani, li mulati, e nati da doi nationi diverse...

[100v] E quando arrivava à qualche villa si posava nella cameretta o stanza del moro più povero e separato dall'altri, e se vi n'era alchuna abbandonata, e che non habitasse alchuno in quella per essere vecchia, e scommoda, in quella si accomodava, e diceva che stava molto bene, e questo Testimonio li dispiaceva perche solevano stare d'ordinario molto sporche, et era necessario che la scopassero et accomodassero, et acciò non li dispiacesse tanto, molte volte il detto Padre lo agiutava à scopare detta stanza, e la causa principale del dispiacere di questo Testimonio era, come hà detto, perche il detto Padre allogiandosi nella casa o stantiole delli Spagnuoli che la tenevano limpida, scopata, et ornata [*sic*], gli toglierebbe il detto travaglio, ma esso non lo voleva fare per mostrarsi povero in tutto e perfetto seguace della somma povertà...

[101r] [Q]uello che fece maravigliare maggiormente questo Testimonio fù la sua gran mortificatione, et il raro soffrire delle zampane delle quali abbondavano assai le dette ville, perche mai le ammazzava, benche molto lo stassero mordendo nella faccia e nelle mani, il che visto da questo Testimonio, se n'andò ad esso e li disse alchune volte perche non le ammazzava, che erano molte quelle che haveva nelle dette parti, et esso rispondeva che non era bene ammazzarle che più tosto li facevano giovamento, per li cavavano il sangue cattivo, et alchune notti, che il detto Padre faceva alchune essortationi spirituali alli detti mori delle dette ville, quando venivano le staggioni delle Rose e delle Semente, erano tante le zampane che se li ponevano sopra la detta faccia, e mani, che di biancho pareva nero, e esso no le amazzava ne faceva movimento ma che le tolerava e soffriva come se fosse stato insensibile proseguendo le dette sue essortationi con molto fervore e spirito, et era tanto il danno, e combattimento che li facevano le dette zampane che il giorno seguente rimaneva con la detta faccia e mani piene di molti segni gonfiate et annegrite, il che visto da questo testimonio compatendolo e conoscendo che ancorche li havessero detto, che ammazzassero le dette zampane, ò che permettesse che con una ventarola gliela stassero scacciando, mentre faceva le dette essortationi, no lo haveva da fare ne permettere, li disse che non si trattenesse molto nelle dette prediche perche li detti negri venivano stanchi di travagliare tutto il giorno, e si annoiarebbero se fosse longo e

non tornarebbero à sentire l'altro giorno, et al detto Padre li parve bene il detto consiglio, e fu più breve nelle dette prediche, con il che lo liberò questo Testimonio in parte dalla gran mortificatione che in soffrire le dette zampane pativa, e non sà questo Testimonio che possa haver maggior mortificatione che la riferita...

Similmente dice questo Testimonio, che ancorche il suo offitio è essere sonatore di trombone, era uno dell'Interpreti della lingua Angola, che haveva il detto P. Pietro Claver, per la qual causa, sà il molto che travagliò e patì in instruire [sic] e insegnare li mori rozzi, che vengono à questa terra, perche subito che sapeva ch'era entrato nel porto, qualche naviglio di quelli, non capeva[2] in se per il gusto et il giubilo [che] se [sic] li conosceva nella faccia, che nelle dette occasioni la teneva allegra e ridente, essendo cosi che d'ordinario la portava pallida, macilente [sic], e melanconica e [101v] le palpebre degli occhi assai mortificate e subito avvisava questo Testimonio, e tutti l'altri mori Interpreti, che teneva, e si preveniva d'alchuni regali in specie di merangoli e limoni et alchuni biscottini e tabacco, il che tutto buscava di elemosina trà suoi divoti e cognoscenti, e con tutto quello e con alchuni Interpreti lo andava a portare alli detti mori, e molte volte lo vidde questo Testimonio andare con la barchetta delli Offitiali Reali quando andavano à visitare il detto naviglio, e se haveva notitia che venivano molti infermi, preparava qualche barca ò navicella nella quale andava à soccorrerli con ogni prestezza, il che tutto sà questo Testimonio per haverlo visto, et aiutato à portare et imbarcare li detti regali, fino alla sponda del mare.

[3][E]t ancorche questo Testmonio mai andò alli detti navigli, con il detto Padre sà che subito, che arrivava à quelli abbracciava et accarezzava tutti li mori di quello con molta volontà e gusto, e subito se ne andava, ove stavano l'infermi pericolosi, et à vedere le creature ch'erano nate nel mare e se alcuno delli detti, ò dette, stava in pericolo, lo battezzava subito, istruendolo al meglio che poteva, per mezzo delli suoi Interpreti e l'instruttione era alli adulti che haveva da battezzare, acciò havessero fede, e ricevessero degnamente il detto battesimo insegnandoli il misterio della Santissima Trinità, che sono Padre, Figlio e Spirito Santo tre persone distinte in un solo Dio, e la Incarnatione del figlio d'Iddio, la sua morte, e passione e il rimedio che li lasciò del sacramento del Santo Battesimo per poterci salvare e limpidare dal peccato originale, il che tutto diceva,

---

[2] Here the testimony uses the verb *capere* from Latin in a turn of phrase common in Spanish but nonexistent in Italian: "no cabía en sí" [he was beyond himself].

[3] Paragraph break added.

teneva un Santo Christo nelle mani avanti li infermo che haveva da battezzare, et erà il detto Santo Christo di bronzo, e lo portava sempre con se, collocato nel seno con una cinta, e doppo per mezzo delli Interpreti, posto in mezzo del detto naviglio li diceva alli detti mori che esso era venuto ivi per essere Padrino e difesa di tutti, et acciò li trattassero bene li Bianchi, che avvertissero che non li portavano per mangiarli, et ammazzarli, come facevano alle loro terre li negri che li facevano priggioni ma per insegnarli la legge d'Iddio, e che quella mediante si salvassero le loro anime ch'erano immortali, et andassero al cielo e non all'Inferno ove havevano d'andare necessariamente se non fossero Christiani, et acciò servissero li Spagnuoli e che esso faria che l'amassero molto, animandoli et disingannandoli dell'errore nel quale venghono imbeverati [*sic*] li detti negri, tenendo per certo che li Bianchi li conducono alle loro terre per acciderli e mangiarli, e di far d'essi oglio e polvere, e questo Testimonio e di natione Angola, conforme ha detto, et intese il medesimo quando lo condussero dalla sua terra à questa di Cartagena, e fu grande l'allegrezza et il giubilo che ricevè quando il detto P. Pietro Claver li disingannò del riferito, dicendoli tutto quello che ha detto e molte altre raggioni di molto amore, et accarrezzamento, e cosi giudica che saria assai particolare il giubilo che haverebbero li detti mori ascoltandolo, il che tutto sà questo Testimonio, per haverglielo detto alchuni mori Interpreti che andavano alli detti navigli con il detto Padre, come sono Ignatio Alvanil, Ignatio Solo e Francesco Jolofo, quali hoggi vivono, e Giovanni Primero, e Antonio Balanta, Domenico Folupo, quali già sono morti, alla presenza del fratello Nicolò Gonzalez Religioso della Compagnia, e Sagrestano di questo Colleggio in varie occasioni, e questo Testimonio tiene per certo et infallibile tutto il sudetto, perche quando non andava il [102r] detto Padre alli navigli, andava subito che sbarcavano alla Casa, ove stavano alloggiati li detti mori, e faceva e li diceva tutto il riferito, battezzando li mori di età e le creature piccole, che stavano in pericolo, doppo il che tutto divideva frà quelli li Regali delle cose già riferite, per accarezzarli et attraherli facilmente ad essere istruiti, e battezzati.

Witness Andrés Sacabuche – May 19, 1659

[100r] He always held Claver to be a religious man of much virtue and exemplary life, very observant of the rules of his religion. This witness knows all of this for having seen it occur behind the doors of this school in which he has lived as its slave. The fathers who knew Claver who are still alive could say the same thing. They are brother Nicolás González, sexton of this church; Emanuel Rodriguez, alms collector;

and Pedro Lamparte, procurator. This witness remembers being sick on one particular occasion, and for the great love Father Claver had for this witness for being one of his interpreters, he took this witness to his bedroom so that this witness could get well and so that Claver would have space to attend to him with whatever was necessary; Claver did this with so much love, will, and candor as if he were another black man like this witness. During this time, this witness saw that every day at four in the morning when the bells rang for all to rise in this School, the Father Pedro Claver would inflict on himself a very rigorous discipline in which he would spend a quarter of an hour, after which he would kneel before a crucifix that he had painted on cloth in his room. This crucifix is today in the possession of this witness because when the said father died, he took it and carried it to his room for his own private devotion...

[4]Similarly, this witness remembers that in the year 1650 after Easter, he accompanied the said father on a mission to spread the word of the Hundredth Jubilee throughout the villages outside of this city until the river that they call Sinú, more than thirty leagues away. In all the villages there, Father Claver confessed all of the black men and women that were in them, just as he did with the Spaniards and the Indians, the *mulatos*, and those born of two different nations...

[100v] When Father Claver would arrive in a village, he would accommodate himself in small room or living space of the poorest and most isolated black person; and if there was an abandoned room that no one lived in because it was old and uncomfortable, he would accommodate himself there, and he would say that he felt very good there. This witness was sorry for this because these rooms tended to be very dirty and it was necessary to sweep and organize them. To not bother this witness so much, often the father himself would help him sweep the room. The principal cause for the displeasure of this witness was that, as he has said, if the father stayed in a house or rooms of the Spaniards who kept them clean, swept, and decorated, it would avoid this witness this work. But the father did not want to do it to show himself to be poor in everything and a perfect follower of extreme poverty...

[101r] What most amazed this witness was Father Claver's great mortification and the strange suffering by mosquitos which abound in these

---

[4] Paragraph break added.

villages, because Father Claver never killed them although they would be biting him a lot on his face and hands. On seeing this, this witness would go to him and sometimes ask why he would not kill them because there were so many all over his face and hands, and he would respond that it was not good to kill them, that they rather helped him because they would take away his bad blood. Some nights in which the father would preach to a group of those blacks from the aforementioned villages, when the harvest and planting seasons would arrive, the mosquitos covering Father Claver's face and hands were so many that though he was white, he looked black. And still he never killed them or scared them away, rather he tolerated them and suffered as if he did not feel them, continuing in his ministry with much fervor and spirit. The harm and damage the mosquitos caused him were so extreme that the next day he was left with his face and hands full of many marks, swollen and blackened. On seeing this, this witness felt sorry for him, knowing that Claver should have allowed them to kill them or use a big fan to blow them away while he did the exhortations, but that Claver would not do it or allow for it to be done. And so, this witness told the father that he should not spend so long preaching because the blacks would arrive tired from working all day and would become bored if he would speak for a long time and would then not return to listen the next day. The father looked favorably on this advice and spent less time preaching. With this, this witness saved the father, to a certain extent, from the great mortification that he experienced enduring the said mosquitos. This witness does not know if there could be a greater form of mortification than this one...

Similarly this witness says that even though his job is to play the trombone, he was one of the interpreters of the language of Angola that Father Pedro Claver had. Because of this, this witness knows how much Father Claver worked and endured to instruct and teach the black *bozales* who come to this land, because as soon as Father Claver would learn of the arrival in the port of any of these ships, he could not contain his joy and delight; it was evident on his face, which in those occasions was happy and full of smiles, when it was normally pale, sickly, and melancholic, [101v] marked by his extremely penitent eyelids. Promptly Father Claver would notify this witness and all of the other black interpreters that he had. He equipped himself with some gifts such as oranges and lemons and some cookies and tobacco, which he collected as alms among his devoted and acquaintances. With all this in hand and with some interpreters, he would send the gifts to the blacks. Many times this witness saw Father Claver go on a skiff of the Royal Officials when they would go visit the said ship, and if he heard news that there were many sick people on board, Claver would prepare a boat or small ship in which he would go help them as soon as possible. This witness knows all of this for having seen it and having helped bring and carry the said gifts to the shore.

[5]Even if this witness never went out to the said ships with the Father, he knows that as soon as he arrived at the ships he would hug and caress all of the blacks of the ship with much will and delight, and he would immediately go to where the dangerously sick were and to see the babies that had been born at sea. If any of these were in danger, he would immediately baptize them, teaching them to the best he could through his interpreters. The instruction would be to the adults that he would have to baptize so that they would believe and receive the baptism with dignity, teaching them the mystery of the Holy Trinity, which is the Father, Son, and Holy Spirit, three different people in only one God, and of the Incarnation of the son of God, of his death, his passion, and the remedy that He left of the sacrament of the holy baptism to be able to save ourselves and clean ourselves of original sin. While saying all of this, he held a holy Christ in his hands before the sick person that he was to baptize. And this holy Christ was made of bronze and he would always carry it with him, on his chest with a cord. And after, through the interpreters, in the middle of that ship, the father told those blacks that he had come there to be the father and protector of all, so that the whites would treat them well and so that they [the blacks] would realize that the whites did not take them there to eat and kill them, as the blacks who had imprisoned them in their lands would do, but to teach them the law of God, through which they would save their souls that were immortal so they would go to heaven and not to hell where they would necessarily have to go if they were not Christian. And so they should serve the Spaniards, which would make the Spaniards love them very much. With this, [the father through the interpreters] would encourage them and disabuse them of the lie with which blacks come imbued, firmly believing that the whites take them to their lands to kill and eat them and turn them into oil and powder. This witness is Angolan, as he has already said, and understood this himself when they brought him from his land to Cartagena. This witness felt great happiness and delight when F. Pedro Claver disabused them of the aforementioned lie, telling them all that this witness

[5] Paragraph break added.

has said and even more things that made them feel loved and cared for. And so this witness believes that the happiness that the said blacks would feel upon hearing Claver is very intense. This witness knows all of this because he was told by some of the black interpreters that went with the said father to those ships, such as Ignacio Albañil, Ignacio Solo y Francisco Jolofo, who are still alive; and Juan Primero, Antonio Balanta, Domingo Folupo, who are now dead, on various occasions in the presence of brother Nicolás González, religious man of the Company and sacristan of this School. This witness considers all that has been said above certain and infallible because when the [102r] father would not go out to the ships, he would go as soon as they had disembarked to the house where the said blacks were being kept and did and said all of the above, baptizing the black adults and the small babies who were in danger, after which he would give out among them the gifts of the abovementioned things to show them care and easily attract them to be instructed and baptized.

Bibliography

Archival Sources

Archivo Franciscano de Lima
[*Vida anónima*] "Espejo de Religiosas, Vida, Virtudes y Muerte de la Venerable Hermana Ursula de Jesuchristo," Registro 17, No. 45, n.d., ff. 585r–607v.

Archivo General de Indias
Patronato 234

Archivo General de la Nación, Lima, Peru
Fondo Compañía de Jesús, Serie Colegios-San Pablo

Archivo Histórico de la Nación (Madrid)
Inquisición

Archivo de Santa Clara de Lima
[*Spiritual diary*] *Diario espiritual de la venerable Úrsula de Jesús, escrita por ella misma*, Archivo de Santa Clara de Lima, 8r–60r
[*Vida breve*] *Vida de la madre Úrsula de Jesús, escrita por una clarisa*, Archivo de Santa Clara de Lima, 3r–6r

Archivum Romanum Societatis Iesu (ARSI)
Novi Regni et Quitensis
Peru
Epistolario General

Biblioteca Nacional de Colombia, Bogota
[*Proceso 1676* manuscript] *Proceso de beatificación de Pedro Claver*, Libros raros y manuscritos, Manuscrito 281 [1658–69], trans. Claudio Louvet [1676]
"Testimonio de diligencias sobre la causa de beatificación y canonización del venerable padre Pedro Claver de la Compañía de Jesús que floreció"

(Cartagena de Indias, 1690), libros raros y manuscritos, libro 401, fols. 1–52

Printed Sources

Abelard, Peter. "Letter 4 to Héloise [ca. 1130–36]," in *Race in Early Modern England: A Documentary Companion*, ed. Ania Loomba and Jonathan Burton (New York: Palgrave Macmillan, 2007), 60–61.

Acosta, José de. *De procuranda indorum salute*, ed. and trans. Luicano Pereña, 2 vols. (Madrid: CSIC, 1984–87).

Adorno, Rolena. *Guaman Poma: Writing and Resistance in Colonial Peru* (Austin: University of Texas Press, 1986).

"The Indigenous Ethnographer: The 'Indio Ladino' as Historian and Cultural Mediation," in *Implicit Understandings: Observing, Reporting, and Reflecting on the Encounters between Europeans and Other Peoples in the Early Modern Era*, ed. Stuart B. Schwartz (New York: Cambridge University Press, 1994), 378–402.

The Polemics of Possession in Spanish American Narrative (New Haven, CT: Yale University Press, 2007).

Aguirre, J. M. "Ensayo para un estudio del tema amoroso en la primitiva lírica castellana," *Cuadernos de Filosofía y letras* 1, no. 54 (1965): 7–34.

José de Valdivielso y la poesía tradicional (Toledo: Diputación Provincial, 1965).

Alberro, Solage. *Inquisición y sociedad en México, 1571–1700* (Mexico: Fonod de Cultura Económica, 1946).

Alcalá, Luisa Elena. "The Image of the Devout Indian: The Codification of a Colonial Idea," in *Contested Visions in the Spanish Colonial World*, ed. Ilona Katzew (New Haven: Yale University Press, 2011), 227–50.

Alfonso X. *Las Cantigas de Santa María. Edición facsímil del códice B.R. 20 de la Biblioteca Nazionale Centrale de Florencia, Siglo XIII*, ed. Ana Domínguez Rodríguez, Agustín Santiago Luque, and María Victoria Chicao Picaza, 2 vols. (Madrid: Edilán, 1989–91).

Alín, José María, ed. *El cancionero español de tipo tradicional* (Madrid: Taurus, 1968).

Almeida, Ronaldo de. "Tradução e mediação: Missões transculturais entre grupos indígenas," in *Deus na aldeia: Missionários, índios, e mediação cultural*, ed. Paula Montero (São Paolo: Globo, 2005), 277–304.

Andrade, Alonso de. *Vida del Venerable y Apostolico Padre Pedro Claver de la Compañia de Jesus* (Madrid: Maria de Quiñones, 1657).

Anghie, Anthony. "Francisco Vitoria and the Colonial Origins of International Law," in *Imperialism, Sovereignty, and the Making of International Law* (New York: Cambridge University Press, 2005), 13–31.

Arenal, Electa, and Stacey Schlau. "Stategems of the Weak: Autobiographical Prose of the Seventh-Century Hispanic Convent," *Tulsa Studies in Women's Literature* 9, no. 1 (1990): 25–42.

Arenal, Electa, and Stacey Schlau, eds. *Untold Sisters: Hispanic Nuns in Their Own Works*, trans. Amanda Powell (Albuquerque: University of New Mexico, Press, 2010).

Ares Queija, Berta. ""Mestizos, mulatos y zambaigos (Virreinato del Perú, siglo XVI)," in *Negros, mulatos, zambaigos: Derroteros africanos en los mundos ibéricos*, ed. Berta Ares Queija and Alessandro Stella (Seville: Escuela de Estudios Hispano-Americanos, 2000), 75–88.

Aristizábal, Tulio. *Los jesuitas en Cartagena de Indias* (Cartagena: Espitia, 2009).

Retazos de historia: Los jesuitas en Cartagena de Indias (Bogota: Antropos, 1995).

Aristotle. *Nicomathean Ethics*, ed. Roger Crisp (New York: Cambridge University Press, 2000).

Astrain, Antonio. *Historia de la Compañía de Jesús en la asistencia de España*, vol. 4 (Madrid: Sucesores Ribadeneira, 1902–9).

Historia de la Compañía de Jesús en la asistencia de España, vol. 5 (Madrid: Sucesores Ribadeneira, 1916).

Avesani, Rino. "La professione dell'umanista nel Cinquecento," *Italia medioevale e umanistica* 13 (1970): 205–32.

Baker, Geoff. "The Ethnic Villancico and Racial Politics in 17th-Century Mexico," in *Devotional Music in the Iberian World, 1450–1800: The Villancico and Related Genres*, ed. Tess Knighton and Alvaro Torrente (Burlington, VT: Ashgate, 2007), 399–408.

Imposing Harmony: Music and Society in Colonial Cuzco (Durham, NC: Duke University Press, 2008).

"Latin American Baroque: Performance as a Post-colonial Act?," *Early Music* 36, no. 3 (2008): 441–48.

Balandier, Georges. *La vie quotidienne au royaume de Kongo du XVIᵉ au XVIIIᵉ siècle* (Paris: Hachette, 1965).

Baranda Leturio, Consolación. "Las hablas de negros. Orígenes de un personaje literario," *Revista de Filología Española* 69, nos. 3–4 (1989): 311–33.

Bartra, Enrique. "Los autores del catecismo del Tercer Concilio Limense," *Mercurio Peruano* 52, no. 470 (1967): 359–72.

Beatty-Medina, Charles. "Between the Cross and the Sword: Religious Conquest and Maroon Legitimacy in Colonial Esmeraldas," in *Africans to Spanish America: Expanding the Diaspora*, ed. Sherwin Bryant, Rachel O'Toole, and Ben Vinson III (Urbana: University of Illinois Press, 2012), 95–113.

"Rebels and Conquerors: African Slaves, Spanish Authority, and the Domination of Esmeraldas, 1563–1621," PhD diss., Brown University, 2002.

Bénassy-Berling, Marie-Cécile. "Alonso de Sandoval, les jésuites et la descendance de Cham," in *Études sur l'impact culturel du Nouveau Monde*, vol. 1 (Paris: L'harmattan, 1981), 49–60.

Bennassar, Bartolomé, and Lucile Bennassar. *Los cristianos de Alá. La fascinante aventura de los renegados*, trans. José Luis Gil Aristu (Madrid: Nerea, 1989).

Bennett, Herman. *African Kings and Black Slaves: Sovereignty and Dispossession in the Early Modern Atlantic* (Philadelphia: University of Pennsylvania Press, 2018).

Africans in Colonial Mexico: Absolutism, Christianity, and Afro-Creole Consciousness, 1570–1640 (Bloomington: Indiana University Press, 2003).

Colonial Blackness: A History of Afro-Mexico (Bloomington: Indiana University Press, 2009).

Benoist, Valérie. "La conexión entre casta y familia en la representación de los negros," *Afro-Hispanic Review* 29, no. 1 (2010): 35–54.

Benton, Lauren. *Law and Colonial Cultures: Legal Regimes in World History, 1400–1900* (New York: Cambridge University Press, 2002).

Beresford, Andrew. "Sanctity and Prejudice in Medieval Castilian Hagiography: The Legend of S. Moses the Ethiopian," in *Medieval Hispanic Studies in Memory of Alan Deyermond*, ed. Andrew M. Beresford, Louise M. Haywood, and Julian Weiss (New York: Boydell and Brewer, 2013), 11–37.

Bermúdez, Egberto. "El archivo de la catedral de Bogotá: Historia y repertorio," *Revista Musical de Venezuela* 16, no. 34 (1997): 53–64.

Historia de la música en Santafé y Bogotá, 1538–1938 (Bogota: Fundación de Música, 2000).

"Organización musical y repertorio en la Catedral de Bogotá durante el siglo XVI," *Ensayos, teoría e historia del arte* 3 (1996): 43–54.

"Sounds from Fortresses of Faith and Ideal Cities: Society, Politics, and Music in Missionary Activities in the Americas, 1525–1575," in *Listening to Early Modern Catholicism: Perspectives from Musicology*, ed. Daniele V. Filippi and Michael Noone (Leiden: Brill, 2017), 301–25.

Bernand, Carmen. *Negros esclavos y libres en las ciudades hispanoamericanas* (Madrid: Tavera, 2000).

Bernard of Clairvaux. "On the Song of Songs [ca. 1136–53]," in *Race in Early Modern England: A Documentary Companion*, ed. Ania Loomba and Jonathan Burton (New York: Palgrave Macmillan, 2007), 61–62.

Beusterien, John. *An Eye on Race: Perspectives from Theater in Imperial Spain* (Lewisburg, PA: Bucknell University Press, 2006).

Bielicke, Federico Beals Nagel. "El aprendizaje del idioma náhuatl entre los franciscanos y los jesuitas en la Nueva España," *Estudios de cultural náhuatl* 24 (1994): 419–41.

Bigelow, Allison. *Mining Language: Racial Thinking, Indigenous Knowledge, and Colonial Metallurgy in the Early Modern Iberian World* (Chapel Hill: University of North Carolina Press, 2020).

Binotti, Lucia. "'La lengua compañera del imperio': Observaciones sobre el desarrollo de un discurso de colonialismo linguistico en el renacimiento español," en *Las gramáticas misioneras de tradición hispánica (siglos XVI–XVII)*, ed. Otto Zwartjes (Portada Hispanica, 2001), 259–88.

Blackburn, Robin. *The Making of New World Slavery from the Baroque to the Modern, 1492–1800* (New York: Verso, 1997).

Block, David. *Mission Culture in the Upper Amazon: Native Tradition, Jesuit Enterprise, and Secular Policy in Moxos, 1660–1880* (Lincoln: University of Nebraska Press, 1994).

Block, Kristen. *Ordinary Lives in the Early Caribbean: Religion, Colonial Competition, and the Politics of Profit* (Athens: University of Georgia Press, 2012).

Blumenthal, Debra. *Enemies and Familiars: Slavery and Mastery in Fifteenth-Century Valencia* (Ithaca: Cornell University Press, 2009).

Bontinck, François, and D. Ndembe Nsasi, eds. *Le catechism kikongo de 1624, Réédition critique* (Brussels: Académie Royale des Sciences d'Outre-Mer, 1978).

Borja Gómez, Jaime Humerto. "Historiografía y hagiografía: Vidas ejemplares y escritura de la historia en el Nuevo Reino de Granada," *Fronteras de la Historia* 12 (2007): 53–78.

Borja Gómez, Jaime Humberto. "Restaurar la salud: La cristianización de los esclavos en el siglo XVII," in *150 años de abolición de la esclavización en Colombia: Desde la marginalidad hasta la construcción de la nación* (Bogota: Aguilar 2003), 292–329.

Rostros y rastros del demonio en la Nueva Granada: Indios, negros, judíos, mujeres y otras huestes de Satanás (Bogota: Ariel, 1998).

Borja Medina, Francisco de. "El esclavo: ¿Bien mueble o persona? Algunas observaciones sobre la evangelización del negro en las haciendas jesuíticas," in *Esclavitud, economía y evangelización: Las haciendas jesuitas en la América virreinal*, ed. Sandra Negro and Manuel M. Marzal (Lima: PUCP, 2015), 83–124.

"La experiencia sevillana de la Compañía de Jesús en la evangelización de los esclavos negros y su repercusión en América," in *La esclavitud negroafricana en la historia de España: Siglos XVI y XVII*, ed. Aurelia Martín Casares and Margarita García Barranco (Granada: Comares, 2010), 75–94.

Borucki, Alex, David Eltis, and David Wheat. "Atlantic History and the Slave Trade to Spanish America," *American Historical Review* 120, no. 2 (2015): 433–61.

Böttcher, Nikolaus, Bernd Hausberger, and Max S. Hering Torres. "Introducción. Sangre mestizaje y nobleza," in *El peso de la sangre: Limpios, mestizos y nobles en el mundo hispánico*, ed. Böttcher, Hausberger, and Hering Torres (Mexico City: El Colegio de México, 2011), 9–28.

Bowser, Frederick. *The African Slave in Colonial Peru, 1524–1650* (Stanford, CA: Stanford University Press, 1976).

Boyer, Richard. "Negotiating *Calidad*: The Everyday Struggle for Status in Mexico," *Historical Archaeology* 31, no. 1 (1997): 64–72.

Brakke, David. "Ethiopian Demons: Male Sexuality, the Black-Skinned Other, and the Monastic Self," *Journal of the History of Sexuality* 10, nos. 3–4 (2001): 501–35.

Branche, Jerome. *Colonialism and Race in Luso-Hispanic Literature* (St. Louis: University of Missouri Press, 2006).

Braude, Benjamin. "The Sons of Noah and the Construction of Ethnic and Geographical Identities in the Medieval and Early Modern Periods," *William and Mary Quarterly* 54, no. 1 (1997): 103–42.

Brewer-García, Larissa. "The Agency of Translation: New Assessments of the Roles of Non-European Linguistic Intermediaries," in *Routledge Companion on Colonial Latin America and the Caribbean*, ed. Santa Arias and Yolanda Martínez-San Miguel (2020, in press).

"Bodies, Texts, and Translators: Indigenous Breast Milk and the Jesuit Exclusion of Mestizos in Late Sixteenth-Century Peru," *Colonial Latin American Review* 21, no. 3 (2012): 365–90.

"Hierarchy and Holiness in the Earliest Colonial Black Hagiographies: Alonso de Sandoval and His Sources," *William and Mary Quarterly* 76, no. 3 (2019): 477–508.

"Imagined Transformations: Color, Beauty, and Black Christian Conversion in Seventeenth-Century Spanish America," in *Envisioning Others: Race, Color, and the Visual in Iberia and Latin America,* ed. Pamela A. Patton (Leiden: Brill, 2016), 111–41.

"Negro, pero blanco de alma: La ambivalencia de la negrura en la *Vida prodigiosa* de Fray Martin de Porras (1663)," *Cuadernos del CILHA* 13, no. 2 (December 2012): 112–45.

Brickhouse, Anna. "Mistranslation, Unsettlement, La Navidad," *PMLA* 128, no. 4 (2012): 938–46.

The Unsettlement of America: Translation, Interpretation, and the Story of Don Luis de Velasco, 1569–1945 (New York: Oxford University Press, 2015).

Bristol, Joan Cameron. *Christians, Blasphemers, and Witches: Afro-Mexican Ritual Practice in the Seventeenth Century* (Albuquerque: University of New Mexico Press, 2007).

Brooks, George E. *Eurafricans in Western Africa: Commerce, Social Status, Gender, and Religious Observance from the Sixteenth to the Eighteenth Century* (Athens: Ohio University Press, 2003).

Brown, Vince. *The Reaper's Garden: Death and Power in the World of Atlantic Slavery* (Cambridge, MA: Harvard University Press, 2008).

Bruslon, Jacques Savary des. *Dictionnaire universel de commerce* [1723], vol. 1 (Paris: Veuve Estienne et fils, 1797).

Bryant, Sherwin. *Rivers of Gold, Lives of Bondage: Governing through Slavery in Colonial Quito* (Chapel Hill: University of North Carolina Press, 2014).

Bryant, Sherwin, Ben Vinson III, and Rachel Sarah O'Toole. "Introduction," in *Africans to Spanish America: Expanding the Diaspora,* ed. Bryant, O'Toole, and Vinson (Urbana: University of Illinois Press, 2012), 1–26.

Burgaleta, Claudio M. *José de Acosta, S.J.: His Life and Thought* (Chicago: Jesus Way, 1999).

Burkhart, Louise M. *The Slippery Earth: Nahua-Christian Moral Dialogue in Sixteenth-Century Mexico* (Tucson: University of Arizona Press, 1989).

Burns, Kathryn. *Colonial Habits: Convents and the Spiritual Economy of Cuzco* (Durham, NC: Duke University Press, 1999).

Into the Archive: Writing and Power in Colonial Peru (Durham, NC: Duke University Press, 2010).

"Unfixing Race," in *Rereading the Black Legend: The Discourses of Religious and Racial Difference in the Renaissance Empires,* ed. Margaret R. Greer, Walter D. Mignolo, and Maureen Quilligan (Chicago: University of Chicago Press, 2007), 188–204.

Bynum, Caroline Walker. *Jesus as Mother: Studies in the Spirituality of the High Middle Ages* (Berkeley: University of California Press, 1982).

Byron, Gay. *Symbolic Blackness and Ethnic Difference in Early Christian Literature* (New York: Routledge, 2002).

Calainho, Daniela Buono. *Metrópole das mandingas: Religiosidade negra e inquisição portuguesa no Antigo Regime* (Rio de Janeiro: Garamond, 2008).

Calepini, Ambrosii. *Dictionarium undecim linguarum* (Basileae: Sebastianum Henricpetri, 1590).

Campana, Augusto. "The Origin of the Word Humanist," *Journal of the Warburg and Courtauld Institutes* 9 (1946): 60–73.

Cañeque, Alejandro. *The King's Living Image: The Culture and Politics of Viceregal Power in Colonial Mexico* (New York: Oxford University Press, 2004).

Cañizares-Esguerra, Jorge. "Demons, Stars, and the Imagination: The Early Modern Body in the Tropics," in *The Origins of Racism in the West*, ed. Miriam Eliav-Feldon, Benjamin Isaac, and Joseph Ziegler (New York: Cambridge University Press, 2009), 313–25.

Carroll, Patrick J. "Black-Native Relations and the Historical Record in Colonial Mexico," in *Beyond Black and Red: African-Native Relations in Colonial Latin America*, ed. Matthew Restall (Albuquerque: University of New Mexico Press, 2005), 245–68.

Carruthers, Mary. *The Book of Memory in Medieval Culture* (New York: Cambridge University Press, 1996).

Cashner, Andrew. "Faith, Hearing, and the Power of Music in Hispanic Villancicos, 1600–1700," PhD diss., University of Chicago, 2015.

Cassani, José. *Historia de la provincial de la Compañia de Jesus del Nuevo Reyno de Granada en la America* (Madrid, 1741).

Castañeda, Paulino, and Pilar Hernández. *La Inquisición de Lima (1590–1634)* (Madrid: Deimos, 1989).

Castellano, Juan. "El negro esclavo en el entremés del Siglo de Oro," *Hispania* 44, no. 1 (1961): 55–65.

Castellanos, Juan de. *Elegías de varones ilustres de Indias*, 3rd ed. (Madrid: Ribadeneira, 1874).

Castillo Mathieu, Nicolás del. *Esclavos negros en Cartagena y sus aportes léxicos* (Bogota: Publicaciones del Instituto Caro y Cuervo, 1982).

La llave de las Indias (Bogota: El Tiempo, 1981).

Cerrón Palomino, Rodolfo. "The Concept of General Language in Garcilaso Inca," in *Garcilaso Inca de la Vega: An American Humanist* (Notre Dame, IN: University of Notre Dame Press, 1998).

"Diversidad y unificación léxica en el mundo andino," in *El quechua en debate: ideología, normalización y enseñanza*, ed. Juan Carlos Godenzzi (Cuzco: Centro de Estudios Regionales Andinos Bartolomé de las Casas, 1992), 205–35.

Cervantes, Miguel. "El [c]eloso e[x]tremeño," in *Novelas exemplares* (Madrid: Juan de la Cuesta, 1613), 137v–158r.

Cesareo, Mario. *Cruzados, mártires y beatos: Emplazamientos del cuerpo colonial* (West Lafayette, IN: Purdue University Press, 1995).

Chandler, David L. *Health and Slavery in Colonial Colombia* (New York: Arno, 1981).

Charles, John. *Allies at Odds: The Andean Church and Its Indigenous Agents, 1583–1671* (Albuquerque: University of New Mexico Press, 2010).

"More *Ladino* than Necessary: Indigenous Litigants and the Language Policy Debate in Mid-colonial Peru," *Colonial Latin American Review* 16, no. 1 (2007): 23–47.

Charney, Paul. "Sense of Belonging: Colonial Indian Cofradías and Ethnicity in the Valley of Lima, Peru," *The Americas* 54, no. 3 (1998): 379–407.

Chasca, Edmund de. "The Phonology of the Speech of the Negroes in Early Spanish Drama," *Hispanic Review* 14 (1946): 323–39.

Chaves, María Eugenia. "La creación del 'Otro' colonial: Apuntes para un estudio de la diferencia en el proceso de la conquista americana y de la esclavización de los africanos," in *Genealogías de la diferencia: Tecnologías de la salvación y representación de los africanos esclavizados en Iberoamérica colonial*, ed. María Eugenia Chaves (Bogota: Javeriana, 2009), 178–243.

Chung, Dong-Hee. "Imagen y función de los negros en la literatura española de la primera mitad del siglo XVI: Enfocado en la *Segunda Celestina* (1534), de Feliciano de Silva," *Revista Asiática de Estudios Iberoamericanos* 27, no. 3 (2016): 67–95.

Cicero, Marcus Tulius. *On Invention: The Best Kind of Orator*, trans. H. M. Hubbell, Loeb Classical Library (Cambridge, MA: Harvard University Press, 1949).

Claro, Samuel. *Antología de la música colonial en América del sur* (Santiago de Chile: Universidad de Chile, 1974).

Cobo, Bernabé. *Obras*, vol. 2, ed. Francisco Mateos (Madrid: Biblioteca de Autores Españoles, 1956).

Cobo Betancourt, Juan Fernando. "Colonialism in the Periphery: Spanish Linguistic Policy in New Granada, 1574–1625," *Colonial Latin American Review* 23, no. 2 (2014): 126–29.

Cohen Suárez, Ananda. *Heaven, Hell, and Everything in Between: Murals of the Colonial Andes* (Austin: University of Texas Press, 2016).

Combes, I. A. H. *The Metaphor of Slavery in the Writings of the Early Church* (Sheffield: Sheffield Academic Press, 1998).

Confessionario para los curas de indios (Lima: Antonio Ricardo, 1585).

Cope, Douglas. *The Limits of Racial Domination: Plebian Society in Colonial Mexico, 1660–1720* (Madison: University of Wisconsin Press, 1994).

Córdova y Salinas, Diego de. *Crónica Franciscana de las Provincias del Perú* [1650], ed. Lino Canedo (Washington, DC: Academy of American Franciscan History, 1957)

Correas, Gonzalo. *Vocabulario de refranes y frases proverbiales* [1627] (Madrid: Olózaga, 1924).

Cortés López, José Luis. *Esclavo y colono: Introducción y sociología de los negroafricanos en la América Española del siglo XVI* (Salamanca: Ediciones Universidad, 2004).

Courtès, Jean Marie. "The Theme of 'Ethiopia' and 'Ethiopians' in Patristic Literature," in *The Image of the Black in Western Art, vol. 2: From Early Christianity to the "Age of Discovery": From the Demonic Threat to the Incarnation of Sainthood* (Cambridge, MA: Harvard University Press, 2010), 199–214.

Covarrubias, Sebastián de. *Tesoro de la lengua castellana* (Madrid: Luis Sánchez, 1611).

Cuadriello, Jaime. "Winged and Imagined Indians," in *Angels, Demons, and the New World*, ed. Fernando Cervantes and Andrew Redden (New York: Cambridge University Press, 2013), 211–48.

Cummins, Tom. "Three Gentlemen from Esmeraldas: A Portrait Fit for a King," in *Slave Portraiture in the Atlantic World*, ed. Agnes Lugo-Ortiz and Angela Rosenthal (New York: Cambridge University Press, 2013), 119–46.

Cussen, Celia L. *Black Saint of the Americas: The Life and Afterlife of Martín de Porres* (New York: Cambridge University Press, 2014).

Daher, Andrea. "De los intérpretes a los especialistas: El uso de las lenguas generales de América en los siglos XVI y XVII," en *Saberes de la conversión: Jesuitas, indígenas e imperios coloniales en las fronteras de la cristiandad*, ed. Guillermo Wilde (Buenos Aires: Bibliografika, 2011), 61–80.

Daza, Antonio. *Quarta parte de la Chronica General de Nuestro Padre San Francisco y su Apostolica Orden* (Valladolid: Juan Godines de Millis y Diego de Cordova, 1611).

de Jaca, Francisco José. *Resolución sobre la libertad de los negros y sus originarios, en estado de paganos y después ya cristianos* (Madrid: CISC, 2002).

de la Fuente, Alejandro. *Havana and the Atlantic in the Sixteenth Century* (Chapel Hill: University of North Carolina Press, 2008).

"Slave Law and Claims-Making in Cuba: The Tannenbaum Debate Revisited," *Law and History Review* 22, no. 2 (2004): 304–69.

de la Puente, José Carlos. "The Many Tongues of the King: Indigenous Language Interpreters and the Making of the Spanish Empire," *Colonial Latin American Review* 23, no. 2 (2014): 143–70.

de Moirans, Epifanio. *Siervos libres: Una propuesta antiesclavista de finales del XVII* (Madrid: CISC, 2007).

Dean, Carolyn. *Inka Bodies and the Body of Christ: Corpus Christi in Colonial Cuzco, Peru* (Durham, NC: Duke University Press, 1999).

del Valle, Ivonne. "José de Acosta: Entre el realismo politico y disparates e imposibles, o por qué importan los estudios coloniales," in *Estudios transatlánticos poscoloniales*, ed. Ileana Rodríguez and Josebe Martínez (Barcelona: Anthropos, 2010), vol. 1, 291–324.

"José de Acosta, Violence, and Rhetoric: The Emergence of Colonial Baroque," *Calíope: Journal for the Society of Renaissance and Baroque Poetry* 18, no. 2 (2013): 46–72.

Delesalle, Simone, and Lucette Valensi. "Le mot 'nègre' dans les dictionnaires français d'Ancien Régime: Historie et lexicographie," *Langue Française* 15 (1972): 79–104.

Devoto, Daniel. *Cancionero llamado Flor de la rosa* (Buenos Aires: Francisco A. Colombo, 1950).

di Camillo, Ottavio. "Humanism in Spain," in *Humanism beyond Italy, Renaissance Humanism: Foundations, Forms, and Legacy*, vol. 2, ed. Albert Rabil, Jr. Philadelphia: University of Pennsylvania Press, 1988), 55–108.

Díaz, Nicolás. *Tratado del Juyzio Final en el qual se hallaran muchas cosas muy provechosas y curiosas* (Valladolid: Diego Fernandez de Cordova y Oviedo, 1588).

Doctrina christiana y catecismo para instruccion de los indios, y de las de mas personas, que han de ser enseñadas en nuestra sancta fé (Lima: Antonio Ricardo, 1584).

Doutrina christãa. Composta pelo P. Marcos Jorge da Companhia de IESU Doutor em Theologia ... De novo traduzida na lingoa do Reyno de Congo, por ordem do P. Mattheus Cardoso Theologo, da Companhia de IESU (Lisbon: Geraldo da Vinha, 1624).

Dronke, Peter. *The Medieval Lyric*, 3rd ed. (Rochester, NY: D. S. Brewer, 1996).

Durston, Alan. "Indigenous Languages and the Historiography of Latin America," *Storia della Storiografia* 67, no. 1 (2015): 51–65.

Pastoral Quechua: The History of Christian Translation in Colonial Peru, 1550–1650 (Notre Dame, IN: University of Notre Dame Press, 2007).

Earle, Rebecca. *The Body of the Conquistador: Food, Race and the Colonial Experience in Spanish America, 1492–1700* (New York: Cambridge University Press, 2012).

Echeverri, Marcela. "Popular Royalists, Empire, and Politics in Southwestern New Granada, 1809–1819," *Hispanic American Historical Review* 91, no. 2 (2011): 237–69.

Edwards, Brent. *Practice of Diaspora: Literature, Translation, and the Rise of Black Internationalism,* (Cambridge, MA: Harvard University Press, 2003).

Egaña, Antonio de, ed. *Monumenta Peruana*, vol. 1 [1565–75] (Rome: Instituto Histórico de la Compañía de Jesús, 1954).

Eguren, Jorge. "Sandoval frente a la raza esclavizada," *Revista de la Academia Colombiana de Historia Eclesiástica* 29-30 (1973): 57–86.

Farriss, Nancy. *Tongues of Fire: Language and Evangelization in Colonial Mexico* (New York: Oxford University Press, 2018).

Fayer, Joan. "African Interpreters in the Atlantic Slave Trade," *Anthropological Linguistics* 45, no. 3 (2003): 281–95.

Fernández, José. *Apostolica y penitente vida del P. Pedro Claver de la Compañia de Jesus* (Zaragoza: Dormer, 1666).

Fernández Fernández, Amaya, et al., *La Mujer en la conquista y la evangelización en el Perú (Lima 1550–1650)* (Lima: Pontificia Universidad Católica del Perú, 1997).

Fisher, Andrew B. "Creating and Contesting Community: Indians and Afromestizos in the Late-Colonial Tierra Caliente of Guerrero, Mexico," *Journal of Colonialism and Colonial History* 7, no. 1 (2006).

Fisher, Andrew B., and Frank O'Hara. "Racial Identities and their Interpreters in Colonial Latin America," in *Imperial Subjects: Race and Identity in Colonial Latin America*, ed. Fisher and O'Hara (Durham, NC: Duke University Press, 2009).

Fiume, Giovanna. "Saint Benedict, the Moor: From Sicily to the New World," in *Saints and Their Cults in the Atlantic World*, ed. Margaret Cormack (Columbia: University of South Carolina Press, 2006), 16–51.

Forbes, Jack. *Africans and Native Americans: The Language of Race and the Evolution of Red-Black Peoples* (Chicago: University of Illinois Press, 1993).

Forcione, Alban K. *Cervantes and the Humanist Vision: A Study of Four Exemplary Novels* (Princeton: Princeton University Press, 1982), 31–92.

Fracchia, Carmen. *"Black but Human": Slavery and Visual Arts in Hapsburg Spain, 1480–1700* (New York: Oxford University Press, 2019).

"(Lack of) Visual Representation of Black Slaves in Spanish Golden Age Painting," *Journal of Iberian and Latin American Studies* 10 (2004): 23–34.

"Metamorphoses of the Self: Slave Portraiture and the Case of Juan de Pareja," in *Slave Portraiture in the Atlantic World*, ed. Agnes Lugo Ortiz and Angela Rosenthal (New York: Cambridge University Press, 2013), 147–70.

Fra Molinero, Baltasar. *La imagen de los negros en el teatro del siglo de oro* (Mexico: Siglo XXI, 1995).

"Los negros como figura de negación y diferencia en el teatro barroco," *Hipogrifo* 2, no. 2 (2014): 7–29.

"Ser mulato en España y América: Discursos legales y otros discursos literarios," in *Negros, mulatos, zambaigos: Derroteros africanos en los mundos ibéricos*, ed. Berta Ares Queija and Alessandro Stella (Seville: Escuela de Estudios Hispano-Americanos, 2000), 123–47.

Francis, J. Michael. "Language and the 'True Conversion' to the Holy Faith: A Document from the Archivum Romanum Societatis Iesu, Rome, Italy," *The Americas* 62, no. 3 (2006): 445–53.

Francis I. "La recita dell'Angelus presso la Chiesa di San Pietro Claver a Cartagena e la visita alla Casa Santuario di San Pietro Claver," Viaggio Apostolico del Santo Padre Francesco in Colombia (6–11 settembre 2017), http://press.vatican.va/content/salastampa/it/bollettino/pubblico/2017/09/10/0582/01237.html.

Francisca Josefa de la Concepción. *Vida de la V. M. Francisca Josefa de la Concepción* (Philadelphia: T. H. Palmer, 1817).

Franklin, Vincent P. "Bibliographical Essay: Alonso de Sandoval and the Jesuit Conception of the Negro," *Journal of Negro History* 158 (1973): 349–60.

Frenk, Margit. "La canción popular femenina en el Siglo de Oro," in *Poesía popular hispánica: 44 estudios* (Mexico, DF: Fondo de Cultura Económica, 2006), 336–37.

"Cancionero de Gaspar Fernández (Puebla-Oaxaca)," in *Literatura y cultura populares de la Nueva España*, ed. Mariana Masera (Barcelona: Azul Editorial, 2004), 19–35.

Frenk, Margit, ed. *Nuevo corpus de la antigua lírica popular hispánica, siglos XIV–XVI* (Mexico, DF: Universidad Nacional Autónoma de México, 2003).

"Símbolos naturales en las viejas canciones populares," in *Poesía popular hispánica: 44 estudios* (Mexico, DF: Fondo de Cultura Económica, 2006), 239–352.

"Villancicos de negro en el siglo XVII novohispano," in *El folclor literario en México*, ed. Herón Pérez Martínez and Raul Eduardo González (Zamora: Universidad Autónoma de Aguascalientes, 2003), 45–54.

Freyre, Gilberto. *Brazil: An Interpretation* (New York: Knopf, 1945).

Fromont, Cécile. *Art of Conversion: Christian Visual Culture in the Kingdom of Kongo* (University of North Carolina Press, 2014).

"Collecting and Translating Knowledge across Cultures: Capuchin Missionary Images of Early Modern Central Africa, 1650–1750," in *Collecting Across Cultures: Material Exchanges in the Early Modern Atlantic World*, ed. Daniela Bleichmar and Peter C. Mancall (Philadelphia: University of Pennsylvania Press, 2011), 134–54.

"Common Threads: Cloth, Colour, and the Slave Trade in Early Modern Kongo and Angola," *Art History* 4, no. 5 (2018): 838–67.

"Paper, Ink, Vodun, and the Inquisition: Tracing Power, Slavery, and Witchcraft in the Early Modern Portuguese Atlantic," *Journal of the American Academy of Religion* (2020, in press).

Fuentes, Marisa. *Dispossessed Lives: Enslaved Women, Violence, and the Archive* (Philadelphia: University of Pennsylvania Press, 2016).

Gálvez Peña, Carlos. "La ciudad letrada y santa: La ciudad de Los Reyes en la historiografía del siglo XVII," in *Urbanismo y vida urbana en Iberoamérica colonial* (Bogota: Archivo de Bogota, 2008), 71–101.

Garcilaso de la Vega, Inca. *Comentarios reales de los incas* [1609] (Mexico: Fondo de Cultura Económica, 1995).

Garofalo, Leo J., and Rachel Sarah O'Toole. "Introduction: Constructing Difference in Colonial Latin America," *Journal of Colonialism and Colonial History* 7, no. 1 (2006).

Gharala, Norah L. A. *Taxing Blackness: Free Afromexican Tribute in Bourbon New Spain* (Tuscaloosa: University of Alabama Press, 2019).

Gilroy, Paul. *The Black Atlantic: Modernity and Double Consciousness* (Cambridge, MA: Harvard University Press, 1993).

Goldenberg, David M. *The Curse of Ham: Race and Slavery in Early Judaism, Christianity, and Islam* (Princeton: Princeton University Press, 2003).

Gómez, Pablo F. "The Circulation of Bodily Knowledge in the Seventeenth-Century Black Spanish Caribbean," *Social History of Medicine* 26, no. 3 (2013): 383–402.

The Experiential Caribbean: Creating Knowledge and Healing in the Early Modern Atlantic (Chapel Hill: University of North Carolina Press, 2017).

Góngora, Luis de. "Letrillas sacras," in *Todas las obras de Don Luis de Góngora en varios poemas* (Madrid: Hoces y Córdova, 1633), 72–76.

Granda, Germán de. *Estudios linguisticos hispánicos, afro-hispánicos y criollos* (Madrid: Gredos, 1978).

Graubart, Karen. "The Creolization of the New World: Local Forms of Identification in Urban Colonial Peru, 1560–1640," *Hispanic American Historical Review* 89, no. 3 (2009): 471–99.

"Los lazos que unen. Dueñas negras de esclavos negros en Lima, siglos XVI–XVII." *Nueva corónica* 2 (2013): 625–40.

Republics of Difference: Racial and Religious Self-Governance in the Iberian Atlantic, 1400–1650 (forthcoming).

"'So color de una cofradía': Catholic Confraternities and the Development of Afro-Peruvian Ethnicities in Early Colonial Peru," *Slavery and Abolition* 3, no. 1 (2012): 43–64.

Gray, Richard. "'Come un vero Prencipe Catolico': The Capuchins and the Rulers of Soyo in the Late Seventeenth-Century," *Africa: Journal of the International African Institute* 53, no. 3 (1983): 39–54.

Greenblatt, Stephen. *Marvelous Possessions: The Wonder of the New World* (Chicago: University of Chicago Press, 1991).

Griffiths, Nicholas. "Inquisition of the Indians?: The Inquisitorial Model and the Repression of Andean Religion in Seventeenth-Century Peru," *Colonial Latin American Historical Review* 3, no. 1 (1994): 19–38.

Groebner, Valentín. *Who Are You?: Identification, Deception, and Surveillance in Early Modern Europe* (New York: Zone, 2007).

Guaman Poma de Ayala, Felipe. *Primer nueva corónica y buen gobierno* [1615], ed. John V. Murra and Rolena Adorno. www.kb.dk/permalink/2006/poma/info/en/frontpage.htm.

Gudeman, Stephen, and Stuart Schwartz. "Cleansing Original Sin: Godparenthood and the Baptism of Slaves in Eighteenth-Century Bahia," in *Kinship Ideology and Practice in Latin America*, ed. R. T. Smith (Chapel Hill: University of North Carolina Press, 1984).

Guerrero Mosquera, Andrea. "Misiones, misioneros y bautizos a través del Atlántico: Evangelización en Cartagena de Indias y los reinos del Kongo y Ngola, siglo XVII," *Memoria y sociedad* 18, no. 37 (2014): 14–32.

Guía artística de Málaga y su provincia, vol. 1, ed. Rosario Camacho Martínez and Isidoro Coloma Martín (Seville: Juan Manuel Lara, 2006).

Guibovich, Pedro. "The Printing Press in Colonial Peru: Production Process and Literary Categories in Lima, 1584–1699," *Colonial Latin American Review* 10, no. 2 (2001).

Guthrie, Malcolm. *Comparative Bantu*, 4 vols. (Farnborough: Gregg International Publishers, 1967–71).

"Western Bantu Languages," in *Current Trends in Linguistics 7, Linguistics in Sub-Saharan Africa*, ed. Thomas A. Sebeok (The Hague: Mouton, 1971), 357–66.

Hahn, Thomas. "The Difference the Middle Ages Makes: Color and Race before the Modern World," *Journal of Medieval and Early Modern Studies* 31, no. 1 (2001): 1–37.

Hair, P. E. H. "The Use of African Languages in Afro-European Contacts in Guinea: 1440–1560," *Sierra Leone Language Review* 5 (1966): 5–26.

Hall, Gwendolyn Midlo. *Slavery and African Ethnicities in the Americas: Restoring the Links* (Chapel Hill: University of North Carolina Press, 2005).

Hall, Kim. *Things of Darkness: Economies of Race and Gender in Early Modern England* (Ithaca, NY: Cornell University Press, 1995), 107–16.

Hanchard, Michael. *Orpheus and Power: The Movimiento Negro of Rio de Janeiro and Sao Paolo, 1945–1988* (Princeton: Princeton University Press, 1994).

Hanke, Lewis. *All Mankind Is One: A Study of the Disputation between Bartolomé de Las Casas and Juan Ginés de Sepúlveda in 1550 on the Intellectual and Religious Capacity of the American Indians* (DeKalb: Northern Illinois University Press, 1974).

Hankins, James. "Humanism, Scholasticism, and Renaissance Philosophy," in *Cambridge Companion to Renaissance Philosophical Thought* (New York: Cambridge University Press, 2007), 30–48.

Hanks, William. *Converting Words: Maya in the Age of the Cross* (Berkeley: University of California Press, 2010).

Harper, John. *The Forms and Orders of Western Liturgy: From the Tenth to the Eighteenth Century* (Oxford: Clarendon Press, 1991).

Harpster, Grace. "The Color of Salvation: The Materiality of Blackness in Alonso de Sandoval's *De instauranda Aethiopum salute*," in *Envisioning Others: Race, Color, and the Visual in Iberia and Latin America*, ed. Pamela A. Patton (Leiden: Brill, 2016), 83–110.

Hawthorne, Walter. *From Africa to Brazil: Culture, Identity, and an Atlantic Slave Trade, 1600–1830* (New York: Cambridge University Press, 2010).

Hazañero, Sebastián. *Letras anuas de la Compañía de Iesus de la provincia del nuevo reyno de Granada. Desde el año de mil seiscientos treinta y ocho hasta el año de mil seiscientos cuarenta y tres* [1638-1643] (Zaragosa, 1643).

Heitzmann, Alfonso Alegre. "El color de la Sulamita en las Biblias medievales romanceadas," *Anuario de Filología* 5 (1979): 239–56.

Helg, Aline. *Liberty and Equality in Caribbean Colombia* (Chapel Hill: University of North Carolina Press, 2004).

Hering Torres, Max. "Cuerpo, misoginia y raza. España y las Américas en los siglos XVI–XVII," in *Desvelando el cuerpo: Perspectivas desde las ciencias sociales y humanas*, ed. Josep Martí and Yolanda Aixela (Madrid: CISC, 2010), 145–56.

"Purity of Blood: Problems of Interpretation," in *Race and Blood in the Iberian World*, ed. Max S. Hering Torres, María Elena Martínez, and David Nirenberg (Zurich: Lit Verlag, 2012), 11–38.

Herzog, Tamar. *Frontiers of Possession: Spain and Portugal in Europe and the Americas* (Cambridge, MA: Harvard University Press, 2015).

Heywood, Linda. *Njinga of Angola: Africa's Warrior Queen* (Cambridge, MA: Harvard University Press, 2017).

Heywood, Linda, and John Thornton. *Central Africans, Atlantic Creoles, and the Foundation of the Americas* (New York: Cambridge University Press, 2007).

Hill, Ruth. "Hearing Las Casas Write: Rhetoric and the Facade of Orality in Brevísima relación," in *MLA Approaches to Teaching Bartolomé de las Casas*, ed. Santa Arias and Eyda Merediz (New York: MLA, 2008), 57–64.

Hierarchy, Commerce, and Fraud: A Postal Inspector's Exposé (Nashville, TN: Vanderbilt University Press, 2005).

Sceptres and Sciences in the Spains: Four Humanists and the New Philosophy, c. 1680–1740 (Chicago: University of Chicago Press, 2000).

Hilton, Anne. *Kingdom of Kongo* (Oxford: Oxford University Press, 1985).

Holler, Jacqueline. *Escogidas Plantas: Nuns and Beatas in Mexico City, 1531–1601* (New York: Columbia University Press, 2005.

Holt, Thomas. "Race Making and the Writing of History," *The American Historical Review* 100, no. 1 (1995): 1–20.

Hood, Robert. *Begrimed and Black: Christian Traditions on Blacks and Blackness* (Minneapolis: Fortress Press, 1994).

Horozco, Sebastián de. *El libro de los proverbios glosados (1570–1580)*, ed. Jack Weiner (Kassel: Edición Reichenberger, 1994).

Ibsen, Kristine. *Women's Spiritual Autobiography in Colonial Spanish America* (Gainsville: University Press of Florida, 1999).

Illari, Bernardo. "Polychoral Culture: Cathedral Music in La Plata (Bolivia), 1680–1730," PhD diss., University of Chicago, 2001.

Instruccion para remediar y assegurar, quanto con la divina gracia fuere possible, que ninguno de los Negros, que vienen de Guinea, Angola, y otras Provincias de aquella costa de Africa, carezca del sagrado baptismo (Lima: Geronymo de Contreras, 1628).

Ireton, Chloe. "'They Are Blacks of the Caste of Black Christians': Old Christian Black Blood in the Sixteenth- and Early Seventeenth-Century Iberian Atlantic," *Hispanic American Historical Review* 97, no. 4 (2017): 579–612.

Irigoyen, Javier. "Diana and Wild Boar Hunting: Refiguring Gender and Ethno-Religious Conflict in the Pastoral Imaginary," *Bulletin of Hispanic Studies* 88, no. 3 (2011): 237–87.

Iwasaki Cauti, Fernando. "Luisa Melgarejo de Soto y la alegría de ser tu testigo, señor," *Histórica* 19, no. 2 (1995): 219–51.

"Mujeres al borde de la perfección: Rosa de Santa María y las alumbradas de Lima," *Hispanic American Historical Review* 73, no. 4 (1993): 581–613.

"Vidas de Santos y santas vidas: Hagiografías reales e imaginarias en Lima colonial," *Anuario de estudios americanos* 51, no. 1 (1994): 57–64.

Iyengar, Sujata. *Shades of Difference: Mythologies of Skin Color in Early Modern England* (Philadelphia: University of Pennsylvania Press, 2004).

Jara, Álvaro. *Guerra y sociedad en Chile* (Santiago de Chile: Editorial Universitaria, 1971).

Jardine, Lisa. "Logic and Language: Humanist Logic," in *Cambridge History of Renaissance Philosophy*, ed. Charles B. Schmitt, Quentin Skinner, Eckhard Kessler, and Jill Kraye (New York: Cambridge University Press, 2008), 173–98.

Johnson, Walter. *Soul by Soul: Life Inside the Antebellum Slave Market* (Cambridge, MA: Harvard University Press, 1999).

Jones, Nicholas R. "Sor Juana's Black Atlantic: Colonial Blackness and the Poetic Subversions of Habla de negros," *Hispanic Review* 86, no. 3 (2018): 265–85.

Staging Habla de Negros: *Radical Performances of the African Diaspora in Early Modern Spain* (University Park: Penn State University Press, 2019).

Jouve Martín, José Ramón. *Esclavos de la ciudad letrada: Esclavitud, escritura y colonialismo en Lima, 1650–1700* (Lima, Peru: IEP, 2005).

"Public Ceremonies and Mulatto Identity in Viceregal Lima: A Colonial Reenactment of the Fall of Troy (1631)," *Colonial Latin American Review* 16, no. 2 (2007): 179–201.

Juan de la Cruz, *Doctrina christiana en la lengua guasteca c[on] la lengua castellana* (Mexico: Pedro Ocharte, 1571).

Kaplan, Paul H. D. "Italy, 1490–1700," in *The Image of the Black in Western Art from the "Age of Discovery" to the Age of Revolution: Artists of the Renaissance and Baroque*, ed. David Bindman and Henry Louis Gates, Jr. (Cambridge, MA: Harvard University Press, 2010), 93–190.

Katzew, Ilona. "White or Black? Albinism and Spotted Blacks in the Eighteenth-Century Atlantic World," in *Envisioning Others: Race, Color, and the Visual in Iberia and Latin America*, ed. Pamela A. Patton (Leiden, 2016), 142–86.

Keniston, Hayward. *The Syntax of Castillian Prose: The Sixteenth Century* (Chicago: University of Chicago Press, 1937).

Kennedy, George A. *A New History of Classical Rhetoric* (Princeton: Princeton University Press, 2009).

Kerpel, Diana Magaloni. *The Colors of the New World: Artists, Materials, and the Creation of the Florentine Codex* (Los Angeles, CA: Getty Museum, 2014).

Kiddy, Elizabeth W. *Blacks of the Rosary: Memory and History in Minas Gerais, Brazil* (University Park: Pennsylvania State University Press, 2005).

Kimmel, Seth. *Parables of Coercion: Conversion and Knowledge at the End of Islamic Spain* (Chicago: University of Chicago Press, 2015).

Klor de Alva, J. Jorge. "Colonizing Souls: The Failure of the Indian Inquisition and the Rise of Penitential Discipline," in *Cultural Encounters: The Impact of the Inquisition in Spain and the New World*, ed. Mary Elizabeth Perry and Anne J. Cruz (Berkeley: University of California Press, 1991), 3–23.

Koerner, Joseph Leo. "The Epiphany of the Black Magus circa 1500," in *The Image of the Black in Western Art*, vol. 3, part 1 (Cambridge, MA: Belknap Press of Harvard University, 2010), 7–93.

Konetzke, Richard. *Colección de documentos para la historia de la formación social de Hispanoamerica, 1493–1810* (Madrid: Consejo Superior de Investigaciones Científicas, 1953–58).

Kristeller, Oskar. "Humanism and Scholasticism in the Renaissance," *Byzantion* 17 (1944–45): 346–74.

Krug, Jessica. *Fugitive Modernities: Kisama and the Politics of Freedom* (Durham, NC: Duke University Press, 2018).

Labrador Herraiz, José J., and Ralph A. DiFranco. "Villancicos de negros y otros testimonios al caso en manuscritos del siglo de oro," in *De la canción de amor medieval a las soleares*, ed. Pedro M. Piñero Ramírez (Seville: Fundación Macado and Universidad de Sevilla, 2004), 163–87.

Laird, Andrew. "Cicero in Colonial Latin America," in *The Afterlife of Cicero*, ed. Gesine Manuwald (London: Institute of Classical Studies, University of London, 2016), 121–43.

Landers, Jane. "The African Landscape of Seventeenth-Century Cartagena and Its Hinterlands," in *The Black Urban Atlantic in the Age of the Slave Trade*, ed. Jorge Cañizares-Esguerra, Matt D. Childs, and James Sidbury (Philadelphia: University of Pennsylvania Press, 2013), 147–62.

Black Society in Spanish Florida (Urbana: University of Illinois Press, 1999).

Lane, Kris. *Quito, 1599: A Colony in Transition* (Albuquerque: University of New Mexico Press, 2002).

Las Casas, Bartolomé de. *Historia de las Indias* [1527–59], ed. Agustín Millares Carlo (Mexico: Fondo de Cultura Económica, 1951).

Lavrin, Asunsión. "Unlike Sor Juana? The Model Nun in the Religious Literature of Colonial Mexico," in *Feminist Perspectives on Sor Juana Inés de la Cruz*, ed. Stephanie Merrim (Detroit: Wayne State University Press, 1991), 61–85.

Lawrence, Jeremy. "Black Africans in Spanish Literature," in *Black Africans in Renaissance Europe*, ed. Thomas F. Earle and Kate J. P. Lowe (New York: Cambridge University Press, 2005), 80–93.

Lawrence, Jeremy N. H. "Humanism in the Iberian Peninsula," in *The Impact of Humanism in Western Europe*, ed. Anthony Goodman and Angus MacKay (London: Longman, 1990), 220–58.

Levy, Evonne. *Propaganda and the Jesuit Baroque* (Berkeley: University of California Press, 2004).

Lewis, Laura. *Hall of Mirrors: Power, Witchcraft, and Caste in Colonial Mexico* (Durham, NC: Duke University Press, 2003).

Li Causi, Pietro. *Generare in comune: Teorie e rappresentazioni dell'ibrido nel sapere zoologico dei Greci e dei Romani* (Palermo: Palumbo, 2008).

Lipski, John M. *A History of Afro-Hispanic Language: Five Centuries, Five Continents* (New York: Cambridge University Press, 2005).

Lopetegui, León. "Influjos de Fr. Domingo de Soto, O.P. en el pensamiento misional del P. José de Acosta," *Estudios Eclesiásticos* 36 (1961): 57–72.

El Padre José de Acosta y las misiones (Madrid: Consejo Superior de Investigaciones Científicas, 1942).

López Fadul, Valeria. "Languages, Knowledge, and Empire in the Early Modern Iberian World (1492–1650)," PhD diss., Princeton University, 2015.

López García, José Tomás. *Dos defensores de los esclavos negros en el siglo XVII. Francisco José de Jaca y Epifanio de Moirans* (Caracas: Universidad Católica Andrés Bello, 1982).

Lott, Eric. *Love and Theft: Blackface Minstrelsy and the American Working Class* (New York: Oxford University Press, 1993).

Lowe, Kate. "'Representing' Africa: Ambassadors and Princes from Christian Africa to Renaissance Italy and Portugal, 1402–1608," *Transactions of the Royal Historical Society* 17 (2007): 101–28.

Lucena Salmoral, Manuel. "Leyes para esclavos: El ordenamiento jurídico sobre la condición, tratamiento, defensa y represión de los esclavos en las colonias de la América española," in *Tres grandes cuestiones de la historia de Iberoamérica*, ed. José Andrés Gallego (Madrid: Fundación Mapre Tavera, 2005).

Lunn, Arnold. *A Saint in the Slave Trade: Peter Claver (1581–1654)* (New York: Sheed & Ward, 1935).

MacCormack, Sabine. "'The Heart Has Its Reasons': The Predicaments of Missionary Christianity in Early Peru," *Hispanic American Historical Review* 65, no. 3 (1985): 443–66.

Religion in the Andes: Vision and Imagination in Early Colonial Peru (Princeton: Princeton University Press, 1991).

MacGaffey, Wyatt. "Dialogues of the Deaf: Europeans on the Atlantic Coast of Africa," in *Implicit Understandings: Observing, Reporting, and Reflecting on the Encounters between Europeans and Other Peoples in the Early Modern Era*, ed. Stuart B. Schwartz (New York: Cambridge University Press, 1994), 249–67.

Religion and Society in Central Africa: The BaKongo of Lower Zaire (Chicago: University of Chicago Press, 1986).

Mannheim, Bruce. *The Language of the Inka since the European Invasion* (Austin: University of Texas Press, 1991).

Martín, Luis. *Daughters of the Conquistadors: Women of the Viceroyalty of Peru* (Dallas: Southern Methodist University Press, 1989).

The Intellectual Conquest of Peru: The Jesuit College of San Pablo, 1568–1767* (New York: Fordham University Press, 1968).

Martínez, María Elena. "The Black Blood of New Spain: Limpieza de Sangre, Racial Violence, and Gendered Power in Early Colonial Mexico," *William and Mary Quarterly* 61, no. 3 (2004): 479–520.

Genealogical Fictions: Limpieza de Sangre, Religion, and Gender in Colonial Mexico* (Stanford, CA: Stanford University Press, 2008).

Martínez Céspedes, Jimmy. "Los jesuitas y la extirpación de las idolatrías: La historia oficial contada desde la Crónica del Padre Jacinto Barrasa, 1674–1680," *Revista Yuyarccuni* 2, no. 2 (2018): 49–103.

Martínez i Àlvarez, Patrícia. *La libertad femenina de dar lugar a dios. Discursos religiosos del poder y formas de libertad religiosa desde la Baja Edad Media hasta el Perú colonial* (Lima: Universidad Nacional Mayor de San Marcos, 2004).

"La oralidad femenina en el texto escrito colonial: Úrsula de Jesús," *Revista Andina* 38 (2004): 201–33.

Martínez i Àlvarez, Patrícia, and Elisenda Padrós Wolff. "Úrsula de Jesús: La palabra de Dios en el cuerpo propio," in *Catequesis y derecho en la América colonial: Fronteras borrosas*, ed. Roland Schmidt-Riese and Lucía Rodríguez (Madrid: Iberoamericana, 2010), 217–34.

Martínez-Osorio, Emiro. *Authority, Piracy, and Captivity in Colonial Spanish American Writing: Juan de Castellanos's Elegies of Illustrious Men of the Indies* (Lewisburg, PA: Bucknell University Press, 2016).

Martínez, Glenn Swaidon. "Los villancicos de negro y el teatro breve. Un primer acercamiento," in *La literatura popular impresa en España y en la América colonial: Formas y temas, géneros, funciones, difusión, historia y teoría*, ed. Laura Puerto Moro, Eva Belén Carro Carvajal, and Laura Mier Pérez (Salamanca: SEMYR, 2006), 161–68.

Massing, Jean Michel. "From Greek Proverb to Soap Advert: Washing the Ethiopian," *Journal of the Warburg and Courtauld Institutes* 58 (1995): 180–201.

"Washing the Ethiopian or the Semantics of an Impossibility," in *Studies in Imagery*, vol. 2 (London: Pindar, 2007), 315–34.

"Washing the Ethiopian, Once More," in *Studies in Imagery*, vol. 2 (London: Pindar, 2007), 335–58.

Maya Restrepo, Luz Adriana. *Brujería y la reconstrucción de identidades entre los africanos y sus descendientes en la Nueva Granada, Siglo XVII* (Bogota: Ministerio de Cultura, 2005).

"Demografía histórica de la trata por Cartagena 1533–1810," in *Geografía humana de Colombia: Los afrocolombianos*, vol. 6, ed. Jaime Arocha Rodríguez, Martha Luz Machado Caicedo, and William Villa (Bogota: Instituto Colombiano de Cultura Hispánica, 2000), 9–52.

McGrath, Elizabeth. "The Black Andromeda," *Journal of the Warburg and Courtauld Institutes* 55 (1992): 1–18.

McKinley, Michelle. *Fractional Freedoms: Slavery, Intimacy, and Legal Mobilization in Colonial Lima, 1600–1700* (New York: Cambridge University Press, 2016).

McKnight, Kathryn Joy. "Confronted Rituals: Spanish Colonial and Angolan 'Maroon' Executions in Cartagena de Indias (1634)," *Journal of Colonialism and Colonial History* 5, no. 3 (2004).

"Elder, Slave, and Soldier: Maroon Voices from the Palenque del Limón (1634)," in *Afro-Latino Voices: Narratives from the Early Modern Ibero-Atlantic World, 1550–1812*, ed. Kathryn Joy McKnight and Leo Garofalo (Indianapolis, IN: Hackett, 2009), 64–81.

"'En su tierra lo aprendió': An African Curandero's Defense before the Inquisition," *Colonial Latin American Review* 12, no. 1 (2003): 63–84.

"Gendered Declarations: Three Enslaved Women Testify before Cartagena Officials (1634)," *Colonial Latin American Historical Review* 12, no. 4 (2003): 499–527.

The Mystic from Tunja: The Writings of Madre Castillo, 1671–1742 (Amherst: University of Massachusetts Press, 1997).

Medina, Bernardo de. *Vida prodigiosa del venerable siervo de Dios Fr. Martin de Porras* (Lima: Juan de Quevedo y Zarate, 1673).

Mejía, Manuel. *San Pedro Claver de la Compañía de Jesús* (Cartagena, 1918).

Meléndez, Juan. *Tesoros verdaderos de las Indias* (Rome: Angel Tinasio, 1681).

Mercado, Pedro de. *Historia de la provincia del Nuevo Reino y Quito de la Compañía de Jesús* [c. 1688] (Bogota: Biblioteca de la Presidencia de Colombia, 1957).

Metcalf, Alida. *Go-betweens and the Colonization of Brazil* (Austin: University of Austin Press, 2005).

Mignolo, Walter. *Darker Side of the Renaissance: Literacy, Territoriality, and Colonization* (Ann Arbor: University of Michigan Press, 1995).

Milton, Cynthia, and Ben Vinson III. "Counting Heads: Race and Non-native Tribute Policy in Colonial Spanish America," *Journal of Colonialism and Colonial History* 3, no. 3 (2002).

Mintz, Sidney, and Richard Price. *The Birth of African American Culture: An Anthropological Perspective* (Boston: Beacon, 1976).

Molina, Michelle. *To Overcome Oneself: The Jesuit Ethic and the Spirit of Global Expansion, 1520–1767* (Berkeley: University of California Press, 2013).

Moll, Jaime V. "Los villancicos cantados en la Capilla Real a fines del siglo XVI y principios del siglo XVII," *Anuario musical* 25 (1970): 81–96.

Montero, Paula. "Índios e missionários no Brasil: Para uma teoria da mediação cultural," in *Deus na aldeia: Missionários, índios, e mediação cultural*, ed. Paula Montero (São Paolo: Globo, 2005), 31–66.

Moore, Denny. "Historical Development of Nheengatu (Língua Geral Amazonica)," in *Iberian Imperialism and Language Evolution in Latin America*, ed. Salikoko Mufwene (Chicago: University of Chicago Press, 2014), 108–42.

More, Anna. "From Lines to Networks: Carl Schmitt's Nomos and the Early Atlantic System," *Política común* 5 (2014).

Morgan, Ronald. "Jesuit Confessors, African Slaves and the Practice of Confession in Seventeenth-Century Cartagena," in *Penitence in the Age of Reformations*, ed. Katherine Jackson Lualdi and Anne T. Thayer (Burlington, VT: Ashgate, 2000), 222–39.

"Postscript to His Brothers: Reading Alonso de Sandoval's *De Instauranda Aethiopum Salute* (1627) as a Jesuit Spiritual Text," *Atlantic Studies* 5, no. 1 (2008): 75–98.

Mujica Pinilla, Ramón. "Hell in the Andes: The Last Judgment in the Art of Viceregal Peru," in *Contested Visions in the Spanish Colonial World*, ed. Ilona Katzew et al. (New Haven, CT: Yale University Press, 2011), 177–201.

Rosa Limensis. Mística, política e iconografía en torno de la patrona de América (Mexico, DF: Fondo de Cultura Económica, 2005).

Mulvey, Patricia A. "Black Brothers and Sisters: Membership in the Black Lay Brotherhoods of Colonial Brazil," *Luso-Brazilian Review* 17, no. 2 (1980): 253–79.

Murakawa, Naomi. *First Civil Right: How Liberals Built Prison America* (New York: Oxford University Press, 2014).

Murillo, Diego. *Instruccion para enseñar la virtud a los principiantes, escala espiritual de la perfeccion evangelica* (Zaragoza: Robles, 1598).

Myers, Kathleen Ann. "Redeemer of America: Rosa de Lima (1586–1617), the Dynamics of Identity, and Canonization," in *Colonial Saints: Discovering the Holy in the Americas, 1500–1800*, ed. Allan Greer and Jodi Bilinkoff (London: Routledge, 2003), 251–75.

Navarrete, Maria Cristina. "Las Cartas Annuas jesuitas y la representación de los etíopes en el siglo XVII," in *Genealogías de la diferencia: Tecnologías de la salvación y representación de los africanos esclavizados en Iberoamérica colonial*, ed. María Eugenia Chaves (Bogota: Javeriana, 2009), 22–57.

Navarrete, María Cristina. *Genesis y desarrollo de la esclavitud en Colombia: Siglos XVI y XVII* (Cali: Universidad del Valle, 2005).

Historia social del negro en la colonia: Cartagena, siglo XVII (Cali: Universidad del Valle, 1995).

"El palenque de limón (Cartagena de Indias, siglo XVII): El Imaginario del poder y sus jerarquias," in *Visicitudes negro africanas en iberoamerica: Experiencias de investigación*, ed. Juan Manuel de la Serna Herrera (Mexico: UNAM, 2011), 101–34.

Nemser, Daniel. *Infrastructures of Race: Concentration and Bio-politics in Colonial Mexico* (Austin: University of Texas Press, 2017).

Netanyahu, Benzion. *The Origins of the Inquisition* (New York: Random House, 1995).

Newson, Linda, and Susie Minchin. *From Capture to Sale: The Portuguese Slave Trade to Spanish South America in the Early Seventeenth Century* (Leiden: Brill, 2007).

Nirenberg, David. "Race and the Middle Ages," in *Rereading the Black Legend: The Discourses of Religious and Racial Difference in the Renaissance Empires*, ed. Margaret R. Greer, Walter D. Mignolo, and Maureen Quilligan (Chicago: University of Chicago Press, 2007), 71–87.

"Was There Race before Modernity? The Example of 'Jewish' Blood in Late Medieval Spain," in *The Origins of Racism in the West*, ed. Miriam Eliav-Feldon, Benjamin Isaac, and Joseph Ziegler (New York: Cambridge University Press, 2009), 232–64.

Olmedo Gobante, Manuel. "'El mucho número que hay dellos': *El valiente negro en Flandes* y los esgrimistas afrohispanos de *Grandezas de la espada*," *The Bulletin of the Comediantes* 7, no. 2 (2018): 67–91.

Olsen, Margaret. *Slavery and Salvation in Colonial Cartagena de Indias* (Gainesville: University Press of Florida, 2004).

O'Neill, Charles. *Diccionario histórico de la Compañía de Jesús: Biográfico-temático I (AA-Costa Rica)* (Rome: Instituto Historicum, S.J., 2001).

Oraciones traducidas en lengua del Reino de Angola. Por orden del P. Mateo Cardoso Teólogo de la Compañía de IESUS natural de Lisboa. Impressos primero para el Reyno de Portugal, y aora de nuevo con la declaración en lengua castellana (Lima: Geronymo de Contreras, 1629).

O'Toole, Rachel Sarah. *Bound Lives: Africans, Indians, and the Making of Race in Colonial Peru* (Pittsburgh: University of Pittsburgh Press, 2012).

"From the Rivers of Guinea to the Valleys of Peru: Becoming a Bran Diaspora within Spanish Slavery," *Social Text* 25, no. 3 (2007): 19–36.

"'The Most Resplendent Flower of the Indies': Making Saints and Constructing Whiteness in Colonial Peru," in *Women, Religion, and the Atlantic World, 1600–1800*, ed. Daniella Kostroun and Lisa Vollendorf (Toronto: University of Toronto Press, 2009), 136–55.

Ovalle, Alonso de. *Historica Relacion del Reyno de Chile* (Rome: Francisco Cavallo, 1646).

Pacconio, Francesco. *Gentio de Angola suficientemente instruido no mysterios da nossa sancta Fé* (Lisbon: Domingos Lopes Reza, 1642).

Pacheco, Juan Manuel. *Los jesuitas en Colombia, Tomo 1 (1567–1654)* (Bogota: San Juan Eudes, 1959).

Pagden, Anthony. *The Fall of Natural Man: The American Indian and the Origins of Comparative Ethnology* (New York: Cambridge University Press, 1982).

Lords of All the World: Ideologies of Empires in Spain, Britain, and France, c. 1500–c. 1800 (New Haven, CT: Yale University Press, 1995).

Spanish Imperialism and the Political Imagination: Studies in European and Spanish-American Social and Political Theory 1513–1830 (New Haven, CT: Yale University Press, 1990).

Page, Carlos A. "Iglesias para negros en las estancias jesuitas del Paraguay," in *Fronteiras e identidades: Encontros e desencontros entre povos indígenas e missões religiosas*, ed. Graciela Chamorro, Thiago Leandro Vieira Cavalcante, and Carlos Barros Gonçalves (São Paolo: Nhanduti Editora, 2011), 205–22.

Pallas, Gerónymo. *Missión a las Indias* [1619], ed. José Hernández Palomo (Seville: Consejo Superior de Investigaciones Científicas, 2006.

Palmer, Colin. *Slaves of the White God: Blacks in Mexico, 1570–1650* (New York: Cambridge University Press, 1976).

Palmié, Stephan. "Ethnogenetic Processes and Cultural Transfer in Caribbean Slave Populations," in *Slavery in the Americas*, ed. Wolfgang Binder (Würzburg: Königshauser und Neumann, 1993), 337–364.

Pan y Agua, Juan Carlos. *Black Bride of Christ: Chicaba, an African Nun in Eighteenth-Century Spain*, ed. and trans. Sue Houchins and Baltasar Fra Molinero (Nashville: Vanderbilt University Press, 2018).

Patterson, Orlando. *Slavery and Social Death* (Cambridge, MA: Harvard Unviersity Press, 1982).

Peabody, Sue. "'A Nation Born to Slavery': Missionaries and Racial Discourse in Seventeenth-Century French Antilles," *Journal of Social History* 38, no. 1 (2004): 113–26.

Pena González, Miguel Anxo. *Francisco José de Jaca. La primera propuesta abolicionista de la esclavitud en el pensamiento hispano* (Salamanca: Universidad Pontificia, 2003).

Perdomo Escobar, José Ignacio. *El archivo musical de la Catedral de Bogotá* (Bogota: Instituto Caro y Cuervo, 1976).

Peterson, Jeanette Favrot. *Visualizing Guadalupe: From Black Madonna to Queen of the Americas* (Austin: University of Texas Press, 2014).

Petrucci, Armando. *Prima lezione di paleografia* (Rome: Editori Laterza, 2002).

Phillips, William D., Jr. *Slavery in Medieval and Early Modern Iberia* (Philadelphia: University of Pennsylvania Press, 2014).

Picón-Salas, Mariano. *Pedro Claver, el santo de los esclavos* (Mexico: Fondo de Cultura Económica, 1950).

Premo, Bianca. *The Enlightenment on Trial: Ordinary Litigants and Colonialism in the Spanish Empire* (New York: Oxford University Press, 2017).

"Familiar: Thinking beyond Lineage and across Race in Spanish Atlantic Family History," *William and Mary Quarterly* 70, no. 2 (2013): 295–316.

Proceso de beatificación y canonización de San Pedro Claver, trans. Tulio Aristizábal and Ana María Splendiani (Bogota: Javeriana, 2002).

Quevedo, Francisco de. *Obras en prosa festivas y satíricas* (Barcelona: Sociedad Editorial La Maravilla, 1862–63).

Quijano, Anibal. "Colonialidad del poder, cultura y conocimiento en América Latina," in *Capitalismo y geopolítica del conocimiento: El eurocentrismo y la filosofía de la liberación en el debate intellectual contemporáneo*, ed. Walter Mignolo (Buenos Aires: Signo, 2001).

Randles, W. G. L. *L'ancien royaume du Congo des origines à la fin du XIXe siècle* (Paris, 1968).

Rappaport, Joanne. "Asi lo paresçe por su aspecto: Physiognomy and the Construction of Difference in Colonial Bogotá," *Hispanic American Historical Review* 91, no. 4 (2011): 601–31.

The Disappearing Mestizo: Configuring Difference in the Colonial New Kingdom of Granada (Durham, NC: Duke University Press, 2014).

Rappaport, Joanne, and Tom Cummins. *Beyond the Lettered City: Indigenous Literacies in the Andes* (Durham, NC: Duke University Press, 2012).

Rarey, Mathew. "Assemblage, Occlusion, and the Art of Survival in the Black Atlantic," *African Arts* 51, no. 5 (2018): 20–33.

Redden, Andrew. "The Problem of Witchcraft, Slavery and Jesuits in Seventeenth-Century New Granada," *Bulletin of Hispanic Studies* 90, no. 2 (2013): 223–50.

Restall, Matthew. *The Black Middle: Africans, Mayans, and Spaniards in Colonial Yucatan* (Stanford, CA: Stanford University Press, 2009).

"A History of New Philology and New Philology in History," *Latin American Research Review* 38, no. 1 (2003): 113–34.

Restrepo, Eduardo. "Eventalizing Blackness in Colombia," PhD diss., University of North Carolina, Chapel Hill, 2008.

"El negro en un pensamiento colonial de principios del siglo XVII: Diferencia, jerarquía y sujecion sin racialización," in *Genealogías de la diferencia: Tecnologías de la salvación y representación de los africanos esclavizados en Iberoamérica colonial*, ed. María Eugenia Chaves (Bogota: Javeriana, 2009), 118–77.

Ripodaz Adarnaz, Daisy. "Influencia del teatro menor español de los siglos XVI y XVII sobre la imagen peninsular de lo indiano," in *Lo indiano en el teatro menor de XVI y XVII*, ed. Ripodaz Adarnaz (Madrid: Ediciones Atlas, 1991), IX–CXXI.

Roa, Martín de. *Estado de los bienaventurados en el cielo* (Seville: Francisco de Lyra, 1624).

Roach, Joseph. *Cities of the Dead: Circum-Atlantic Performance* (New York: Columbia University Press, 1996).

Romano, Giovanni Battista. *Dottrina christiana, nella quale si contengono i principali Misteri della nostra Fede* (Rome: Giorgio Dagano, 1591).

Rowe, Erin Kathleen. "After Death, Her Face Turned White: Blackness, Whiteness, and Sanctity in the Early Modern Hispanic World," *American Historical Review* 121, no. 3 (2016): 726–54.

Black Saints in Early Modern Global Catholicism (New York: Cambridge University Press, 2019).

"Visualizing Black Sanctity in Early Modern Spanish Polychrome Sculpture," in *Envisioning Others: Race, Color, and the Visual in Iberia and Latin America*, ed. Pamela A. Patton (Leiden: Brill, 2016), 51–82.

Ruiz de Elvira Serra, Isabel. "Introducción," in *Catálogo de Villancicos de la Bilbioteca Nacional, siglo XVII* (Madrid: Ministerio de la Cultura, 1992).

Russel-Wood, A. J. R. "Before Columbus: Portugal's African Prelude to the Middle Passage and Contribution to Discourse on Race and Slavery," in *Race, Discourse, and the Origins of the Americas: A New World View*, ed. Vera Lawrence and Rex Nettleford (Washington, DC: Smithsonian, 1995), 134–68.

Russo, Alessandra. *The Untranslatable Image: A Mestizo History of the Arts in New Spain, 1500–1600* (Austin: University of Texas Press, 2014).

Sac. Rituum Congregatione sive Eminentissimo et Reverendissimo Domino Card. De Abdua. Cartagenen. Beatificationis, et Canonizationis Ven Servi Dei Petri Claver Sacerdotis Societ. Iesu (Rome: Typis Rev. Camerae Apostolicae, 1696).

Sacra Rituum Congregatione Eminentisimo et Reverendissimo D. Card. Zondedario Indiarum seu Carthaginen. Beatificationis et Canonizationis ven servi

Dei Petri Claver Sacerdotis Professi Societatis Iesu (Rome: Typis Rev. Camerae Apostolicae, 1720).

Sahagún, Bernardino de. *Historia general de las cosas de la Nueva España* (Mexico, DF: Porrúa, 2016).

Salvadore, Matteo. *The African Prester John and the Birth of Ethiopian-European Relations, 1402–1555* (New York: Routledge, 2017).

Sánchez-Godoy, Ruben. "Early African-Amerindian Subjectivities in Miguel Cabello Balboa's *Verdadera descripción de la provincia de Esmeraldas* (1583)," *Comparative Literature* 49, no. 2 (2012): 167–85.

"Mercanía, gentes pacíficas y plaga: Bartolomé de las Casas y los orígenes del pensamiento abolicionista en el Atlántico," PhD diss., Pennsylvania State University, 2009.

El peor de los remedios: Bartolomé de las Casas y la crítica temprana a la esclavitud en el Atlántico ibérico (Pittsburgh, PA: Iberoamericana, 2016).

Sánchez Romeralo, Antonio. *El Villancico (Estudios sobre la lírica popular en los siglos XV y XVI)* (Madrid: Gredos, 1969).

Sanders, James. "'Citizens of a Free People': Popular Liberalism and Race in Nineteenth-Century Southwestern Colombia," *Hispanic American Historical Review* 84, no. 2 (2004): 233–312.

Sandoval, Alonso de. *De instauranda Aethiopum salute: El mundo de la esclavitud negra en América* (Bogota: Empresa Nacional de Publicaciones, 1956).

Historia de la Aethiopia: Tomo primero de De instauranda Aethiopum salute (Madrid, 1647).

Naturaleza, policia sagrada i profana, costumbres i ritos, disciplina i catechismo evangelico de todos etiopes (Seville: Francisco de Lyra, 1627). http://gallica.bnf.fr/ark:/12148/bpt6k737763z.

Un tratado sobre la esclavitud: De instauranda Aethiopum Salute, ed. Enriqueta Vila Vilar (Madrid: Alianza Editorial, 1987).

Santamaría, Carolina. "Negrillas, negros, y guineos y la representación musical de lo africano," *Cuadernos de música, artes visuales y artes escénicas* 2, no. 1 (2006): 4–20.

Santos Morillo, Antonio. "La expresión lingüística de los esclavos negros según Alonson [sic] de Sandoval," in *Actas del Congreso Internacional América Latina: La autonomía de una región*, ed. Heriberto Cairo Carou et al. (Madrid: Trama Editorial, 2012), 1086–93.

Sás, Andrés. *La música en la Catedral de Lima durante el virreinato, primera parte* (Lima: Universidad Nacional Mayor de San Marcos, 1971).

Scarry, Elaine. *The Body in Pain: The Making and Unmaking of the World* (New York: Oxford University Press, 1985).

Scott, David. "That Event, This Memory: Notes on an Anthropology of African Diasporas in the New World," *Diaspora* 1 (1991): 261–84.

Scott, James C. *Domination and the Art of Resistance* (New Haven, CT: Yale University Press, 1990).

Seigel, Micol. *Uneven Encounters: Making Race and Nation in Brazil* (Durham, NC: Duke University Press, 2009).

Sellassie, Sergew Hable. *Ancient and Medieval Ethiopian History to 1270*, (Addis Ababa: United Printers, 1972).

Sierra Silva, Pablo Miguel. "From Chains to Chiles: An Elite Afro-Indigenous Couple in Colonial Mexico, 1641–1688," *Ethnohistory* 62, no. 2 (2015): 361–84.

Silverblatt, Irene. *Modern Inquisitions: Peru and the Origins of the Civilized World* (Durham, NC: Duke University Press, 2004).

Smallwood, Stephanie. *Saltwater Slavery: A Middle Passage from Africa to American Diaspora* (Cambridge, MA: Harvard University Press, 2007).

Solano, Francisco. *Documentos sobre política lingüística en Hispanoamérica (1492–1800)* (Madrid: Consejo Superior de Investigaciones Científicas, 1991).

Solórzano y Pereira, Juan de. *Política Indiana* (Madrid: Diego Diaz de la Carrera, 1648).

Sotuellus, Anathanaele. *Bibliotheca Scriptorum Societatis Jesu* (Rome, 1676).

Souza, Laura Mello e. *The Devil in the Land of the Holy Cross: Witchcraft, Slavery, and Popular Religion in Colonial Brazil*, trans. Diane Grosklaus Whitty (Austin: University of Texas Press, 2004).

Spaulding, Rachel. "Mounting the Poyto: An Image of Afro-Catholic Submission in the Mystical Visions of Colonial Peru's Úrsula de Jesús," *Early American Studies* 17, no. 4 (2019): 519–44.

Spivak, Gayatri Chakravorty. *Death of a Discipline* (New York: Columbia University Press, 2003).

Splendiani, Anna María, José Enrique Sánchez Bohórquez, and Emma Cecilia Luque de Salazar. *Cincuenta años de inquisición en el Tribunal de Cartagena de Indias 1610–1660*, vol. 1 (Bogota: Centro editorial Javeriano, Instituto Colombiano de Cultura Hispánica, 1997).

Stark, Thomas C. Smith. "Rincón y Carochi: La tradición jesuítica de descripción del náhuatl," in *Las gramáticas misioneras de tradición hispánica (siglos XVI–XVII)*, ed. Otto Zwartjes (Portada Hispanica, 2001), 28–71.

Steinberg, Justin. *Accounting for Dante: Urban Readers and Writers in Late Medieval Italy* (Notre Dame: University of Notre Dame Press, 2007).

Stevenson, Robert. "The Afro-American Musical Legacy to 1800," *The Musical Quarterly* 54 (1968): 475–502.

Latin American Colonial Music Anthology (Washington, DC: Organziation of American States, 1975).

The Music of Peru: Aboriginal and Viceroyal Epochs (New York: Pan American Union, 1959).

"La música colonial en Colombia," *Revista musical chilena* 16, nos. 81–82 (1962): 153–71.

Stoichita, Victor. "The Image of the Black in Spanish Art: Sixteenth and Seventeenth Centuries," in *The Image of the Black in Western Art, vol. 3: From "Age of Discovery" to the Age of Abolition: Artists of the Renaissance and Baroque* (Cambridge, MA: Harvard University Press, 2010), 191–234.

Swadley, John. "The *Villancico* in New Spain 1650–1750: Morphology, Significance and Development," PhD diss., Canterbury Christ Church University, 2015.

Sweet, James. *Domingos Álvares, African Healing, and the Intellectual History of the Atlantic World* (Chapel Hill: University of North Carolina Press, 2011).

"The Iberian Roots of American Racist Thought," *William and Mary Quarterly* 54, no. 1 (1997): 143–66.

Recreating Africa: Culture, Kinship, and Religion in the African-Portuguese World, 1441–1770 (Chapel Hill: University of North Carolina Press, 2003).

Talavera, Gabriel de. *Historia de Nuestra Señora de Guadalupe* (Toledo: Imprenta Tomás de Guzmán, 1597).

Tannenbaum, Frank. *Slave and Citizen: The Negro in the Americas* (New York: Vintage, 1946).

Tardieu, Jean-Pierre. "Du bon usage de la monstruosité: La vision de l'Afrique chez Alonso de Sandoval (1627)," *Bulletin Hispanique* 86, nos. 1–2 (1984): 164–78.

"Los inicios del 'ministerio de negros' en la provincia jesuitica de Paraguay," *Anuario de estudios americanos* 6, no. 2 (2005): 141–60.

"L'integration des noirs dan le discours de Felipe Guaman Poma de Ayala," *Revue de CERC* 4 (1987): 40–60.

"Los jesuitas y la 'lengua de Angola' en Perú (siglo XVII)," *Revista de Indias* 53, no. 198 (1993): 627–37.

El negro en la Real Audiencia de Quito, ss. XVI–XVII (Quito: Abya-Yala, 2006).

Los negros y la Iglesia en el Perú: Siglos XVI–XVII (Quito: Centro Cultural Afroecuatoriano, 1997).

Taylor, Diana. *Archive and the Repertoire: Performing Cultural Memory in the Americas* (Durham, NC: Duke University Press, 2003).

Tello, Aurelio, ed. *Cancionero musical de Gaspar Fernándes* (Mexico: Centro Nacional de Investigación, Documentación e Información Musical Carlos Chávez, 2001).

Tenorio, Martha Lilia. *Los villancicos de Sor Juana* (Mexico: El Colegio de México, 1999).

Tercero cathecismo y exposicion de la doctrina christiana, por sermones para que los curas y otros ministros prediquen y enseñen a los Yndios y a las demas personas (Lima: Antonio Ricardo, 1585).

Teresa de Jesús. *Libro de la vida* (Madrid: Cátedra, 2006).

The Life of Teresa of Jesus: The Autbiography of Teresa of Ávila, trans. E. Allison Peers (New York: Doubleday, 2004).

Thierren, Monika. "Más que distinción, en busca de la diferenciación: Arqueología histórica de Cartagena de Indias en el siglo XVII," in *Cartagena de Indias en el siglo XVII*, ed. Adolfo Meisel Roca and Haroldo Calvo Stevenson (Cartagena: Banco de la República, 2007), 17–66.

Thornton, John K. *Africa and Africans in the Making of the Atlantic World, 1400–1800*, 2nd ed. (New York: Cambridge University Press, 1998).

"The Development of an African Catholic Church in the Kingdom of the Kongo, 1491–1750," *The Journal of African History* 25, no. 2 (1984): 147–67.

The Kongolese Saint Anthony: Dona Beatriz Kimpa Vita and the Antonian Movement, 1684–1706 (New York: Cambridge University Press, 1998).

"On the Trail of Voodoo: African Christianity in Africa and the Americas," *The Americas* 44, no. 3 (1988): 261–78.

"Perspectives on African Christianity," in *Race, Discourse, and the Origin of the Americas: A New World View*, ed. Vera Lawrence Hyatt and Rex Nettleford (Washington, DC: Smithsonian, 1995), 169–98.

Tiffany, Tanya J. "Light, Darkness, and African Salvation," *Art History* 31, no. 2 (2008): 33–56.

Townsend, Camilla. *Malintzin's Choices: An Indian Woman and the Conquest of Mexico* (Albuquerque: University of New Mexico Press, 2006).

Triana y Añorveza, Humberto. *Las lenguas indígenas en la historia social del Nuevo Reino de Granada* (Bogota: Instituto de Caro y Cuervo, 1987).

Twinam, Ann. "Purchasing Whiteness: Conversations on the Essence of Pardoness and Mulatto-ness at the End of the Empire," in *Imperial Subjects: Race and Identity in Colonial Latin America*, ed. Andrew B. Fisher and Matthew D. O'Hara (Durham, NC: Duke University Press, 2009), 141–66.

Purchasing Whiteness: Pardos, Mulattos, and the Quest for Social Mobility in the Spanish Indies (Stanford, CA: Stanford University Press, 2015).

Urreta, Luis de. *Historia eclesiastica, politica, natural, y moral, de los grandes y remotos Reynos de la Etiopia, Monarchia del Emperador, llamado Preste Juan de las Indias* (Valencia, 1610).

Valdivielso, José de. *Primera parte del romancero espiritual* (Toledo: Loarte, 1612).

Valensi, Lucette. "Nègre/Negro: Recherches dans les dictionnaires français et anglais du XVIIème au XIXème siècles," in *L'Idée de race dans la pensée politique française contemporaine*, ed. Pierre Guiral and E. Temime (Paris: Editions du Centre National de la Recherche Scientifique, 1977), 157–70.

Valla, Lorenzo. *De linguae latinae elegantia* (Rome: Phelippe de Lingamine, 1471).

Valtierra, Ángel. *Cuarto centenario del nacimiento de San Pedro Claver: 24 de junio 1580–24 de junio de 1980* (Bogota: Banco de la República, 1980).

El esclavo de los esclavos: San Pedro Claver, S.J., tercer centenario de su muerte (1654–1954) (Bogota: Antares, 1954).

"El padre Alonso de Sandoval, S.J.," in *De instauranda Aethiopum salute. El mundo de la esclavitud negra en América* (Bogota: Empresa Nacional de Publicaciones, 1956), v–xxxvii.

El santo que libertó una raza: San Pedro Claver, S.J., su vida y su época (Bogota: Imprenta Nacional, 1954).

van Deusen, Nancy. "The 'Alienated' Body: Slaves and Castas in the Hospital de San Bartolomé in Lima, 1680–1700," *The Americas* 56, no. 1 (1999): 1–30.

Las almas del purgatorio: El diario espiritual y vida anónima de Úrsula de Jesús, una mística negra del siglo XVII (Lima: Pontificia Universidad Católica del Peru, 2012).

"Diaspora, Bondage, and Intimacy in Lima, 1535–1555," *Colonial Latin American Review* 19, no. 2 (2010): 247–77.

Embodying the Sacred: Women Mystics in Seventeenth-Century Lima (Durham, NC: Duke University Press, 2018).

Global Indios: The Indigenous Struggle for Justice in Sixteenth-Century Spain (Durham, NC: Duke University Press, 2015).

"God Lives among the Pots and Pans: *Donadas* (Religious Servants) in Seventeenth-Century Lima," in *Africans to Spanish America: New Directions*, ed. Sherwin Bryant, Rachel O'Toole, and Ben Vinson III (University of Illinois Press, 2012), 136–60.

Souls of Purgatory: The Spiritual Diary of a Seventeenth-Century Afro-Peruvian Mystic, Úrsula de Jesús (Albuquerque: University of New Mexico Press, 2004).

Vargas Arana, Paola. "Pedro Claver y la evangelización en Cartagena: Pilar del encuentro entre africanos y el Nuevo Mundo, siglo XVII," *Fronteras de la historia* 11 (2006): 293–328.

"Pedro Claver y la labor de evangelización en Cartagena de Indias (siglo XVII): Fuentes claves para analizar a los africanos en el Nuevo Mundo," *Revista de Historia* 155, no. 2 (2006): 43–79.

Vaughn, Alden, and Virginia Vaughn. "Before Othello: Elizabethan Representations of Sub-Saharan Africans," *William and Mary Quarterly* 54, no. 1 (1997): 19–44.

Vicuña Guengerich, Sara. "The Witchcraft Trials of Paula de Eguiluz, a Black Woman in Cartagena de Indias, 1620–1636," in *Afro-Latino Voices: Narratives from the Early Modern Ibero-Atlantic World, 1550–1812*, ed. Kathryn Joy McKnight and Leo Garofalo (Indianapolis, IN: Hackett, 2009), 175–94.

Vieira, Antônio. "'Children of God's Fire': A Seventeenth-Century Jesuit Finds Benefits in Slavery but Chastises Masters for Their Brutality in a Sermon to the Black Brotherhood of Our Lady of the Rosary," in *Children of God's Fire: A Documentary History of Black Slavery in Brazil*, 2nd ed., ed. Robert Edgar Conrad (University Park: Pennsylvania State University Press, 1994), 163–74.

"Sermão Vigesimo Setimo" [ca. 1633], in *Obras completas do Padre Antonio Vieira: Sermões*, vol. 12 (Porto: De Lello & Irmão, 1908), 301–34.

"'Two Slaveries – The Sermons of Padre Antônio Vieira, Salvador, Bahia (ca. 1633) and São Luís do Maranhão (1653)," in *Colonial Latin America: A Documentary History*, 2nd ed., ed. Kenneth Mills, William B. Taylor, and Sandra Lauderdale Graham (Wilmington, DE: Scholarly Resources, 2002), 218–33.

Vignaux, Hélène. "Palenque de Limón: ¿Subversión o sumisión? Un caso de cimarronaje en el Nuevo Reino de Granada," *Memoria* 7 (2000): 30–57.

Vila Vilar, Enriqueta. "Cimarronaje en Panamá y Cartagena: Es costo de una guerrilla en el siglo XVII," *Caravelle* 49 (1987): 77–92.

"En torno al padre Sandoval, autor de un tratado sobre la esclavitud," in *Église et politique en Amérique Hispanique* (Bordeaux: Presses Universitaires de Bordeaux, 1984), 65–76.

"Introducción," in *Un tratado sobre la esclavitud* (Madrid: Alianza Editorial, 1987), 15–44.

Vilaça, Aparecida, and Robin M. Wright. *Native Christians: Modes and Effects of Christianity among Indigenous Peoples of the Americas* (Farnham: Ashgate, 2009).

Villa-Flores, Javier. *Dangerous Speech: A Social History of Blasphemy in Colonial Mexico* (Tuscon: University of Arizona Press, 2006).

Vincent, Bernard. "Saint Benoît de Palermo et L'Espagne," in *Schiavitù, religione, e libertà nel Mediterraneo tra mediovo ed età moderna* (Cosenza, 2009), 201–14.

Vinson, Ben, III. *Bearing Arms for His Majesty: The Free-Colored Militia in Colonial Mexico* (Stanford, CA: Stanford University Press, 2002).

"Race and Badge: The Free-Colored Militia in Colonial Mexico," *The Americas* 56, no. 4 (2000): 471–96.

Vinson, Ben, III, and Cynthia Milton. "Counting Heads: Race and Non-native Tribute Policy in Colonial Spanish America," *Journal of Colonialism and Colonial History* 3, no. 3 (2002).

Vinson, Ben, III, and Matthew Restall. "Black Soldiers, Native Soldiers: Meanings of Military Service in the Spanish American Colonies," in *Beyond Black and Red: African-Native Relations in Colonial Latin America*, ed. Matthew Restall (Albuquerque: University of New Mexico Pres, 2005), 15–52.

Von Germeten, Nicole. *Black Blood Brothers: Confraternities and Social Mobility for Afro-Mexicans* (Gainesville: University Press of Florida, 2006).

"Corporate Salvation in a Colonial Society: Confraternities and Social Mobility for Africans and their Descendants in New Spain," PhD diss., University of California Berkeley, 2003.

Von Germeten, Nicole, ed. and trans. *A Treatise on Slavery: Selections from De instauranda Aethiopum salute* (Indianapolis, IN: Hackett, 2008).

Violent Delights, Violent Ends: Sex, Race, and Honor in Colonial Cartagena de Indias (Albuquerque: University of New Mexico Press, 2013).

Wade, Peter. "Images of Latin American Mestizaje and the Politics of Comparison," *Bulletin of Latin American Research* 23, no. 1 (2004): 355–66.

Race and Ethnicity in Latin America, 2nd ed. (London: Pluto, 2010).

Wadell, Maj-Brit. "The Evangelicae Historiae Imagines: The Designs and Their Artists," *Quaerendo* 10, no. 4 (1980): 279–91.

Waisman, Leonardo J. "Características y límites de la alfabetización musical en las misiones jesuíticas sudamericanas, siglos XVII–XVIII," *Revista de Musicología* 40, no. 2 (2017): 427–48.

Wardropper, Bruce. "The Color Problem in Spanish Traditional Poetry," *Modern Language Notes* 75, no. 5 (1960): 415–21.

Wardropper, Bruce W. "The Impact of Folk Song on Sacred and Profane Love Poetry in Post-Tridentine Spain," *The Sixteenth Century Journal* 17, no. 4 (1986): 483–98.

Warner, Marina. *Alone of All Her Sex: The Myth and Cult of the Virgin Mary* [1976] (New York: Random House, 1983).

Weber, Alison. *Saint Theresa and the Rhetoric of Femininity* (Princeton: Princeton University Press, 1996).

Weber de Kurlat, Frida. "Sobre el negro como tipo cómico en el teatro español del siglo XVI," *Romance Philology* 7, no. 2 (1963): 380–91.

"El tipo cómico del negro en el teatro prelopesco: Fonética," *Filología* 8 (1962): 139–68.

Weissbourd, Emily. "'I Have Done the State Some Service': Reading Slavery in Othello through Juan Latino," *Comparative Drama* 47, no. 4 (2013): 529–51.

Welmers, William E. *African Language Structures* (Berkeley: University of California Press, 1973).

Wheat, David. "The Afro-Portuguese Maritime World and the Foundations of Spanish Caribbean Society, 1570–1640," PhD diss., Vanderbilt University, 2009.

  Atlantic Africa and the Spanish Caribbean, 1570–1640 (Chapel Hill: University of North Carolina Press, 2016).

White, Richard. *The Middle Ground: Indians, Empires, and Republics in the Great Lakes Region, 1650–1815* [1991] (New York: Cambridge University Press, 2011).

Whitford, David M. *The Curse of Ham in the Early Modern Era: The Bible and the Justifications for Slavery* (New York: Routledge, 2009).

Wilde, Guillermo. *Religión y poder en las misiones guaraníes* (Buenos Aires: SB, 2009).

Winant, Howard. *Racial Conditions: Politics, Theory, Comparisons* (Minneapolis: University of Minnesota Press, 1994).

Wright, Elizabeth. *The Epic of Juan Latino: Dilemmas of Race and Religion in Renaissance Spain* (Toronto: University of Toronto Press, 2016).

Yannakakis, Yanna. *The Art of Being in-between: Native Intermediaries, Indian Identities, and Local Rule in Colonial Oaxaca* (Durham, NC: Duke University Press, 2008).

Yerushalmi, Yosef ayim. *Assimilation and Racial Anti-Semitism: The Iberian and the German Models* (New York: Leo Back Institute, 1982).

Zafra, Esteba de. *Villancicos para cantar en la Natividad de nuestro Señor Jesu Christo* (Toledo: Juan Ruyz, 1545).

Zamora, Margarita. *Language, Authority, and Indigenous History in the* Comentarios reales de los Incas (New York: Cambridge University Press, 1988).

Zúñiga, Jean-Paul. "'Morena me llaman ...' Exclusión e integración de los afroamericanos en Hispanoamérica: El ejemplo de algunas regiones del antiguo virreinato del Perú (siglos XVI–XVIII)," in *Negros, mulatos, zambaigos: Derroteros africanos en los mundos ibéricos*, ed. Berta Ares Queija and Alessandro Stella (Seville: Publicaciones de la Escuela de Estudios Hispano-Americanos, 2000), 105–22.

Zwartjes, Otto. "The Missionaries' Contribution to Translation Studies in the Spanish Colonial Period," in *Missionary Linguistics V: Translation Theories and Practices* (Amsterdam: John Benjamins, 2014), 1–50.

Index

Acosta, José de, 10, 39–40, 62–73, 217
Africa
  central, 1, 77, 102, 107–12, 135–37
  lower Guinea, 89–90
  northeastern, 8–9, 26
  Senegambia, 89–90, 125, 130–31, 133
African diaspora studies, 17–18, 162
Anchico
  ethnonym, 90, 126
  language, 1, 156, 178
Anchico, Domingo, 156, 160
Anchico, Sebastián, 156, 160
Andrade, Alonso, 119, 121, 131, 139, 176
Angola, 1, 49, 70, 74, 89, 93, 102, 107–8,
  110, 112, 123, 126–27, 129, 136–37
  ethnonym, 90, 101, 126, 225, 256, 264,
  267
Angola, Alonso, 129, 142
Angola, Ignacio, 125, 127, 129–30, 141–42,
  145, 160, 176, 179, 268
Angola, Lucía, 225
Angolans, 101–2, 253–54, 258
Arda (ethnonym), 90
Artiagame, Bartolomé de, 197–98, 199–200
Augustine of Hippo, Saint, 97–98, 216
Aymara, 78, 83, 101, 252, 257

Balanta (ethnonym), 90
Bañún (ethnonym), 89
baptism, 2
  in Africa, 27
  celebrations after, 203–4
  in Iberian territories, 70–72
  with interpreters, 95–96, 104

  missionary language for, 205
  painting of, 176–88
  on ships, 98–99
  on slave ship, 267
  against a slaveholder's wishes,
  151–53
barracoons, 133, 143, 149, 165, 166
beatas, 208–9
beatification inquest for Pedro Claver, 119.
  See also Proceso 1676 manuscript;
  Proceso 1696 book
Benedict of Palermo, Saint, 195–98, 200,
  202, 222–23
Bennett, Herman, 18, 245
Berbesí (ethnonym), 89
Bermúdez, Gonzalo, 83–84
Biafara (Biafada)
  ethnonym, 32, 90, 95–96, 125, 127–28,
  131–32, 254, 258
  language, 95–96
Bigelow, Allison, 16–17
Bioho (Bijago)
  ethnonym, 90, 131
  language, 127, 131
black conquistadors, 3, 34, 36
black Madonnas, 189–91
black magus, the, 22, 26, 192–95, 198, 233
black musicians, 50–51, 54–55, 126, 129,
  145, 160
blackness, 21–30
  beauty of, 179–81, 187–88, 191–92,
  200–2, 204, 206, 222–23, 226–27,
  229, 244, 246
blanco/a, 31–32